from storm to
FREEDOM

from storm to
FREEDOM

America's Long War with Iraq

JOHN R. BALLARD

NAVAL INSTITUTE PRESS
Annapolis, Maryland

Naval Institute Press
291 Wood Road
Annapolis, MD 21402

Library of Congress Cataloging-in-Publication Data

Ballard, John R., 1957–
   From storm to freedom : America's long war with Iraq / John
R. Ballard.
      p. cm.
   Includes bibliographical references and index.
   ISBN 978-1-59114-018-4 (acid-free paper) 1. Persian Gulf
War, 1991—United States. 2. Iraq War, 2003—United States.
3. United States—Foreign relations—Iraq. 4. Iraq—Foreign
relations—United States. I. Title.
   DS79.724.U6B354 2010
   956.7044—dc22

                              2010004368

Printed in the United States of America on acid-free paper

15 14 13 12 11 10   9 8 7 6 5 4 3 2
First printing

Book layout and composition: Alcorn Publication Design

For those—over 4300 American men and women—who gave their lives
in the conflict between the United States and Iraq,
and for my father, veteran of another, equally complex war:
Military service is the ultimate form of patriotism.

CONTENTS

MAPS AND ACRONYMS

Maps and Charts

Acronyms

ACR	Armored Cavalry Regiment
BCT	Brigade Combat Team
CENTCOM	U.S. Central Command
CFACC	Coalition Forces Air Component Command
CFLCC	Combined Forces Land Component Command
CONUS	Continental United States
COP	combat outpost
CRAF	Civil Reserve Air Fleet
DoD	Department of Defense
EFP	explosively formed projectile
FOB	forward operating base
GCC	Gulf Cooperation Council
IED	improvised explosive device
IIS	Iraqi Intelligence Service
INTERFET	International Force East Timor
IRGC	Iranian Republican Guard Corps
ISCI	Islamic Supreme Council of Iraq
ISF	Iraqi Security Forces
JFC	Joint Forces Command
JSAT	Joint Strategic Assessment Team
JSCP	Joint Strategic Capabilities Plan
JSOC	Joint Special Operations Command
JSS	joint security station
KKMC	King Khalid Military City

KTO	Kuwaiti Theater of Operations
MEB	Marine Expeditionary Brigade
MEF	Marine Expeditionary Force
MEU	Marine Expeditionary Unit
MiTT	Military Transition Team
MLRS	Multiple Launch Rocket System
MNF-I	Multi-National Force-Iraq
MoD	Ministry of Defense [Iraq]
MoI	Ministry of the Interior [Iraq]
MPSRON	Maritime Preposititioned Shipping Squadron
MRE	Meals Ready to Eat
MSC	Military Sealift Command
NSS	National Security Strategy
NATO	North Atlantic Treaty Organization
NSC	National Security Council
ODA	Operational Detachment Alpha
OIF	Operation Iraqi Freedom
PSU	port security unit
QRF	Quick Reaction Force
RCC	Revolutionary Command Council
RCT	Regimental Combat Team
RGFC	Republican Guard Forces Command
ROE	rules of engagement
RRF	Ready Reserve Force
RSLF	Royal Saudi Land Forces
SANG	Saudi Arabian National Guard
SAS	Special Air Service
SCIRI	Supreme Council of the Islamic Revolution in Iraq
SFA	Strategic Framework Agreement
SOCOM	Special Operations Command
SOF	special operations forces
SOFA	Status of Forces Agreement
SSO	Special Security Office
UNAMET	UN Mission in East Timor
UNMIH	United Nations Mission in Haiti
UNMOVIC	United Nations Monitoring, Verification and Inspection Commission
UNOSOM	United Nations Operation in Somalia
UNPROFOR	United Nations Protection Force
UNSCOM	United Nations Special Commission
UNSCR	United Nations Security Council Resolution

UNSMIH	United Nations Support Mission in Haiti
UNTAET	United Nations Transitional Administration in East Timor
UNTMIH	United Nations Transition Mission in Haiti
VBIED	vehicle born improvised explosive device
WMD	weapons of mass destruction

PREFACE

I n its infinite complexity, war scars everything that it touches and, despite the best efforts of mankind, always remains powerfully out of control. War is both the creator and destroyer of modern states and yet is the source of much national allure. The decision for war remains the ultimate test of any national leader, but going to war more commonly shapes the leader than it is shaped by the decision-maker. Ultimately war kills and requires intensive and serious study.

Many American analysts and policymakers were quite surprised when Saddam Hussein's military forces attacked Kuwait in 1990. Unfortunately, many other surprises followed during the twenty-year conflict that the United States conducted in and around Iraq. This book is designed to explain the key strategic and operational actions that made the long war with Iraq so complex; it also is intended to highlight the critical decisions, both political and operational, made during combat operations, which dramatically affected the outcome of the war.

One of the controversial aspects of this book will most certainly be the decision to view the strife of over two decades as a single prolonged conflict. Traditionally, wars have been viewed simplistically, as brief periods when the normal commerce of nation-states was interrupted by the abnormal, bellicose actions of one or more countries. In this traditional view, a "state of war" was formally declared by one or both parties when such periods occurred and all the belligerents were nation-states. Regardless of what occurred during the state of war, eventually one side would cease behaving belligerently and all the participating nations would resume normal diplomatic and commercial activities. Frequently a punishment was meted out to the instigator or to the nation identified as the loser in the war, and though peace (normal nation-state activities) returned, some costs of the war were acknowledged.

Since the end of World War II in 1945, this traditional view of war has changed dramatically. War has incorporated a wide variety of actions over the course of history, so this period of change has not been unique, but what has been significant is the seemingly irrevocable nature of the change. Due to the loss of supremacy of the nation-state as the key actor in war, and the lack of significant resolution of the wars that have occurred since 1945, our traditional view has become increasingly passé. Now non–nation-states have engaged in war in a significant way, and the once fairly distinct division between the conditions of war and peace has become significantly blurred. (Four clear examples of this blurring of status can be found in the interventions by the United States in Lebanon in 1983, Somalia in 1993, Haiti in 1994 and 2001, Bosnia in 1995, and Kosovo in 1999.) Some in fact say the clear distiction between war and peace has been lost.

The use of the term "global war on terror" (GWOT) by the United States has only added to the complexity of this general trend. One can understand why President George W. Bush and key members of his administration began to use the term in late 2001 to indicate the novel nature of the conflict they had been forced to wage against the terrorist organization Al Qaeda. The use of the term "war" incited a whole-of-nation approach, highlighted the significance of the attacks in New York City and Washington, D.C., and demonstrated in advance the seriousness of the response envisioned. The effort was certain to be global in reach and would hopefully become an international response against a common threat to so many nations. Having no other easy moniker, since the effort was clearly seen as opposing terrorist acts, and because no one could rationally support terrorism, it could correctly be labeled a war on terror.

Even as this seemed understandable and even appealing at the time, the GWOT soon became fraught with difficult challenges. The international nature of the war was confusing to nations that had been fighting terrorists with legal and security tools for years. The status of combatants from an international legal perspective was overly vague, and of course the spectacle of the sole superpower, the United States, attacking nation-states simply because they were suspected of harboring terrorists appeared a gross violation of the new, UN-based international order. Though a number of coalition partners signed up to assist the United States in the immediate aftermath of the attacks, after the Bush administration linked an "axis of evil" to the war in the president's State of the Union speech in January 2002, some nations began to distance themselves from the administration's policies. When President Bush decided to include responses to Iraq in the overall context of the global war, even normally staunch allies such as France reduced their support for the war effort.

Military theorists and doctrine writers most frequently use a continuum of actions, starting with battles at the tactical level of conflict, to characterize war. Operationally, military activities are grouped into campaigns, which have the same objective but synchronize multiple battles to achieve desired effects on the enemy. Strategies most frequently coordinate the elements of national power (diplomacy, economics, information, law enforcement, and military) in order to accomplish national security goals and, when necessary, to compel other nations to act in a certain way. Yet, none of these overly simplistic organizing principles match well when attempting to describe the approach taken by the United States toward Iraq from 1990 to 2010, unless one comes to understand that the Ba'athist government of Saddam Hussein did not accept or follow any of these approaches. And it was most often Saddam who kept the pot boiling with the United States.

Over time, the United States also acted more and more uncharacteristically in its festering relationship with Iraq. The reason for the return to active combat in 2003 demonstrates this fact well. Two rationales seemed plausible at the time: preventing Iraq from exporting weapons of mass destruction to terrorists in general and to Al Qaeda in particular (as was then reported by Secretary of State Colin Powell), or continuing hostilities in response to the continual, flagrant violations of the no-fly zones established under the aegis of the United Nations after the 1991 Safwan cease-fire. Both were justifiable reasons for a return to active military operations. However, in truth, it is much more accurate to understand that America went back to war primarily because Saddam Hussein naively continued to proclaim capabilities and intentions which the newly attacked United States saw as threats it could not leave unanswered. Perceived Iraqi threats during a period when the American government was already anticipating a second terrorist attack generated a fatal defensive riposte by the United States. What is even more disconcerting, there was apparently no specific decision to go to war on the part of President George W. Bush; there was instead a defensive escalation in the threat to use military force that eventually passed the tipping point when force had to be used, for doing otherwise would have entailed backing down in the face of a decade-long menace posed by Saddam in league with global terrorism. This was an unacceptable situation for the post–9/11 United States.

Legally, many would support the idea that Iraq's continual violations of United Nations Security Council Resolution 687 of April 1991 provided sufficient justification, in an international legal sense, for the resumption of hostilities. Why the Bush administration did not use this justification as its principal rationale for going to war remains a mystery. Still, the decision to effect regime change in Iraq unleashed a number of secondary effects there that forced the United States to confront an unanticipated style of war along with its international campaign against terrorism. For that reason alone, the lessons of the long conflict with Iraq should be crucial for a better understanding of conflict in the future.

This is primarily the study of the use of military power as an element of statecraft, so the focus will be on military action, but this is in no way intended to give precedent to the use of military power over diplomatic, economic, or other tools of statecraft. In fact, quite the reverse is true, for with the focused study of the use of military force, one quite naturally understands that it should only be used with greatest reluctance and that all other tools should be used to the maximum extent possible before a nation places the lives of its citizens at risk.

ACKNOWLEDGMENTS

This book was inspired by the inquiring minds of my students at the National War College during 2007, 2008, and 2009. Ongoing combat operations served for them as a great case study of national power, but as we sought to make sense of the war that was continuing in Iraq they questioned why its portrayal in the global media was so very different from their experiences "on the ground." They also wrestled with the fog and friction of the war and struggled to identify the causal factors that made the conflict so fascinating. The sophisticated questioning of so many astute students led me to develop a different, if somewhat more controversial, way of understanding the war at hand. I can only hope this effort will add clarity for those that follow in their wake.

As with all my work, this book was also inspired by my wife Rosaline, my partner in all things. It was only through her support and gentle encouragement that it came to be written over too many weeks and months. As veterans, she and I are grateful to be Americans and for the many blessings in our lives, but mostly we are thankful for our Renée and her Lauren—they are the real reason why we do what we do, and to them this book is dedicated.

Although it has benefited from a great deal of government information, this book does not reflect the opinions of the U.S. Department of Defense or the National Defense University, nor does it reflect their policies. The views expressed in this book are mine alone, as are any errors or omissions.

PRELUDE

American Military Power in the Post–Vietnam Era, 1975–1989

Memories of Vietnam are very sharp, clear to me, I mean with every other step I take I'm reminded of Vietnam. . . . [It's] never far from my mind and especially during the Gulf War, we didn't say it to each other but I think we all felt that we're going to do it right this time.
—LIEUTENANT GENERAL FRED FRANKS,
COMMANDING GENERAL VII CORPS, OPERATION DESERT STORM[1]

America wages war like no other nation in history. The tremendous economic power of the United States fused with the powerful esprit of patriotic democracy and a predilection for direct approaches, massed combat power, and technological solutions has created a particularly dominating and unique American way of war. Over the last century, the United States has developed the capacity to wage its unique way of war across the globe, but even with its wide reach and its wealth of military assets, the United States still has encountered difficulty dealing with unconventional conflicts, particularly those that are prolonged and irregular in nature. The long conflict with Iraq comprised both conventional and unconventional phases, and was marked by both striking successes and puzzling defeats. In many ways the conflict with Iraq may be the most instructive of America's wars and it certainly should serve as an important standard of comparison for years to come.

For its part, the conflict with Iraq was most consistently compared with the last war that proceeded it—the Vietnam conflict that raged from the early 1960s until the middle of the following decade. Many of the strategic decisions pertaining to the long conflict between the United States and Iraq are rooted in the American experience in Vietnam. As Secretary of Defense Donald Rumsfeld ignominiously said in December 2004, "As you know, you go to war with the Army you have. They're not the Army you might want or wish to have at a later time."[2] And the American military of the 1990s was largely the product of the Vietnam era and the changes that it brought to America.

Although World War II provided the dominant image of combat for Americans for several decades after that war ended, the Vietnam conflict clearly exerted a much greater influence over American strategic thinking and the execution of American security policy in the last decade of the twentieth century. Vietnam changed the way the United States organized its military forces and it also altered the way the American people interact with their government during wartime. Most significantly, Vietnam was the first military action that brought the real costs of war home to the living rooms of all citizens of the United States. As a result, combat in Vietnam became a media experience and was both much less romanticized and much more politicized. And, because American involvement in the conflict there ended without a clear military victory, the Vietnam experience established a sort of "never-again" benchmark for American military doctrine and force employment. Vietnam era veterans were also key framers of the strategic outlook of the United States and many exerted significant influence over the development of national security policy through the end of the century. Finally, and most literally, Vietnam veterans provided the greatest bulk of the uniformed leadership for the generation of men and women who would carry out combat in Iraq. With romantic ideas of World War II in their hearts, Americans approached war with Iraq in the 1990s with military weapons systems designed for high intensity combat with the Soviet Union, but a senior uniformed military dominated by the negative experiences of the conflict in Vietnam.[3]

Dave Palmer has called the Vietnam conflict an "incomprehensible war."[4] It was complex, unfitted to mold, and an experience both extremely frustrating and inordinately painful to many in America, combatants and family members alike. It brought many small victories but no satisfaction and left a generation of American servicemen and women feeling misunderstood and underappreciated. In the aftermath of the Vietnam conflict the United States military underwent significant changes in organization, doctrine, and attitudes designed to ensure that the errors made in Vietnam were not to be repeated. In many ways these changes were a reaction to feelings within the military that the armed services had been poorly organized and poorly employed in Vietnam. Unfortunately, even as these changes were being put in place, there endured within the U.S. military a malaise rooted in the feeling that the civilian population misunderstood the sacrifices they had made during the war. Some military leaders retained a feeling of shame associated with failing to secure a win in Vietnam that matched the victory made famous by World War II. The changes in structure and organization would have a profound impact on the capability of the U.S. military to fight in Iraq in 1990, and the strategy employed during Desert Storm was at least in part a reflection of the desire, born of the Vietnam experience, to ensure that military capabilities would be fully employed and well focused on victory.

One shortfall in Vietnam had resulted from the fact that the U.S. Army had been organized and trained primarily for conventional warfare in Europe. This meant that most of the senior leaders who served in Vietnam had little understanding of unconventional warfare; they most frequently responded to unconventional enemy actions with conventional "European-focused" responses. Thus conventional war responses fostered by the World War II experience developed a mentality among many officers that placed great emphasis on search-and-destroy operations as means of achieving success and body counts as a metric of success; neither of which proved very successful in Vietnam.

Also in Vietnam, the primary ground services of the U.S. military—the Army and Marine Corps—had not been fully integrated within a single strategic approach to war. Units of the two services were assigned to different sectors in Vietnam, with the Marines operating primarily in the northern (I Corps) sector, and the Army in the South. The Marines did attempt to bring some of their unconventional warfare experiences to the fight in Southeast Asia (with the employment, for example, of Combined Action Platoons); but the Army—with the notable exception of the newly formed Green Beret force—remained for the most part committed to conventional warfighting methodologies. The one significant evolutionary response within the ground forces in Vietnam was the airmobile (or for the Marines, heliborne) assault.

One of the strongest positive legacies of the Vietnam conflict was the emergence of special operations forces (SOF), a significant and lasting development. Even though the Army did not really bring SOF soldiers into the fold until the 1980s, the organizations within the SOF (both the Special Forces battalions of Green Berets, and the Ranger regiment of assault troops) were firmly structured and resourced after the Vietnam conflict. With the further development of special forces aviation in the Army and Air Force following the disastrous Eagle Claw raid to recover the American hostages inside Iran in 1980, the special operations forces as a whole became much better trained and better funded. In 1986 they gained their own unified combatant command, the U.S. Special Operations Command (USSOCOM), which made these gains permanent.

Integration of Reserve and Guard Forces

Another change resulting from the conflict in Vietnam that shaped the U.S. military for decades to follow was the decision to place many of the combat service support units required in time of war within the Reserve and National Guard structure, thus making mobilization of units all across the nation a prerequisite for effective execution of any large-scale war. This was known as the

Abrams Doctrine after its author, General Creighton Abrams, the vice chief of the Army during the Vietnam conflict, who later led the movement to change the Army force structure to ensure the entire nation shared responsibility for wartime operations.[5] The key concept behind this effort was the idea that a democracy at war must be actively supported by its citizens and, with a professional military—which could be somewhat isolated from its citizenry—the best way to ensure that the people are fully involved with any conflict was to base large segments of required force structure in the Reserve component. As a result the mobilization of American citizens—and, by extension, gaining popular support for mobilization—became prerequisites for going to war. Additionally, the army would have to devote training funds to ensure Reserve and National Guard forces were ready to fight.

World War II had witnessed a huge mobilization in both the military and civilian/industrial spheres; by contrast, the Korean conflict saw a steep decline in the percentage of Americans directly involved in the war effort. This was also true of the Vietnam War, where most combat was experienced by the professional military and a large number of very short-term draftees. On the ground especially, the Vietnam War was largely a draftee conflict. The point being that a significant portion of the populace—young men in their late teens and twenties—were indeed subject to mass mobilization. The fact that many young men were able to avoid service does not mean that they were unaffected. So, mobilization, albeit limited, did take place; but it proved unpopular. And therein lay the problem. Thankfully, the Abrams Doctrine reversed this trend and caused the military services to put more training effort, including both dollars and time, into their Reserve and National Guard components. These component forces would still be under-ready for combat during Operation Desert Storm some fifteen years later, but would be fully ready by the time Operation Iraqi Freedom required their service in large numbers and for long periods of time.

Air-Land Battle Doctrine and Generals Depuy and Starry

After Vietnam, the American military began searching for new approaches that would better accommodate the kinds of warfare that had dominated the globe since 1945. The 1973 Arab-Israeli War influenced the development of weapons and equipment, which changed tactics and employment practices and resulted in the need for new doctrinal manuals to educate the force concerning these new ways of operating. Although the effort to adapt did not begin with any idea that doctrinal revision would in fact revolutionize the force, by the late 1970s, the advent of Army Field Manual 100-5 had done just that.

Two key leaders in this movement were Generals William Depuy and Don Starry, who commanded the U.S Army Training and Doctrine Command (TRADOC) from 1973 to 1981. These efforts of these two generals, both Vietnam combat veterans, had a huge impact on the U.S. Army and indirectly on the entire armed forces of the United States.[6] Depuy began a debate about the doctrinal approaches of the United States to war which eventually resulted in a study that concluded that the two main possibilities for future conflicts by the United States were a major armored conflict in Europe, and a primarily infantry-centric fight in other locations around the world. Among other things, the study helped to develop the concept of the Rapid Deployment Force.

This healthy debate set the stage for General Starry to formulate a new "Air-Land Battle" doctrine, which prepared the Army for warfighting into the twenty-first century. Air-Land Battle emphasized close coordination between forces, aggressive maneuver in the defense, and air forces attacking the rear-echelon forces of the enemy. Although it was developed for warfare in Europe, it took full advantage of the lessons learned from the 1967 and 1973 Arab-Israeli Wars. Starry also introduced the new doctrinal concept of the extended battlefield, where there were not only geographical dimensions to combat (as had been the norm previously), but a time dimension as well; in Starry's mind, brigade commanders had different time horizon requirements in order to respond effectively to enemy actions than did division and corps commanders, who had to think much farther ahead in time to better anticipate the moves of their corresponding enemy commanders. Starry helped senior military leaders to understand that they had to anticipate events and developments, sometimes weeks ahead, in order to fight effectively at high levels of command. It was this coordination both in space and time that redefined the battlefield of the 1970s. All of these improvements would be vital to the conduct of operations in the Middle East in the years to come.

Iran, Lebanon, and Grenada—The Reforms of the 1980s

Still, even with new weapons systems and new doctrines altering the armed forces, old attitudes about commanding warfighting organizations still hampered the United States during the 1980s. That decade saw the United States employ its military power in a number of ways, primarily in small interventions, but not always with small goals. Unfortunately, the decision-making processes that resulted in the use of military force often lagged behind the capability of the forces that would be placed in harm's way.

The first challenge of the decade of reforms was the Iranian hostage rescue mission in April 1980, code-named Eagle Claw. Conceived to rescue the

American hostages taken when the embassy in Teheran was stormed, the operation was plagued by bad weather, bad timing, bad luck, and even incompetence at senior levels of leadership. It failed to accomplish its intended mission and left a literal black mark on the Iranian desert and a figurative black mark on the reputation of the United States.[7] Eagle Claw demonstrated the need for a specially trained hostage rescue team with air-ground and sea capability, and underscored the long-understood need for unity of command in high-risk operations.

In October 1983 American intervention in the war-torn Lebanese capital of Beirut, undertaken as a stabilizing mission, took a tragic turn when a suicide truck bomber destroyed a Marine battalion headquarters in the city, killing 243 Marines and sailors. The Beirut experience revealed a convoluted chain of command, insufficient national strategy development, and failure at Joint Staff and theater command levels to plan for unexpected outcomes.

Also in 1983 Operation Urgent Fury in Grenada demonstrated poor Army-Marine cooperation, uncoordinated mission changes, poor intelligence, and inefficient command and control. It was in Grenada that General H. Norman Schwarzkopf first experienced post–Vietnam era combat; he was chosen at the last minute to become deputy Joint Task Force commander. He was given little authority and took away from the experience the need to adapt joint command arrangements in order to improve operational effectiveness.

Each of these operations underscored the need for reforms within the U.S. military establishment. Fortunately, in the latter half of the 1980s some senior leaders in the Pentagon and a few members of the U.S. Congress began studying past military shortfalls. Once begun in earnest, those studies would result in legislation and organizational changes that would significantly improve the performance of American forces in Operations Desert Storm and Iraqi Freedom.

The Goldwater-Nichols Reforms[8]

In a historic act the Chairman of the Joint Chiefs of Staff, General David C. Jones of the U.S. Air Force, sparked a firestorm of change when on February 3, 1982, he "told a closed session of the House Armed Services Committee that restructuring the JCS would be his priority for the rest of his tenure as chairman and in his retirement. . . . With a weak chairman unable to force a resolution, this JCS system, according to Jones, produced advice that was 'not crisp, timely, very useful or very influential. And that advice is often watered down and issues are papered over in the interest of achieving unanimity.'"[9]

The changes proposed by General Jones and also by General Edward "Shy" Meyer of the Army spurred Congress to craft legislation aimed at reorganizing the Department of Defense and creating new authorities that would eventually prove crucial for the successful execution of all operations in Iraq. The House of Representatives Committee on Armed Services report that accompanied the legislation cited several historical examples of the need for change going back into the foundation of the American republic, but focusing most specifically on the post–World War II era.[10] That resulting law, the Goldwater-Nichols Department of Defense Reorganization Act of 1986, created a structure that permitted the chiefs of the four military services to focus on organizing, training, and equipping the armed forces, and allowing the newly created combatant commanders to focus solely on the exection of operational missions assigned by the National Command Authority. The law also created a new command authority, Combatant Command, which gave those designated as combatant commanders power over all service organizations assigned to them for operations by the secretary of defense.

Neither Desert Storm nor Iraqi Freedom could have been conducted without the improvements of the Goldwater-Nichols Act of 1986. Although inefficiencies, service rivalries, and even logistics constraints would remain through the long conflict with Iraq, the decade of the 1980s produced significant and lasting improvements for the conduct of military operations by the United States. Specifically, the empowerment of the senior military commands in each of the designated regions of the world to better perform their duties was an important legacy. One of these combatant commands, the U.S. Central Command (CENTCOM) had only just evolved, but would benefit most from the creation of these new authorities.

The Carter Doctrine and Central Command from the RDJTF

Over the same period that the American military was being reorganized, U.S. national strategy in the Middle East was developing as well. As a first step, President Jimmy Carter announced on October 1, 1979, that he was creating Rapid Deployment Forces (RDF) that could operate independently, without the use of forward bases or the facilities in other nations. Although the RDF was conceived with a global mission in mind, it was soon focused primarily on the Persian Gulf region, the one place in the world were the United States had few friends and even fewer facilities from which to conduct military activities. The subsequent announcement of the "Carter Doctrine" only increased the value of the RDF concept. The Carter Doctrine, announced in Jimmy Carter's State of the Union address on January 23, 1980, changed the approach of the United States toward threats in the Middle East. In his speech President Carter said, "Let our position be absolutely clear: an attempt by any outside force to gain control of the Persian Gulf region will be regarded as an assault on the vital interests of the United States of America, and such an assault will be repelled by any means necessary, including military force."[11]

That statement required a military capability to back it up, and the RDF headquarters (formally known then as the Rapid Deployment Joint Task Force, or RDJTF) was officially established at MacDill Air Force Base in Tampa, Florida, on March 1, 1980. The organization was first commanded by Marine Corps Major General Paul X. Kelly. Then, in April 1981, Secretary of Defense Casper Weinberger announced that the RDJTF would become a separate command with specific geographic responsibilities in the Middle East. This decision to focus the attention of the RDJTF principally on the Gulf region caused some concern, but it was fairly evident that this region was the most significant area of the world that was not adequately serviced by military capability. Then, in a final evolution, in 1983 the RDJTF became a separate unified command known as the U.S. Central Command (CENTCOM), reporting directly to the secretary of defense.

Weak Partners: The Tanker War in the Gulf, 1988–1989

CENTCOM's first real post–Goldwater-Nichols test came in the last two years of the 1980s during the war between Iraq and Iran. Four crucial incidents demarcated the "Tanker War," which was in a sense a quasi-war between the United States and Iran during 1987 and 1988, while Iran was in the midst of an eight-year war with Iraq. The principle interest of the United States in that conflict was security of the threatened oil transport routes leading from the Persian Gulf. But that rather limited concern eventually resulted in President Ronald Reagan's decision to reflag and escort Kuwaiti tankers in the Gulf in 1987. As a consequence of that decision, American military forces came into direct contact with the forces of the two Middle Eastern belligerents for the first time.

The first of the four major incidents was the Iraqi missile attack on the USS *Stark* on May 17, 1987, which actually preceded the first escort missions in the Gulf. The second was the mine strike on the SS *Bridgeton* on July 24, 1987. This marked the beginning of the active phase of Operation Earnest Will— the escorting of Kuwaiti oil tankers through the Persian Gulf. The third major incident was the U.S. counterattack on Iranian oil platforms and ships in the gulf on April 18, 1988, known as Operation Praying Mantis. The fourth was the tragic shoot-down of an Iranian airliner by the USS *Vincennes* on July 3, 1988. These four incidents show very clearly the complexity of the conflict and the difficulty military forces would encounter in attempting to provide air and maritime security in such closely contested waters over a twenty-six–

month period. It was also a challenging introduction of the Central Command to conflict in the region.

Of these four events, the mine warfare and maritime convoy escort preparations for Earnest Will and the joint force integration of the Praying Mantis attacks provided the most valuable lessons for American commanders, even though they were primarily tactical in nature. The far more useful take-away from the Iranian and Iraqi actions in the Gulf was the need to better understand the strategic motivations and operational techniques of the two belligerents. Unfortunately, the American military did not profit very well or deeply from its introduction to warfare in the Persian Gulf and it would have a very steep learning curve in the buildup for a more conventional war less than two years later.

Chapter 1

THE DECISION TO GO TO WAR

At one in the morning on August 2, 1990, a company of Iraqi commandoes of the Republican Guard's Hammurabi Division slipped across the border into Kuwait to attack Fort Sideriya on the border between the two countries. Two hours later the division's armored columns were advancing through Kuwait at 20 mph toward its capital on the coast. By 9:30 AM the Iraqis had reached the Persian Gulf coast, and by the end of the following day the Hammurabi and its Republican Guard sister divisions had completed the occupation of Kuwait. It seemed to Iraqi commanders that they had accomplished a nearly perfect coup de main.

Saddam Hussein shocked the American government when he deployed his army to annex Kuwait. Despite the fact that the United States had generally favored Iraq in the Iran-Iraq War; even though the Iraqi dictator had, on July 25, assured the U.S. ambassador to Baghdad, April Glaspie, that he had no hostile intentions; and even though Prince Bandar, the Saudi family's ambassador in Washington, had received similar assurances from Saddam in a face-to-face meeting the previous April, no one in the highest levels of government anticipated the Iraqi attack.[1]

Under most circumstances, conflict between Iraq and the tiny emirate on its southern border would have raised little concern in the West. The emir of Kuwait was no friend of democracy, and although his government had supported U.S. desires during the "Tanker War" two years before, few in America had any affection for the Kuwaitis. In truth, few Americans had ever heard of Kuwait, and had it not been for the peculiar circumstances surrounding the Iraqi attack on the small emirate, the history of U.S. involvement in the Middle East might have been very different indeed.

Strategic Surprise

Potential enemies of the United States should learn the lesson that surprise is not something Americans adapt to easily or graciously. Even more characteristically, America seems to support the weak over the strong and to condemn violations of national sovereignty, when it is in its national interest to do so. The media coverage of the violence perpetrated against Kuwaiti noncombatants by Iraqi soldiers disgusted many observers. Finally, the fact that Saddam Hussein had menaced Israel in a speech the previous spring also added to the eventual groundswell of American emotion against his move on Kuwait.

From a completely dispassionate perspective, Iraq had frequently claimed Kuwait as a part of its national territory. The Kuwaiti government and its leader, Sheikh Jaber III al-Sabah, had also snubbed Saddam in a very public way with its continued exportation of oil in excess of its OPEC quota, thus driving prices down when Saddam needed much higher oil prices to pay for his national expansion projects following the long and costly war with Iran. The United States only received 3 percent of its foreign oil from Kuwait in 1989.[2] So, America would have been hard to nudge into a response had it not been for Saddam's audacity and the personal ethic of President George H. W. Bush.

President George H. W. Bush—Key Determination and Commitment

The most instructive incident of America's decision to go to war in 1990 occurred on August 2, when the National Security Council (NSC) was convened in the White House by National Security Advisor Brent Scowcroft. Over the long sleepless night previous, Scowcroft, General Tom Kelly in the Pentagon, and several other senior officials of the government had worked to make initial response preparations in reaction to the invasion by Iraq the day before.[3] In fact, Scowcroft had awakened President Bush at 5 AM to obtain a signature on documents freezing both Iraqi and Kuwaiti financial assets in the United States—so the government had already acted very quickly to make a credible response against Saddam's actions.[4] But no one knew exactly what the president would want to do.

After a fairly lengthy, detailed discussion by the staff, during which the president asked several key questions and made very clear his desire to get diplomatic support, to include the United Nations, and to implement financial sanctions immediately, the meeting ended with no clear decision about the endgame. In fact the major tone of the meeting was more one of resignation against a fait accompli.[5] This was not out of the ordinary for a first meeting of the NSC. Many presidents have used the NSC, but they have used it in very different ways. President Bush was a very hands-on leader with vast government experience, and he used his NSC as a tool *to develop consensus and coordinate actions*. He clearly felt that the United States could not stand idly by, and although General Colin Powell, the Chairman of the Joint Chiefs of Staff, had asked for General Norman Schwarzkopf, the commander of CENTCOM, to attend the meeting, no definitive military actions were discussed. Schwarzkopf had proposed two very broad potential military options, but had stressed the limitations on military power without significant staging bases in the region.[6] Powell and Schwarzkopf left the meeting thinking that only a continued Iraqi penetration in Saudi Arabia would be a cause for war.[7]

After the NSC meeting Scowcroft had a follow-up with the president, who then met with his White House Council, Boyden Gray, concerning the presidential authority for the use of force.[8] Scowcroft was concerned that the other policymakers within the NSC were not seeing the bigger picture—he felt that this first major intervention of the post–Cold War world had enormous ramifications, and in their discussions the president agreed with him. At Scowcroft's urging President Bush would allow him to depart from his usual style during the next NSC meeting to begin the discussion with a statement of the fundamental importance of the situation in Kuwait.[9]

Clearly President Bush favored action, but at that early juncture his views were unknown to the rest of the government. President Bush and Scowcroft then flew to Aspen, Colorado, where the president was scheduled to make a speech after meeting with Prime Minister Margaret Thatcher of the United Kingdom. Thatcher did not mince words when she met with Bush, telling him that "aggressors must never be appeased"—a lesson the free world had learned, at great cost, from the policies of the 1930s. She went on to point out that if Saddam Hussein were to cross the border into Saudi Arabia he could go right down the Gulf in a matter of days, whereupon he would control 65 percent of the world's oil reserves and "could blackmail us all." It was therefore necessary to stop Saddam's aggression, and "stop it quickly."[10]

President Bush seemed at first inclined to delay action in order to see an Arab solution to the problem, but it soon became apparent that such a solution was unlikely. Scowcroft was very concerned that an Arab solution would really mean a compromise and therefore a victory for Saddam.[11] Bush did not immediately rule out the use of force, but at least publicly he did not indicate it was likely either. (President Bush did discuss the immediate deployment of an F-15 fighter squadron to Saudi Arabia with King Fahd, but the Saudi ruler demurred.)[12] Later during the conference at Aspen Thatcher made her views public, saying, "Iraq's invasion of Kuwait defies every principle for which the United Nations stands. If we let it succeed, no small country can ever feel safe again."[13] Though control of the world's oil resources was an important factor affecting the decision to go to war, the central issue for Bush and Thatcher was the sovereignty of nations and the role of the United Nations in the post–Cold War era.

Upon his return from Aspen, President Bush held a second NSC meeting on August 3 attended by Scowcroft, Secretary of Defense Dick Cheney, Deputy Defense Secretary Paul Wolfowitz, General Powell, Deputy Secretary

Lawrence Eagleburger representing State, Under Secretary of State for Political Affairs Robert Kimmett, Secretary James Watkins of the Department of Energy, Attorney General Richard Thornburgh, and William Webster of the CIA. President Bush opened the discussion by noting his agreement with Thatcher and the fact that he had spoken with many leaders in the region, but had mostly detected "hand-wringing"; "the status quo," he told the assemblage, "is intolerable."[14] Scowcroft then commented that in his judgment accommodating the Iraqi attack should not be a policy option, saying, "We have to seriously look at the possibility that we can't tolerate him [Saddam] succeeding."[15] Deputy Secretary of State Eagleburger agreed, and unknowingly echoed Bush's own concerns, saying, "This is the first test of the [post–Cold War] system."[16] Secretary Cheney then observed that the conquest of Kuwait put Saddam in a position to menace Saudi Arabia while providing him with the financial means to acquire additional weapons, including nuclear arms; he concluded by outlining the American resource requirements for any potential military response. Later in the meeting General Powell laid out two basic military options, a defensive deployment of U.S. forces to deter aggression into Saudi Arabia, and "to deploy U.S. force against Iraqi forces in Kuwait to defend Saudi Arabia or possibly go against Iraq." He continued by saying, "Looking at this option, this is harder than Panama or Libya. This would be the NFL, not a scrimmage."[17]

At its conclusion, the second NSC meeting still did not determine a national response, but the official notes of the meeting reflect that the president had made it clear that any U.S. deaths or the taking of American hostages by Iraq would fundamentally alter the nature of the crisis. President Bush was heard to say that if Americans suffered in such ways, the United States would demonstrate "whatever resolve it takes, with or without our friends."[18] The president's views were hardening. Later in the day, Brent Scowcroft met in the White House with Prince Bandar to discuss the deployment of the F-15 squadron but Bandar demurred; pressed by Scowcroft to explain his reluctance to accept such easy assistance, Bandar said that such easy offers from the United States had been retracted just as quickly in the past![19] The commitment of the United States was viewed with much suspicion in the Arab world; many Arabs did not trust the United States to act in their best interests. At the end of their meeting President Bush entered the room unexpectedly, and after noting that Saddam had tricked both the Americans and the Saudis, Bush told Bandar, "I give you my word of honor: I will see this through with you."[20] Bandar then left the White House to meet with Secretary Cheney at the Pentagon to discuss specific assistance options that could be made available to the Saudis.[21]

By August 3, only about forty-eight hours into the crisis, President Bush had already spoken personally with the leaders of Kuwait, Saudi Arabia, Egypt, Jordan, the United Kingdom, France, Turkey, Germany, and Japan. Outside the Arab world nearly every leader agreed that something needed to be done; many spoke of avoiding another Munich. Even the Russian government issued a statement condemning the invasion—a key comment indicating that Saddam's most significant international backer was no longer in support.[22] In the Middle East concerns were equally high, but trust in American involvement and confidence in the utility of confronting Saddam was much lower; resolve among Arabs in the region then seemed quite uncertain.

Journalist Robert Woodward determined that the August 3 NSC meeting also produced a mission for the CIA to develop an option to destabilize the Iraqi regime and perhaps topple Saddam. The context of the minutes of the subsequent NSC meeting confirms that this kind of effort was in planning, but on August 4, as the president traveled to the presidential retreat at Camp David, Maryland, specifically to hear more about military options, it is clear that he had several ideas under consideration, and his mind had not yet been made up.[23]

Executive Commitment

The next day, Saturday, August 4, another NSC meeting was held at Camp David, with Secretary of State James Baker in attendance.[24] General Powell gave General Schwarzkopf the entire morning to brief the president on the details of military planning—specifically on the execution of Operations Plan 90-1002 (OPlan 1002). As Powell prefaced the overview, 1002 was "doable"; it could defend Saudi Arabia from Iraqi attack and could repel such an attack, but any movement north into Iraq would require additional forces. Schwarzkopf provided an overview of Iraqi strengths and weaknesses and said that it would take seventeen weeks to deploy the force necessary to defend the Saudi border; should the president want Iraqi forces pushed out of Kuwait, it would take eight to twelve months to deploy sufficient force to gain an advantageous ratio of combat power over the Iraqis.[25] The discussion returned several times to address the likelihood that an air campaign would be sufficient to deter and defend, but no one felt air power alone offered any guarantee of success.[26] The meeting adjourned and a smaller group stayed behind to discuss sensitive intelligence issues with President Bush. Later on Saturday, Bush again contacted world leaders to develop support. One of the leaders he spoke to was the Kuwaiti emir, Sheik Jabir al Ahmed al Sabah. According to Woodward, Bush promised to liberate Kuwait and restore the emir to power.[27]

By the time President Bush returned to the White House the following day, Sunday, August 5, he had decided to use military power to stop Saddam

Hussein; he had not, however, determined the full measure of the military requirement because he did not yet know if Saddam would invade Saudi Arabia. As he met with reporters on the south lawn of the White House, he responded to questions from the media and concluded by saying, "This will not stand. This will not stand, this aggression against Kuwait."[28] Even Colin Powell was surprised by the president's forceful reply. Bush later said he did not intend to voice anything greater than commitment to resolution of the crisis, but in reality he had made up his mind.[29] It had taken him three days to decide that Saddam's attack on Kuwait warranted war.

On Sunday afternoon Defense Secretary Cheney departed Andrews Air Force Base for Jiddah, Saudi Arabia, to brief King Fahd and try to obtain basing rights for U.S. forces to flow into the region. That evening, in another NSC meeting held in the Cabinet Room of the White House, President Bush made two points that demonstrated he understood the problem quite well. First he noted that the situation would not truly end until Saddam was gone: "All will not be tranquil until Saddam Hussein is history." Then he emphasized that there was a critical difference between defending Saudi Arabia and liberating Kuwait, saying, "It is one thing to defend and quite another to liberate."[30]

President Bush had made the decision for war with a full understanding of the economic, diplomatic, and military options available to him. He had emphasized the role of the United Nations and had worked ceaselessly to develop an international consensus on the problem by personally speaking with leaders around the world. Though he understood the basic geometry of the military problem, he had not directed specific actions of his generals; rather, he had asked questions to determine in his own mind if the options available could achieve the ends that he desired, and left the details of how to accomplish those ends to his generals—largely within the rubric of OPlan 1002, which Secretary Cheney was to monitor.

President Bush met again with Margaret Thatcher on Monday, August 6, and during that meeting they received word that the United Nations had passed its second resolution (UNSCR 661) condemning the Iraqi invasion and directing an embargo of all goods (but not foodstuffs) going in or out of Iraq and Kuwait. Thatcher had a strong supportive effect on President Bush and the discussions they later had with the press clearly indicated that the two leaders were of the same mind and committed to ending the threat posed by Saddam.

Though President Bush clearly understood that Saddam Hussein could not be trusted and that the Iraqi dictator was the heart of the problem, he still did not understand the reason for Saddam's actions or what his real objectives were. There had been discussion in the NSC meetings about Saddam's potential to control the oil markets, but little was discussed about the internal domestic motivations of the Iraqi leader.

American Naiveté

Some analysts contend that the United States fought Saddam from a Western perspective rather than understanding the Iraqi motivations and then fighting the Iraqi ruler in a way he would understand. This theory contends that the failure to fight the war in a way that Saddam understood undercut every major effort by the coalition. Because the Western powers did not understand Saddam's motivations and value system their efforts at deterrence were fatally flawed from the beginning, and any hope that they had of using a coalition of forces to defeat Saddam would be doomed to failure.

This is vitally important because an understanding of Saddam's motivations and outlook might have increased the effectiveness of non-military efforts (diplomacy and international pressure), thus avoiding combat. Those who really understood the Iraqi experience in the long Iran-Iraq War could draw many useful lessons from that conflict, including some that showed Saddam claiming victory even though his forces had never achieved any degree of tactical or operational success against their enemies on the field of battle (because the Iraqi forces had protected their territory against Iranian threats). Such lessons should have aided in the development of a more accurate view of Saddam's thinking and therefore to the development of more effective persuasive efforts on the part of the United States and the coalition it led.

For example: since the motivations for Saddam's attack on Kuwait were predominantly economic, and his justifications for the move were humanitarian and cultural, the West could have developed economic aid packages designed for the Kuwaitis, knowing full well that any financial aid sent to Kuwait would have eventually flowed to Saddam. Such a payout might have induced him to depart from a more secure Kuwait without combat, with his coffers enlarged as well as his international reputation increased.

Unfortunately, after the invasion, there was very little understanding that meeting force with force would only harden Saddam's resolve, and even less inclination to use economic leverage particularly if it would actually "reward" the Iraqis for their attack. Nevertheless, these issues were still very much under consideration in the early days of the crisis, until it became known that Saddam had taken Western (and American) hostages in late August. This action was a "red line" in the eyes of President Bush which, once crossed, obviated the use of diplomacy and sanctions as means for resolving the issue. Nations need to develop mature and realistic expectations of their own national values. They also must understand the values of other states and their leaders, if military confrontations are to be effectively avoided and conflicts eventually solved for the longer term.

Coalition Warfare and the Role of the United Nations

Although President Bush was determined enough to "go it alone" if necessary to defend Saudi Arabia, his strong inclination from the beginning was to confront Saddam from a united international position. As a former U.S. ambassador to the United Nations, he understood the functioning of the UN very well and also valued its role in the post–World War II world. President Bush wanted the United Nations Security Council fully engaged in crisis resolution and also sought the support of friends and allies of the United States from around the world in the early days of the crisis to generate global condemnation.

Still, as much as the President wanted to develop an international response to Saddam's aggression, actually forming a global partnership among like-minded nations and operating in a coalition environment was much more difficult than simply gathering promises from international partners. Military action remains overwhelmingly a unilateral act; nations that undertake military action do so under their own unique laws, in their own national interests, and the rules for the employment of military force are among the most sacrosanct of national prerogatives. With the forty-year-old North Atlantic Treaty Organization (NATO) alliance as its only working model, the United States still had to develop a very different and much less constrained coalition if it was to fight alongside regional partners from outside Europe, particularly the all-important regional partner nations from the Middle East, which did not share the common juridical tradition that made the often frustrating but workable NATO alliance functional as a supra-national military organization.

Bush seemed to understand intuitively that the coalition needed to include members from the Arab states of the Middle East, even though military coordination among such potential partners would be extremely difficult to gain and maintain because the level of training and the equipment of many of the Middle Eastern nations was vastly different from that of the U.S. military. Many of the forces from Arab states were in fact equipped with Soviet military equipment, just like the Iraqis.

However, the campaign against Saddam Hussein was to be much more than an international military response to aggression. In many ways both President Bush and his national security advisor, Brent Scowcroft, saw the response as the first step in establishing a new world order wherein the UN could become a guiding force in world affairs through the promotion of democratic principles. And of course the United States would be the leader of this new order around the globe and share richly in the development and progress that it would foster. Bush and Scowcroft conceived this vision while on a fishing trip at the Bush home in Kennebunkport, Maine, and they worked diligently to bring it to fruition throughout the following months.[31]

Ends, Ways, and Means—National Goals

Any coherent national security decision has to be framed by the national interests of the countries involved and a realistic appraisal of the anticipated risks and expected costs of any action. These factors clearly drove the dialog within the National Security Council in the early weeks of August. Ultimately, however, a decision has to be made either to act or to ignore a specific threat, and President Bush decided on August 5 that the United States would act to defend other nations against Iraqi aggression. Once that decision was taken, the goals established by the Commander in Chief for the American response would dominate all subsequent actions. Thankfully, the Bush administration understood the importance of formulating and communicating clear goals for its actions, and to that end it produced "National Security Directive 45."[32]

Signed on August 20, 1990, the directive spelled out four national goals: the immediate, complete, and unconditional withdrawal of Iraqi forces from Kuwait; the restoration of Kuwait's legitimate government; restoration of the security and stability of the Gulf region, and finally the protection of the lives of American citizens abroad.[33] The document identifying these goals also provided—in fact, began with—an assessment of American interests around the globe, and included a list of national capabilities that were to be employed in areas of economic, diplomatic, military, energy, and coalition activity.

From this document it was quite easy for the cabinet agencies of the U.S. government to develop their own objectives that could support the overall national effort. The entire U.S. government was involved in the response to Iraqi aggression in 1990; though it often appears that military activity predominated, during the early months of the crisis diplomacy, economics, and informational leverage were actually the most frequently used tools of statecraft. Within the Department of Defense, it was clear that goal of unconditional withdrawal might entail the use of military force, but the document also made clear that any use of force would be made as a coalition effort, with clear importance given to regional stability. President Bush's decision to include the protection of American citizens was clearly aimed at Saddam's tactic of hostage-taking but, as a specified national goal, it also compelled military planners to develop options that could accomplish the expulsion of the Iraqi forces while retaining some capability to protect citizens that remained *in harm's way.*

Elements of Statecraft

With the clear strategic direction provided in NSD 45, a host of cabinet officials began to work on a solution to the crisis. The individual departments of the U.S. government each had a supporting role to play, but most prominent among the agencies outside Defense were efforts by the State Department, the Department of Transportation, and the Department of Energy.

Secretary James Baker's State Department bore the brunt of the non-military activity that supported President Bush's resolve to act against Iraq. The department's efforts were continuous and broad-based throughout the period following the invasion and until the operation to repel the Iraq attack commenced in January 1991. A summary of the efforts of Secretary Baker show in outline the major actions of the diplomatic element of national power during this period. His efforts can be broken into three major platforms: exerting pressure to bring the Soviet Union into opposition with the Iraqi invasion; convincing the members of the UN Security Council to support the coalition effort against Saddam with powerful resolutions; and, finally, an effort to develop broad-based coalition support from around the globe, even including nations that could not normally commit military forces to the coalition effort.

Baker's initial efforts with the Soviet Union began as early as the day of the invasion, when he happened to be meeting with his Soviet counterpart, Edward Shevardnadze, in Irkutsk, Siberia, and became the first to announce the invasion to the Soviet foreign minister. Within twenty-four hours the two diplomats had forged an understanding condemning the invasion.[34] Baker then flew to Moscow for a second meeting where the two issued a joint statement saying, "Today, we take the unusual step of jointly calling upon the rest of the international community to join with us in an international cutoff of all arms supplies to Iraq," and calling on the Security Council to "'promptly and decisively condemn the brutal and illegal invasion of Kuwait by Iraqi military forces.''[35] Because the Soviet Union sat as a member of the permanent five on the council and particularly due to the significant support that the Soviets had provided to Saddam Hussein, the joint statement was a huge signal to the Iraqi leader. Coming as it did in 1990, just after the fall of the Berlin Wall, the joint statement also seemed to indicate that President Bush's hopes for a new world order were actually realistic.

Baker's efforts with the Soviets continued for months afterwards, and he visited Moscow twice before November, but he soon turned his major efforts to convincing the other members of the Security Council that resolutions offered an important answer to the Iraqi crisis. President Bush's emphasis on using the United Nations to support the international response was a challenge, as gaining the needed votes was always far from a foregone conclusion. The Security Council was influenced from many sides and the United Nations General Assembly was also prone to sway toward the views of several influential blocs, some of which were traditionally reluctant to consider intervention in the affairs of member states. So, gaining the necessary votes in the Security Council was a battle each time a resolution was proposed. Some in the Bush administration feared that using the council could backfire, but Secretary Baker remained confident that each vote could be managed to ensure support.[36]

In actuality, according to Dennis Ross, "the administration operated at three different levels in managing the Security Council. Tom Pickering, the U.S. ambassador to the United Nations, worked his counterparts in New York; in Washington, the ambassadors from the countries on the Security Council were called in for meetings at the State Department; and in the foreign capitals of the countries on the Security Council, our ambassadors discussed every resolution with their host countries."[37] These efforts were just as intense and fatiguing as the parallel actions used to deploy military forces to the crisis region. Secretary Baker has said, "I met personally with all my Security Council counterparts in an intricate process of cajoling, extracting, threatening, and occasionally buying votes. Such are the politics of diplomacy."[38]

The third major task executed by the diplomats in the State Department was the formation and maintenance of the international coalition which actually opposed the Iraqi invasion. Eventually the coalition consisted of forces from thirty-one countries: Afghanistan, Argentina, Australia, Bahrain, Bangladesh, Belgium, Canada, Denmark, Egypt, France, Greece, Italy, Kuwait, Morocco, The Netherlands, New Zealand, Niger, Norway, Oman, Pakistan, Portugal, Qatar, Republic of Korea, Saudi Arabia, Senegal, Singapore, Spain, Syria, the United Arab Emirates, the United Kingdom, and the United States itself. And just as importantly those forces were supported by financial contributions totaling $10 billion from Japan and $6.6 billion from Germany.

Each of these nations had unique interests and concerns, so every national commitment had to be nurtured differently. For example, Turkey had to close the oil pipeline from Iraq to participate in the international embargo—an extremely expensive proposition for which compensation had to be developed. Japan could not constitutionally provide forces, but had the economic resources and the national interests at stake to support fully as a financial partner. And Syria, which brought huge dividends to the coalition as an Arab member, had to be handled very carefully as well. President Bush met with every key leader of the coalition and maintained a remarkable effort of telephone diplomacy—earning him the nickname the "Mad Dialer."[39]

The Department of Transportation was still relatively new in 1990, but participated in two very meaningful ways to the success of America's response to Iraqi aggression. On August 10, the Maritime Administration activated sealift ships from the Ready Reserve Force (RRF); then, one week later, on August 17, the Federal Aviation Administration oversaw the activation of part of the Civil Reserve Air Fleet (CRAF) for airlift to the Middle East for the first time in the history of the program. These two actions provided the commander of the U.S. Transportation Command within the Defense Department critical transport assets that could not be matched with regular military assets. Throughout the following months, RRF ships and CRAF aircraft would continue to carry the bulk of the American military contingent to combat in the region.

On the same day, Transportation Secretary Skinner and Coast Guard Admiral Kime also committed Coast Guard law enforcement boarding teams to support Operation Desert Shield. Later that same month, on August 22, President Bush authorized the call-up of selected members of the Coast Guard Reserve to active duty in support of operations in the Persian Gulf region. Three port security units (PSUs), consisting of 550 Coast Guard Reservists, deployed to the Gulf, as the first involuntary overseas mobilization of Coast Guard Reserve units in the fifty-year history of the organization.

Secretary James Watkins and his subordinates at the Department of Energy also played a rare strong role in the crisis because of the importance of oil to all three principal nations involved and the regional dynamics of the Middle East. The department's initial priorities were to calm the domestic oil markets, reassure the public concerning oil issues, enhance energy coordination with international partners (particularly the International Energy Agency), and decrease consumption and stimulate domestic production to meet the nation's needs. The department also made recommendations concerning the use of the Strategic Oil Reserve.[40]

Strategic Commitment

Once the decision to use military force had been taken, the United States faced a number of hurdles. It had very little capacity to act immediately against Saddam's forces half a world away, but would instead have to deploy forces capable of repulsing Saddam, while building consensus among the American people that tiny Kuwait was worth the effort, as well as creating a coalition that could demonstrate that other nations supported the stand against the Iraqi leader. The decision for war was not easy, but preparing for combat would be much harder and would test President Bush, Saddam Hussein, and the United Nations in a host of ways over the period of months to come.

Chapter 2

THE IRAQI CONTEXT

Because secrecy and layers of control were integral to the way Saddam Hussein ruled Iraq, we may never know the full rationale behind his decision to invade Kuwait in August 1990. Still, there can be no doubt that three factors significantly influenced his decision to use military force.

The first factor that impelled Saddam to act was the economic and financial crisis in Iraq that had resulted from the long war with Iran and the untimely decrease in the global price of oil in 1989 and 1990. The second stimulus for war was the burden on the Iraqi economy of maintaining the large army that was developed to fight Iran and, even more problematic from Saddam's standpoint, the negative impact of demobilizing that army and the resulting increase in unemployment on the already under-burdened Iraqi work force.

Finally, and perhaps most importantly, Saddam seemed to sense an opportunity to seize for himself a larger place among the leadership of the Arab world by resisting the influence of outsiders and calling for renewed influence on the part of the Muslim nations in the Middle East. Though Saddam Hussein's faith cannot be judged to have had a significant place in his life, he was still undoubtedly influenced by the most common Muslim worldview of the time, which held that the Islamic world had suffered long under persecution by the West in particular and Western phenomena such as liberalization, democracy, and industrialization in general. In the face of this onslaught, Muslim leaders in the Middle East had far too frequently failed to oppose these negative influences on their society and had most commonly chosen to profit from the Western ways, to the disadvantage of the people.

Saddam was certainly more interested in his own power and influence than he was in the plight of the individual Iraqi, yet he also understood that the need to satisfy Arab and Muslim pride would very likely bring many outside Iraq to support any effort he made against the influences of the West. He had defended his fellow Arabs from Iran for nearly a decade and he felt justified in continuing to call for the support of other Arab states as he acted to denounce a wide range of issues, many of which were focused increasingly after January 1990 on Israel and on his former quasi-ally, the United States.

Finally, beneath the stated reasons that Saddam Hussein sought a more prominent role for Iraq in world affairs was the very real, but more rarely understood rationale that lay with the creation of modern Iraq itself. No one should have considered conducting a war with Iraq without understanding the unique cultural and national characteristics that grew there from the very creation of the Iraqi state.

The Creation of Modern Iraq

As is true of most nations, the cultural, religious, and ethnic aspects of Iraqi society have had a powerful influence on the course of Iraqi history. But the very nature of the creation of the Iraqi state incited a distrust of foreigners and distaste for democratic processes. Few modern nations with such proud ancient histories and with so many important contributions to world society have such inauspicious beginnings as does modern Iraq.

The Sumerians, whom we identify among the early inhabitants of Iraq, created one of the earliest forms of written communications, cuneiform. Ziggurats, the epic of Gilgamesh, and other great advances followed in Sumerian society between the Tigris and the Euphrates. The Babylonian period then gave the world the code of Hammurabi, astronomy, and much of the original foundation for modern economic and social networks. The Assyrian period brought the development of the professional army to the world and the Chaldeans that followed re-established Babylon as the greatest city in the Near East and created the Hanging Gardens there, known forever after as one of the Seven Wonders of the Ancient World.

Unfortunately, from the ancient period through the modern era, Iraq has been ruled by foreign powers, and foreign domination has had a strong, negative impact on modern Iraq. First the Persians under Alexander and his successors, then the Abbasid Caliphate controlled Iraqi territory following the Arab domination of the area in the seventh century. It was in fact the advent of Arab Muslim control in the region that first signaled a significant break with the area's storied past, as among a host of momentous changes, the advent of Islam partially erased the affinity many people still held for the ancient Babylonian glory. Then the Ottomans took control in the sixteenth century, ruling Iraq for hundreds of years. What became modern Iraq was finally delivered out of the Ottoman Empire as a result of the First World War; but only through a thinly disguised and somewhat disruptive period of British domination.

The occupying Ottoman Turks had ruled the modern territory of Iraq as three separate provinces, Mosul, Baghdad and Basra. Shortly after declaring war on the Ottomans, the British landed military forces in Basra to create an outpost linking the far reaches of their empire and to gain a foothold in the oil-rich region. Nearly a million soldiers of the British Empire would eventually serve in the area and in March 1917, the British forces entered Baghdad on their way to establishing control of all three provinces. The British theater commander at the time, General Sir Frederick Stanley Maude, promised the local people, "Our armies do not come into your cities and lands as conquerors or enemies, but as liberators."[1]

The British effort to establish their authority in Iraq was not easy. Although they gained control of Basra and Baghdad with relative ease, they encountered resistance from the Kurds in the north and in the primarily Shia cities of Najaf and Karbala in the south. These areas would remain volatile during the entire period of British rule. The British imported their style of colonialism from nearby India as they sought to pacify the three provinces, but in doing so they overturned one of the hallmarks of the rather effective Ottoman rule and reinforced the authority of the local sheiks in order to minimize the number of British local administrators. The sheiks under British rule were empowered to provide security in the areas under their control and to collect taxes. Thus, from the earliest days, the British reinforced two of the hallmarks that mark Iraqi society today: the empowerment of the sheiks and continuing divisions between the ethnic Kurdish and Shia regions.[2]

During the Great War, Sharif Hussein of the holy city of Mecca had organized and led an Arab revolt against the Ottomans in support of the Allied war effort in the region; and, as a result, Hussein was promised a leadership position after the war by the British. Hussein sent his son to lead the armed forces of the revolt, and it was the son, Faisal (ably assisted by T. E. Lawrence) who wrecked such havoc on the Ottomans for the Allied cause.

After the war, American President Woodrow Wilson strongly supported the creation of an independent Arab state in the region with the twelfth of his "Fourteen Points" stating, "The Turkish portion of the present Ottoman Empire should be assured a secure sovereignty, but the other nationalities which are now under Turkish rule should be assured an undoubted security of life and an absolutely unmolested opportunity of autonomous development, and the Dardanelles should be permanently opened as a free passage to the ships and commerce of all nations under international guarantees."[3] Faisal even traveled to Paris to attend the peace conference at Versailles, seeking the promised reward, only to find something rather different in the offing—the throne of Syria.

Unfortunately for Faisal, the French and British had other more complex motivations and desires for the region and they developed a political system between self-determination and colonization, known as a mandate in the San Remo Accords of 1920. A mandate was in effect a colonial administration, but one designed to eventually foster self-rule. After the mandate system was

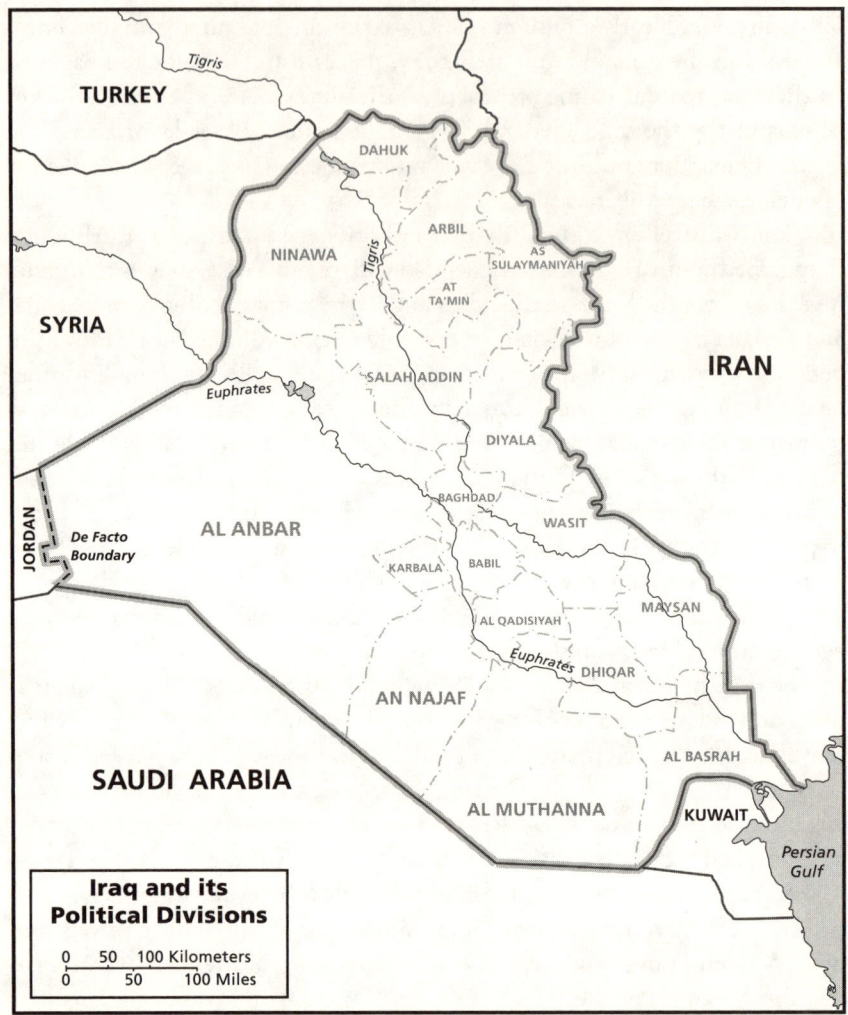

TURKEY

Tigris

DAHUK

ARBIL

NINAWA

Tigris

AS SULAYMANIYAH

AT TA'MIN

SYRIA

Euphrates

SALAH ADDIN

IRAN

DIYALA

JORDAN

De Facto Boundary

AL ANBAR

BAGHDAD

WASIT

KARBALA

BABIL

AL QADISIYAH

MAYSAN

Euphrates

DHIQAR

AN NAJAF

AL BASRAH

SAUDI ARABIA

AL MUTHANNA

KUWAIT

Persian Gulf

Iraq and its Political Divisions

| 0 | 50 | 100 Kilometers |
| 0 | 50 | 100 Miles |

created, the territories of the Ottoman Empire were split up as had been previously (and secretly) agreed upon in the Sykes-Picot Agreement in 1916, wherein much of modern Iraq was awarded to the British.

On November 11, 1920, the three former Ottoman provinces were joined to become a League of Nations mandate, under British control, labeled the "State of Iraq." (See map.) Winston Churchill, then the British colonial secretary, was the cabinet official who had to work out how the new state would actually be governed. He met with a group of Middle East specialists, including T. E. Lawrence and Gertrude Bell (colonial secretary in the British High Commission in Baghdad), in Cairo to address the governance of the new mandate. From that conference Churchill rather reluctantly determined that

Faisal was the right man to lead Iraq. It is also from this period that the Sunnis in Iraq, though a minority of the total population in the three former provinces, were selected to be the primary sector of Iraqi society entrusted with government authority.

While the details of the mandate were being worked out, however, the Iraqi people did not remain idle, nor were they particularly happy with the process that appeared to be awarding them to yet another colonizing power. Opposition to the British had been growing over time, and beginning in April an open revolt broke out in Rumaitha, where a sheik was imprisoned for refusing to pay a debt. Over a three-month period, the revolt never reached too deeply into the cities, but did cost the British four hundred lives and nearly 40 million pounds.[4] The revolt eventually failed, but it did send a strong signal to the British and set some important precedents for the future, in particular the need to exert strong central authority across the provinces. It was to be only the first of several Iraqi revolts against foreign rule.

The British formally installed King Faisal in a new Iraqi state on August 23, 1921. Faisal was not an Iraqi, but the British felt that he was well qualified for the job: as the Arab leader of the revolt against the Ottoman sultan during the war he was well known and highly respected, especially in Baghdad; he was also a member of the Sunni Hashimite family from Mecca, and had formerly been named king of Syria. Once nominated by the British, however, Faisal still had to be elected. As Phebe Marr points out: "There followed a well managed plebiscite which indicated that 96 percent of the population favored Faisal. In fact, his real support was nowhere near that figure. The Kurdish portion of the population and the pro-Turkish groups in the north wanted no part of Faisal. . . . The shi'i religious leaders wanted a theocratic government. Yet there is no little doubt that no other candidate had his stature or could have received anywhere near the acclamation he did."[5]

The New Iraqi State

The multi-ethnic and religious nature of Iraq had long been a problem, and compounded by the lack of clearly identifiable borders and the nomadic nature of many of the inhabitants, it was obvious that Iraq would pose a governance challenge. Although Faisal was legitimized by a plebiscite in 1921, in reality Iraqi independence was a sham until the 1930s, when the British mandate officially ended. Even more importantly, during this mandate period, elections in Iraq were regularly rigged to keep control of Iraq in the hands of a few oligarchs (Baghdadis allied with wealthy landowners), all with the support of the British administration. Though nominally a constitutional monarchy, this sham democratic government was soon completely discredited in the eyes of many Iraqis. "From their perspective, constitutional democracy in Iraq had become a tool of colonialism."[6] The other impact of Faisal's rule was the institution of his largely Sunni supporters within the administration of Iraq—and as a result the beginning of clear Sunni domination over the other religious segments of Iraqi society from a very early time in its national life.

The Cairo Conference that delivered King Faisal also gave impetus to three other significant influences in Iraq: the treaty through which Britain exercised indirect rule in Iraq, the constitution, and the Iraqi army. The treaty required the king to take fiscal guidance from the British, which allowed Britain to control the country economically, and to appoint British administrators to a number of important posts within the country, thus giving Britain a powerful intelligence scheme and influence in key regions and departments. The constitution of Iraq was designed to give the king and the British high commissioner dominant power over the national assembly. It was never accepted by the Iraqi people because it failed to give them real influence over their own affairs and was always viewed as an "instrument of foreign manipulation and control."[7] Finally, the Iraqi army was envisioned by the British as a means to help control the population but it also soon became a bastion of Sunni control.

In 1927, oil in the Kirkuk area brought some economic improvement, but the exploration rights were still controlled by a British oil compan. In 1930, as the British were easing control of everyday affairs in Iraq to the monarchy, they still retained military bases in Iraq and had control of both economic and foreign policy. It was not until October 1932 that Iraq truly became self-governing—after eleven years of foreign domination.

Rising Iraqi Nationalism and a Cycle of Coups

The same sentiments that gave rise to the 1920 revolt against the British only simmered as time passed under King Faisal's rule. When the treaty that gave the British their authority in Iraq came up for review in 1922, the revolt gained new life, as it did again in 1924 when a constituent assembly met to consider government organizational reforms. In each of these cases there was a sort of alliance of convenience between the Sunni urban elites and the Shia religious leaders in the south—though neither favored the other, both were working for better representation in the Iraqi government. Unfortunately, none of the opposition groups or their leaders seemed to be able to build a base of power sufficient to make changes in the government. Through the 1920s only the growing Iraqi army seemed to offer a real base of support for the nationalist cause.

In 1929, after a change of government in London, the British decided to reduce their influence in Iraq and move toward Iraqi independence. By 1930 a new treaty had been negotiated by Iraqi Prime Minister Nuri al-Said.[8] The treaty gave the British extensive permissions for the stationing of military forces in Iraq, but also demonstrated Iraqi independence from British control, and in 1932 Iraq joined the League of Nations as the first mandate state to achieve self-determination. Unfortunately, as the British withdrew from Iraq, the new county's weaknesses only became more evident, when many largely inexperienced Iraqi politicians were forced to face a variety of internal problems for the first time. Among these problems were a gradual dissolution of the weak unity engendered by British efforts, a resurgence of Shia tribalism, and a general disaffection with the government by Iraqis who had long before seen through the sham constitutional monarchy.[9]

King Faisal was succeeded by his twenty-one-year-old son Ghazi in 1933. The new king, who ruled until 1939, was even less effective than his father; his only noteworthy accomplishment was to proclaim Iraqi authority over Kuwait during a period that witnessed a number of small but well publicized tribal revolts, a coup led by General Bakr Sidiqi, a Kurd, and an increase in the influence of the Iraqi army on national politics on the model of Turkey's Mustafa Kamal. In 1936 the Iraqi army conducted a coup to dispose the prime minister and replace him with a more sympathetic politician. The new government represented a complete change of the ruling elite beneath the king in Iraq and it brought the military to a position of great influence behind the scenes. Upon the king's early death in an automobile accident the following year, Ghazi's four-year-old son Faisal II followed him in the line of succession, and Iraq was governed for years by a weak regent—Ghazi's cousin Abd al-Ilah.

The single most influential factor in this period was the halting but clear increase in nationalistic sentiment over time and the tendency of the Iraqi government to drift frequently toward more conservative methods and to military leaders. Ministers and generals came and went, but two, Nuri al-Said and Rashid Ali, returned to government many times, illustrating the contest between Iraqi nationalist and pro-British and pro-Western approaches.

Mid-Century Return of Colonialism

In March 1940 World War II ushered in a second period of British influence even though sentiment in Iraq was more open to the ideas of national socialism and Arab nationalism.[10] The Iraqi government, led by ardent nationalist Prime Minister Rashid Ali,[11] seeking to distance itself from British influence, inflamed London by a series of missteps which resulted in a return of significant

British forces to Iraq.[12] When Rashid Ali refused to assist the British in compliance with the terms of the 1930 treaty, London gave Baghdad an ultimatum. After a short period of crisis, Rashid Ali and his nationalistic administration, with the strong support of the army, soon deposed Abd al-Ilah as regent and prepared to oppose the British.

In response, the British landed additional forces in Iraq, which caused Rashid Ali's government to fall. Subsequently, the Iraqi military performed dismally trying to defend the country in what some call the Anglo-Iraqi War and, after a major battle near Fallujah, the British forces under Lieutenant General Edward Quinan entered Baghdad in June 1941 to restore the influence of pro-British Iraqis in the national government, including Abd al-Ilah and Nuri al-Said; it was a second British occupation.

British forces remained in Iraq until October 1947. In London's eyes, the occupation of Iraq was necessary to ensure access to the oil resources in Iraq and to keep the lines of communication and transport through Iraq to the Indian subcontinent open. Rashid Ali and many of his nationalist supporters were tried and convicted and a number of Iraqi army officers were retired; many other Iraqis considered a threat to the new pro-British government were also interned. These actions significantly broadened the gulf between the new Iraqi government and the majority of its citizenry, many of whom viewed the nationalists as martyrs. The war also brought inflation and scarcity of everyday supplies, making life in Iraq even more difficult for the people.

Postwar Iraq

In 1945, Iraq joined the United Nations and also became a founding member of the Arab League the same year. The following year, Nuri al-Said returned as premier but regent Abd al-Ilah continued to press for more distance from Great Britain and more liberalization of politics within Iraq. Eventually, a new treaty was signed in January 1948 which ended the stationing of British forces on Iraqi soil and signaled the return of Iraqi sovereignty, but still required Baghdad to support the United Kingdom in time of war.

Meanwhile, the people of Iraq had watched the activity in the British mandate of Palestine with increasing concern. Beginning in 1946, strikes and demonstrations in support of the Palestinian Arabs were conducted by IraqiSunni and Shia Arab populations as well as its ethnic Kurdish peoples. Similar demonstrations occurred throughout the next year as the United Nations struggled with partition plans. Then in May 1948, with the establishment of the state of Israel, Iraq enthusiastically entered the first Arab-Israeli War along with other members of the Arab League in order to defend the rights of the Palestinians. Iraq sent some five thousand troops into Israel but found only disappointment with the performance of the Arab forces deployed in the war, not the swift victory that was expected. Iraq was not a party to the cease-fire agreement signed in May 1949, but was very much affected by the soul-searching that resulted from the lack of Arab success in the war.

In May 1953, Faisal II finally acceded to the throne, though he still looked to Abd al-Ilah and the long-serving Nuri al-Said for advice. Iraq's social and economic problems were growing, as was the influence of both the national-ist and communist movements inside the country, which made Faisal's rule increasingly unpopular. Elections in 1954 returned a surprisingly broad-based, representative government, but internal problems soon combined with for-eign affairs tensions to dampen democratic trends and retain the dominance of the conservative and military figures in Iraq.

In an attempt to gain more regional security and freedom of action from its British allies, Iraq supported the concept of the so-called Baghdad Pact linking it with its neighbors, Turkey and Iran, and perhaps even Pakistan. The pact was advocated by the United States and acceptable to the British, so in 1955 Iraq and Turkey signed an agreement for reciprocal military support and basing relationships. Later in the fall, Iran and Pakistan joined the pact as well. The United States participated in the committee relationships estab-lished under the pact.

In February 1958, King Hussein of Jordan proposed a union of Hashimite monarchies to counter the recently formed Egyptian-Syrian union, and later that same summer King Hussein asked for Iraqi military assistance during the escalating Lebanon crisis. Inspired by the rise to power of Egypt's Nasser, and dissatisfied with their own government's weakness, units of the Iraqi army under the command of General Abdul Karim Qasim chose to march on Baghdad instead, where Qasim and Colonel Abdul Salam Arif mounted a coup on July 14, 1958. King Faisal and several members of his family were shot in the gardens of the palace. The British-inspired Iraqi experiment with royalty was finally over, to be replaced by another form of authoritarian rule in Iraq.

The impact of the two British invasions on Iraq stood as a backdrop to almost everything that happened there through the first decade of the century to follow. Following several hundred years of foreign domination, the British twice showed the Iraqis how their strategically important land would be used by others if they did not resist foreign control. These memories would be rekin-dled when the United States took up a similar stance to the British in the two decades following the 1990 campaign. From 1958, only Ba'athist nationalist leaders would control Iraq, until the party was toppled in 2003.

The Qasim Years

The government initially established in Baghdad by Qasim and Arif was surprisingly broad-based, with all three major faiths and an array of professions represented in its ruling council and cabinet. The government's platform was decidedly anti-colonial and indicated a shift away from the West and toward the Soviet Union. The coup leaders even drafted a constitution for Iraq, but they soon fell away from each other over the issue of union with the United Arab Republic (Egypt and Syria) and with their disagreement over pan-Arabism. Qasim pushed out Arif to assume control, but he was eventually the target of an assassination attempt by a group of Ba'ath party thugs, including a then largely unknown Saddam Hussein in October 1959.[13]

Over time, the Iraqi Communist Party had gained ever greater influence in the country and by 1959 Qasim was persuaded to end the Baghdad Pact and align Iraq with the Soviet Union. Qasim started his revolution with liberal intentions and he did accomplish many much-needed reforms. In particular he changed the land distribution and inheritance laws, gave women more rights, and greatly expanded funding for education. He also took on the Iraq Petroleum Company to gain more control over the nation's natural resources. But at the same time, he was consolidating power into his own hands and growing ever more isolated from the Iraqi people.

As Qasim was liberalizing many aspects of life in Iraq, the Shia leadership in the country grew increasing worried about the infringement of the new national laws on the religious life and practices of Islam. As a consequence, two Shia parties grew increasingly important in Iraq, and one of them, the Dawa Party, would remain a powerful institution in Iraq for the remainder of the century and into the next.

Just as Qasim's government caused many changes in the social and political structure inside Iraq, it had a similarly significant impact in foreign affairs, as Qasim moved Iraq away from the West and toward the Soviet Union. This meant that both Great Britain and the United States ceased providing support to Iraq and also implied that the stability that they and the Baghdad Pact had brought to the region was at risk. Relations between Iran and Iraq soon soured (principally over control of the Shatt al Arab, but also over an Arab-populated province in Iran). Then in 1961, Kuwait gained independence from Britain and Iraq claimed sovereignty over the small state. Not surprisingly, London reacted strongly to Iraq's claim and sent troops to Kuwait to deter Qasim; he was eventually forced to back down and in October 1963, Iraq formally recognized Kuwaiti sovereignty.

The Ba'ath Party Comes to Power

Although Qasim had accomplished perhaps more than any other Iraqi leader since independence, his erratic foreign policy, preference for the Communist Party, and increasing isolation made him extremely unpopular among the power brokers in Iraq. Plus, he was particularly detested by pan-Arabists. For these reasons he was eventually assassinated following a Ba'ath Party coup in February 1963—an act which eventually brought some stability to Iraq and also led to the rule of Saddam Hussein.

The Ba'ath Party, formally the Arab Socialist Ba'ath Party, was founded by Michel Aflaq and has its origins in Syria in the 1940s. It began as a secular Arab movement focused predominately on core tenets of nationalism, socialism, and belief in pan-Arabism. The name Ba'ath itself means rebirth or resurrection—perhaps reflective of the strong anti-colonial sentiment and Arab pride that inspired its original members. The Ba'ath Party started as a very small organization, but soon spread widely around the Middle East, eventually to include non-Muslims among its ranks. It grew through the late 1940s and 1950s, fueled by Arab nationalism and reaction to the foundation of the state of Israel; it grew most prominently in both Syria and Iraq, where the Ba'ath Party took power in the same year.

The Ba'athists took power in Iraq under the leadership of General Ahmed Hasan al-Bakr, a Tikriti and long time pan-Arabist who had participated in the 1941 revolt against Nuri al-Said and was also one of the leaders of the 1958 coup that brought Qasim to power. al-Bakr became prime minister and vice president of Iraq and Colonel Abdul as-Salam Muhammad Arif—another veteran of the 1958 coup—was installed as president. In the immediate aftermath of the coup, the Ba'athists conducted purges that killed thousands of Iraqis, particularly those sympathetic to the communists. Nine months later, Arif led a successful coup against his own Ba'ath government to displace al-Bakr. [14] President Arif ruled for three years, but then in April 1966 he died in a helicopter crash and was succeeded by his brother, General Abdul Rahman Arif, who retained power for an even shorter period.

Following the Arab-Israeli Six-Day War of 1967, the Ba'ath Party finally became strong enough to retake control and on July 17, 1968, returned Ahmad Hasan al-Bakr to power in a precedent-setting bloodless coup. al-Bakr became president and chairman of a newly created Revolutionary Command Council (RCC) of the Ba'ath Party of Iraq. [15] The new Iraqi president moved to nationalize the Iraq Petroleum Company and introduced wide-ranging socioeconomic reforms designed to move Iraq toward a national socialist society. al-Bakr improved diplomatic relations between Iraq and Egypt and also strengthened Iraqi ties with the Soviet Union.

Saddam Hussein, President al-Bakr's Tikriti "cousin," was always an influential part of the al-Bakr government, yet he held no official position in the early days of the administration (though his uncle was appointed the governor of Baghdad); instead he agreed to work on forming a state security apparatus.[16] Members of the Ba'ath Party (particularly men from Tikrit) assumed key roles in the government and the RCC became more dominant. Internal security measures grew more extreme in response to alleged coups and all other supposed threats to the regime. House raids, disappearances and the use of torture in Iraqi prisons became commonplace.

In 1969, the RCC membership was expanded to fourteen and Saddam Hussein became an official part of the government for the first time, as the council's vice chairman.[17] Saddam also became the point man for an increasingly wide range of government initiatives in both the domestic and international spheres. He led an effort to reform Iraqi education in order to increase the influence of the Ba'ath party and he began to play an important role internationally, even leading a delegation to Moscow in 1972. When the Iraq Petroleum Company was nationalized later that same year, Saddam became the head of the new Iraqi National Oil Company's steering committee.[18]

In 1976, Saddam (who had never served in the armed forces) also assumed the title of General in the Ba'ath Party's Popular Army. As al-Bakr aged into his late sixties and became less able to execute his duties, Saddam took on increasingly more power and authority as the face of the government, eventually becoming the day-to-day leader of Iraq years before he officially became president.

On July 16, 1979, sixty-five-year-old al-Bakr stepped down as the president and chairman of the RCC of Iraq, ostensibly on health grounds, and Saddam Hussein assumed both of the most powerful offices in the country in a move that was well understood as a mere formality. It is probable that Saddam forced al-Bakr to step down under threat of force, but it is even more likely that the Iraqi president was wise enough to move out of Saddam's way.

Saddam Hussein and the War with Iran

Saddam possessed a grandiose sense of not only his role in history, but also his responsibility to write the region's history through action.
—KEVIN M. WOODS, *THE MOTHER OF ALL BATTLES*[19]

Much has been written about the background and psychology of Saddam Hussein.[20] In nearly every case, analysts focus on the poverty and alienation of his earliest years and the barbarism and tenacity he exhibited in his rise to influence in the Ba'ath Party. Much of his style was demonstrated in his first official act as president, when he called some four hundred members of the party together in a large meeting and summarily called out the names of party members to be purged. Eventually some five hundred people were executed, some reportedly by Saddam himself.[21] He had studied the country and its security for over a decade and he knew exactly what to do to consolidate power completely in his hands.

Saddam did not ignore international affairs as he moved to make his mark on Iraqi society, and he also increased his standing in the Arab world. In the aftermath of the Camp David Accords, Saddam became one of the most vocal defenders of Palestinian rights and he soon pressed to take up the mantel of the leader of the Arab world as the fortunes of Egypt's Presiden Anwar Sadat declined. When the Ayatollah Khomeini took power in Iran, Saddam's security forces rounded up Persians and even Shia Iraqi's by the thousands in an effort to forestall any possible Iranian threat to the Iraqi regime. As the crackdown progressed Saddam even had the Shia Grand Ayatollah Sayyid Muhammad Baqir al-Sadr and his sister arrested and executed in 1980.[22]

The execution hardened the already difficult relations between the two neighboring countries, and in response Ayatollah Ruhollah Mousavi Khomeini, the Iranian "Supreme Leader," began to speak of war. Saddam saw an opportunity to demonstrate his Arab leadership by seizing the bordering Iranian province of Khuzistan, which was oil rich, inhabited by a large Arab population, and key to the river access to the Persian Gulf. The Iran-Iraq War then began with air strikes designed to defeat the Iranian air force in advance of a ground invasion of the Shatt al-Arab region on September 22, 1980. The Iranian cities of Abadan and Khorramshahr are situated along the river and witnessed the brunt of the initial fighting. This war would devastate both nations for nearly a decade.

A few days after the Iraqi invasion, the Iranian navy attacked Basra and the Iranian air force began air strikes against Iraqi targets, including oil facilities, dams, petrochemical plants, and targets in Baghdad.[23] In response to these air attacks, Iraq launched a number of air strikes against Iranian targets. On October 24, Khorramshahr was captured by the Iraqi forces, but the Iranians mobilized additional forces, including many members of the shah's old armed forces, and some two hundred thousand troops were soon at the front by the end of November. Iran then slowly began a series of counteroffensives in January 1981 with both its regular soldiers and revolutionary militiamen eager to fight, the former seeing an opportunity to regain some of the prestige lost after the fall of the shah's regime.[24]

Iran's first counterattack failed due to poor coordination between the units of the regular army and those of the Pasdaran (commonly referred to as the IRGC or Iranian Republican Guard Corps). Fortunately for Iran, however, the Iraqi forces failed to follow up with another attack. Iran then unveiled its "human wave" assaults, which used thousands of Popular Mobilization Army volunteers in attempts to overwhelm the Iraqi forces. Iran finally gained its first major victory when Khomeini brought the army and the Pasdaran together to lift the Iraqi siege of Abadan in September 1981.

In the spring of 1982 Iran began a new offensive near Susangerd, and for the first time the Iraqis were forced to retreat. Within a week, the Iranians had destroyed nearly three Iraqi divisions and regained the strategic initiative. In May the Iranians finally retook Khorramshahr and were able to keep the pressure on Iraq until Saddam Hussein had to announce the Iraqi withdrawal from Iranian territory. That summer Iran launched an offensive into Iraq near Basra. As they approached the city, the Iranian forces launched human-wave attacks against the city's defenders, hoping to provoke a coup to overthrow Saddam. The result was one of the biggest land battles since the end of World War II; like the Red Army in the war against Germany thirty years before, Iranian soldiers swept over minefields and fortifications to clear approaches for tanks. The casualty toll was enormous on both sides, but eventually the Iraqis were able to repulse the Iranian invasion.

The following year, Iran launched three more major offensives along the border, none of which were successful. By the end of the year, some 120,000 Iranians and 60,000 Iraqis had been killed. After so much blood was shed for no gain, in 1984 Saddam was forced to alter his strategy; no longer capable of penetrating into Iranian territory, he went on the strategic defensive. Saddam purchased new weapons from the Soviet Union and France and also created barrier zones in flooded areas near Basra designed to help stop the Iranian attacks. According to some sources, Saddam used chemical weapons against Iranian troop concentrations in an effort to force Iran to negotiate an end to the conflict.[25]

By 1984 nearly three hundred thousand Iranian soldiers and almost as many Iraqi troops had been killed or wounded in the conflict. Between February and March 1984, the Iraqis reportedly killed forty thousand Iranians and lost nine thousand of their own men, but the year ended with no change in the relative positions of the two belligerents. The only major offensive in 1985 was another Iranian attempt to take Basra, but it only resulted in more heavy casualties. In February 1986, Iraq suffered a major loss when Iran successfully conducted a surprise amphibious assault by thirty thousand soldiers across the Shatt al-Arab to capture the Iraqi port. Saddam Hussein vowed to eliminate the bridgehead but it took Iraq two years to recover the territory.

The Iraqis conducted an offensive into Iran in May 1986 only to lose the terrain they had seized later in July. They then began to conduct air strikes on Kharq Island which forced Iran to shift its bases farther south in the Gulf to Sirri and Laraq Islands, which were then also struck by the Iraqis. As a result, over one hundred neutral ships were attacked accidentally by such raids in the Gulf by one side or the other during 1986.

To better defend itself during this period of see-sawing attacks, Iraq built defensive fortifications along the contested zone, with particular attention paid to Basra, where concrete bunkers, minefields, and an artificially flooded lake thirty kilometers long and eighteen hundred meters wide were constructed. In late May 1987, the fighting shifted to the north where Iranian units backed by Iraqi Kurdish rebels attacked Mawat in Iraq, threatening the Iraqi oil fields near Kirkuk. In the north, Iraq could only remain on the defensive and try to inflict as many casualties as possible.

From April to August 1988 the Iraqis defeated the Iranians in four major battles. In a first move, Iraqi Republican Guard and regular army units recaptured the al-Faw peninsula. Three subsequent operations followed in the Fish Lake and Shalamjah areas near al-Basrah where the oil-rich Majnun Islands were recaptured. In a last major engagement, Iraqi forces attacked deep into Iran, before Iran accepted United Nations Security Council Resolution 598, leading to a cease-fire on August 20, 1988.

The Military, Economic, and Diplomatic Impacts of the Iran-Iraq War

The war cost more than 1.5 million casualties to both sides and forced millions to become refugees due to the incessant and inconclusive fighting.[26] Yet at the war's end, none of the major issues that caused the fighting had been resolved; although Iraq may have won the war militarily by positioning forces inside Iran at the end of hostilities, the UN-arranged cease-fire failed to resolve the problems or reduce the animosity between the two states. The Iraqi military had grown to number more than a million men with an arsenal of chemical weapons, and the missiles to employ them, plus a large air force.

Although the Iran-Iraq War did not result in any tangible Iraqi gains outside the growth in size of the its armed forces, it did cost a great deal in a host of other ways. Iraq increased its debt significantly, particularly to France and the Soviet Union which had supplied Saddam with his major arms purchases. The war's total cost, including military supplies and civilian damages, probably exceeded $500 billion for each side. Both Iran and Iraq sacrificed considerable oil wealth to prosecute the war for nearly a decade, and Iraq was forced to borrow heavily, especially from its allies on the Arabian Peninsula (most particularly Kuwait, which had loaned Saddam some $8 billion to finance his arms improvements).[27]

Traditionally Iraq had been free of foreign debt and had even accumulated foreign reserves that reached nearly $35 billion by 1980, but these reserves were exhausted in the early stages of the war which Saddam had misguidedly expected to be short in duration. After the war

> Iraq was faced with the dilemma of paying off short-term debts to western creditors estimated between $35 to 45 billion at high interest rates. However, the Regime resisted western attempts through the International Monetary Fund (IMF) and World Bank to reschedule the debt primarily because Baghdad believed it could negotiate more favorable terms dealing with countries bilaterally. . . . Although the Gulf States considered the financial support provided to Iraq to be a loan, Iraq believed that the Gulf States were required to provide help to Iraq in its fight to prevent the spread of radical Iranian fundamentalism.[28]

This uncommon debt, when combined with the potential for big unemployment problems should Saddam have demobilized his huge army, placed Iraq in very difficult circumstances in the immediate aftermath of the war. Those circumstances were worsened by a significant fall in the global price of oil, which devastated Iraqi economic productivity at the very worst time in its modern history.

Shifting American Relationships and the State of Iraq in 1990

The end of the Cold War changed the dynamics of the United Nations, in particular the impact and role of the Security Council, once the Soviet Union and the United States were no long using their vetoes to block efforts by the other to exert influence around the world during their global confrontation. The end of superpower confrontation also liberalized international affairs to a degree unknown since the early 1950s. America's shift in alignment from Iran to Iraq following the 1979 capture of the U.S. embassy in Tehran also played an important role in the choices made by Saddam Hussein. Prior to that date the twin pillars of American policy in the region were based in support to Iran and Saudi Arabia.[29] The United States took Iraq off its list of states sponsoring terrorism in 1982 and restored diplomatic relations in 1984. Between 1985 and 1990 the U.S. government approved sales of military equipment and technology to Iraq worth over $1 billion.[30] Annual trade between Iraq and the United States had increased from $500 million to $3.5 billion by 1990.[31]

By 1990, the Ba'ath Party was in complete control of most of Iraq (a limited degree of independent action was still permitted in the Kurdish north of the country) and the RCC was the supreme organ of a bureaucracy that controlled every facet of daily life in Iraq. The police and the army were part of the party hierarchy, as were the vast majority of the professional tradesmen in the country. Conflicts with the Kurds had worsened significantly during the Iran-Iraq War, but relations between the Sunni and Shia religious sects in Iraq had generally improved as both worked together to prosecute the war effort (though the Sunnis dominated the decision-making and the Shia soldiery dominated the casualty lists.) The country was at an important crossroads, and as usual, Saddam Hussein moved the nation in a direction that became disastrous.

The Iraqi Plan for Conquest: A Coup de Main with Limited Objectives

Less than two years after the Iran-Iraq War ended, Saddam Hussein approached the chief of staff of the Iraqi Republican Guard and asked him to "take a look at the Iraq/Kuwait border" in the early summer of 1990.[32] Very quickly thereafter a small cell began to meet regularly with Saddam to plan the "retrieval" of Kuwait. Their deliberations produced what became known as "Plan 17." An operation of such size, though considered relatively small in the context of the Iran-Iraq war which had just finished, was still extremely complex, particularly because it needed to be planned in complete secrecy. It would require the forces of the entire Republican Guard Forces Command (RGFC), plus assets from the Iraqi air force, navy, and regular army, and appeared to be something that the Iraqi president intended to execute relatively soon. Saddam in fact kept most of his government, and even the army chief of staff, completely ignorant of the planning effort as it progressed through the summer months.

Through the previous year, anti-Kuwaiti rhetoric had been growing in intensity, along with general anti-Western proclamations. Rising tensions and frequent discussion of generic Zionist conspiracies— which added to the justifications for force preparedness—had become increasingly obvious to members of the Iraqi military. It is also important to realize that the Iraqi military shared a sense of resentment toward their Arab neighbors because the other nations of the Middle East had not shared sufficiently in the heavy burden of the long war with Iran. Many Iraqis saw the Iraqi role in the war as a shield against Persian threats to the Arab world. They had suffered mightily over the entire ten years of fighting and knew that Iraq was poorer economically due to both the cost of waging war and the inflation resulting from it. Saddam Hussein had made it very clear that other Middle Eastern nations should pay to ease the Iraqi burden and had embarked on a series of diplomatic initiatives in order to gain financial support from his neighbors. The Saudis had in fact paid off Saddam by forgiving Iraq's debts to the kingdom after the Iran-Iraq War, but the Kuwaitis refused to do the same.

Initial movements to stage forces began as early as July 15, but the detailed planning required for what would be a large-scale mechanized assault did not begin until the end of the month.[33] The Iraqi air force was probably brought into the planning process in mid-July, primarily in order to provide photo reconnaissance support and to develop ways to protect the assault forces from the relatively potent Kuwaiti air force; only later was it tasked to develop air defense for the Kuwait theater. The Iraqi navy, the least capable of Saddam's armed forces, was not even told of the impending assault until two days prior to its commencement.[34]

The overall concept of operations for the Iraqi invasion can be viewed as a three-pronged armored assault from north to south preceded by air support operations to establish some degree of air control, commando raids on key positions along the route, and naval attacks on the port of Kuwait City. The main attack axis was to belong to the Hammurabi Division, with supporting attacks from the west conducted by the Medina and Baghdad Divisions. Nearly simultaneous with the main assault, a commando raid to capture the Kuwaiti royal family and justify the attack as being in support of a local movement for self determination would be executed.

Iraqi Operational Execution in 1990

Plan 17 kicked off (as previously described) in the early morning hours of August 2, largely as conceived. The initial commando operations were for the most part successful (although the Kuwaiti royal family evaded capture) and the main penetration of the Hammurabi Division was proceeding even better than was expected as dawn broke. It appears that the Kuwaitis were surprised by the size of the offensive and generally failed to understand that the main attack was in multi-division strength.

Naval operations succeeded despite the lack of detailed planning largely because the Kuwaiti defenders were completely surprised. Iraqi air force operations, however, achieved disappointing results because planners had badly misjudged the complexity of the airspace control problem; consequently the air force contributed very little to the operation as a whole. Despite having received little advanced notice of the operation, the Iraqi navy and commando forces performed adequately and had their objectives well in hand at the end of the second day.

The main attack by the mechanized Hammurabi, Nebuchadnezzar, and Medina Divisions of the Republican Guard Forces Command seemed well executed but was fraught with problems.[35] The three divisions suffered from very poor tactical intelligence and had little idea what they would encounter in Kuwait—they actually had to use tourist maps. Communications between the divisions was so poor that the three had little idea of each other's progress. The advancing brigade columns were also poorly coordinated, resulting in massive traffic jams inside urban areas. Due to the courage of the Kuwaiti forces, the Medina Division, tasked with the taking the coastal areas south of Kuwait City, was delayed by over twenty-four hours, thus enabling many Kuwaiti citizens to escape to Saudi Arabia. Many Iraqi units ran completely out of fuel as they approached their objectives.

The Failure of Deterrence and Compellance— Differing Worldviews

Over a period of months following Saddam Hussein's invasion of Kuwait, several countries brought diplomacy, economic leverage, and even regional pressures to bear in a rather broad range of actions designed to avert war. From August until November 1990 the primary emphasis of the U.S. government was deterrence. Deterrence theory held that once it became obvious to Saddam Hussein that the United States was willing to use force to counter the invasion, he would have to review his commitment to incorporating Kuwait into Iraq.[36] In order to deter war, diplomacy is normally the most useful tool; however, diplomacy is fundamentally rooted at least in part in the ability to effectively communicate disparate goals and objectives in a rational, understandable, and acceptable manner.

Mitigation of the impact of war should have also been tried in an attempt to back both Iraq and the United States out of positions of direct confrontation. However, the fact that the United States was the world's only superpower made mitigation by another like power nearly infeasible. The Soviet Union attempted on several occasions to mitigate the march to war. France also did what it could, in time becoming a full partner in the coalition against Iraq.

Compellance came to the fore once the United States began its second, and more significant, force buildup. With additional forces in the field, and augmented by the visible support of the United Nations and other regional players, the United States expected that its additional leverage would have helped convince Saddam Hussein of the costs of war in a way which should have caused him to back down and leave Kuwait, or at least negotiate away his formal occupation of the country. Both deterrence and compliance failed to slow the march to wider war.

Chapter 3

DESERT SHIELD:
THE LINE IN THE SAND

From a cold start operational planners deployed a force that was able to successively deter, delay, defend, and attack its Iraqi opponent. Given that the Iraqis had their deployment challenges as well, the window of likely allied defeat was narrow indeed.

—JOHN S. BROWN, "THE MATURATION
OF OPERATIONAL ART"[1]

The U.S. military response to Saddam Hussein's invasion of Kuwait was neither long-planned nor well rehearsed. Although American military leaders normally develop a wide range of contingency plans designed to anticipate aggression in "hot spots" around the globe, Kuwait was never deemed important enough to be designated as key terrain and Iraq had not been considered a potential enemy long enough for even the most prudent of planners to have designed a full operations plan to deal with it as a military threat. Interestingly, the United States had long had a rather robust plan designed to confront Soviet aggression in the region, but beginning in early 1990, General Schwarzkopf began to reorient his staff's planning toward a possible attack by Iraq in the region.

General Schwarzkopf told the Senate Armed Forces Committee in January 1990 that "Iraq is now the preeminent military power in the Gulf, and it is assuming a broader leadership role throughout the Arab world. Iraq has the capability to militarily coerce its neighboring states should diplomatic efforts fail to produce the desired results."[2] The U.S. Army began to shift its planning assumptions back in 1989 and by March of that year had begun to conduct war games to better understand the potential threat. By February 1990, Exercise Persian Tiger 89 was being conducted to anticipate the force requirements to prevent an Iraqi invasion of Saudi Arabia. In July 1990, the basic army plan for the CENTCOM region was focused on "counter[ing] an intra-regional conflict on the Arabian Peninsula to protect United States and allied access to Arabian Peninsula oil."[3] It was that plan that CENTCOM's staff was rehearsing during their annual command post exercise "Internal Look" immediately prior to Iraq's invasion of its neighbor.

Through this period of wargaming and assessment two things became very clear to the senior commanders and key staff members. They learned a great deal about the problems of time and space in deploying significant forces to the region, and they began to understand better the force requirements needed to mount a credible defense of the key ports and facilities in Saudi Arabia. Even if not long-planned or rehearsed, the plan to defend Kuwait ended up being a masterpiece of operational design. In part that was due to the great advantage of having clearly defined objectives, a clear national focus of effort, and presidential backing for plan development.

Deployment and Defense

The first, and in many ways the greatest, challenge of the initial campaign of the war with Iraq was undertaking the rapid deployment of sufficient U.S. forces to deter Saddam Hussein from continuing his attack into Saudi Arabia without sending those forces into a situation that would only place them at unacceptable levels of risk.[4] There is no evidence today that Saddam intended to attack the Saudi kingdom and its important oil fields in 1990. But the number of the forces he sent into Kuwait would have made it a relatively simple thing to continue his attack south and eventually occupy the Saudi Ghawar oil field—the largest conventional field in the world and the source of 60–65 percent of all Saudi oil produced since World War II. American strategic analysts were also acutely aware that a further Iraqi advance down the east coast of the Arabian Peninsula would have given Saddam control of the most important ports needed to transship arriving U.S. troops and equipment to defensive positions in the kingdom.

General Schwarzkopf's first major task then was the rapid deployment of sufficient combat power to the peninsula to deter any southward movement of Iraqi forces into Saudi Arabia. Initially this was done by flying the ready 2nd Brigade of the 82nd Airborne Division, commanded by Colonel Ronald Rokosz, with only its light antitank weapons and M551 Sheridan tanks, to Dhahran, Saudi Arabia, where the fighter aircraft of the 1st Tactical Fighter Wing from Langley Air Force Base in Virginia were also arriving in the very early days. "Rokosz's first troops established defenses around the airfield to provide security for the other arriving units. As additional troops came into the country, the perimeter expanded. By the afternoon of 13 August, when the ready brigade reported 100 percent of its troops deployed from Fort Bragg, with 88 percent of them already in Saudi Arabia, it had expanded its area of operations to provide security at Al Jubayl, the port through which the Marines would enter the theater."[5]

The U.S. Navy had aircraft carriers USS *Eisenhower* in the Red Sea and USS *Independence* in the Gulf of Oman along with more than one hundred fighter and attack aircraft, plus a surface action group and command ship in the Persian Gulf—though these Navy forces had very little deterrent effect since they were invisible to the Iraqi leadership. At that early stage, the only military option open to Schwarzkopf would have been to trade space for time, and gradually fall back into Saudi Arabia in the face of an Iraqi attack, with the goal of defending the critical ports and airfields needed to continue the flow of his reinforcements. This approach would not have found favor with the Saudis, but Schwarzkopf had no other realistic course.

Press coverage, which became increasingly influential as time passed, ensured that everyone concerned with the crisis knew that U.S. military forces had begun deploying to the Persian Gulf region. Once the initial army and air force forces were in place, they began to develop defensive postures (the airborne forces were largely defenseless against Iraqi armor), and the fighters beginning to fly air patrols over the deployment positions.[6] Luckily, the first arriving forces were very quickly joined by the fifteen thousand Marines of the 7th Marine Expeditionary Brigade and its heavy equipment which had been deployed from Diego Garcia by Maritime Prepositioned Shipping Squadron (MPSRON) 2 on August 25.[7] The remainder of the 82nd Airborne had also finished arriving in theater by that week, so Schwarzkopf had nearly thirty thousand ground troops in Saudi Arabia. Though the Marines could finally mount a reliable defense of the port of Al Jubayl, by the end of the month the ground forces deployed in Saudi Arabia still remained a largely symbolic capability and were realistically incapable of defending Saudi Arabia from a deliberate attack by the far more numerous Iraqi forces—should that have been their goal. This nerve-wracking period became famous for the image of America's finest forces used as nothing more than a "speed-bump" to slow the advance of Saddam's armor.

Thirty days later, by the end of September, the initial deterrence force had grown fantastically in size and the CENTCOM staff began to think of how they might actually conduct operations against the Iraqis. With the 24th Mechanized Division, the 1st and 4th Marine Expeditionary Brigades, two more Navy carrier battle groups and a host of combat aircraft in place, and the 101st Airborne Division, the 3rd Armored Cavalry Regiment, an Egyptian Division, and a French mechanized Brigade soon to arrive, the initial concerns about the ability of the coalition to defend against a further incursion by the Iraqis had been replaced by questioning how the invasion might be reversed.[8]

In mid-September, Schwarzkopf had begun a top secret refinement of his plan, aided significantly by a small group of four operational planners: graduates of the Army's School of Advanced Military Studies in Fort Leavenworth led by Lieutenant Colonel Joe Purvis.[9] (Later, they became known as the Jedi Knights after characters from the popular movie *Star Wars*.) Any plan to eject Saddam's forces from Kuwait had to take into account the size of the Iraqi occupying force, the advantage it had gained from being able to reinforce defensive positions since August, and the need to employ all forces of the coalition to ensure coalition solidarity.[10] The senior military leaders also understood that the coalition had many technological advantages working in its favor. Quite obviously, from an operational perspective, the planners did not want to attack the Iraqis head on—that would only reinforce Iraqi positional strengths and reduce the technological advantage that the Americans wanted to maximize. Plus, "they felt Iraq had the capability to unleash anthrax, botulism, cholera, equine encephalitis, tularemia, and typhoid," which added significantly to the planning challenge.[11]

From the beginning, the operational concept had sought to focus coalition combat power on the western flank of the Iraqi Republican Guard Forces Command (RGFC) in Kuwait. In the Kuwaiti Theater of Operations (KTO), the RGFC comprised eight divisions with a combined total of 110,000 troops—a significant armored capability that would be very difficult to match in conventional combat, particularly as the Iraqis had learned how to fight well in the defense during the war with Iran.[12] The key to coalition success would necessarily entail minimizing risk and maximizing speed and firepower, using both ground and aviation assets.

The recent development of Army Field Manual FM 100-5 and the renaissance in operational study had fostered a heightened level of thinking about conventional combat operations. The planners from Leavenworth were among the best in the United States. They knew they needed to avoid a direct assault and that their relatively small available force structure had to be focused on the essentials. As Colonel Purvis later commented:

> At the strategic level, we decided that Saddam was the key, but that we could do nothing about him legally and ethically. We could and did isolate him and cause the battle to be fought without centralized command. The Republican Guard was the focus at the operational level. If we could mass our ground forces on the RG without fighting any other force, we had perfect success. Also, if the RG left the theater, surrendered, or were defeated, we still had, to our opinion, dealt appropriately with the "C.G." (center of gravity).[13]

The Jedis quickly decided that a flanking attack near the heal of the Kuwaiti boot offered significant advantages, but once they did a more detailed study of troops available to accomplish the tasks required for such an attack it became obvious that they would exhaust the entire force then available in the assault, leaving no reserve capability and no room for error—a recipe for disaster in modern war. Plus the terrain in that area was highly questionable— no one knew if it could even be used effectively by modern mechanized forces. The Jedis briefed General Schwarzkopf on their plans on October 6 with little enthusiasm. The CENTCOM commander expressed disappointment in what he also recognized was a high-risk plan and asked what would change the balance of forces in his favor. Purvis and his team recommended the addition of another army corps![14]

The coalition already had one operational concept at work, however— that was an air campaign plan that was conceived by a small section of the Air Staff in Washington under the direction of Air Force Brigadier General Buster Glossen way back in the second week of August. Ideologically, it was driven by the strategic air power ideas of Colonel John Warden, who was then assigned to the Air Force office known as Checkmate.[15] Warden had begun planning on August 8 in the Pentagon by outlining five concentric circles representing Iraq's centers of gravity.[16] For Warden, victory could be found in isolating the enemy field forces (in this case the Republican Guard Forces Command in Kuwait) from the strategic structures that supported it: the Iraqi senior leadership and the national infrastructure that sustained the deployed divisions.

Checkmate's assigned task was to develop a plan that could be executed quickly and the team soon named its concept "Instant Thunder"—a throwback to and rejection of the famous "Rolling Thunder" bombing campaign of the Vietnam conflict. On August 10 Glossen and Warden had flew to Tampa to brief Schwarzkopf, and Warden used the occasion to plant the idea that Schwarzkopf could execute an "air Inchon," in reference to the famous Korean War amphibious operation conducted by General Douglas MacArthur that turned the tide of the Korean conflict in 1950.[17] Given CENTCOM's paucity of forces in the region and the very real risk Schwarzkopf must have felt at the time, the Checkmate concept of operations at least provided some method of effectively employing military power against Saddam.

Schwarzkopf was interested, and after another brief a few days later, so was Colin Powell; the Checkmate staff accordingly intensified their efforts and after even more plan development returned to Tampa on August 17 to brief the CENTCOM staff again on their ideas. Schwarzkopf and his key staff liked what they heard—though they most likely still saw the use of air power as a critical adjunct to the early arriving ground forces. As a result of their ideas, Warden, Lieutenant Colonel Dave Deptula, and two other members of Checkmate deployed to Saudi Arabia at Schwarzkopf's request, to work for General Charles Horner, the CENTCOM air component commander, in what came to be known as the "Black Hole" in Riyadh.[18]

The Checkmate planners were developing a brilliant targeting strategy designed to win the war but, as conceived, its intent was fundamentally different from the effort led by the Leavenworth Jedis. Most essentially, the air planners did not see the Republican Guard as their focus of effort—the Jedis did. Although both concepts of operations could become complementary, initially they seemed to pull scarce resources in two different directions. Much of the ideological steam expended over the following months would be aimed at reconciling these two ways of thinking about warfare and making them both as effective as possible. Along the way the Black Hole planning cell integrated staff from all four services and the air attack plan became larger, more extensive, and fully joint.

Three days after Schwarzkopf had determined another corps was required to manage the risk in an assault on Kuwait he was tasked with providing an update brief in Washington. He sent his chief of staff, Marine Major General Bob Johnston, along with General Glossen and Colonel Purvis to brief the status of the "One Corps" planning effort. The response in Washington was dismay. Brent Scowcroft, Secretary Cheney, and Under Secretary Wolfowitz were all confused and disappointed with what they saw as an uninspired and risky concept.[19] As a result, Schwarzkopf took a verbal pummeling in Washington, with some even comparing him to General George B. McClellan, President Abraham Lincoln's reluctant commander. In response, General Powell flew to the theater to get a first-hand impression of what was going on in CENTCOM. Powell met with all of Schwarzkopf's subordinate commanders and heard an improved version of the Jedi brief, one which did employ additional forces to advantage. The chairman pushed for even more creative ideas and reassured Schwarzkopf that the president would support him completely with all the assets needed. Powell came away reassured about Schwarzkopf and, more importantly, convinced that a second reinforcing corps of forces was necessary for success. His encouragement in Riyadh reduced some of the pressure on Schwarzkopf, and he pushed the planners to be even bolder, consistent with his belief that America needed to use overwhelming force to make any combat operation as fully successful as possible.[20] Thus the poor response to the One Corps brief actually engendered greater support for a troop increase, and the addition of four more divisions, plus the deployment of additional aircraft and aircraft carriers, was approved by President Bush on October 31.[21]

Conventional force options were not the only ideas being circulated in military planning circles in September and October 1990. The full array of capabilities was considered and both the nuclear option and direct attacks against Saddam Hussein were studied in detail. The attacks against Saddam ran against legal concerns as the U.S. government had previously determined that targeting government leaders was not an acceptable option (although air planners and special technical operations staffers continued to develop options that might catch Saddam within the effective kill radius of a weapon). Secretary Cheney and General Powell discussed the employment of nuclear weapons against Iraqi forces in Kuwait, but the initial studies by the Joint Staff dissuaded Powell of the effectiveness of a nuclear response.[22]

Fortunately, "by mid-September the operational picture had again changed. The debarkation of the 24th Infantry Division (Mechanized) put a force on the ground that could stand fast, rather than retire, in the face of all but the most massive of Iraqi attacks."[23] That meant that the confrontation over Kuwait would not fade away without some substantial effort—either military or diplomatic. Saddam Hussein may have assumed that he could deal with the United States in the same way that he had dealt with Iran for nearly a decade and still walk away with his forces intact; the United States, however, viewed the use of military force as sacrosanct, acceptable only after the decision to risk decisive combat had been justified and validated. Once its forces were in the field, America intended to fight to a decisive result.

Iraqi Military Activities

Once Kuwait was occupied the Iraqi military had to turn its attention to a very different task—the pacification of the small emirate. From the evidence, there seems to have been little effort expended on considering where the Iraqi forces should be employed and how they would serve as an occupying force once inside Kuwait. They were not well dispersed and there were numerous instances of looting, inability to control curfew, and lack of basic sustainment supplies.[24] Throughout August and September the situation inside Kuwait remained quite chaotic. First Saddam appointed his half brother to be chief of security in Kuwait, then the Iraqis mandated that the entire population of Kuwait had to use Iraqi security documents—or else they lost their rights to food and cooking fuel.[25] Then Saddam directed his ministries of trade and transportation to work with the army in order to move all the wealth out of Kuwait.

Over time the Iraqi intelligence services infused their brutal forms of control in the "nineteenth province" and the soldiers there began to conduct typical security operations, except that they had the power to use deadly force for many small infractions. As a consequence, six months after the invasion the native population of Kuwait had largely slipped away—reduced from a normal 2.4 million to less that half of that. Many areas of the occupation were uninhabited by the time the recovery of Kuwait began.

It was clear as time passed that the most forward deployed Iraqi divisions really had no logistics or sustainment capability on site and could not have operated effectively outside of their defensive locations. Plan 17, the Iraqi blitzkrieg into Kuwait, had cost Saddam Hussein much more than most people realized at the time. Though the personnel losses had been relatively light (some one hundred dead and three hundred wounded in one frontline division) the Iraqi forces had lost nearly half of their helicopters and exhausted their supplies in the rapid assault. It was a spent military force almost as soon as its objectives were accomplished.

As the coalition forces began to flow into nearby Saudi Arabia, the Iraqis also began to develop plans for dealing with any actions the coalition might undertake. There never seemed to be any question of an evacuation of Kuwait but there were three significant developments which demonstrate how the Iraqi military and Saddam Hussein viewed coalition possibilities for a countermove in the early months.

First, a series of spoiling attacks were developed in case the coalition forces made an early assault to retake Kuwait.[26] These were to be rather limited in their effect, most likely developed as simple efforts to confuse and delay the coalition. Such a spoiling attack was actually executed in late January of the following year, so it is clear that they were an integral part of Iraqi strategy.

The second and by far more significant action conducted by the Iraqi military was the shift of forces in Kuwait. Over the month of September, as the coalition forces grew in size to nearly match the number of Republican Guard force in Kuwait, the Republican Guard formations were replaced in the KTO by regular Iraqi army divisions and units of the Popular Army and moved to a general reserve position just north of Kuwait.[27] This shift of forces would do three things: first it returned the Republican Guard to its more normal position as a response force ready to counterattack in the event of a coalition attack or able to respond elsewhere in Iraq as it had been used more traditionally to put down civil unrest.

The third major action was accomplished not in Kuwait but in Baghdad, where Saddam Hussein replaced both his defense minister and army chief with less political and more militarily skilled officers. Saddam may have seemed erratic to Western observers but he was no fool.

The National Effort to Compel

As the size of the coalition defense force grew and the operational plan evolved, the international diplomatic activity increased in intensity. Both sides in the crisis probably had fleeting opportunities to resolve it diplomatically, but as emotions and the force commitments on the coalition side grew, the viability of a diplomatic solution waned significantly.

Among the most important of the early issues that made negotiating much more difficult by September 1990 was the taking of civilian hostages by the Iraqi regime. As summer turned to fall in 1990 the issue of Saddam Hussein's "human shields" began to take on increased importance. At a time when forces were still incapable of conducting significant offensive operations and when diplomacy was really the only national tool in play, Saddam Hussein unwittingly did probably the worst thing he could have imagined by taking American citizens hostage in Kuwait and bringing some of them to Baghdad to place them on display before the international media.

President Bush was incensed by the act and it drove his conviction to use force more than any other factor as the months passed. This was a key example of crucially different perceptions between Saddam Hussein and President Bush that increasingly minimized any chance to avert war.

The question remained: if Saddam did not order his forces from Kuwait, how was the tiny emirate to be freed? The answer to that question was soon to be provided by the addition of another corps of ground forces, which could decisively eject the Iraqi occupier from Kuwait. That additional corps stretched the deployment capacity of the American military to new post-Vietnam limits and allowed for the application of overwhelming force, the ruling principle of the so-called Powell Doctrine.

The Shift from Defense to Offense—November 1990

By the time the mid-term congressional elections were held in the United States in November 1990, the Bush administration had already garnered sufficient international support to continue its military buildup of forces in the Persian Gulf. Following General Colin Powell's visit to Riyadh in October and the presidential approval of an additional corps-sized deployment to the region, the U.S. Army's VII Corps was alerted for movement and a number of other Army Reserve and National Guard units from all fifty states also received mobilization orders. "Among the National Guard units eventually federalized were the 48th Infantry Brigade from Georgia; the 155th Armored Brigade from Mississippi; the 256th Infantry Brigade (Mechanized) from Louisiana; the 142d Field Artillery Brigade from Arkansas and Oklahoma; and the 196th Field Artillery Brigade from Tennessee, Kentucky, and West Virginia."[28]

The active duty VII Corps units selected to deploy from Germany included the 1st Armored Division, the 3rd Armored Division; the 2nd Armored Cavalry Regiment; the 11th Aviation Brigade; and the 2nd Corps Support

Command. The 1st Infantry Division at Fort Riley, Kansas, also received deployment orders to serve as the fourth combat division of the VII Corps. This decision to send the VII Corps eventually raised the troop level of U.S. forces in the Persian Gulf to over four hundred thousand. At a news briefing on November 8, President Bush publicly announced his decision to increase the troop strength in Southwest Asia to ensure "an adequate offensive military option."[29] The idea of defending Saudi Arabia had been supplanted by the need to eject Saddam Hussein's forces from Kuwait through the use of military force.

On November 10, several members of VII Corps based in Germany arrived in Saudi Arabia to assess the situation. General Franks traveled to the Persian Gulf a few days later to confer with General Schwarzkopf, and on November 13, during a strategy review session of the CENTCOM staff, the CENTCOM commander told General Franks that his mission would be to attack the Republican Guard, thus assigning Franks with the key movement of the campaign: the attack on the Iraqi center of gravity.

In about seven weeks the U.S. Army, Europe, moved more than 122,000 soldiers and civilians and 50,500 pieces of equipment from Germany to Saudi Arabia. The tight schedule, coupled with the unpredictable German winter weather conditions, made it essential to use all available modes of transportation. Thousands of tracked and wheeled vehicles, hundreds of aircraft, and tons of equipment and supplies deployed every way possible—421 barge loads from the primary loading sites at Mannheim and Aschaffenburg; 407 trains, with 12,210 railcars; and 204 road convoys, totaling 5,100 vehicles. In a deliberate effort to reduce the burden of increased traffic on the autobahns and to expedite the move, the large majority of vehicles, both tracked and wheeled, traveled by rail or barge. Once at the three ports, the equipment was assembled in staging areas and subsequently sent in 154 shiploads to Saudi Arabia. The soldiers flew out of Ramstein, Rhein Main, Nuremberg, and Stuttgart. It took 1,772 buses to move the troops to the airports, 1,008 vehicles and drivers from the 37th Transportation Group to carry the baggage, and 578 aircraft to fly them all to Southwest Asia.[30]

About 90 percent of all these forces arrived in theater and were reassembled in their tactical assembly areas by the target date of January 15—a fantastic and commendable achievement. It was made possible through the many annual Reforger exercises that had practiced the reinforcement of American forces in Europe, the support of the German government, and some extremely professional transportation planning by staff members of the Army Military Transportation Management Command.

The mobilization and deployment of the three combat round-out brigades of the National Guard—(the 48th Infantry Brigade from Georgia; the 155th Armored Brigade from Mississippi; the 256th Infantry Brigade (Mechanized) from Louisiana— and the two artillery brigades were an even more complex problem. There had been much debate over the utility of such National Guard units through the fall; many believed that they were not well enough trained to be able to serve in combat operations, particularly operations as high intensity as what was envisioned by General Schwarzkopf. But the way the U.S. Army was organized required the mobilization of Reserve and National Guard forces once a certain size force package (larger than the XVIII Corps) was determined.

> The Army set the same deployment criteria for reserve combat units as for regular component units at its highest C-1 standard.[31] A unit could have no deficiencies in the prescribed levels of wartime resources and training and had to have 90 percent of its personnel and equipment. Occasionally a unit at a C-2 readiness level, with minor deficiencies and 80–90 percent of its personnel and equipment, also deployed. For the three round-out brigades, a detailed training program and personnel plan was established to upgrade the units, when necessary, to C-1.[32]

Although all three of these round-out brigades received additional, post-mobilization training at the Army's National Training Center (under the command of Brigadier General Wesley Clark, a future four-star general) none were deployed to Saudi Arabia in time to be integrated into the Desert Storm scheme of maneuver. The two artillery brigades were deployed and served with distinction, but the capabilities of the three maneuver brigades—particularly the 256th Infantry Brigade—were so poor that the entire concept of Reserve integration into modern combat came into question within the Army. Among Marine Reserve units these problems were far less evident, although in general the Marine Corps mobilized battalion-sized units with the intention of employing them within larger active duty units. A large portion of the Marine Reserve was deployed to Southwest Asia and its units were fully integrated into I MEF's combat operations, with very little difference observable between the two types of units.[33]

The addition of a second maneuver corps to the ground component of CENTCOM's force was precedent-setting in several ways. Not only did it require the first mobilization of Reserve and National Guard forces since the Korean conflict, but it also severely tested the deployment and integration doctrines that had been developed within the Army since Vietnam. Still, these problems were necessary if the American military was going to be able to field a force sufficient to outmaneuver the Iraqi forces occupying Kuwait with any numerical advantage in combat power. Ideally, attacking forces desired a three-to-one advantage over an enemy ensconced in prepared defenses. One way of developing such a force-on-force ratio was to field a larger force; another was to attrite the enemy force through indirect means prior to the start of conventional combat.

CENTCOM wanted to do both. It also wanted to avoid significant casualties in the process. Casualty avoidance would be relatively easy during any precursor campaign primarily focused on air power due to the great technological advantages of the coalition air forces and the relative paucity of Iraqi air defense assets in Kuwait. The same would not be true for a ground assault as the defenses in Kuwait would require breaching minefields and obstacles and at least some urban conflict—both of which could be large casualty producers. Therefore the CENTCOM concept evolved toward a maneuver that would outflank the Iraqi forces in the west and force their retreat from Kuwait without significant frontal attacks.

> By November 1990 the Iraqis had matured a layered defense, with line infantry entrenched behind protective barriers along the border backed up by local mobile reserves of regular army tank and mechanized divisions. These local reserves were themselves backed up by the operational reserves of the heavily mechanized Republican Guard. Of these Iraqi forces, the line infantry was considered brittle, the regular army heavy divisions reliable, and the Republican Guard formidable.[34]

Final Diplomatic Efforts and Authorization for War

Even as the movement of forces came to a close, the diplomatic efforts to avert their use continued across multiple avenues: in the United Nations, among a small group of interested nations (including the Russian Federation), and between Iraq and the United States. In early October, the Soviet Union—long an ally of Saddam Hussein's—launched a new diplomatic effort to solve the crisis without the use of force. However, the ongoing debate over the civilian shields continued to harden international conviction against Iraq and in late October United Nations Security Council Resolution 674 passed, holding Iraq responsible for any breaches of Geneva and Vienna Conventions protocols pertaining to the internationals being held in Iraq. Late the following month, on November 27, Soviet President Mikhail Gorbachev even gave up the notion of moderating Saddam's behavior and began to support the use of force to free Kuwait.

Secretary of State Baker flew to Geneva on January 9 for a final attempt to end the occupation of Kuwait diplomatically. The Iraqis were represented by Foreign Minister Tariq Aziz, who refused to even accept a letter offered by Baker from President Bush. On January 12, 1991, the United States Congress authorized the use of military force to drive Iraq out of Kuwait; the votes were 52–47 in the Senate and 250–183 in the House of Representatives. These were very close votes when one considers that they would certainly result in the loss of American lives. Still, once cast, these votes began a countdown for combat.

National Security Directive 54

Diplomatic efforts could have continued for months in 1991, but on January 15 President Bush issued a second directive on Iraq that made his decision for war evident and his goals and objectives for the campaign very clear. National Security Directive 54, "Responding to Iraqi Aggression in the Gulf," listed four overarching purposes for the combat operations to come: to effect the immediate, complete, and unconditional withdrawal of all Iraqi forces from Kuwait; to restore Kuwait's legitimate government; to protect the lives of American citizens abroad; and, finally, to promote the security and the stability of the Persian Gulf region. He also specified six military objectives towardswhich General Schwarzkopf and his staff should focus their efforts: defend Saudi Arabia and the other Gulf Cooperation Council (GCC) states against attack; preclude Iraqi launch of ballistic missiles against neighboring states and friendly forces; destroy Iraq's chemical, biological, and nuclear capabilities; destroy Iraq's command, control, and communications capabilities; eliminate the Republican Guard as an effective fighting force; and conduct operations designed to drive Iraq's forces from Kuwait, break the will of Iraqi forces, discourage Iraqi use of chemical, biological, or nuclear weapons, encourage defection of Iraqi forces, and *weaken Iraqi popular support for the current government.*

Although these goals and objectives were clearly written after the war planning was completed, they remain instructive because they provided an essential framework for the conduct of the campaign directly from the hand of the Commander in Chief. Of note, later in the directive, President Bush also specified that if Saddam Hussein should "resort to using chemical, biological, or nuclear weapons, be found supporting terrorist acts against U.S. or coalition partners anywhere in the world, or destroy Kuwait's oil fields, it shall become an explicit objective of the United States to replace the current leadership of Iraq."

The basic plan to retake Kuwait can be seen as three major coordinated ground offensives designed to deceive, fix, and finally destroy the Iraqi Republican Guard units. The southern-most offensive would begin first and consist primarily of Marine and Arab coalition forces. The western-most offensive, largely comprising the American XVIII Airborne Corps and its attached French Division *Daguet*, was designed to shape the battlespace and prevent the Iraqi forces from escaping destruction. The main attack force was to be commanded by Lieutenant General Fred Franks and was based on the VII Corps.[35] His target remained the Republican Guard.

By December 1990 the base plan was well established and the forces needed to execute it successfully were rapidly arriving in theater. Though some of the units would not arrive in time for the contemplated start date for combat operations, there was no doubt that sufficient combat power would be on hand to eject Iraq from Kuwait if necessary. The real questions at that point centered more on the level of risk and cost factors (in human lives and in unit effectiveness) in execution. For example, would the Iraqis use chemical weapons in the defense of Kuwait—thus significantly increasing both military and civilian casualties and significantly slowing the pace of any coalition attack? Was the air campaign plan too focused on attacking Saddam Hussein's strategic targets and not sufficiently focused on attriting the center of gravity of his fielded forces in Kuwait? Would the coalition partner units fight effectively with the Americans on their flanks? Much of the American concept of operations was based upon a philosophy of indirect operational maneuver, primarily because the CENTCOM staff believed its own worst estimates and still feared the specter of Vietnam-era casualties. Only time would demonstrate if these critical assumptions would weigh heavily during combat.

The Relevance of Desert Shield

It would be a mistake to disregard the importance of Operation Desert Shield as a distinct phase within the long war between Iraq and the United States. The operation was far from perfect, but as a distinct action it was a critical enabler for the effectiveness of the Desert Storm campaign to follow and in itself "the deployment also represented considerable operational finesse, allowing thoughtful progression from forces capable of deterrence alone through those capable of delay, of defense, and, finally, of attack."[36]

The clearly defined political objectives provided by President Bush made the development of understandable military objectives relatively easy. No member of the coalition had any doubts about the role of military force during

Desert Shield. The American investment in forward deployed and rapidly deployable forces made it possible for the United States to establish a credible deterrent capability in theater quickly and to build upon that capacity rapidly thereafter. The CENTCOM command structure was clear and flexible, allowing General Schwarzkopf to maximize the service and national capabilities of all forces, while ensuring unity of effort in a coalition environment. These relationships established during Desert Shield were fundamental to the level of cooperation needed during the execution of Desert Storm the following year.

Chapter 4

DESERT STORM:
THE 1991 GULF WAR CAMPAIGN

Soldiers, Sailors, Airmen and Marines of the United States Central Command: This morning at 0300 we launched Operation Desert Storm, an offensive campaign that will enforce United Nations Resolutions that Iraq must cease its rape and pillage of its weaker neighbor and withdraw its forces from Kuwait. The President, the Congress, the American people, and indeed the world, stand united in their support of your actions. . . . Our cause is just! Now, you must be the thunder and lightning of Desert Storm.
        —GENERAL NORMAN SCHWARZKOPF, JANUARY 17, 1991[1]

W hen Iraq invaded Kuwait in the summer of 1990, few thought that the resulting crisis could only be resolved by sending American troops into combat in the deserts of the Middle East. Even so, it had been General Schwarzkopf's task since August to develop the most effective military solution to Iraqi aggression. By January 1991 every other means to avert fighting had been tried and CENTCOM was poised to use deadly force and put thousands of lives at peril by countering the Iraqi invasion with coalition combat power.[2]

Although Americans tend toward the use of direct, mass-intensive approaches to combat (which maximizes the industrial capacity and technological strengths of the United States) the CENTCOM staff had worked diligently through 1990 to develop a counterattack that would surprise and overwhelm the Iraqi forces in Kuwait while at the same time avoiding as much as possible attrition-style engagements. Achieving this goal entailed the use of deception and indirect actions by aviation and special operations forces to shape the early phases of combat operations, leaving the Iraqi forces so vulnerable that any conventional operations would be of very short duration.

In 1991, few analysts would have believed that the six-month deployment would be followed by a relatively short, three-week air campaign phase and cumulate in a ground operation that would last only one hundred hours. Operation Desert Storm shattered much of the post–Vietnam era military mindset, but it did not completely erase the wounds created in Southeast Asia, nor did it decisively change the American way of war to something less direct or less conventional.

The Coalition Air Campaign Shifts Perceptions

Most people date the beginning of the campaign to recover Kuwait with the coalition air sorties that started on January 17, 1991. These operations were planned and coordinated by Lieutenant General Charles Horner from King Khalid air base in Saudi Arabia. Horner had coordinating authority, though not command in a service-specific sense, of the great majority of the aircraft that flew missions during Operation Desert Storm. Horner and his key planners had worked to integrate air power deeply into the operation, so that by January the air campaign plan was fully synchronized and ready for implementation—though it was not completed without much compromise and at least a few hard feelings.[3] When the final ultimatum expired and Secretary Baker's final diplomatic efforts to avert combat ended without an Iraqi withdrawal from Kuwait, President Bush gave the approval for General Schwarzkopf to begin ejecting the Iraqi military by force, initially with air power.

Starting combat operations against Iraq with air power was significant for four reasons. First, Iraq had no significant air capability and only rudimentary air defense systems, so the use of air power was a relatively safe, asymmetric means to damage Iraqi forces without risking the loss of many coalition lives. Second, Iraq was an easy geographic location to employ air power; its openness and the lack of many hardened defenses for its forward deployed forces made most targets vulnerable to air strikes. Third, air strikes did not require the taking of Iraqi territory, and at least some planners still believed that as long as ground forces had not entered Iraq a ground clash could be avoided. Finally, the coalition's technological advantage was most evident in its air power and the impact of a devastating air campaign was expected to be localized enough against military forces to maintain international support and crushing enough in its effect to press Saddam to withdraw.

Air Campaign Execution

"No plan ever survives initial contact" remains a well-respected refrain among military planners. And although the coalition air campaign dazzled the world, it was changed significantly in the very early days of its execution in response to two dominating factors: its own rapid success, and eventually the Iraqi launch of Scud missiles against Israel.[4]

The assault began with the infiltration of ten American helicopters from the 160th Special Operations Aviation Squadron, commanded by Lieutenant Colonel Dick Cody.[5] Those aircraft destroyed a series of Iraqi radar sites near the border with Saudi Arabia that would have warned Iraq of the pending main air attack. Then another package of attack jets (F-15E Eagles) conducted attacks against two Iraqi airfields (labeled H-2 and H-3) in western Iraq.[6] A short time later, ten F-111 Stealth fighters attacked Baghdad to take out a series of strategic command and control and air defense targets. Immediately afterwards, U.S. Navy Tomahawk cruise missiles struck additional targets in Baghdad. These preparatory strikes blinded Saddam Hussein and severely crippled his meager air defenses, opening the door for a massive air assault and enabling other less-capable coalition aircraft to participate in the pre-planned series of attacks following throughout Iraq with much less risk.

These sorties were launched from airfields in Saudi Arabia and from the six American aircraft carriers in the Persian Gulf and Red Sea. (The carriers were USS *Midway*, USS *John F. Kennedy*, USS *Ranger*, USS *America*, USS *Theodore Roosevelt*, and USS *Saratoga*.) The effort required to intricately coordinate the interwoven strikes of rotary and fixed-wing aircraft from multiple locations, different services, and even different members of the coalition was one of the first and most impressive acts of what would become a very innovative campaign.

The intended goals of the air strikes were to reduce the effectiveness of Iraqi command and control, demoralize and attrite the capability of the ground forces, and if possible collapse the Iraqi regime. Saddam Hussein's tendency to micromanage the Iraqi forces during the war with Iran was well understood and it was hoped that the Iraqi resistance would quickly collapse if deprived of effective command and control from the top.

Iraq did not take the pounding from the air campaign without response.[7] Ground based antiaircraft was employed all over Iraq and most importantly, as promised, Saddam Hussein did strike back with the only strategic weapons system that he had available: his Scud missile forces. On January 17, Iraqi Scuds struck both Haifa and Tel Aviv. The missiles were so imprecise that they were highly unlikely to hit any specific target, but the psychological impact on the Israeli population exerted tremendous pressure on Jerusalem to fight back.[8] Over the weeks that followed, a total of thirty-nine missiles struck Israel, causing some property damage and killing at least two Israeli civilians. In response, the United States deployed two of its new Patriot missile battalions to Israel, and the Netherlands also sent another Patriot unit, to deflect future attacks (the Patriot was never intended to be an anti-missile system) and to reassure the Israelis and keep the Israeli Defense Forces out of the fight. Generals Schwarzkopf and Horner diverted a full third of their planned air sorties to address the Scud problem.[9] Soon a range of allied aircraft were flying in the Iraqi desert hunting Scuds, in particular by trying to locate the camouflaged erector trucks used to set up the missiles before they were fired at Israel or Saudi Arabia. These Scud attacks were strategically menacing because they threatened to split the coalition by bringing Israel into the fight, but they were also a real tactical threat; one of the last Scuds to be fired hit Dhahran, Saudi Arabia, on February 25, killing twenty-eight U.S. soldiers when the missile destroyed their barracks.

In mid-February, Iraq offered to withdraw from Kuwait on four conditions: that Israeli forces withdraw from the Palestinian Territories and Syrian forces withdraw from Lebanon, that all coalition forces withdraw from Saudi Arabia, and that the UN sanctions against Iraq be terminated.[10] No nation took that offer seriously. The Iraqi offer was later amended to a simple request for access to the sea, but the United States refused to act on either proposal because President Bush had established the complete Iraqi withdrawal from Kuwait as a *precondition* to stop the ongoing operations.[11] The American administration was determined that Iraq not only pull out of Kuwait, but that its ability to threaten its neighbors and its standing in the region be reduced.

Command and Control—Little Benefit from Goldwater-Nichols

The headquarters that was to be used by General Schwarzkopf to conduct the Desert Storm campaign was organized differently from the structures that had previously been traditional for the U.S. military.[12] It was still primarily organized around Army, Navy, Marine, and Air Force service components staffs, but the creation of General Horner's Coalition Forces Air Component Command (CFACC) signaled the first truly joint and combined approach to warfighting within the CENTCOM organization and it soon became the most operational joint component within the headquarters. Even so, it was critiqued for several shortfalls that limited the integration of naval air power within the campaign, and there were some who argued that it brought a focus on strategic attack that did not fully support Schwarzkopf's operational concept focused on the RGFC. The differing approaches were reconciled over time, in execution, but they represented conflicting ideologies that were still hotly contested even after the combat phase of the campaign ended.[13]

Though the staff in Tampa and the forward headquarters in Riyadh were manned by members of all the services, CENTCOM was not a fully joint organization in execution. No fully joint command structure existed beneath Schwarzkopf's own headquarters and even the Special Operations Component Command—which did include both Army and Air Force officers, was not fully trusted for operations. General Schwarzkopf entered the campaign against Iraq with a structure that was more closely aligned with the one General Dwight Eisenhower used for the Normandy invasion than that which was used by General MacArthur for the Inchon landing—which was in many ways the inspiration for the Desert Storm plan.

General Schwarzkopf retained operational command of all the ground forces involved in operations in the Kuwaiti theater of operations. This was not a particularly controversial act at the time—though it was questioned by some—but it proved to be contentious in execution, as the only major criticism of the main battle against the Iraqis was rooted in his later decision to accelerate the initiation of his main attack and the ill-prepared effort to transition to conflict termination after the main effort had decimated the enemy forces it was designed to destroy.

SOF Enters the Battle

One of the key changes resulting from the Goldwater-Nichols legislation was the creation of a separate command headed by a four star general to coordinate all special operations forces development and deployment. That organization, Special Operations Command, or SOCOM, was charged from the beginning of the invasion of Kuwait with planning for rescue raids to return American diplomats captured by the Iraqis and to execute contingency operations against strategic Iraqi targets. The SOCOM commander, Army General Carl Stiner aggressively lobbied Schwarzkopf for a role in the execution of CENTCOM's plan, but Schwarzkopf was a skeptic; he had little interest in employing special operations forces under his own Special Operations Forces (SOF) component commander, Colonel Jesse Johnson, and he was even less attracted to the involvement of Stiner and his CONUS-based "snake eaters."[14] Among the CENTCOM senior commanders, only Sir Peter de la Billière, who was a previous commander of Britain's 22 Special Air Service (SAS) Regiment, had any real trust in SOF.

The coalition effort began with the insertion of some British special operations forces into Iraq and Kuwait, but these units were primarily intended for reconnaissance missions. However, beginning on January 30, 1991, American SOF entered the battle to find and destroy Saddam's Scud missiles before they could do any more damage against Israel or the coalition soldiers that were massed for the ground assault. These operations were executed not by the CENTCOM SOF component, but instead by the U.S. Joint Special Operations Command (JSOC), under the command of Army Major General Wayne Downing. The four hundred–man JSOC team arrived outside the western Iraqi town of Ar'ar on January 30 to establish a base of operations. They began their full-time Scud hunting on February 7.[15] The main JSOC objective was to find Scuds before they could be launched, but it also stood ready to rescue any downed fliers that were lost in the Iraqi desert during the numerous air sorties flown each day. JSOC mastered the insertion of small teams of special operations warriors using sophisticated dune buggies for transport and special helicopter assets.

The major accomplishments of the SOF campaign within Desert Storm were said to include the destruction of a dozen Scud missiles, but after the fighting was over very few of those attacks could be substantiated. It is likely that many of the sites attacked by JSOC housed dummy missiles designed as decoys. Still, the special operations forces did harass the Iraqis and they were able to provide useful intelligence about the state of play in western Iraq. Had they been better integrated into the planning prior to the start of the air operations, their utility would certainly have proven to be far greater.

Saddam's Repost: The Iraqi Response against Khafgi

After a second week of withering strikes, the air campaign orchestrated by General Horner was affecting more than its tactical and operational goals by the end of January. "In Baghdad the lights went out at the beginning of the war and did not come on again until its end. . . . The damage was not just to infrastructure. The air campaign brought the war home to the population, especially the urban middle-class inhabitants of Baghdad who provided some of Saddam's political base. Daily life was becoming unbearable. There was no electricity or running water in most of Iraq's cities."[16] Not only were these effects exerting pressure on Saddam, but they were also affecting the odds of his basic strategy succeeding.

The Iraqi leader had understood that the American-led coalition had much superior firepower, but he had counted on the Western aversion to casualties playing to his advantage; and he expected to be able to engage the coalition with such severity on the ground that he could shake open an Iraqi doorway of escape. The indirect nature of the air campaign doomed that strategy because Iraq and its forces were suffering terrible looses with no way of responding in kind. As the air strikes continued, Saddam grew increasingly desperate. He had to act in some way that would shift the focus on the coalition attack and give Iraq some way of demonstrating its military power—if for no other reason than to be able to say that Iraqis had fought honorably.

We now know that Saddam Hussein executed a unique and quite desperate gamble midway through the execution of the coalition air effort to dramatically alter the tempo of the campaign. The result has become known as the battle of Khafgi. The Iraqi-initiated battle reveals much about Saddam's intentions and the real capability of the deployed Iraqi forces in Kuwait. It also reveals a very different combat perspective from that held by the key member states of the coalition.

Because the town of Khafgi was within Iraqi artillery range from units stationed in Kuwait, its residents had been evacuated in late January in anticipation of the coalition thrust. (See Map 2.) The town itself was largely undefended and only a few Saudi Marine units were left to patrol the roadway, supported by U.S. Marine and Navy fire support units. According to senior Iraqi officers, Saddam Hussein had directed the development of several plans calling for penetrations into Saudi Arabia, but he only chose to execute the attack toward Khafgi; the operation was ordered after the coalition air campaign had already severely weakened the Iraqi forces in Kuwait, but while they could still fight effectively.[17] In Western parlance, the operation should be viewed as a spoiling attack or raid, designed to unhinge the impending coalition attack before it was fully prepared and perhaps to disrupt its execution.[18]

On January 29, the Iraqi forces attacked and briefly occupied the lightly defended Saudi city with a two-division sized force of tanks and infantry (the 5th Mechanized Infantry Division and the 3rd Armored Division). The Iraqi III Corps was the main attack force, with a second Iraqi corps, the IVth, in support. In Iraqi terms, it was a major attack. As had become common, Saddam had not given the orders for execution until January 27—ten days after the start of the air campaign and only two days before the operation was to commence.

Iraqi commanders did everything they could think of to conceal their attack from air strikes and to conduct their thrust as rapidly as possible—they fully appreciated the risk they were taking by attacking while their opponents had complete air superiority. The Iraqi assault forces did manage to occupy the town, but then started to suffer from the full effects of the coalition's fires in its extended and vulnerable position. The Iraqi 5th Division commander requested permission to withdraw on the 31st. However, the battle of Khafgi only ended when Iraqis were driven back by Saudi and Qatari forces supported by U.S. Marine close air support over the following two days.

As it withdrew the division was subjected to even more damaging fires and by the time it completed its retrograde movement it had been rendered combat ineffective from the coalition perspective. Other forces involved in the attack suffered similarly. Despite this outcome, the Iraqis pronounced the Khafgi operation to be a success. Official Iraqi combat reports extolled the valor of their troops in repulsing repeated Allied attacks, using their heroism as justification for claiming victory—it did not matter that Iraqi's position was only weakened by the operation.

As far as the Iraqis were concerned, the fight for Khafgi was more about pride than achieving victory—but it cost them dearly and showed the coalition something very important. Though the Iraqi reluctance to commit several armored divisions to the occupation and subsequent use of Khafgi as a launching pad into the vulnerable east of Saudi Arabia is considered by many as a grave strategic loss of opportunity, the battle is more instructive for what it shows about the Iraqi philosophy of battle. Saddam understood well that his forces could not fight unit against unit and win, but he felt that it was necessary to shed the blood of his soldiers to develop conditions for an honorable peace. Such ideas were completely foreign to General Schwarzkopf and his senior Army commanders. The fighting in and around Khafgi showed that the Iraqis had a lot of trouble mounting coordinated ground operations. And it should have been evident to the planners at CENTCOM headquarters in Riyadh that the Iraqis had major deficiencies that prevented them from coordinating complex operations; in particular, air and ground coordination was lacking. At Khafgi it became clear that the Iraqis were probably not going to be difficult opponents, and just as importantly that the Arab forces within the coalition were willing to fight. Finally, the Iraqi raid demonstrated to both sides that air power was going to be a decisive factor in hindering the movement of Iraqi forces.

Logistics to the Fore—The Massive Shift to the West

In order to execute the plan as designed and crush the Iraqi Republican Guard Forces Command from the rear, the main body of the coalition, including the French Division *Daguet*, the American XVIII Airborne Corps and its British armored division, and the main effort, the American VII Corps, had to shift over two hundred miles to the left of the coalition lines deep into the Saudi Arabian desert. Most importantly, this movement had to be accomplished with the millions of tons of supplies required to sustain the mechanized mailed fist of the coalition and done in secret so that the Iraqis would not know about the massive force in their rear until it was attacking them.

With the start of the air war, the Army supply experts moved to areas west of the Wadi al Batin to set up a forward logistics base for each corps. CENTCOM'S Army component (Third U.S. Army, commanded by Lieutenant General John Yeosock) was responsible for supplying both corps and sought to fill those bases with sixty days of supplies by G-day—a formidable task given the shortage of heavy trucks and drivers, the lack of railroads, and the heavy civilian traffic on the roads. For five weeks supply vehicles rolled northwest to the corps logistic bases on the main supply route, or Tapline Road (the highway alongside the pipeline from the ports to Jordan), bearing the huge quantities of ammunition, fuel, water, and food required for combat operations executed by such a large and mobile force.

1. French Forces
2. 82nd Airborne Div.
3. 101st Airborne Div.
4. 25th Infantry Div.
5. 3rd Armored Div.
6. 1st Armored Div.
7. 1st Infantry Div.
8. 1st Cavalry Div.
9. 2nd Marine Div.
10. 1st Marine Div.

Iraq: the *Desert Storm* Campaign

0   50   100 Kilometers
0   50   100 Miles

The massive westward shift of the units assigned to the XVIII Airborne Corps and VII Corps into their attack positions began on January 20, and continued for about three weeks. Both corps had to move long distances, more than 500 miles for XVIII Corps and over 330 miles for VII Corps. This movement of massive amounts of military equipment and supplies over the expanses of the Arabian desert strained the capacity of the theater transportation units to a degree unknown since World War II. To save tracked combat vehicles from wear and tear, the 22nd Support Command acquired almost four thousand heavy trucks and distributed them to the corps in direct and general support. Among those vehicles were about 1,300 heavy equipment transporters, 450 lowboys, and 2,200 flatbeds.[19]

The Effects of the Media, Psychological Operations, and Deception

The air attacks on Baghdad signaled more than the beginning of conventional operations against Iraq; they also helped create a new powerful media phenomenon. For the first time in history, viewers worldwide watched televised images, broadcast in real time, of bombs and missiles hitting their targets and aircraft maneuvering through Iraqi antiaircraft fire over the Iraqi capital. In the United States, television networks updated news of the war continuously, from the moment the air strikes began on January 16. Correspondents reporting live from Baghdad described in wonder the flashes of light from missile strikes and tracer fire over the skies of Baghdad. It was the beginning of the Cable News Network (CNN) revolution in media affairs and CNN's wartime coverage was clearly influential in shaping public perceptions of the war.[20] Newspapers from all over the world also covered the war.

Most of the press information came from briefings organized by the American military, either in the Pentagon or in CENTCOM's forward headquarters. In comparison to their treatment in previous wars, journalists were restricted in their ability to observe combat operations or to conduct interviews with soldiers. And their activities were normally subject to both prior approval by the military and censorship afterward. These measures, ostensibly taken to prevent sensitive information from being revealed to Iraq, were in fact an unfortunate result of the U.S. military's negative experiences with the media during the Vietnam War. Still, even with restrictions, the coverage of the campaign was often instantaneous and extremely eye-catching, due to the superb technology of the American forces and the well planned series of briefings conducted from Schwarzkopf's forward headquarters.

By the time the coalition air campaign entered its second week, the impact of modern media had already made itself felt. General Schwarzkopf had begun giving media briefings on the conduct of military operations on January 18 and CENTCOM continued to provide daily televised media updates for the remainder of the combat phase of the campaign. General Powell or his operations deputy also gave a significant number of media briefings in the Pentagon that reinforced the overall message of overwhelming success given by the CENTCOM commander in Riyadh. These media briefings convinced the world that the coalition had greater firepower, greater weapons system accuracy, and a dominating technological advantage over the Iraqi forces.

Psychological operations (PSYOPS) also made a major contribution. Radio and TV broadcasts, leaflets, and loudspeakers used the themes of Arab brotherhood, dominating allied air power, and Iraqi isolation to induce large numbers of enemy soldiers to desert. One of the most effective tactics involved the dropping of leaflets on a particular unit, informing it that it would be bombed within twenty-four hours and could avoid destruction only by surrendering immediately.[21]

Deception was given great importance by the coalition and played a very strong role in the lead-up to conventional combat as a method of shaping Iraqi expectations of the fight to come. Deception had played a role in the previous year's activities, but with many more forces available after January 1, much more was possible in the following months.

Maneuver

In January 1991, the 1st Cavalry Division began its shift toward offensive action by moving its seventeen thousand soldiers five hundred kilometers to the west to another assembly area near King Khalid Military City (KKMC) in northern Saudi Arabia. This repositioning put the division in a key strategic location covering the historic Wadi al Batin approach into Saudi Arabia and threatening Iraq along the same avenue into western Kuwait along the Tapline Road.

The division tied in with the French Division *Daguet* to the left and the 101st Airborne Division to its right. Then the division began a calculated war of deception along the Saudi border. "The goal was to lure Saddam Hussein into believing the main ground attack of the Allies would come up the Wadi al Batin, a natural invasion route, causing him to reposition additional forces there."[22] This deception effort consisted of three major actions: Multiple Launch Rocket System (MLRS) attacks battering targets deep in Iraq; conventional cannon artillery batteries firing Copperhead rounds (computer-controlled, rocket-assisted projectiles) and thousands of high explosive along with improved conventional munitions into Iraq; and, finally the division's aviation brigade flying obstacle reduction and serial reconnaissance missions, identifying and designating targets for destruction by the division's artillery units.

The 2nd (Blackjack) Brigade of the 1st Cavalry Division conducted a covert reconnaissance mission into Iraq on February 9, 1991, to test the Iraqi reaction and ensure that mechanized forces could maneuver effectively in the deserts of Kuwait and Iraq. Then, on February 19, in one of the first conventional ground operations of the campaign, the brigade, commanded by Colonel Randy House, conducted Operation Knight Strike I to make it look like a reconnaissance in force was in progress up the Wadi, moving some ten kilometers into Iraq and destroying an Iraqi battalion in the process. That night and for the next four days heavy air strikes also pounded the route up the Wadi. Then on February 24, General John Tilelli's 1st Cavalry Division conducted another feint up the Wadi al Batin, Operation Deep Strike, creating the illusion that it was the main ground attack of the coalition.[23] That attack was supported by the 3rd Battalion, 82nd Field Artillery, reinforced by a MLRS (Multiple Launch Rocket System) battery, which laid down heavy fire in support of the feint.[24] This action apparently tied down four Iraqi divisions, leaving their flanks thinned and allowing the VII Corps to attack virtually unopposed in the western part of their sector.

By that time, the impressive array of forces provided by some twenty-nine coalition member nations to Generals Schwarzkopf and Khalid bin Sultan were basically ready to start combat operations. There was always the desire for more time to prepare, but with the force fully deployed there was also the risk that coalition's scheme of maneuver would be revealed or that the Iraqis would conduct another spoiling attack. They could not reasonably remain tactically deployed for long.

Negotiations during Combat

Despite what many may believe, diplomatic and economic activity aimed at resolving the crisis did not stop once the military operations to retake Kuwait began. Many states continued to press for alternatives to military action. Although the air campaign was clearly succeeding, nations around the word remained concerned about the eventual results of the fighting, and for some, including the Soviet Union, the destruction of their former ally was not a desirable outcome.

On February 21, just days before the ground attack was due to begin, Iraqi Foreign Minister Tariq Aziz arrived in Moscow seeking Soviet support to end hostilities and to give Saddam a final chance to save his honor. Aziz met with Gorbachev and told the Soviet leader that Saddam would not accept the UN resolutions that called for Iraq to recognize Kuwait's independence and pay it compensation. But he would withdraw from Kuwait. Gorbachev thought this was good enough. He called President Bush to urge a halt to operations.[25]

For the Americans, unconditional withdrawal was a pre-condition for terminating the air campaign. Avoiding a ground war was in everyone's interest, but Saddam Hussein could not be allowed to walk away unpunished with his army still a threat to regional security. Bush decided the offer was unacceptable.

Still, as the Iraqis maneuvered diplomatically the international coalition was beginning to fragment. With a ground assault looming, the French and Egyptian presidents both pressed for more time. Just then intelligence sources revealed that the Iraqi forces in Kuwait had set the oil wells on fire. That outrage decided the issue for most of the heads of state. President Bush issued a final ultimatum that required Iraq to unconditionally withdraw starting within forty-eight hours. The ground invasion was set to begin the following morning on February 24. What the president probably did not know is that his forces had already penetrated into Kuwait and that the Iraqi forces were already disappearing—through death but mostly through desertion.

On February 25, as previously mentioned, Iraq launched an Al-Hussein (Scud) missile that impacted on an American military barracks in Dhahran, Saudi Arabia, killing twenty-eight American soldiers from a Pennsylvania reserve unit—the most fatalities suffered by American forces in a single incident of the campaign. The missile strike certainly hardened American opinions against Iraq, but in truth the major movements of the ground campaign had already begun and there was little incentive to stop the coming thrust into Kuwait.

The Marines, Their Coalition Partners, and Amphibious Deception Operations

The forces facing the Iraqi army in Kuwait most directly were the U.S. Marines of the I Marine Expeditionary Force (I MEF) and the Arab members of the coalition units contributed by Egypt, Saudi Arabia, and other Gulf Cooperation Council (GCC) states on the Marines' flanks.[26] The terrain south of Kuwait was divided among three commands. On the right flank, along the Gulf coast, Joint Forces Command (JFC)-East anchored the coalition line. JFC-East was under the direct command of Saudi Lieutenant General Khalid bin Sultan and consisted of units from the GCC states. There were three task forces: TF Omar, comprising the 10th Infantry Brigade (Royal Saudi Land Forces, RSLF) and an United Arab Emirates Motorized Infantry Battalion; TF Othman, consisting of the 8th Mechanized Infantry Brigade (RSLF), an Omani Motorized Infantry Battalion, a Bahraini Infantry Company, and the Kuwaiti Al-Fatah Brigade; and TF Abu Bakr, with the 2nd Saudi Arabian National Guard (SANG) Motorized Infantry Brigade and a Qatari Mechanized Battalion. Just to the west of JFC-East in the center of the sector South of Kuwait was I MEF. JFC-North, also commanded by Lieutenant General Khalid bin Sultan, situated in the center of the coalition and just to the west of the Marines, comprised the 3rd Egyptian Mechanized Division, the 4th Egyptian Armored Division, the 9th Syrian Division, the Egyptian Ranger Regiment, the Syrian Special Forces Regiment, the 20th Mechanized Brigade (RSLF), the Kuwaiti Ash-Shahid and Al-Tahrir Brigades, and the 4th Armored Brigade (RSLF).[27] These forces had been defending Saudi Arabia since the other coalition forces shifted to the west and would be the first units to begin the recovery of Kuwait.

The coalition forces of JFC-East and the embarked U.S. Marine Expeditionary Brigade (MEB) stationed on ships in the Gulf were assigned to clear the coastal approaches to Kuwait City. The MEF and JFC-North would simultaneously attack directly north to clear the remainder of the emirate. Between these coalition forces and their objective was a formidable series of minefields and defensive berms constructed by the Iraqis to aid in their defense. The Marines argued again and again with General Schwarzkopf that they needed to have an amphibious assault capability to reinforce in zone or at a minimum to deceive the Iraqis into keeping a sizable force contingent in Kuwait City proper to defend against such an assault.[28] The CENTCOM naval component had conducted an amphibious landing in mid-August and other highly visible exercises in Oman (in late October) and on the east coast of Saudi Arabia (in November and December). Schwarzkopf never thought the risk associated with a modern amphibious operation into Kuwait was acceptable, but in the end, the deception effect did work strongly in the coalition's favor—particularly after a high publicized "rehearsal" exercise, Sea Soldier IV, was conducted in Oman on January 24. In response, the Iraqis built some large-scale coastal defense fortifications and kept six infantry divisions in defensive positions in the expected landing area with two other mechanized divisions nearby acting as a reserve—a corps-sized formation kept largely out of the fight due to deception.[29]

Still, even with the amphibious option, and despite the overall success of the air campaign in decreasing the combat effectiveness of the Iraqi units in Kuwait, Lieutenant General Walter E. Boomer, commander of the Marine forces, still feared that storming the minefields and barbed wire of southern Kuwait would be a murderous affair fought under a barrage of Iraqi chemicals and nerve gas. Therefore he had developed a plan using his two Marine divisions in column (one behind the other) to force a penetration in a relatively small frontage in order to maximize his combat power while minimizing his exposure in the breach.

The Marines, however, had learned a great deal by participating in the repulse of the Iraqi attack on Khafgi, and at least one of their senior commanders, Major General Bill Keys, was convinced by what he observed in that fight that the Iraqi army was in fact far less formidable than had been previously estimated. General Keys then pressed to change the Marine plan from two divisions in column approach to one wherein the two divisions would take advantage of infiltration to seep through the Iraqi defensive works and attack abreast. This change was designed to spread the force more widely and would emphasize speed over combat power. General Boomer initially resisted the change, but in the end accepted its logic and reoriented his forces accordingly. He did not specifically brief General Schwarzkopf on the change, viewing it as an internal Marine component matter only.

On February 8 Secretary Cheney and General Powell traveled to Riyadh to meet with the CENTCOM staff and review the final assessment of readiness for combat prior to the kick off of the ground phase of the campaign. During this meeting it became clear to General Schwarzkopf that his subordinate generals had very different ideas about fighting the Iraqis; he also became concerned that the plan General Franks had developed for the VII Corps main effort was much too ponderous and deliberate for what he wanted to achieve. Schwarzkopf noted in his biography that he specifically told General Yeosock that "I do not want a slow, ponderous pachyderm mentality. This is not a deliberate attack. I want VII Corps to *slam* in to the Republican Guard."[30] Secretary Cheney was also said to be concerned about the uninspired nature of the VII Corps plan.[31]

It was clear that some of the American generals overestimated Iraq's military capabilities. Or perhaps they were too stronly influenced by the years they had spent focused on the Soviet threat to Western Europe to have developed any realistic appreciation of the actual capabilities of the Iraqi forces.

No army in history has had as precise and accurate a picture of how its adversary laid out on the ground as did the American Third Army on 24 February 1991. Prior to the 1st Infantry Division breach, for example, battalion commanders received aerial photos detailing Iraqi platoon positions in their sectors. Narrative descriptions concerning where units were and when one could expect to encounter them proved remarkably accurate. Satellite imagery, aerial photography, unmanned aerial vehicle (UAV) feedback, and information drawn from a fistful of other sensors fed huge amounts of material into the voracious appetites of military intelligence analysts.[32]

Still, Saddam's military was not nearly as formidable as most senior officers believed.

The air campaign continued its unrelenting punishment of a wide variety targets inside both Iraq and Kuwait. Despite being somewhat sidetracked by the foray of Scud hinting, the coalition air forces continued to take out ever smaller but nonetheless critical nodes of the Iraqi strategic command structure and to hit other key force and installation targets that were connected to the Iraqi capacity for combat. Overall, the campaign was startlingly accurate, but there were mistakes in identification and in tactical execution. One of the most significant of those mistakes took place on February 13 when the Al Firdos bunker site in Baghdad was attacked by F-117s.

Intelligence traffic and satellite photography of limousines and trucks parked outside the facility in a middle class section of the Iraqi capital suggested to the air planners that it had been constructed as an Iraqi senior leadership shelter or alternate command post. (There is also evidence that an Iraqi spy contributed to the focus on the Al Firdos bunker.) The facility was hit by two 2,000-pound laser-guided bombs in the early morning hours, piercing the concrete steel reinforced roof. In any case, in truth, the bunker was occupied by some four hundred civilians; perhaps two hundred were killed in the strike. Not only was the attack later proven to be based on weak justification, but the deaths of so many innocent civilians during a campaign that had been so prominently portrayed as surgical became a media disaster and began the process of sensitizing senior policymakers against the continued, one-sided destruction of the war.[33]

Once it was clear that the ground war was imminent, the Iraqi forces began to set the Kuwaiti oil platforms on fire. These oil fires were part of a scorched earth effort, but were mostly viewed as a way of obscuring the battlefield to reduce the effectiveness of the coalition and its technological approach to combat, while giving the Iraqi forces some concealment from attack. The fires burned for months[34] afterward and did obscure the battlefield to a significant degree, even though American night vision goggles helped units to compensate for the thick smoke that turned sections of the Kuwait landscape into a dark forbidding inferno and covered much of the operating area traversed by the coalition forces.

Setting the oil platforms on fire was one of the special conditions that had been outlined in President Bush's directive authorizing the campaign. According to NSD 54, "Should Iraq resort to using chemical, biological, or nuclear weapons, be found supporting terrorist acts against U.S. or coalition partners anywhere in the world, *or destroy Kuwait's oil fields*; it shall become an explicit objective of the United States to replace the current leadership of Iraq." In February 1991 that decision had yet to be made, but the setting of the oil fires definitely instigated the coalition ground campaign. After some additional discussions about changing the time of the main attack, General Schwarzkopf ordered the ground assault to commence at 0400 on February 24, but by that time two regiments of Marines were already behind the Iraqi lines primed to advance north toward Kuwait City.

Commanded by Major General Mike Myatt, the 1st Marine Division, led by Task Force Ripper and covered by the two task forces that had infiltrated into Kuwait earlier (Grizzly and Taro), kicked off its attack from a position just west of the "elbow" on Kuwait's southern border. Keys' 2nd Marine Division with the reinforced 6th Marines in the lead blasted its way through the obstacle belts against moderate resistance ninety minutes later. The lead regiment advanced in three battalion columns through mortar and artillery fire. Against sometimes stiff resistance, I MEF quickly succeeded in breaching two defended defensive belts, opened fourteen lanes in the east and six lanes in the west, and established a solid foothold inside Kuwait.

To the west of the MEF zone, the 2nd Marine Division cleared its first obstacles with M-154 mine clearing line charges and M60A1 tanks with forked mine plows and rakes to clear lanes in the division sector. Once through, the 6th Marine Regiment advanced to its objectives, overrunning elements of the Iraqi 7th and 14th Infantry divisions. The division noted in its after-action report that the regiment captured more than four thousand Iraqis including the Iraqi 9th Tank Battalion with thirty-five operational tanks.[35] As the Marines moved into Kuwait, Iraqi troops proved to be fairly effective defenders when attacked frontally, but quickly surrendered when flanked or attacked from the rear. By end of the first day of combat, I MEF had broken the Iraqi defensive line, penetrated twenty miles into Kuwait and eliminated the better part of three infantry divisions. The MEF effort had also successfully diverted the attention of the senior Iraqi commanders and ensured that they remained largely ignorant of the envelopment soon to strike them from the far west.

JFC-East had begun its attack at 8 AM in the east of the coalition line on G-day. As expected, the 8th and 10th Saudi Mechanized Brigades secured their respective objectives during the initial attacks with fire support provided by the 16-inch guns of the battleships USS *Missouri* and USS *Wisconsin*. JFC-East then managed to seize the remainder of its initial objectives by the end of the first day, also capturing large numbers of Iraqis. On the Marines' left flank at 4 AM on G-day, JFC-North commenced its part of the coalition effort when the 3rd Egyptian Mechanized Division, including TF Khalid and TF Muthannah, began to attack Iraqi positions in Kuwait with the Egyptians in the lead. They encountered Iraqi fire trenches, minefields, barriers, and harassing fires as they crossed the border in their zone. The Egyptian division made good progress but soon became concerned about an Iraqi armored counterattack and halted its advance to establish a blocking position short of its initial objectives for the night.

By midday of the first day of the ground offensive, it was already obvious to General Schwarzkopf that his forces were meeting with great success. In fact, they were performing so well that his carefully formulated plan was coming apart. The attack in the south of Kuwait was after all designed as a fixing action, so that the Iraqi Republican Guard forces would be held in place, right in the path of the VII Corps juggernaut that was tasked to destroy it. That end goal could only be fully realized if the southern and western attacks were well coordinated in time and space. The Marines at the end of first day were clearly on a path that would bring them much deeper into Kuwait than the CENTCOM planners had expected and the JFC-North forces on their left flank were not well positioned to support their penetration. Schwarzkopf was concerned that the Marines might run into trouble, but he was even more worried that their success might destabilize the timing of the main attack.

Rather than hold the Marines back, the CENTCOM commander decided to attempt to accelerate his intricate attack timetable.[36] Schwarzkopf called General Yeosock and asked the army general if his forces could attack early. Once the surprised Yeosock had obtained the acceptance of both his corps commanders (Lieutenant Generals Gary Luck and Fred Franks), he agreed, and at 1 PM Schwarzkopf directed the Third Army to begin its attack two hours later at 3 PM—fully fourteen hours earlier than planned.[37]

The extent of the Iraqi defensive effort's defeat was obvious to more than just General Schwarzkopf. As the sun set on G+1, "Baghdad Radio reported that Saddam Hussein had ordered his forces to withdraw from Kuwait."[38] Still, though the Iraqi defense of Kuwait was clearly failing, that issue was never really in doubt. The coalition commanders knew that they could recapture Kuwait City; the questions were at what cost in people and materiel would the restoration take place and would the coalition forces be able to defeat Saddam Hussein's ability to threaten the region in the process. With the first question being answered in very favorable terms for the coalition, the CENTCOM commander was still worried about the second issue, the defeat of the Republican Guard.

Before dawn on February 25, helicopters from the 4th Marine Expeditionary Brigade embarked in Navy ships conducted an amphibious feint off Ash Shuaybah to hold Iraqi forces along the coast. The second day of combat in the eastern half of the coalition saw continued progress across all sectors in the southern and eastern parts of Kuwait, but also witnessed the first significant Iraqi efforts to counterattack in zone as they were pushed north. Several individual Iraqi battalions attempted to attack the advancing coalition units but were very quickly destroyed by the lethal fires that the better equipped coalition forces could coordinate against them. In particular, coalition close air support exacted a huge casualty toll on the Iraqi forces every time they moved. JFC-North also resumed offensive operations at daybreak with the 4th Egyptian Armored Division and the 9th Syrian Armored Division following the lead Arab units as the JFC-North reserve.

"By the third day of the ground war the I Marine Expeditionary Force had isolated Kuwait City, secured Kuwait International Airport, and seized Mutla Ridge, the dominant terrain feature overlooking Kuwait City, and roads north from it. Nothing that they encountered could cope with the Marines' carefully synchronized and tightly focused supporting attack."[39] In general the coalition forces that fought along both sides of the Marine penetration did so with skill and drive, though the great success of the penetration did start to unnerve some commanders. As an example, even though the Iraqi defenses were clearly melting away, the Saudi Forces nearing Kuwait City became reluctant to enter the

Kuwaiti capital without the expressed direction of the Saudi government.[40] The official report to Congress on the war stated:

> During this period, the massive exodus of Iraqi forces from the eastern part of the theater began. Elements of the Iraqi III Corps were pushed back into Kuwait City by I MEF and JFC-East. They were joined by Iraqi occupation troops from Kuwait City. Iraqi units became intermingled and disordered. During the early morning of 26 February, military and commandeered civilian vehicles of every description, loaded with Iraqi soldiers and goods looted from Kuwait, clogged the main four lane highway north from Kuwait City. To deny Iraqi commanders the opportunity to reorganize their forces and establish a cohesive defense, these forces were struck repeatedly by air attacks.[41]

The "piston effect" likely had already provided sufficient pressure to break up the already weak geometry of the Iraqi occupation forces in Kuwait. Certainly the flow north along the Basra road on the night of February 25–26 indicated that many of the forces in Kuwait had lost cohesion and were disintegrating in the face of prolonged air attacks and the more recent ground penetration by the Marines and their coalition partners.

Unleashing the Main Attack: Desert Saber and VII Corps

The main effort of the coalition's assault to recover Kuwait was conducted neither by the air campaign nor by I MEF and JFC-East operating in Kuwait, but instead by the American VII Corps' armored thrust deep inside Iraq and behind the bulk of the Iraqi forces occupying Kuwait. This drive, commanded by Lieutenant General Fred Franks, was code-named Operation Desert Saber. As intended in the 1002 operations plan, the ground assault to eject Iraqi forces from Kuwait required the first attack to deceive the Iraqis as to the location and composition of the main thrust so that when the latter struck their flanks it would have a crushing effect. The Marine and coalition forces of JFC-East would cut through the Iraqi defensive barriers in order to maintain the deception of a main effort coming from the south. Then the left wing of Schwarzkopf's coalition forces (XVIII Corps under Lieutenant General Gary Luck, spearheaded by the 24th Mechanized Division under the command of Major General Barry McCaffrey and VII Corps under General Franks) would also begin to attack. Luck's Corps VIII would establish blocking positions to protect Franks' flank as the VII Corps penetrated deep into the Iraqi forces to destroy the Republican Guard—the center of gravity of the Iraqi occupation force. Frank's VII Corps was an entirely mechanized force, led by the 2nd

Armored Cavalry Regiment (ACR), and including the 1st and 3rd Armored Divisions, the 1st Infantry Division, the British 1st Armored Division, and the U.S. 11th Aviation Brigade. "This massive steel fist . . . boasted over 146,000 soldiers and almost 50,000 vehicles. Its divisions advanced with footprints twenty-four kilometers wide by forty-eight kilometers deep. Never before had so much firepower been concentrated into such an organization, and never before had such an organization featured such extraordinary tactical mobility."[42]

The main Desert Storm land assault thus began at 3 PM on Sunday, February 24, with the VII Corps attack spearheaded by the 2nd Armored Cavalry Regiment driving north and then east from its assembly areas in the Saudi desert. VII Corps consisted of American and British soldiers in essentially five divisions (three armored, one mechanized infantry division, and one cavalry division). Included in this force were some sixteen hundred tanks, American and British, and eight hundred helicopters. Supporting them were logistics units and other formations totaled over twenty-six thousand troops. Fifteen hospitals stood ready to accept casualties. In the course of operations VII Corps consumed over two million gallons of fuel per day. The corps had to pass through the Iraqi defenses, push north to gain maneuver space, and then wheel to the east before it could bring all its impressive firepower to bear on the RGFC.

On February 23, the 2nd ACR had already bypassed Iraqi defenses to the west and crossed into Iraq in preparation for the VII Corps attack. Early on February 24, the 1st Infantry Division (Mechanized) also penetrated the Iraqi defenses east of the 2nd ACR while the latter pushed another thirty kilometers to the north. Following through the openings created by these actions were the 1st and 3rd Armored Divisions.

Franks' attack took the Iraqi forces in VII Corps' sector completely by surprise—the deception operations conducted by the Marines and the rapid sweep of forces and logistics to the western desert had worked magnificently. The attack's 3 PM start-time gave VII Corps only a few hours of daylight, and because the complicated passage-of-lines maneuver that would shift the British 1st Armored Division through the U.S. 1st Infantry Division was considered too dangerous to complete in the dark, the corps attack halted for the night. On its flanks, both the Marines and the XVIII Airborne (in the open western desert) continued the attack through the night. In particular, Major General Barry McCaffrey's 24th Division was making extremely rapid progress pounding through the desert to the northwest.

In support of the main attack, General Luck's XVIII Airborne Corps launched a sweeping attack across the largely uninhabited desert of southern Iraq, led by the 3rd Armored Cavalry Regiment and the 24th Infantry Division. The left flank of the XVIII Corps attack was protected by the French Division *Daguet*. The French force quickly overcame the Iraqi 45th Infantry

Division and took up blocking positions to secure the far left flank of the coalition attack from any Iraqi counterattack. Once the two fast moving corps had penetrated into Iraqi territory, the VII Corps continued eastward to conduct its primary assault into the flanks of the Iraqi Republican Guard.

By the morning of G+1 all the forces except VII Corps had made significant advances overnight. VII Corps' slow movement infuriated General Schwarzkopf.[43] Further delays came as a result of General Franks' decision to pass both of his lead divisions through the frontline Iraqi defenses to continue the attack instead of leaving the 1st Infantry back while pushing the British 1st Armored Division through. Although the decision seemed to take advantage of the lack of strong Iraqi resistance and would normally have resulted in getting more forces into the fight faster, on that morning the two divisions ended up in a "huge rolling traffic jam" rather than the well organized assault that had been envisioned.[44]

On the far left of the VII Corps lineup, at the edge of the huge wheeling movement, Major General Ron Griffith's 1st Armored Division had the farthest distance to go in order to engage the Republican Guard. After defeating the Iraqi division in its zone, Griffith decided at the end of day one to conduct a deliberate attack on the town of al Busayyah during the morning of G+2. Later it turned out that the town was only weakly defended and Griffith was criticized for not continuing his attack vigorously. There is no doubt that a combination of factors, including imprecise intelligence, overestimations of enemy strength, excessive caution to preserve the force, and a training history that engrained a more deliberate attack philosophy—based upon anticipated combat with Soviet forces—all combined to make the VII Corps attack slower than anyone desired.

The Iraqis failed to mount significant resistance to the coalition forces largely because they were overwhelmed by the direction and the speed of the leading American, British, and French attacks.

> The few Iraqi counterattacks that did occur seem to have been local and reflexive—certainly they were unsuccessful. The air campaign had seriously degraded Iraqi command and control at all levels, further aggravating inherent leadership shortcomings. The Iraqi command style was already ponderous and set piece. The line infantry divisions were virtually incapable of operational maneuver, and only the Republican Guard had ever demonstrated a capacity for it. Unsuccessful generals tended to be shot, so daring, creativity, and risk taking were unlikely Iraqi command attributes. Iraqi expectations were not for victory in the traditional sense, but rather to defend stubbornly enough that bloodied Americans opted for a diplomatic resolution.[45]

Still, on the second day of the ground war, February 25, General Schwarzkopf publicly expressed frustration over what he characterized as VII Corps' slow pace, because in his view. General Franks' attack was allowing elements of the Republican Guard to escape destruction and flee toward Basra. It should be noted, however, that Franks was changing the execution of his plan on the move with very imprecise information about the exact location of his target—in fact, he had chosen to issue a fragmentary order that was based upon the assumption that the Republican Guard had remained basically in the same position that it had occupied at the start of the ground offensive. Franks assumed that if those key elements changed, Schwarzkopf and Yeosock—both of whom should have been aware of the "big picture"—would tell him so.[46] Schwarzkopf complained that "the window of opportunity is rapidly slamming shut."[47]

Once all the VII Corps forces had spread into their attack positions on the morning of February 26, Franks could finally unleash the full power of his corps. But Schwarzkopf was still angry at the slow pace of the VII Corps and that morning, with Baghdad announcing a withdrawal, he had also taken a phone call from General Powell to discuss the possibility of a cease-fire. "Schwarzkopf was worried that the war might be ended prematurely."[48] The CENTCOM commander spoke with General Franks and told him to attack through the night. February 27 then became the key day of the war. The XVIII Airborne Corps forces, in particular General McCaffrey's division, were tearing up the Iraqi forces in their zone, and finally the VIII Corps was decisively engaged with all its forces (plus the recently committed 1st Cavalry Division) in one of the most intense combat engagements of the ground campaign.

Meanwhile, Generals Schwarzkopf and Powell were talking much more seriously about a cease-fire the following day. In the meantime VII Corps continued destroying the Iraqi forces in its zone while a series of powerful coalition air attacks shredded Iraqi forces retreating toward Basra. Media coverage of those attacks, featuring dramatic images of the death and devastation suffered by the Iraqis, revealed the truly overwhelming nature of the force brought to bear against them. In doing so the media created the impression that too much force had been used. That afternoon President Bush met with his key advisors to deliberate over the terms of a cease-fire and that evening General Schwarzkopf effectively announced the campaign was over during his press briefing in Riyadh. Later that evening, Powell called Schwarzkopf and then the CENTCOM commander notified his subordinate commanders that a cease-fire could go into effect at 5 AM on the 28th.[49] In one hundred hours of maneuver and combat, General Franks' VII Corps units had engaged and defeated the Iraqi forces along their route of advance in a series of short battles that came to be called the Battle of Al Busayyah, the Battle of 73 Easting, the

Battle of Norfolk, and the Battle of Medina Ridge. Nevertheless, and despite Schwarzkopf's pronouncements to the contrary, coalition forces had not decisively defeated the key elements of the Iraqi army.

The Iraqi View: "The Mother of All Battles"

The Iraqi Republican Guard Forces Command was led in 1991 by Lieutenant General Aayad Futayyih Khalifa al-Rawi. Thanks to the translation of the Iraqi documents in the Defense Intelligence Agency's Harmony database, we now know a great deal about how he and his fellow commanders viewed the campaign they called "The Mother of All Battles." The first key event in the preparation for that battle from the Iraqi perspective was the shift in forces that occurred in September, replacing the Republican Guard forces that had occupied Kuwait with Iraqi regular army divisions. The RGFC moved north to become a theater reserve and the defensive posture of the Iraqi forces in Kuwait was shifted from a static defense to a more mobile defense. Then, in November 1990—about the same time that the Americans were starting to deploy the VII Corps—the Iraqi high command shifted the RGFC mission again and added four new divisions to its structure.[50] At that point the Republican Guard had been shifted to a strategic reserve role in anticipation of the coalition counterattack into Kuwait. Each of these moves increased the depth of the Iraqi defensive scheme of maneuver and, importantly, freed up the RGFC to react more flexibly to the coalition attack.

Saddam Hussein and his intelligence analysts had predicted accurately that the coalition campaign would begin with the extensive use of air power, so the RGFC and the Iraqi divisions in Kuwait used the passing months to minimize their exposure to attacks from the air. Once the air campaign began in earnest, the Iraqi forces minimized movement in order to reduce their exposure, but the Iraqi leadership still harbored significant doubts that the Americans would risk a ground attack.

The Iraqis could not remain unresponsive in the face of the coalition air attacks and Saddam traveled to Basra to personally brief his commanders in preparation for the Khafgi operation. Although General Schwarzkopf found the attack in Khafgi to be "perplexing" and even General Khalid bin Sultan thought it came "like a bolt from the blue," Saddam understood the move to be "exactly what an Arab warrior would be expected to achieve" against such overwhelming odds.[51] It was a demonstration of capability despite the huge odds. In retrospect, the Iraqis considered Khafgi one of the high points of the campaign and one of the major reasons they could justifiably claim to have performed well in combat and prove that the American forces were timid.[52]

Initially, the Iraqi high command expected the coalition to attack along the Kuwaiti coastal road. Around February 5 the Iraqis obtained some information about the shift of Schwarzkopf's forces to the west, and by February 15 they were certain that there would be a "left hook" attack.[53] Although the Iraqis were fooled into thinking that the feints up the Wadi- al- Batin signaled the start of the ground campaign, they realized very quickly on February 24 that the real assault was much more significant. They still believed, however, that the coalition had been intimidated by their resolve during the probes of the previous few days. The commander of the III Iraqi Corps in Kuwait, Lieutenant General Salah Aboud Mahmoud, lost the tactical picture of the battle on the first day, but was able to organize a two-division pincer counter-attack against the Marine advance on February 25. Once that effort failed, resulting in the destruction of most of both divisions, he ordered his corps to fall back toward Kuwait City late in the same day. At that point, three of his divisions, the 7th, 14th, and 29th, were largely ineffective.[54] Saddam and his senior generals, including General al-Rawi of the RGFC, understood fairly well what would take place once the coalition attacked and a two-phase withdrawal plan was developed by the Iraqi army headquarters on the night of February 25–26.[55]

Saddam then ordered all Iraqi forces to retire from Kuwait and organize the defense of Basra, with only the Tawakalna Division of the RGFC remaining to cover the withdrawal. The announcement was made in Baghdad that the Iraqi forces had "proven their ability to fight and stand fast" and were in the process of complying with UNSCR 660.[56] It soon appeared that the elements of the XVIII Corps that had attacked deepest into Iraq were turning to withdraw (in reality the 24th Division was simply heading east to join the VII Corps advance) and this gave some credence to Iraqi claims concerning the ability of their forces to defend in the south of the country. President Bush's offer of a cease-fire confirmed in many minds that the risk-averse Americans had seen enough dying for the restoration of Kuwait.[57]

One American view held that "the Republican Guard—outflanked, surprised, outranged, and in any given exchange generally outgunned—had no more chance of reversing this inexorable advance than vegetation in the path of a magma flow. Their choices were to die, surrender, or flee."[58] *Certain Victory*, the official Army account of the war, said of this period, "By the 28th [of February, the third day of the ground war], with the exception of the Hammurabi Division, the majority of the remaining Guard armor had already reached or passed through the Basra sanctuary en route to positions well inside Iraq."

In reality, the Euphrates River and the decision to withdraw his RGFC forces to a position of strategic reserve saved the Republican Guard from destruction. In other words,

> The Iraqis benefitted from the gap that grew between the two corps as VII Corps swept east and XVIII Airborne Corps reduced enemy resistance in the Euphrates Valley. The two-corps attack against the Republican Guard that ARCENT envisioned turned into a sequential affair with the XVIII Airborne Corps trailing Franks' VII Corps. By 1300 on the 27th, lead elements of the 1st Armored Division were almost 50 kilometers ahead of XVIII Airborne Corps. But the Adnan, Nebuchadnezzar, and al-Faw Republican Guard Infantry Divisions north of VII Corps were little threat to VII Corps' flank, and as XVIII Airborne Corps turned east, most of their units escaped north across the Euphrates or turned back to Basrah. The time to kill Saddam's armor was before it reached the Basrah pocket, but once al-Rawi ordered a withdrawal, the chance to do so was fleeting.[59]

The complexity of the coalition attack and the lack of visibility and solid intelligence, particularly once the Iraqi formations started to both fall apart and be withdrawn from their original positions, made identification of the Iraqi defensive scheme of maneuver very challenging. It would have helped if CENTCOM had employed a separate ground component headquarters to control that portion of the battle, but even with a functional ground commander it might have been too much to shift the axis of the VII Corps once it had commenced the attack.

Kuwait Restored

A British crew from CBS News (David Green and Andy Thompson) equipped with satellite transmission equipment traveled with the frontline coalition forces and, after transmitting live TV images of the fighting en route, arrived in Kuwait City a day ahead of coalition forces. Thus they were able to cover the entry of Arab forces the following day. Their live broadcast, beamed around the world, showed thousands of jubilant Kuwaitis greeting their triumphant liberators in a scene reminiscent in Western minds of the liberation of Paris in World War II.

In what had been a hugely successful and very short operation, Kuwait was liberated with an astonishingly low loss of life—at least on the winning side. According to one unit history:

In a panorama extending beyond visual limits 1,500 tanks, another 1,500 Bradleys and armored personnel carriers, 650 artillery pieces, and supply columns of hundreds of vehicles stretching into the dusty brown distance rolled east through Iraqi positions, as inexorable as a lava flow. By 28 February 1991, when the cease-fire ordered by President Bush went into effect, the Iraqis had lost 3,847 of their 4,280 tanks, over half of their 2,880 armored personnel carriers, and nearly all of their 3,100 artillery pieces. Only five to seven of their forty-three combat divisions remained capable of offensive operations. In the days after the cease-fire the busiest soldiers were those engaged in the monumental task of counting and caring for an estimated 60,000 prisoners.[60]

By March 2, 1991, the VII Corps had largely achieved its objectives. It had, however, failed to destroy three of the five Republican Guard divisions; moreover, the failure of coalition forces to close the escape route north for the remaining, unengaged units of the Iraqi army would eventually pose serious problems for both the coalition and the Iraqi people. The fact that those units had survived the war relatively intact would prove immensely beneficial to Saddam Hussein, enabling him to stay in power during the turbulent period that followed the cessation of hostilities.

The Strategic Political Decision to Halt and the Cease-Fire at Safwan

Although both General Schwarzkopf and General Powell had discussed the idea of a cease-fire at least twice during the final two days of ground combat, neither had a clear idea of what the specific terms for the end of hostilities needed to be. In fact, each general probably expected the other to have a better idea and the dominate voice in developing the terms for the ending of combat operations in Kuwait.

Iraq formally agreed to the coalition's terms for a cease-fire at a meeting at Safwan airfield on March 3, 1991. Safwan is located in southeastern Iraq, and is the first town north of the Kuwait-Iraq border. General Schwarzkopf wanted to conduct the meeting as deep as possible inside Iraq to demonstrate to the Iraqis that they truly had been defeated. The location also had to be road-accessible to permit the Iraqi delegation to reach it from Baghdad. Therefore the airfield at Safwan seemed to be an ideal choice. But even the location of the meeting had a tragic-comic aspect to it, as some confusion existed concerning whether the coalition actually had occupied the site. When the CENTCOM commander was told by General Franks that the airfield was not yet under U.S. control, one of the units from VII Corps was dispatched to capture the airfield and prepare it for the ceremony. Franks soon realized Safwan was being protected by a Republican Guard armored brigade, and other Iraqi units were also located nearby. Threatened with continued combat if they refused to leave, the Iraqi troops eventually retreated from the airfield just in time for the meeting to be held.

The Iraqi delegation of seven generals arrived at a coalition checkpoint several miles from the airfield, and was then was transported to the airfield in U.S. military vehicles escorted by Bradley Fighting Vehicles, two M1A1 Abrams tanks, and two Apache attack helicopters. The head of the Iraqi delegation was Lieutenant General Hashim Ahmad, chief of operations for the Iraqi Ministry of Defense. He was seconded by Lieutenant General Salah Aboud Mahmoud, commander of the Iraqi III Corps.

The meeting began at 11:30 AM and lasted two hours. Generals Schwarzkopf and bin Khalid basically dictated terms to the surprised Iraqis after telling their former opponents some of the facts about the state of their army. The meeting was also attended by senior officers from Saudi Arabia, Britain, France, Kuwait, Egypt, and Syria. The meeting resulted in the Iraqi generals accepting all of the coalition's conditions for a permanent cease-fire. They had little choice in the matter. The terms offered by General Schwarzkopf were relatively simple: all prisoners of war and abducted Kuwaitis were to be returned; all hostile and provocative actions were to cease; the annexation of Kuwait was to be rescinded; the locations of Iraqi minefields and booby traps in the Kuwaiti theater of operations were to be disclosed; and, finally and most significantly, Iraq was to accept liability under international law for war damages in Kuwait and elsewhere, return all seized property, and help in the rebuilding of Kuwait. These same terms were also outlined in UN Security Council Resolution 686, which had been passed in New York by a vote of 11–1, with three abstentions, the previous day. Though both forces remained wary of one another, and a few clashes between units occurred, the coalition and the Iraqi army shifted from combat operations to an ill-defined and uneasy truce.

Although Kuwait had been restored and the Iraqi forces expelled, the military conditions that had been identified for success had not been accomplished in a way that would prevent Saddam Hussein from menacing his neighbors over the longer term. President Bush spoke fairly frequently about his decision to halt the advance largely outside Iraq and not pursue regime change in 1991, even though his own guidance to the U.S. government agencies under NSD 54 had made destruction of the Kuwaiti oil infrastructure a cause for potential regime change. He explained in a speech at the Naval War College in 2000 that he was certain that the coalition would have disintegrated under a continued march north and was equally sure that the political conditions for the coalition action had been met by the expulsion of the Iraqi forces. It was a new era in the world in 1991 and President Bush held a wider and longer view of world affairs when he decided to halt the destruction of the Iraqi army and end the fighting.

Matching military goals to national strategic objectives will always be challenging, if for no other reason than the fact that the stakes and the time horizons can be so completely different. Schwarzkopf wanted to destroy an enemy force that he felt was slipping through his fingers after nearly a year of confrontation; President Bush wanted to demonstrate American resolve and maintain international good will. The problem with the cease-fire itself was enforcement, and more critically perhaps the fact that to the Americans and their coalition partners, the terms of the cease-fire agreement were legally binding, whereas to the Iraqis in general and for Saddam Hussein in particular the terms were only incidental to a process that would enable him to stay in power. The impact of the cease-fire terms on his regime was never really limiting.[61] Even as coalition force began to plan for their post-victory redeployments, Saddam was positioning his forces to deal with likely internal threats to his regime.[62] The issue of helicopter overflights, which has become well celebrated in the Western press, was only a small part of the significant difference in attitudes between the two sides at Safwan and in Washington and Baghdad.

In part the overwhelming victory of the Desert Storm campaign only added to the philosophical chasm that separated the two belligerents. Most people who paid attention to media coverage of the war knew the extent of the coalition's victory, but the Iraqi population, at least the parts north of Basra and outside Baghdad, had very little appreciation for what had really happened in the campaign. Iraqi views of the war reflected the belief that Saddam had conducted a successful defense of Iraq when faced by an attack from a global coalition of co-opted opponents of Iraqi nationalism. Saddam could justifiably argue that he had saved the army and preserved the territorial integrity of Iraq.

The Impact of the First Gulf War on Iraq

Although most of the ground fighting took place in Kuwait, much of Iraq was affected by the coalition bombing campaign. Significant parts of the Iraqi national infrastructure, particularly roads and communications systems, had been severely degraded. The Iraqi people had been subjected to near-continuous bombing by coalition forces for over a month and they had been under great internal pressure the entire time. For a nation such as Iraq, these pressures were bound to strain the already overstretched bonds that held the various religious, tribal, and sectarian parts of the country together. While the attack solidified control of the Iraqi government by the Sunni minority, it also opened a brief window of opportunity in the wake of the Iraqi army's withdrawal for the Shia population in the south of Iraq to attempt an overthrow of the government. President Bush and his administration had encouraged such an uprising in the past and may have hoped the revolt that began in late March would succeed, but they did nothing to help, leaving Shia and later the Iraqi Kurds in the lurch.

Chapter 5

INTERREGNUM:
IRAQ AND THE UN SANCTIONS
DURING THE 1990s

We have to defend our future from these predators of the 21st century. They feed on the free flow of information and technology. They actually take advantage of the freer movement of people, information and ideas. And they will be all the more lethal if we allow them to build arsenals of nuclear, chemical and biological weapons and the missiles to deliver them. We simply cannot allow that to happen. There is no more clear example of this threat than Saddam Hussein's Iraq. His regime threatens the safety of his people, the stability of his region and the security of all the rest of us.
—PRESIDENT BILL CLINTON, MARCH 1, 1998[1]

I raq had begun the conflict over Kuwait largely because its economy had been weakened by the loss of oil revenue and because Saddam wanted to show the world that his nation was a power to be reckoned with. After the cease-fire, Iraq's economy was in significantly worse condition and its global reputation had been destroyed. It was more isolated than ever before. Saddam's claims that Iraq had proven itself in "the mother of all battles" fell on deaf ears almost everywhere, even in Iraq. The only positive effect of the conflict was that Saddam's army had been largely destroyed, and the Iraqi leader no longer had a problem with unemployment resulting from peacetime demobilization—his army had largely vanished. "By March, 1991, it was apparent to all, inside and outside Iraq . . . that the occupation of Kuwait had been a miscalculation of breathtaking proportions and that the Gulf War . . . had been the most damaging act in Iraq's history."[2] These conditions were dire in every sense, and most significantly they served to loosen the cork containing popular discontent in Iraq.

Past Economic Sanctions against Iraq

Shortly after Saddam Hussein invaded Kuwait in August 1990, the United Nations Security Council approved Resolution 660, and within four days another resolution, 661, which effectively isolated Iraq economically from the rest of the world. As the weeks passed, Iraq began to feel the effects, and in November CIA Director William Webster told the U.S. Congress that "economic sanctions and the embargo against Iraq . . . have dealt a serious blow to the Iraq economy. . . . In late November, Baghdad cut civilian rations for the second time since the rationing program began. . . . In addition, services ranging from medical care to sanitation have been curtailed."[3] Webster also said that the Iraqi military was only being marginally affected at that point.

When Operation Desert Shield became Operation Desert Storm, Iraq was the target of a massive air campaign that severely damaged its infrastructure; "the worst civilian suffering, senior officers say . . . resulted not from bombs that went astray but from precision-guided weapons that hit exactly where they were aimed—at electrical plants, oil refineries and transportation networks."[4] Following the cease-fire in March 1991, Under Secretary General of the United Nations Martti Ahtisaari reported to the Security Council on the humanitarian situation in Iraq saying, "The recent conflict had wrought near-apocalyptic results upon what had been, until January 1991, a rather highly urbanized and mechanized society. Now, most means of modern life support have been destroyed or rendered tenuous. Iraq has, for some time to come, been relegated to a pre-industrial age."[5]

These sanctions were seen as a containment policy that would keep Saddam weak and hopefully lead to his downfall.[6] Although the removal of Saddam Hussein from power was not a stated objective in any of the Security Council resolutions, it did became the pseudo-policy for many in the United States after President Bush stated on February 15, 1991, that "there's another way for the bloodshed to stop, and that is for the Iraqi military and the Iraqi people to take matters into their own hands and force Saddam Hussein, the dictator, to step aside and then comply with the United Nation's resolution."[7] Unfortunately, this insistence on the removal of Saddam Hussein by the Iraqi people was not reflective of the realities in Iraq (even in the face of sanctions, his security structure was both strong and oriented on regime survival above all other concerns). It was also not reflective of the power of economic sanctions, which tended to hurt the people and do little damage to regimes in power.

The Effects of Sanctions

While the actual target of the economic sanctions was Saddam Hussein and his regime, the people who suffered most under the sanctions regime were the most vulnerable Iraqis: women and children, and the poor, sick, and elderly. Following a report in March 1991 describing the developing humanitarian crisis, the Security Council attempted the first oil-for-food program in July 1991 with UNSCR 712, allowing Iraq to sell a limited amount of oil (earning $1.6 billion over six months, of which only $900 million would be available for Iraq as more than 30 percent of that amount would be taken to cover UN expenses and to make retribution payments to Kuwait.[8]) The Iraqi government rejected this first offer of oil for food, which they saw as an affront to its sovereignty. It would not be until 1995 that another resolution would be passed allowing Iraq to sell oil in a way that would allow it to feed its people.

The massive Desert Storm air campaign laid waste to a great deal of Iraqi infrastructure. The severe damage inflicted by the coalition bombing campaign, coupled with the embargo against Iraq, had significant and lasting negative effects. Prior to the invasion of Kuwait, Iraq had one of the best health care systems in the region, but the effects of the economic sanctions resulted in a severe reduction in Iraqi health.[9] This in turn increased infant mortality rates. Malnutrition and disease also increased, particularly among the youngest and oldest Iraqis, and among the poor. This situation only worsened and became increasingly scrutinized around the world. The public outcry, including a plea from Pope John Paul II to end the economic sanctions, finally resulted in a stop-gap oil-for-food program in 1995.[10]

Still, much damage had already been done and the oil-for-food program could barely sustain the livelihood of most Iraqis and not repair the degraded infrastructure in Iraq. Without replacement parts to repair water and sewage treatment plants, and electric power facilities, Iraqis suffered in increasing numbers from malaria, cholera, and dysentery. The sale of oil did ease the worst of the food shortages, but with ongoing Iraqi government intransigence, the coalition continued to damage Iraqi infrastructure, which resulted in more deaths and the suffering of thousands of Iraqis. On May 12, 1996, U.S. Ambassador to the United Nations Madeleine Albright appeared on a CBS News 60 *Minutes* where she was asked if she thought the results of the sanctions were worth the lives of nearly half a million Iraqi children; Albright replied "we think the price is worth it."[11] In 1999 a humanitarian panel from the United Nations reported a significant increase in "juvenile delinquency, begging, prostitution, a rising sense of isolation, and a 'parallel economy' with profiteering and criminality."[12] Such problems were extremely rare in Iraq prior to 1990. Even United Nations Secretary General Boutros Boutros-Ghali lamented the ill-effects of the policy, noting in 1995 that the use of sanctions against Iraq "raise(s) the ethical question of whether suffering inflicted on vulnerable groups in the targeted country is a legitimate means of exerting pressure on political leaders whose behavior is unlikely to be affected by the plight of their subjects."[13] Because Iraq was such a closed society little of this damage was known by the American people and, as a result, few of them questioned why their government continued to punish Iraq over the decade following Desert Storm.

The Impact of the First Gulf Campaign on Iraq

Within Iraq the repercussions of the cease-fire agreement were significant and swift. Iraqis in the south reacted almost immediately by rising up against the Ba'ath regime. The inhabitants of southern Iraq had borne a good deal of the actual combat, and being predominately Shia, they were never well wedded to the regime. Compounding the situation was the return of thousands of defeated, demoralized soldiers to their home towns, the urgings of the American president to overthrow Saddam, and the reception of free radio transmissions clarifying Saddam's abuses of power. The inhabitants of Basra soon rose up in revolt, and this Iraqi "intifada" spread quickly to Najaf and Karbala and eventually northward to Hilla and Kut.

Most believe the uprising was spontaneous, started by demobilized soldiers, but it soon involved a broad swath of the local population. Almost always the symbols of the regime and government buildings were the initial targets, but looting and general destruction of property were also widespread. In the initial stages of the fighting the regime's military and security forces were attacked and quickly overwhelmed, surprised and weakened as they were by the impacts of Desert Storm, but they soon regrouped to put down the uprising in the south.

The revolt itself was weakened by its spontaneous nature and the severity of the destruction in the cities—both of which startled the more conservative elements in Baghdad and even many in the south of Iraq. Lack of organized outside support was also a factor—few Iraqi expatriates assisted the rebels and even Iran (which could have aided its fellow Shia participants) failed to provide aid. Ultimately, however, as was so often the case in Iraqi history, it was the Iraqi military that saved the day for the ruling regime. Though many soldiers participated in attacks on the government, and some individuals even led major attacks, large army units simply did not support the rebellion.[14] Eventually, the remaining army units and particularly the Republican Guard forces that had escaped destruction in the war turned in force against the rebels and put down the uprising with great violence. Thousands were killed or executed and by the end of the month the rebellion in southern Iraq had been extinguished.

The Kurdish area in northern Iraq was certainly not immune from the feelings that had given motive to the uprising in the south and, by the end of the first week of March, the population in the north also rose up spontaneously against the regime. The Kurds were even less inclined than the Shia Arabs in the south to support the Ba'ath regime and with bitter memories of the 1986–89 Anfal campaign still fresh in their minds, sentiment against Saddam was easy to arouse. (A series of military operations led by Saddam's cousin, Ali Hassan al-Majid, the Anfal campaign included the destruction of civilian settlements, mass deportations, the use of firing squads, and chemical warfare—all designed to push the Kurds off their oil-rich lands.) The big difference with the rebellion in the Kurdish regions was that there traditional political parties and the better-organized militia forces (the Fursan tribal forces in particular) strengthened the core of the northern movement.[15] The Kurds were able to limit looting and to arrange the surrender of many army units in the northern half of Iraq; in addition their leadership reached out to the international community in a way that gained much more enthusiastic and functional support. On March 20, the Kurdish rebel forces were able to take Kirkuk and force the surrender of the Iraqi I Army Corps.[16]

The rising tides of discontent in the north and south never had much of an effect within the Sunni heartland and center of Iraq around Baghdad. The population there held firm to the regime, clearly the lesser of two evils when the rebellion was seen to menace Sunni domination and, for many, even their personal survival. Under pressure, the regime rebounded from the secure center of the country in mid-March and began to brutally put down the remaining opposition in the south before turning at the end of the month to deal even more forcefully with the much more organized revolt in northern Iraq. The battles to retake the southern cities went on for days and cost tens of thousands of lives; some sixty-eight thousand refugees fled across the border into Iran.[17] Southern Iraq was again devastated, with Basra particularly hard hit. In the north, counterattacking Iraqi forces soon took Kirkuk and then recaptured other cities. The Kurds were amazed to see that the regime not only survived, but fought back powerfully; the result was widespread panic and another even more debilitating explosion of refugees.

The coalition commanders were well placed to observe these events within Iraq over the month of March—a no-fly zone in the south (see map, page 84), established under the terms of the cease-fire, provided clear views of the fighting below—but they did little to help the Shia population, being concerned that their assistance would provoke Iranian interference. In the north, however, the refugee problem generated by the government counterattack quickly drew significant international attention. Faced with a humanitarian nightmare and the brutality of the Ba'ath regime, the Kurdish leadership began to negotiate both with the West, where they had cultivated friendships for years, and with Baghdad to develop solutions to the crisis. Turkey certainly could not accept any increase in the humanitarian problems on its border and

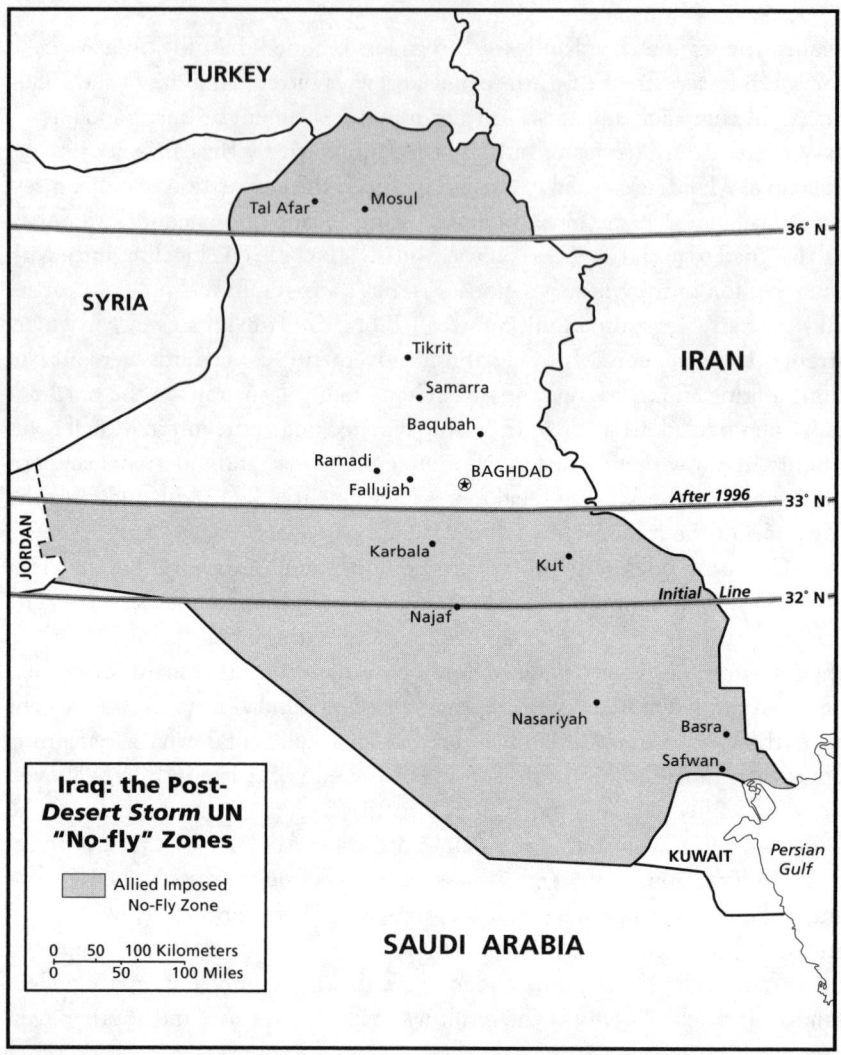

Iraq: the Post-*Desert Storm* UN "No-fly" Zones

Allied Imposed No-Fly Zone

0   50   100 Kilometers
0   50   100 Miles

although the coalition had no forces operating in the north, it could not stand idly by as the crisis grew more severe.

Operation Provide Comfort

In response, Operation Provide Comfort was developed by the coalition to provide humanitarian relief to displaced persons and to induce the Kurds to return to their homes.[18] On April 5, the United Nations passed Security Council Resolution 688, calling on Iraq to end the repression of its population. The following day the coalition began deploying forces into Turkey and northern Iraq and dropping airlifted humanitarian supplies to the Kurdish refugees.[19] Eventually, when it also became apparent that security forces would be required to ensure the successful delivery of the aid packages, and to ensure the protection of the refugees and the overall safety of the operation in the face of potential Iraqi interference, a second, northern no-fly zone was created, limiting Iraqi military flights to an area south of the 36th parallel.

Another part of the operation, known as JTF Bravo, was commanded by Army Major General Jay Garner and included the 24th Marine Expeditionary Unit (MEU) commanded by then Colonel Jim Jones. JTF Bravo's mission was to construct a series of resettlement camps where dislocated civilians could find food and shelter in a secure environment and to prepare the town of Zakho, in northern Iraq, for the returning Kurds. In reality the JTF Bravo effort created a safe haven in northern Iraq for the Kurdish refugees that lasted until July 1991 and established a precedent for continued violation of Iraqi sovereignty.

Thus, in the months immediately following the liberation of Kuwait, no-fly zones existed within Iraq's northern and southern borders. Saddam Hussein had demonstrated that he still had sufficient military power to crack down hard on his own people and he was already maneuvering to avoid or reduce the cost exacted on Iraq for the war. However, because of the manner in which the war was conducted, it would be the United Nations and not the United States that would have to lead the effort in the coming years to ensure he met the conditions stipulated in the Security Council's resolutions.

The UN Sanctions Regime: Goals and Modalities in Concept

The sanctions regime placed on Iraq had actually begun with the economic restrictions instituted after the invasion of Kuwait, but after the cease-fire the UN effort included monitoring the elimination of Iraqi weapons of mass destruction (WMD) as well as economic restrictions. The WMD monitoring mission grew from UNSCR 687, which stated that Iraq should "submit to the Secretary-General and the Director-General of the International Atomic Energy Agency within fifteen days of the adoption of the present resolution a declaration of the locations, amounts, and types of all items specified . . . to place all of its nuclear-weapons-usable materials under the exclusive control, for custody and removal, of the International Atomic Energy Agency, with the assistance and cooperation of the Special Commission as provided for in the plan of the Secretary-General . . . to accept . . . urgent on-site inspection and the destruction, removal or rendering harmless as appropriate of all items specified above; and to accept the plan . . . for the future ongoing monitoring and verification of its compliance with these undertakings."

Those requirements sounded fairly straightforward, and might have endured in a nation that wanted to comply, but Saddam Hussein did not view the resolution as anything more than an irritant to be avoided. Plus, the UN had no organization available to conduct or manage the inspections regime outlined in the resolution.

In order to monitor Iraqi compliance with the resolution, the United Nations Secretary General created the United Nations Special Commission (UNSCOM) in April 1991.[20] From 1991 to 1997, UNSCOM was directed by Rolf Ekéus; he was succeeded in 1997 by Richard Butler, who led the organization until it was dissolved in 1999.[21] UNSCOM's mandate was "to carry out immediate on-site inspections of Iraq's biological, chemical and missile capabilities; to take possession for destruction, removal or rendering harmless of all chemical and biological weapons and all stocks of agents and all related sub-systems and components and all research, development, support and manufacturing facilities; to supervise the destruction by Iraq of all its ballistic missiles with a range greater than 150 km and related major parts, and repair and production facilities; and to monitor and verify Iraq's compliance with its undertaking not to use, develop, construct or acquire any of the items specified above."[22]

Crucially important, and with Iraq's agreement, UNSCOM would have "unrestricted freedom of entry and exit without delay or hindrance of personnel, property, supplies, equipment, spare parts and other items as well as means of transport; unrestricted freedom of movement without advance notice within Iraq of the personnel of the Special Commission and its equipment and means of transport; unimpeded access to any site or facility for the purpose of the on-site inspection; request, receive, examine and copy any record, data or information or examine, retain, move or photograph, including videotape, any item relevant to the Special Commission's activities and to conduct interviews; and to designate any site whatsoever for observation, inspection or other monitoring activity and for storage, destruction or rendering harmless of the items described in operative paragraphs 8, 9 and 12 of resolution 687."[23] These were immensely powerful and broad authorities to be granted by a sovereign state. Still, even with such power, UNSCOM faced many challenges, even under the best of conditions.

UNSCOM had to create itself, deploy inspectors to Iraq, and develop a comprehensive inspections regime on short notice, and do all of these things in a country that actively opposed its work. Almost everyone assumed that the process would proceed as desired, but one thoughtful observer, future U.S. Secretary of Defense Robert Gates, hit the real issue on the head by saying, "We destroyed Iraq's recent nuclear program, and we have now put in place a system of controls that makes it most unlikely that program will be restarted again, at least as long as the UN is paying attention."[24] Paying attention would come to involve not just weeks, but years of focused effort.

UNSCOM was able to begin its first deployment of inspectors to Iraq in June 1991, but even in its first month of operations, it found its inspectors threatened by Iraqi soldiers.[25] Later, in September, Iraq attempted to block UNSCOM's use of helicopters and was embroiled in a four-day standoff with Iraqis who refused to hand over documents concerning their country's nuclear program. The president of the Security Council publicly rebuked the Iraqis for their intransigence and the council passed UN Security Council Resolution 715, which reconfirmed the absolute obligation of Iraq to "accept unconditionally the inspectors and all other personnel designated by the Special Commission."[26] Iraq replied that it considered the resolution unlawful. That exchange began a contest of wills that continued for seven years.

The No-Fly Zones: Operations Northern Watch and Southern Watch

Meanwhile, President George H. W. Bush had announced the coalition's decision to begin surveillance operations in Iraq below the 32nd parallel on August 26, 1992. The goal of those operations was to help protect Iraq's civilian population from ongoing reprisal attacks by the Iraqi military and to ensure Iraq's compliance with UNSCR 688. To facilitate its monitoring efforts, the coalition determined that it needed to bar all Iraqi fixed- and rotary-wing aircraft from the surveillance area. Joint Task Force Southwest Asia was created by U.S. Central Command to control the coalition forces monitoring the no-fly zone, and that mission was dubbed Operation Southern Watch. It began within twenty-four hours of the president's announcement. Initially, Iraq complied with the no-fly restriction, but Saddam Hussein began challenging Southern Watch operations after the UN's decision, taken on November 24, 1992, to retain sanctions against Iraq.

Saddam's challenge came to a head on December 27 when a U.S. Air Force F-16 on patrol in the southern no-fly zone encountered an Iraqi MiG-25 Foxbat. "When the MiG pilot locked his air-to-air radar on the F-16, the American pilot destroyed the Foxbat with an air-to-air missile. Shortly after the shoot down, Hussein positioned surface-to-air missiles in Southern Iraq below the 32nd parallel. Since these missiles threatened pilots flying Southern Watch missions, the coalition ordered Hussein to move them above the 32nd parallel. Hussein ignored the ultimatum, even after warnings from the UN."[27]

Then, on January 6, 1993, four allies—the United States, Russia, France, and the United Kingdom—agreed to work together in enforcing UNSCR 688. A week later, coalition aircraft destroyed surface-to-air missile sites and their command and control units in southern Iraq. Ten days later, on January 17, 1993, U.S. naval forces struck eight buildings at the Zafraniyah nuclear fabrication facility, located just outside Baghdad, in response to Iraq's refusal to cooperate with UN inspectors. Because they wanted to avoid the potential loss of pilots and aircraft and to minimize damage to civilian infrastructure, the president and his advisors chose to use Tomahawk cruise missiles for the strike. U.S. forces at sea fired forty-six missiles, and most of them impacted on the complex, though one was apparently struck by Iraqi antiaircraft fire and crashed into the Al Rasheed Hotel in Baghdad, killing two civilians.[28]

Then on June 26, 1993, U.S. naval forces launched another Tomahawk cruise missile strike on the Iraqi Intelligence Service's (IIS) headquarters in Baghdad. The IIS had been found culpable by the new U.S. administration of President Bill Clinton in a failed attempt to assassinate former President Bush during a visit to Kuwait the previous April. President Clinton ordered the attack after an investigation by U.S. intelligence and law enforcement agencies concluded that the attack on President Bush was directed by the Iraqi Intelligence Service in retaliation for President Bush's involvement in the Gulf War.[29]

Just two months later, on August 31, the Iraqi army attacked the town of Irbil in the Kurdish autonomous region of northern Iraq. The attack was a clear violation of UNSCR 688 (which prohibited Iraqi repression of both the Kurds in the north and the mostly Shia Arabs in the south), and put the United States and coalition forces in the region on alert. Iraqi air defense forces also launched surface-to-air missiles against coalition fighter aircraft patrolling the northern and southern no-fly zones. The August attack was a significant escalation of an ongoing struggle between Saddam and Kurdish factions for control of the autonomous region. "Saddam's actions confirmed a consistent pattern of callous disregard for suffering of the Iraqi people, and a new willingness to use overwhelming conventional forces to continue their oppression. This willingness increased the threat of aggression against allied forces enforcing United Nations resolutions and international relief workers delivering humanitarian supplies."[30] President Clinton ordered an immediate military response, and CENTCOM developed a menu of possible options. To send a clear signal of international condemnation for the continual violation of UN resolutions, and to restrain the oppression of Iraqi citizens, the United States executed Operation Desert Strike.

Ongoing Warfare: Operation Desert Strike

The CENTCOM commander, General James "Binnie" Peay, developed a focused attack plan that would address a range of targets in Iraq, from command and control to air defense in several locations, including Tallil, Nasariyah, and Kut. And on September 3, 1996, a coordinated cruise missile attack was launched against missile sites and communications nodes in southern Iraq.[31] U.S. Navy ships in the Persian Gulf fired fourteen of the twenty-seven cruise missiles employed in the operation, while Air Force B-52s, flying from Barksdale Air Force Base in Louisiana through a staging base in Guam, fired the remaining thirteen missiles early the following morning. Then a second naval strike by seventeen Tomahawks was conducted later that day. To reinforce the message, the aircraft carrier USS *Enterprise* conducted a well publicized, high-speed transit through the Suez Canal, arriving in the region two days later.

Follow-on aircraft deployments, the movement of a heavy brigade task force into Kuwait, and the deployment of a second aircraft carrier to the region backed up diplomatic efforts to deter further action by the Iraqi military. Senator Robert Dole commented that "America and its allies and friends around the world can no longer tolerate Saddam's repeated attempts to erode the restraints that have been placed on his regime, and to violently reassert his authority."[32]

Linked to the operation were two United States and United Kingdom demarches that expanded the southern no-fly zone from the 32nd parallel north to the 33rd parallel and promised further action if Iraqi air defense sites were repaired. This expanded no-fly zone pushed near the outskirts of southern Baghdad and forced relocation of Iraqi tactical aircraft to more northerly bases, reducing the Iraqi air threat to coalition aircraft. Saddam denied that much damage had been done during the strike, but he got the message and over the following weeks his forces stood down and withdrew to their bases.

The Oil-for-Food Program

On April 12, 1995, the Security Council approved Resolution 986 allowing Iraq to sell oil with a restrictive cap. This established a way for Iraq to sell its primary commodity in order to secure food for its people. The oil-for-food program was not humanitarian assistance; no government or NGO donated any food or medical supplies, and Iraq paid for all the food it obtained with cash generated by the limited sale of oil. From 1996 to 2002, Iraq sold a total of $55.4 billion worth of oil with all sales being controlled by the UN. Yet nearly 33 percent of the sale profits were deducted to pay for UN weapon inspectors, UN expenses, and war reparations to Kuwait. Of the remaining money, the Security Council approved $35.8 billion in contracts to support the program.[33] By July 2002, only $23.5 billion worth of actual goods—food and medicine—had been delivered to Iraq. The remaining $10 billion was held up by objections by Security Council members about the content of the sales. The disputed content included water purification systems, sewage pipes, certain medicines, hospital equipment, fertilizers, and electrical and communication system components.[34] Most of the objections were made by the United States.

The program was plagued with scandal. First, while the procedures and policies of the UN managers of the program were often suspect,[35] and the program's former executive director, Benon V. Sevan of Cyprus, was eventually indicted for taking some $160,000 in bribes,[36] Saddam Hussein and the government of Iraq also abused the program. For example, in 2000, oil traders, controlled by the UN, started selling Iraqi oil on the open market at marked-up prices. The traders would give 25–45 cents per barrel to Iraq (Saddam and his regime) as a kickback for the latter's cooperation. Had the kickbacks not been discovered, it is estimated that Saddam could have received some $100 million annually. Indeed, while his people suffered under the economic sanctions regime, Saddam spent some $500 million on lavish "pleasure palaces for himself and his family."[37] Although Iraqi officials would claim these new facilities were national symbols destroyed during the war that had to be built for Iraqi prestige, there was little doubt that they were built for Saddam's enjoyment, and to gratify his ego and demonstrate the power of the Ba'ath regime. In addition to the palaces, Saddam also built a stadium, a safari park, and a lake, even though the country was then suffering from a severe drought.[38]

Yet despite the graft, theft, and abuse committed by UN officials and the Iraqi government, the program did help the Iraqi people. Overall, the oil-for-food program provided about $177 annually to each Iraqi. This income amounted to roughly fifty cents a day and was used to pay for their health care, food, electricity, sewage, and other essential services.[39] It also provided a framework for care that produced the only useable census figures for Iraq that would exist for years.

The Cat and Mouse Game Continues

Saddam Hussein had never been willing to cede sovereignty in Iraq to the United Nations and did everything he could over the years of the sanctions regime to evade compliance with restrictions to his weapons program. As time passed, however, and as the inspectors grew savvier, it became harder for the Iraqis to obstruct the inspections process. By late 1997 both sides were fully engaged in efforts to entangle each other in red tape. On September 13, 1997, an Iraqi military officer attacked a UNSCOM weapons inspector on board a UNSCOM helicopter while the inspector was attempting to take photographs of the unauthorized movement of Iraqi vehicles inside a site designated for inspection. Later the same month, while waiting for access to a site, UNSCOM inspectors witnessed and videotaped Iraqi guards moving files, burning documents, and dumping waste cans into a nearby river. Then at the end of September UNSCOM inspected an Iraqi "food laboratory" only to encounter several men running out with suitcases. The suitcases contained log books for the creation of illegal bacteria and chemicals.[40] The paperwork seems to have come from the office of Saddam Hussein and from his Special Security Office (SSO). In response, UNSCOM attempted to inspect the SSO headquarters but was blocked by the Iraqis. These actions by Iraqi pushed even the UN too far and on October 23, 1997, the Security Council passed yet another resolution, demanding again that Iraq cooperate with UNSCOM inspectors. In response, two days later, Iraq demanded that U.S. citizens working on UNSCOM inspection teams leave the country immediately. Iraq also threatened to shoot down American U2 surveillance planes (which had been working in support of UNSCOM).

In early November, Iraq prevented three American weapons experts from entering the country, and on November 12 the Security Council passed Resolution 1137, condemning Iraq's continued violations of the earlier resolutions, and demanding that Baghdad comply with UNSCOM requests. UNSCOM ended up withdrawing all of its weapons inspectors because of the Iraq expulsion of its American inspectors. On November 18 Russian President Boris Yeltsin met with Iraqi officials and two days later Saddam Hussein agreed to allow all the UNSCOM weapons inspectors to return to Iraq, but shortly thereafter he refused to let UNSCOM inspect the Iraqi presidential palaces. Finally, on February 20, 1998, Saddam Hussein negotiated a deal directly with UN Secretary General Kofi Annan, allowing weapons inspectors to return to Baghdad, preventing likely military action by the United States and Great Britain.

In April, UNSCOM reported that Iraq's declaration concerning its biological weapons program was incomplete and inadequate. Another UNSCOM inspection team discovered a dump containing destroyed Iraqi missiles which upon further analysis revealed that Iraq had weapons armed with the VX nerve agent.[41] Then in July 1998 UNSCOM found documents showing that Iraq had overstated the number of chemical bombs it told the UN it had used during the Iran-Iraq War by at least six thousand, which meant that those bombs remained unaccounted for. On August 3, 1998, UNSCOM Director Butler met with Iraqi Deputy Prime Minister Tariq Aziz, who demanded that the UN weapons inspections end immediately and that Iraq must be certified as free of weapons of mass destruction. Butler refused and as a consequence, on August 5, Iraq suspended all cooperation with UNSCOM teams. This was another signal to American policymakers that Iraq would never comply.

The Iraq Liberation Act

The ongoing intransigence of Iraq was not unknown to the U.S. Congress or the American people. In May 1998, President Clinton had signed Public Law 105-174, which made $5 million available for assistance to the Iraqi democratic opposition for training, communication and dissemination of information, developing and implementing agreements among opposition groups, compiling information to support the indictment of Iraqi officials for war crimes, and other purposes. After Iraq ceased all cooperation with UNSCOM, and subsequently threatened to end long-term monitoring activities by the International Atomic Energy Agency and UNSCOM on August 5, 1998, Congress enacted legislation aimed at spurring the president to be more forceful in seeking a long-term resolution of the problem. In response, on August 14, 1998, President Clinton signed Public Law 105-235, which declared that "the Government of Iraq is in material and unacceptable breach of its international obligations" and urged the president "to take appropriate action, in accordance with the Constitution and relevant laws of the United States, to bring Iraq into compliance with its international obligations."

But even this legislation was deemed insufficient for Congress and several of its members (including sponsor New York Representative Benjamin A. Gilman and his co-sponsor, Representative Christopher Cox of California) pushed forward a new bill on September 29 which affirmed that Iraq had "systematically sought to deny weapons inspectors from the United Nations Special Commission on Iraq (UNSCOM) access to key facilities and documents, [and] has on several occasions endangered the safe operation of UNSCOM helicopters transporting UNSCOM personnel." The act, which passed 360–38 in the U.S. House of Representatives and unanimously in the Senate, declared that it was the policy of the United States to support "regime change" in Iraq.

President Clinton signed the Iraq Liberation Act into law on October 31, 1998. The law's stated purpose was "to establish a program to support a transition to democracy in Iraq." Specifically, Congress pointed to past Iraqi military actions in violation of international law and Iraq's refusal to allow the entry of United Nations Special Commission on Iraq (UNSCOM) inspectors into the country to look for weapons of mass destruction. Congress found that "it should be the policy of the United States to support efforts to remove the regime headed by Saddam Hussein from power in Iraq and to promote the emergence of a democratic government to replace that regime." The act also authorized $97 million to arm and finance opposition groups. The legislative and executive branches of the U.S. government were aligned toward ending the ongoing threat from Saddam Hussein.

Ongoing Warfare: Operation Desert Fox

In the autumn of 1997 CENTCOM, responding to Iraq's non-compliance of UN resolutions, established a force comprising air, land, and sea components totaling thirty-five thousand personnel. The CENTCOM commander, General Anthony Zinni, also established a permanent Coalition/Joint Task Force (C/JTF) at Camp Doha, Kuwait, under command of Lieutenant General Tommy Franks. Operating under the code name Desert Viper, the coalition task force consisted of units from Argentina, Australia, Canada, the Czech Republic, Hungary, New Zealand, Poland, Romania, the United Kingdom, the United States, and Kuwait. The U.S. deployed additional forces to the Persian Gulf region in January and February 1998 as part of Operation Desert Thunder. That deployment included four thousand soldiers from the U.S. 3rd Infantry Division at Fort Stewart, Georgia, as well as members of the 32nd Air and Missile Defense Command, a theater support command, and a Marine air support operations center from the 1st Marine Expeditionary Force (I MEF). It was during this buildup that UN Secretary General Kofi Annan flew to Baghdad to meet with Saddam Hussein and negotiate another round of inspections.

In November 1998, President Clinton publicly warned the Iraqi leadership that force would be used if they continued to hamper the United Nations Special Commission (UNSCOM) inspectors' efforts. In fact, he deployed B-52 bombers to Iraq on November 14 and only called them off minutes before their scheduled attack, when Saddam Hussein agreed to allow UN monitors back into the country.[42] Iraq continued to stymie the UNSCOM inspectors, and UNSCOM submitted a report on December 15 describing how Iraq was continuing a pattern of obstructing weapons inspections by not allowing access to records and inspections sites, and by moving records and equipment from one site to another. On December 16, President Bill Clinton ordered the execution of Operation Desert Fox, a major four-day bombing campaign of targets in Iraq, stating that "the international community gave Saddam one last chance to resume cooperation with the weapons inspectors. Saddam has failed to seize the chance. So we had to act and act now."[43]

The bombing campaign was conducted by CENTCOM on December 16–19, 1998, by the forces from the United States and the United Kingdom under the overall command of Marine General Anthony Zinni. Desert Fox was a rapid and intense use of air power that included manned aircraft as well as cruise missiles attacking fifty separate Iraqi military targets on December 16 in the opening volley of strikes. On the second night CENTCOM forces struck seventy-five targets, including twenty-seven surface-to-air missile sites, eighteen command-and-control facilities, nineteen sites housing security details for Hussein's WMD program, eleven WMD industrial and production facilities, eight Republican Guard facilities, and five airfields.[44] Desert Fox ended on the first day of Ramadan, the Muslim holiday.[45] Defense Secretary William Cohen said of the operation, "We've degraded Saddam Hussein's ability to deliver chemical, biological and nuclear weapons. We've diminished his ability to wage war against his neighbors. Our forces attacked about 100 targets over four nights, following a plan that was developed and had been developed and refined over the past year. We concentrated on military targets and we worked very hard to keep civilian casualties as low as possible. Our goal was to weaken Iraq's military power, not to hurt Iraq's people."[46]

The End of UNSCOM

Iraq stopped cooperating with the UN Special Commission during the same period that the Iraq Liberation Act was signed by President Clinton, but continued diplomatic efforts by UN Secretary General Kofi Annan brought fresh agreement and new modalities for the inspection of sensitive sites at the end of the year. Deputy Prime Minister Tariq Aziz had earlier accused UNSCOM officials of acting as spies for the United States, charges that were later supported by statements from former UNSCOM employees. In addition the Iraqis claimed that use of the American U2 aircraft to develop overhead imagery of Iraq proved that UNSCOM was a tool of the United States.[47] In December 1998 the UNSCOM weapons inspectors departed from Iraq based upon information from Washington that suggested Butler remove them from Iraq in order to protect them from the forthcoming U.S. and British air strikes. The UNSCOM inspectors would not return to Iraq. Following Operation Desert Fox, on December 17, 1999, the passage of Security Council Resolution 1284 provided for the creation of the United Nations Monitoring, Verification and Inspection Commission (UNMOVIC), which replaced UNSCOM.[48] Iraq was once again ordered to allow inspection teams immediate and unconditional access to any weapons sites and facilities. Iraq rejected that resolution as it had done so many times before.

The Second Inspections Regime and UNMOVIC

UNMOVIC replaced UNSCOM, but continued with the same mandate to verify Iraq's compliance with ending its weapons of mass destruction program, and to operate a system of monitoring and verification to ascertain that Iraq did not reacquire the weapons prohibited by the Security Council. The secretary general of the United Nations appointed Dr. Hans Blix of Sweden to be the commission's executive chairman. He served from March 1, 2000, to June

30, 2003, when the mandate was ended and a final report submitted. The UNMOVIC staff included weapons specialists, analysts, scientists, engineers and operational planners, and unlike UNSCOM, the staff of UNMOVIC were employees of the United Nations.[49] The executive chairman was required to report to the Security Council on the activities of UNMOVIC every three months. Although its inspectors were withdrawn from Iraq in March 2003, UNMOVIC continued to operate with respect to those parts of its mandate it could implement outside of Iraq and maintained a degree of preparedness to resume work in Iraq. More than three hundred experts stood ready to serve and continued to conduct training.[50] UNMOVIC issued a comprehensive report on the entire weapons monitoring regime in June 2007.[51]

Saddam's continual undermining of the weapons inspection programs and his repeated human rights violations were the basis upon which the United States and the United Kingdom insisted on maintaining economic sanctions against Iraq. France and Russia, initially fully supportive of those sanctions, eventually expressed reservations concerning their effectiveness and even the morality of the sanctions as continued reports detailing the suffering of the Iraqi people were presented. In June 2000, French Foreign Minister Hubert Vedrine stated that his country considered the Iraq sanctions to be "cruel, ineffective, and dangerous."[52] Russia, China, and France would abstain during most votes in opposition to the sanctions but they did not utilize their veto authority and directly challenge the United States and Great Britain. The intentions of these three countries were not completely humanitarian, however, as all three had "substantial interests in commercial relations with Iraq."[53] Out of the first $18.29 billion of oil sold in the oil-for-food program, $5.48 billion went to France, Russia, and China. All three countries had national oil companies that were negotiating with the Iraqi government to develop the oil fields prior to 1990.[54] Additionally, all three countries were owed significant amounts of money for weapon programs, parts, and systems sold to Iraq prior to 1990. It was obviously in their interests for the sanctions to be lifted so the government of Iraq could pay its debts.

A Never-Ending Conflict?

By the time George W. Bush was elected to succeed Bill Clinton as president of the United States, there was already among the ranks of senior policymakers in Washington a feeling that among the many issues around the globe, Saddam Hussein and his Ba'ath Iraq posed the most immediate threat to the nation. After three major military operations, a number of small but politically risky missile strikes, sixteen hard-fought UN Security Council Resolutions and an ongoing battle in front of the Security Council over sanctions enforcement, Saddam continued to bluster and threaten the sole global superpower. At the end of a decade of humanitarian operations across the globe, where Americans risked their lives to assist the people of Haiti, Somalia, and Bosnia, only Saddam continued to threaten real military action against the U.S. and its allies.

With this perspective, and with the Iraqi assassination attempt on the new president's father well in mind, it is easy to see why officials in the new Bush administration felt in 2001 that Iraq would be one of the key issues they needed to confront in the first year of the new administration. The outgoing Clinton administration had been severely vexed by Saddam for years.[55]

The Results of the Sanctions Regime

The comprehensive economic sanctions against Iraq from 1991 to 2003 by the United Nations were a failure overall. While the inspection program did effectively stop Iraq from continuing its weapons system programs, the sanctions exacted a huge cost for those limited objectives—those costs being the deaths of thousands of Iraqis and the suffering of many more as the Iraqi economy, its health care services, and other governmental aid programs largely collapsed without sufficient resources to repair critical infrastructure and purchase the requisite supplies. The sanctions did not change the behavior of their real target, Saddam Hussein. If anything, they may have served to strengthen his position as the master of Iraq. Sanctions against an authoritarian regime, such as that of Iraq under Saddam Hussein, where the leaders care little about the welfare of their people, are doomed to fail.[56]

The United States' policy of regime change also failed to give Saddam Hussein any incentive to comply with the UN weapons sanctions. Instead, Saddam portrayed himself as fighting for his people, resisting the Western powers, refusing to allow the violation of Iraq's sovereignty, and standing as a hero within the Arab world. This strategy did bear some fruit. The suffering of the Iraqi people under the sanctions was well publicized in the Middle East, and by 2000, most of the Arab world was against the sanctions and had great sympathy for the Iraqi people; Saddam Hussein's reputation was even growing steadily in the region. Positive views of the United Nations and the United States, however, declined during this same period. The increasing support for Saddam and the public international condemnation of the sanctions encouraged him to assume greater risks in thumbing his nose at the United Nations and, in particular, the United States. His boldness and increasing popularity only entrenched his hold on Iraq. Saddam's position in Iraq was so firm by 2000 that the only viable method to remove him was by force.

The economic sanctions also had another effect on the conduct of the coming war. Instead of being greeted as liberators by a happy population, and being able to quickly turn the country back to Iraqi control, coalition forces would be faced in 2003 with a country whose people were weakened in all the ways that mattered most—physically, economically, morally, spiritually—and which would need billions of dollars in aid just to rebuild its critical infrastructure. Paul Bremer, the man chosen to lead Iraq in the aftermath of the 2003 invasion, would later say, "Even more importantly, the information that we had about the state of the Iraqi economy was not good. The economy was in much worse shape than I had been led to believe. . . . I'm not even sure, if the assumptions on the planning had been better, [if] we would have still had a plan that would have helped us, because the fundamental situation of the economy was so much worse than we thought."[57] "Nobody had given me a sense of how utterly *broken* this country was."[58]American forces would also face an untrusting and largely suspicious population from which a violent insurgency would form and fight for the better part of four years before American forces could earn enough trust to receive the needed cooperation of the Iraqi people to suppress it.

UBL, Terrorism, and Iraq

One additional aspect needs to be addressed to fully understand the mindset of the senior officials who would take the United States to war in 2003—the threats posed by terrorism in general and Osama bin Laden in particular, especially in regard to bin Laden's relationship with Iraq and that nation's support for his activities. Many believed that Saddam Hussein had close ties with terrorists such as bin Laden:

> The evidence linking Iraqi state support directly to al Qaeda and the attack of Sept. 11 is not conclusive but strong, in the form of a reported meeting in April 2001 between Sept. 11 ringleader Mohamed Atta and an Iraqi diplomat in the Czech Republic. Iraq has for years reportedly maintained a training camp for anti-American terrorists. Hussein's regime pays $25,000 per death (a huge sum in context) to the families of Palestinian suicide bombers, thus directly bankrolling and fomenting the frequent killing of American allies, sometimes the killing of Americans themselves, and strongly encouraging the conflict that is the prime cause of Middle Eastern enmity toward America.[59]

Yet, in reality there was little direct evidence that linked Iraq and Al Qaeda. In 2008, a Congressional Research Report noted that "some Administration officials, including President Bush, have virtually ruled out Iraqi involvement in the September 11 attacks while others, including Vice President Cheney, have maintained that issue is still open."[60] According to Professor Joseph Collins, writing in the aftermath of Operation Iraqi Freedom:

> Years later analysts would argue about whether Saddam had an operational relationship with Al Qaeda, but in truth, his relationships with many terrorist groups was active and never in doubt.[61] He was among the most active supporters of Palestinian terrorism. The MeK, a leftist, anti-Iranian terrorist/military force, was resident in Iraq, conducted operations against Iran, and cooperated with Saddam's paramilitary and armed forces. Also, Abu Musab al-Zarqawi, who became Al Qaeda's leader in Iraq, was resident for a time in a remote, Kurdish-controlled section of northern Iraq with his group, Ansar al-Islam before the U.S. invasion. He had visited Baghdad and received medical treatment there.[62] Zarqawi did not have an operational relationship with Saddam's intelligence force, but they clearly had communications and a symbiotic coexistence. Initially, Zarqawi was independent and not a subordinate of bin Laden. However, the Zarqawi organization's similarity to bin Laden's attracted the attention of U.S. friends in Kurdistan who brought that group to the attention of U.S. planners. In the run-up to the war, the radical Zarqawi was cooperating with both the Ba'athist regime and Al Qaeda. After establishing his reputation as the most energetic Salafist terrorist leader in Iraq, he merged his group with Al Qaeda and became its emir in post–post–Saddam Iraq.[63]

Ultimately, the truth about Saddam Hussein's links with terrorism remains murky, but the reality was that most Americans felt that there was some connection between the two and that strong measures needed to be taken in order to prevent terrorists from acquiring weapons of mass destruction. After the September 11 attacks, Saddam Hussein was viewed by many Americans as the one person who, through his support (real or potential) of non-state terrorist actors, could make a second attack on the territorial United States a reality.

Chapter 6

TURNING BACK TO WAR

I believe that Bush went to war for the reasons—and only the reasons—he gave at the time: because he believed Saddam Hussein posed a threat to the United States that was far greater than the likely cost of removing him from power. To recall his thinking we must go back to 9/11—which was, for Bush's foreign and security policy, the beginning of time.

—RICHARD PERLE, "AMBUSHED ON THE POTOMAC"[1]

When George W. Bush was sworn in as president of the United States in January 2001, he knowingly assumed responsibility for the confrontation that was still ongoing with Saddam Hussein. In fact, on inauguration day Iraq was the only nation in the world actively confronting the United States with hostile fire. For the first few months of the new Bush administration, the Iraqi problem seemed to be a major topic of discussion, as members of the outgoing Clinton administration felt quite frustrated by their inability to handle Saddam's truculent attitude and to staunch the intermittent but rising tide of American vitriol generated against Saddam Hussein in reaction to the constant Iraqi efforts to interfere with the sanctions regime, then nearly ten years old. But the new president did not initially make his approach to Iraq clear. He certainly had no idea that his two terms in office would be dominated by combat in Iraq.

A New Administration Addresses Strategy

As with any change of administration in the United States the government brought to power after the election of 2000 had a great deal of foundation work to do in order to bring American policies in line with the very different world view of its new leader, George W. Bush. The Republican Party had been out of power for eight years and many of its most prominent members had been outside of government for the entire period. Vice President Richard Cheney had led the Bush administration transition team and he had advocated for a return to influence of many staunch Republican warhorses, men and women who had served President Ronald Reagan and then President Bush's father well in a very different world—in a time dominated by the Cold War rivalry of the two superpowers.

President George W. Bush had been elected by the closest of margins and had barely survived a legal contest over the voting results in the key state of Florida, yet despite wining less of the popular vote than his opponent, Al Gore,. Bush's single electoral vote majority gave him all the incentive he needed to remake government in several policy areas. Among these were repudiation of the 1972 anti-ballistic missile treaty, rejection of the Kyoto protocol and the International Criminal Court, changes to the stance on the China-Taiwan dispute, and a decidedly less affectionate approach to the United Nations, among others.

However, in some areas the Bush platform reinforced the efforts undertaken by the Clinton administration, albeit with a much more realist bent toward action; one of these areas was U.S. policy toward Iraq. Beginning with the Iraq Liberation Act, which had been signed into law by President Bill Clinton in 1998, official U.S. government policy clearly called for the end of the Saddam Hussein regime in Iraq. The Republican Party's campaign platform of 2000 called for full implementation of the act and the removal of Saddam, with an added focus on rebuilding the coalition, instituting tougher sanctions, pressing for more effective inspections, and continued support for the Iraqi National Congress.[2]

During the first eight months of the Bush administration, the major policy efforts of record concerned the economy, faith-based initiatives such as opposition to the use of human embryos for medical research, relations with North Korea and its nuclear development, and relations with China after the shootdown of a U.S. reconnaissance plane over Hainan Island in April. But, at the level of the Deputies Committee, according to Douglas Feith, lower-level officials also "reviewed in depth the existing devices for pressuring Saddam's regime: economic sanctions, WMD inspections, and the no-fly zones in northern and southern Iraq. All the national officials viewed Saddam as a problem, but there were important differences among us: first, concerning containment versus regime change, and second, concerning whether "regime change" should mean merely a coup against Saddam Hussein or a more thorough removal of the Ba'athist government."[3] In fact, the CIA held a very different view, and argued that toppling Saddam would produce even more instability in the region, hence keeping him in power was the better choice among bad options.[4] The deputy secretary of Defense, Paul Wolfowitz, favored action against Saddam, while his counterpart in the State Department, Richard Armitage, along with John McLaughlin, the deputy at the CIA, downplayed the severity of the threat posed by the Iraqi leader.[5] Wolfowitz argued that the threat posed by Saddam would only worsen with time, since sanctions and inspections had proven increasingly futile over the previous decade and Saddam had grown commensurately more vocal in his opposition to the United States and Israel as efforts to contain him proved insufficient.

The basic arguments settled over time into those who favored continued containment and those who saw regime change as the only answer—seemingly irreconcilable options. But in the late spring of 2001, the National Security Council staff developed a more middle-of-the-road option which envisioned that the United States would increase military assistance to the Iraqi opposition parties in order to undermine Saddam or perhaps even stimulate a coup. That proposal was reviewed in detail during a Deputies Committee meeting held on June 22, 2001, but no recommendation was developed at that time. In a second such meeting on July 13, Armitage actually proposed that a recommendation be made to the president that action against Saddam should be made the top U.S. priority.[6] The discussion turned to other options that would make the Iraqi opposition the main player in any international effort against Saddam but, in the end, the meeting did not result in any consensus concerning a future approach or a recommendation to the president.

Still, Secretary Rumsfeld did not want to continue the no-fly zone activity against Iraq without confirming the president's real end-state goal for Iraq, so Wolfowitz and Feith drafted a memo for him to send to Secretary of State Condoleezza Rice, Powell, and the vice president outlining the Defense Department's concerns and urging a formal policy review and consideration of a new set of options. The possible options listed in Rumsfeld's memo ranged from the United States "rolling up its tents" to seeking greater Arab engagement against Iraq and finally even to a possible accommodation with Saddam.[7] "When the 9/11 hijackers struck, President Bush and his National Security Council had not yet resolved any of these issues."[8]

The president was sitting in an elementary school reading class in Sarasota, Florida, when the two aircraft hit the World Trade Center in New York City on September 11 (9/11). From that date, the very essence of the administration's activity changed in order to confront global terrorism as well as those who could possibly have aided terrorists, including the three regimes that President Bush later identified within the "Axis of Evil," North Korea, Iran, and Iraq.[9]

Planning the 2003 Campaign

A lot of poor commentary has framed the Iraq war as a conflict of "choice" rather than of "necessity." In fact, President George W. Bush chose to remove Saddam Hussein from power because he concluded that doing so was necessary.[10]

In 1991, the international coalition conducted Operation Desert Storm in response to the invasion of Kuwait by Saddam Hussein; by the summer of 2001, it was a deeply held conviction by many in Washington that the threat posed by Saddam had not only increased, but was in fact an even more pressing menace to international security than ever before. Amplified a hundredfold in urgency by the climate of shock that followed the September 11, 2001, attacks on the United States, the question in Washington soon became not if, but how to stop Saddam from carrying out his threats. American national security attitudes quickly evolved from defensive mindsets to a form of offensive defense that changed many of the fundamental assumptions about the use of U.S. military power around the globe.

Such a change in attitudes was extremely significant for the United States, a nation that had previously viewed itself as a non-aggressor. Although going to war had not always been a response to aggression in American history, the recent policies of the United States, particularly during the Cold War, suggested that such a great democracy would not make war on another state without due cause. Also by 2001, in the minds of many around the world, only the United Nations held the moral authority to authorize an attack on another member state. For these reasons, the *unabated momentum* toward the use of military force again against Iraq in 2002 remains one of the most potentially important aspects of the long conflict between Iraq and the United States.[11]

The Strategic Impact of 9/11 and the Iraqi Context

Self-defense is a valid basis for preemptive action. The evidence is clear that Hussein continues to amass weapons of mass destruction. He has also demonstrated a willingness to use them against internal as well as external targets. By now, the risks of inaction clearly outweigh the risks of action. If there is a rattlesnake in the yard, you don't wait for it to strike before you take action in self-defense. The danger is immediate. The making of weapons of mass destruction grows increasingly difficult to counter with each passing day. When the risk is not hundreds of people killed in a conventional attack

but tens or hundreds of thousands killed by chemical, biological or
nuclear attack, the time factor is even more compelling.[12]

Although no one understood it at the time, 9/11 was a crucial turning point for
Saddam Hussein. The attacks on the World Trade Center and the Pentagon
on September 11, 2001, changed many of the most fundamental aspects of
strategic decision-making in the United States. Almost imperceptibly, the
attitudes of American policymakers toward Iraq changed as well. The impact
of the 9/11 attacks, like the impact of the attack on Pearl Harbor on December
7, 1941, changed overnight the normally isolationist-pacific mindset of the
American people, first to one of shock, and second to anger, and eventually
to a fatalistic acceptance that war might be necessary to counter the terrorist
threat. During the first few days following the attacks, the Bush administration
had to take stock of the events that had occurred and formulate a national
response. President Bush had already used the term "war"—what kind of war
it was to be still needed to be determined.

The U.S. national response to the September 11 attacks could have been
quite limited—focused, for instance, directly against the individuals who perpetrated the attacks. Or it might have been more broad in scope, designed to
encompass both the attackers[13] and the Taliban—the national government
in Afghanistan that had harbored (and assumingly at least tacitly) supported
the attacks by Al Qaeda. What is more interesting for the purposes of this
study is the fact that even in the earliest days of strategy formulation, prior
to any useful intelligence being available that could precisely identify the
attackers and their support mechanisms, many in the Bush administration
were openly discussing the inclusion of Saddam Hussein's Iraq on the target list of terrorist-supporting nations.[14] By the fall of 2001, distrust and distaste for Iraq, merged with the likelihood of Iraqi support for global terrorism,
made some policymakers much more willing to use force against the regime
of Saddam Hussein.

As previously mentioned, Iraq had funded Palestinian suicide bombers
and was believed to be a supporter of international terrorism. Saddam Hussein
had used chemical weapons against his own people during the Anfal campaign,
and blatantly alluded to the use of weapons of mass destruction against Israel.
Any one of these actions by Iraq would have been cause for serious concern.
The repeated violations of the Gulf War cease-fire were sufficient to cause the
United States to view Iraq as a threat.[16] Still, it was the radically more emo-
tion-charged mindset resulting from the first direct attacks on the American
homeland since 1942 that completely changed the decision-making calcu-
lus in 2001. Like a young soldier who has just experienced the searing pain of
a first bullet strike from an unseen enemy, American leaders recoiled into a

defensive crouch in full anticipation of a second perhaps fatal strike for many months after September 2001. This caused every decision in Washington to be framed by the fear of a potential "second strike on the homeland."

American decision-makers did not push to make Iraq a threat, but took an understood, but often unstated yet dominating mindset into their deliberations that placed Iraq into a special category of *intrinsic threats* to the United States. The United States had conducted air strikes against Iraq on two occasions previously the same year—on February 16 and again on August 30—so the specter of Iraq as a military threat was both real and proximate.[17]

Douglas Feith, then the under secretary of defense for policy, the key defense policy formulator of the Bush administration, makes the pervasive sense of an intrinsic Iraqi threat clear in his book, *War and Decision*. He describes how, in the first meeting he attended with the president on the day after the 9/11 attacks, the supportability of attacking Iraq while conducting operations against the Taliban in Afghanistan was openly discussed.[18] And as early as September 13, during the first formal deliberations to determine a response to the 9/11 attacks, several members of the president's cabinet (including Secretary of Defense Rumsfeld, Chairman of the Joint Chiefs of Staff General Hugh Shelton, and then-National Security Advisor Condoleezza Rice) and the president himself began to explore the connections between Saddam Hussein and terrorism, and the potential need for military responses.

President Bush was just as influential in formulating U.S. policy toward Iraq in 2001 as his father had been in 1990. In fact, history may well show that the convictions of "George W. Bush" with respect to Iraq were the most influential factors in determining the course of the war over the long term even though he did not outwardly appear to be a driven personality. Bush was a man of fervently strong beliefs, one who often exhibited great self-confidence stemming from his conviction that good would win out over evil. And he had a tendency to view the world's problems in such simplistic black-and-white terms.[19]

Planning for Combat

Almost immediately after the attacks in New York and Washington were understood to be the work of Muslim terrorists, the U.S. military was energized to respond. However, there was no immediately clear conventional target toward which the mighty American military could turn its guns. Although technically a response to attacks from terrorists using civilian airliners as weapons was outside the normal expectations of the armed forces, many expectations were shattered in the those days in mid-September, including several resulting from the order to shoot down any other airliners, even those carrying American civilian passengers, which might be part of follow-on strikes. General Richard Meyers was the senior military officer in the Pentagon on 9/11 and he demonstrated the pressure and immediacy that sprang from the attacks by choosing to wear a still-dirty uniform reeking of smoke from the Pentagon in a White House meeting with the president the following day. His appearance signaled both the seriousness of the continuing threat and the commitment of the uniformed military to work ceaselessly to defend the nation; he had no need to increase the tone of seriousness once he arrived, for the entire White House staff seemed to share his level of concern.[20] In the immediate aftermath of the attack, the whole U.S. government was seriously engaged in efforts to identify the attackers and better defend against possible follow-on strikes, but it seemed clear that the military would bear the primary responsibility for any reaction.

Although military decisions emanated from Washington, the center of action for all military planning in the United States is not the Pentagon, but in the headquarters of the regional combatant command; for Iraq this remained the U.S. CENTCOM, which by 2001 was commanded by U.S. Army General Tommy Franks. As with all combatant commands, CENTCOM had been simultaneously conducting operations in its assigned region of the world and developing and refining plans for future operations. Franks and his team had already been worried about Iraq, and they were surprised when the gunsights of America were trained on Afghanistan.

Unlike General Schwarzkopf ten years before him however, General Franks was not aggressively preparing for a potential conflict with Iraq. He had a wide variety of concerns on his mind. Franks had been traveling in Cyprus when the attacks took place and had experienced difficulty returning to Tampa; but he quickly realized the implications of the 9/11 attacks for the CENTCOM region and, by the time he arrived back in Tampa, Florida, he had already ordered an increase in military defensive levels all across the Middle East.

Many analysts have criticized the leadership of Tommy Franks in the Iraq campaign. He was perhaps a surprising choice to be the combatant commander, but he came recommended by his predecessor and his previous post as head of the army forces in the region had prepared him well to understand the AOR and its principal issues. Franks could be difficult to work with and was not the most imaginative senior officer on active duty—which was quite a contrast from his dynamic predecessor, Marine General Tony Zinni—and most would sum him up as a simple "muddy-boots soldier."

Strategic Guidance

The most significant source of planning guidance for CENTCOM and the other combatant commands around the world was the Joint Strategic Capabilities Plan (JSCP), which had last been updated in 1999. The JSCP tasked CENTCOM with planning operations in Iraq (as either the first or second of two potentially near-simultaneous large-scale conflicts) and for keeping the sea-lines of communication open through the Suez Canal and the Straits of Hormuz. More generally the National Security Strategy (NSS) of the United States indicated that "for the foreseeable future, the United States, preferably in concert with allies, must have the capability to deter and, if deterrence fails, defeat large-scale, cross-border aggression in two distant theaters in overlapping time frames."[21] That same NSS outlined the importance of the terrorist threat to the United States. Thus the concept of fighting multiple conflicts around the globe was well accepted, if still acknowledged as difficult, by strategists within the Pentagon. The potential for a terrorist attack was anticipated, but no plans had been formulated specifically for dealing with simultaneously occurring conventional and unconventional attacks.

Subsequent to the attacks on September 11, the United States developed a very hasty counterattack plan designed to respond to the terrorist attacks emanating from Taliban-controlled Afghanistan.[22] The Taliban were known supporters of Osama bin Laden and his terrorist organization, Al Qaeda, which conducted the attacks. Operation Enduring Freedom, as it came to be known, was designed to end Taliban support for Al Qaeda and replace the Taliban with a government that would not allow Afghanistan to offer safe haven for terrorists. The campaign in Afghanistan was challenged by extremely long distances, few logistics bases, extremely difficult terrain, and no pre-existing relationships with the indigenous forces that would form a crucial part of the coalition effort.

With the attacks of 9/11, CENTCOM had to develop a plan out of thin air to respond to the attacks originating in Afghanistan. The Taliban simply had not posed a sufficient threat to be acknowledged as a strategic menace to the United States and no one had specifically linked Al Qaeda with state sponsorship.[23] Given the task to destroy Al Qaeda and rid Afghanistan of the Taliban, military planners at CENTCOM headquarters in Tampa, Florida, had to work through some extremely difficult challenges, not the least of which was the great distance that separated Kabul and other key areas in Afghanistan from U.S. bases and the significant paucity of forces that could be rapidly inserted into such a large and underdeveloped country far from the sea (America's traditional avenue of attack).[24]

The Enduring Freedom Campaign in Afghanistan

Using great diplomatic skill, the United States managed to develop agreements with Kyrgyzstan for the use of Manas Air Base in order to deliver forces and support into Afghanistan from the West. America also deployed maritime forces to the Arabian Sea so that combat power could be projected into Afghanistan from the south. Within weeks, special operations soldiers and members of the CIA had also been transported to the region and had linked up on the ground with the forces of the Afghan opposition, the Northern Alliance.

Enduring Freedom combat operations began with air strikes on Taliban targets in Afghanistan on October 7, 2001, just three weeks following the attacks in New York City. The United States led a large coalition of more than sixty-eight nations in this effort, all united against the perpetrators of the terrorist attacks. In fact, NATO even considered the attacks justification for the invoking of Title 5 of the alliance charter—it was perhaps the most emotionally unified coalition since the World War II.

By late October 2001, the U.S.-led coalition forces had destroyed most of the opposing Taliban air defenses and had executed a series of highly successful missions including striking at but not killing the Taliban leader, Mullah Omar, in the Taliban capital of Kandahar. Coalition special operating forces linked up with groups of anti-Taliban militia and coordinated fire support and provided significant financial and logistical support to instigate their attacks on the key areas of Afghanistan under Taliban control. On November 9, the coalition began an attack on the key city of Mazar-i-Sharif, and only three days afterward began the final attack on the Afghan capital. The Taliban, however, had already been so damaged by the coalition that it evacuated the city without a fight. Very quickly thereafter, all of the western Afghan provinces, including the city of Herat, fell to anti-Taliban forces. Afghan warlords also returned to power throughout northeastern Afghanistan and the Taliban was forced back to the northern city of Kunduz. By November 16, the Taliban's last stronghold in northern Afghanistan was under attack by forces of the Northern Alliance. At that point the Taliban had been forced back to their original heartland in southeastern Afghanistan near the city of Kandahar.

By November 13, Al Qaeda and the Taliban had been forced back into a pocket in the Tora Bora area near the Pakistani border and were organizing for a last stand against the Northern Alliance and U.S./NATO forces. Within weeks the Taliban and Al Qaeda had been reduced to isolated pockets of fighters.[25] By mid-December, U.S. Marines under the command of General Jim Mattis had secured Kandahar airport and the Taliban capital was in the hands of the Northern Alliance.

Although the operational concept employed in Afghanistan was rather unconventional, General Franks and CENTCOM had directed the campaign from Tampa largely in the manner they had practiced during exercise Internal Look in November 2000 and in exercise Lucky Sentinel the previous spring. Enduring Freedom was a unique and highly successful approach driven largely by the circumstances of time and distance in Afghanistan.[26] Although Osama bin Laden and many of his supporters would eventually escape from the Tora Bora pocket, the operation in Afghanistan was a highly successful example of the employment of special operations forces, strategic firepower, and indigenous forces to topple a repressive regime. Many of the lessons learned in Afghanistan would lead to changes in both the planning and conduct of operations in Iraq. Before the fighting in Afghanistan was completely finished however, General Franks and his staff were asked to direct more of their focus on possible operations against Saddam Hussein's Iraq.

Iraq Mission Development

By December 1991, the tide in Afghanistan had clearly turned. Although the conflict was far from being won, and in fact a major contest in Tora Bora was soon to go quite wrong, General Franks in Tampa and several senior officials in the Pentagon were already turning their attention to the other potential adversaries in the so-called War on Terror. Secretary Rumsfeld had reminded Franks not to forget about Iraq back in the early days in September 2001,[27] but he seems to have not returned to the subject until the end of November, when he asked General Franks to develop a commander's concept for potential combat operations in Iraq. Franks would become increasingly embroiled in that task in December, devoting ever more time to Iraq issues as combat in Afghanistan continued.

The Enduring Freedom campaign was related indirectly to the ongoing conflict with Iraq in four important ways. First, both Afghanistan and Iraq are assigned within the Central Command area of responsibility within the U.S. Defense Department's Unified Command Plan. General Franks and his staff would therefore command operations conducted in either country and manage all associated actions and activities, including deployment, resupply, and coordination of intelligence assets needed in both areas of operations. Second, concurrent operations in both countries would frequently stretch sparse military assets beyond their normal operating capability. This was particularly true of airborne reconnaissance and special operations forces. (Many such units would eventually serve in both countries and some level of learning during a deployment and combat on one area could often contribute to an increase in proficiency when the unit was eventually assigned to the other country, but the operational environments in Afghanistan and Iraq were often very different.) Third, the conflict in Afghanistan was directly related to the attacks of September 11, making Operation Enduring Freedom central to prosecution of the war on terrorism—the war in Iraq not only preceded 9/11, but it also was only tangentially linked to terrorism. Finally, some policies designed for one crisis did eventually affect the conduct of operations in the other country, either because people assumed the two operating environments were more alike, or because it became too difficult to develop different policies for concurrent operations. One example of this problem was the development of heavier fully armored combat vehicles for Iraq that were then insufficiently mobile for effective use in Afghanistan.[28]

Donald Rumsfeld's Pentagon

The Defense Department in the early years of President Bush's administration was a very different place than it had been in 1990. Whereas Colin Powell had enjoyed near-equal standing in the administration hierarchy with Secretary of Defense Dick Cheney, the current Chairman of the Joint Chiefs had a very different relationship with his secretary of defense, Don Rumsfeld. Rumsfeld had previously served as secretary of defense under President Gerald Ford from 1975 to 1977 and was an old hand, well experienced in the ways of Washington, D.C.; he had also served (from 1974 to 1975) as President Ford's chief of staff , with Cheney as his assistant.[29]

Rumsfeld was known as a hard taskmaster who was naturally suspicious of Pentagon culture. He drove his senior staff to think unconventionally and challenged anything considered conventional wisdom. He could also be very intimidating for those who did not understand his personality. As events in Iraq would play out, his feisty character would contribute much to the early success of the military effort but would also begin to foster discontent and eventually distrust among his uniformed subordinates.

The Generated Start

General Franks had been a busy man in late 2001 and he seems to have focused only intermittently on the Iraq problem until December 4, when he gave his first Iraq briefing to Secretary Rumsfeld.[30] He was concerned about many aspects of the plan for operations in Iraq, but dominant among his concerns were the possibility of terrorist safe havens and the potential for the use of WMD. After careful consideration of the matter, he proposed making regime change and removal of Saddam's WMD capability the main objectives of any military undertaking in Iraq.

Franks compared Iraq and its security apparatus to that of Nazi Germany in World War II. He later wrote, "The organizations that kept Saddam in power included the Iraqi intelligence service—the dreaded Mukhabarat—and the Special Security Service, the *Al Amn al-Khas*. The Special Republican Guard provided physical security for regime leadership. And the core of Iraq's military power resided in the combat formations of the Republican Guard. These organizations were analogous to Hitler's Gestapo, SS security forces, and his Waffen SS armor and mechanized infantry divisions—with a good measure of Soviet KGB internal security thrown in."[31]

During his initial Video Teleconference (VTC) with Secretary Rumsfeld, General Franks formally advanced several critical assumptions concerning a conflict with Iraq in order to establish in his own mind that he fully understood the mission and scope of operations. Franks specifically asked the secretary if removing the Saddam Hussein regime from Iraq was the correct objective, and he also sought and received confirmation that the key mission requirements would include ending Iraq's capacity to threaten its neighbors with either conventional forces or WMD.[32] Franks seemed to feel that the version of the war plan that was then held at CENTCOM (numbered 1003-98)—a plan honed by his predecessor General Zinni—did not reflect the current balance of forces between Iraq and the United States and had not benefited from the most recent lessons learned in Afghanistan. Franks therefore set out to have his staff conceive a new plan that would better reflect the current military balance of power between Iraq and the United States, and also incorporate the lessons learned in Afghanistan.

General Franks felt that the 1003-98 plan was "based on Desert Storm-era thinking" and was "troop-heavy."[33] So, the force totals listed in the previously existing plan were among the first areas slated for revision. Franks wanted a smaller, faster plan. In particular, he was concerned about the amount of time it would take to deploy sufficient forces to accomplish his mission, without completely sacrificing the element of surprise and placing forces at risk of counterattack (as they had been during Desert Shield). Franks was also very concerned about the linkages between terrorism and WMD in Iraq. He believed that the Jordanian-born, Al Qaeda terrorist Abu Musab Zarqawi was then training in Iraq and was convinced that there was a real connection between Iraq and terrorism—a connection that would necessarily influence his thinking on the conflict to come.[34]

When Franks next formally briefed Rumsfeld he had already cut the size of the force and had begun to focus more on speed than on combat power. After presenting his initial ideas in the VTC to Rumsfeld and General Meyers, he went on to present the basic framework for operations in Iraq to the president at the latter's ranch in Crawford, Texas, on December 27, 2001. Franks felt his one-on-one meeting with the president was something of a test; apparently President Bush gained a feeling of trust for Franks, for he seemed very support-ive of the general's ideas afterwards.[35]

The Legacy of "Desert Crossing"

The plan that Franks rejected so quickly was based on a very different con-cept of warfare. The large number of forces it included reflected an approach that called for overwhelming force to be used in order to maximize flexibility of units and minimize risk to individual troops. Although it was never fully accepted as a plan for war in the Middle East, it strongly influenced think-ing about how to fight in the region, particularly given the success of Desert Storm, upon which it was modeled. Even so, there were several lessons from the earlier conflict that needed to be integrated into the plan, and although General Schwarzkopf's successors (first General Joseph Hoar, then General J. H. Peay, and finally and most influentially, General Anthony Zinni) had each made small changes to the series of contingency plans developed in the event war broke back out in Iraq, much more work remained to be done if the plan was to reflect the military circumstances existing in 2001. General Zinni pushed for a serious reconsideration of the plan based upon the effects of the sanctions against Iraq and changing international policies during his period of command in the late 1990s. As a part of this review process he hosted an inter-agency planning exercise named "Desert Crossing" in late April 1999. Desert Crossing was designed to assess the range of potential outcomes of any inva-sion of Iraq designed to remove Saddam Hussein.

Desert Crossing reviewed the worst case and most likely scenarios of a post–Saddam Iraq under the assumptions contained in OPlAN 1003-98. The review was an interagency effort that included representatives from the depart-ments of defense and state, as well as the National Security Council and the Central Intelligence Agency, among others. The Desert Crossing assessment formed several quite pessimistic conclusions regarding the likely outcomes of any attempt to remove Saddam Hussein from power. Some of these conclu-sions proved to be very similar to what actually occurred after Saddam was overthrown, but with the change of administration in 2000, few then in the government were fully aware of the implications of Desert Crossing.[36]

The "Axis of Evil" and the Role of President George W. Bush

In his State of the Union Address in January 2002, President Bush introduced a new strategic construct that would play a large role in the future of American and Iraqi relations:

North Korea is a regime arming with missiles and weapons of mass destruction, while starving its citizens. Iran aggressively pursues these weapons and exports terror, while an unelected few repress the Iranian people's hope for freedom. Iraq continues to flaunt its hostility toward America and to support terror. The Iraqi regime has plotted to develop anthrax and nerve gas and nuclear weapons for over a decade. This is a regime that has already used poison gas to murder thousands of its own citizens, leaving the bodies of mothers huddled over their dead children. This is a regime that agreed to international inspections then kicked out the inspectors. This is a regime that has something to hide from the civilized world. States like these, and their terrorist allies, constitute an axis of evil, arming to threaten the peace of the world. By seeking weapons of mass destruction, these regimes pose a grave and growing danger. They could provide these arms to terrorists, giving them the means to match their hatred. They could attack our allies or attempt to blackmail the United States. In any of these cases, the price of indifference would be catastrophic.[37]

Component Planning and the Advent of "Shock and Awe"

By the end of January, General Franks and his staff had developed what they called a "generated start" plan for an invasion of Iraq. It was a generated start because for the first time in recent history, America was to go to war on its own timeline, without a specific provocation, and with some secrecy (which was required in order to employ force effectively against the Iraqi regime). Due to the amount of time that was required to mass a decisive amount of force near Iraq, the early deploying phases of any generated start operation would be fraught with risk—just as Desert Shield had been a decade before. One of Franks' early recommendations was that the United States triple the amount of forces it had stationed in Kuwait, using the still ongoing effort in Afghanistan as a cover. Although Secretary Rumsfeld reminded Franks that no decision for war had been made and that the United States could not even signal such a possibility without a presidential decision, he approved Franks' recommendation along with an increase in the Gulf region's support infrastructure.[38]

Franks briefed the president on the planning process on December 28, 2001, at the Crawford ranch. In that meeting he pointed out to President Bush that Iraqi military capability had deteriorated markedly since the sanctions had been put into place even as American military power had increased significantly; hence the force sizes in the current war plan were excessive. Franks also outlined four phases of operations for his concept, including a deployment phase of some six months, and a phase four post-hostilities effort that would take "years not months" to complete.[39] The total number of troops was still about four hundred thousand. After Franks had outlined three broad approaches to the amount of force to be employed (including a unilateral option without allies), President Bush closed the discussion by noting, "The worst thing that could happen to America would be a combination of WMD and terrorism. . . . We don't know what kind of weapons they've developed, and we don't know Saddam's intentions . . . but we do know he has used WMD before. . . . We can not allow weapons of mass destruction to fall into the hands of terrorists. I will not allow that to happen."[40]

With that guidance and concurrence on its basic concept, over the spring of 2002 the Central Command staff continued to hone its plan, in concert with its component command staffs from the four services. As the plan matured it began to take on characteristics of a new warfighting approach that had been pioneered by a group of retired senior officers in the mid-1990s. This construct, named "Shock and Awe" after their book,[41] emphasized shattering the cohesion of an enemy force using a rapid tempo of operations, much like the impact of the highly mobile Wehrmacht on the French forces in the campaign of 1940 in France. It fit well into the desire by Rumsfeld, Franks, and others in the Pentagon to reduce the number of forces in the plan but to still achieve a decisive effect.[42] During February, March, and April 2002, Franks would brief Rumsfeld several times, and each time the number of forces in the plan would be reduced. The expectation was that the lower number of troops would facilitate surprise and rapid deployment, while the technological advantage held by American forces would fill the resulting gap in force-on-force firepower ratios.

At the end of January, the CENTCOM staff started to work on a contingency plan in case Iraq attacked in the midst of their main force deployment. Based again on plans developed previously, this can be known as the "Running Start" variant of 1003V. In subsequent briefings Franks discussed a deployment phase of only four months to develop a force of 160,000 troops for the main assault. Although this was a significant reduction in the forces needed to oust Saddam Hussein, the post-hostilities phase of Franks' plan still envisioned some 250,000 men and women.[43] Meanwhile, a study indicated that the ideal time for any attack would be in the winter months of January, February, and March, when the Iraqi army was at its lowest state of readiness.

Then on March 21, General Franks convened his component commanders to conduct a rehearsal of the plan to date in the Warrior Prep Center near Ramstein Air Force Base, Germany (the site and wearing civilian clothes provided excellent operations security). During that meeting he was able to reveal the seriousness of the president's intentions and to work face to face with his key leaders. The planning effort up to that point had been highly classified and compartmented (labeled TOP SECRET, codeword "Polo Step") and the meeting provided the first forum for all the key players to work through the intricacies of the plan and their mutual support needs. During the meeting, Franks discussed his concept to confront Saddam with multiple crises at the same time—attacking from several directions—including Turkey in the north, Kuwait, in the south, and the air campaign. This was very much in the style of Shock and Awe. The air component commander, Lieutenant General Buzz Moseley, argued for a longer air campaign; the land forces component commander, Lieutenant General Paul T. Mikolashek, also proposed starting before the air assault in order to surprise the Iraqis—Mikolashek voiced concerns about the numbers in the plan.[44] The CENTCOM staff still had multiple issues to resolve.

Franks conducted another briefing with the president on May 11, 2002; by that time the CENTCOM staff had come up with a way to help hide the increasing activity around Iraq by spiking air activity in the no fly-zones to desensitize the Iraqis. Moseley and his air planners had also developed an inside-out air attack scheme that would help keep the Republican Guard out of Baghdad so the Iraqi capital would not become another Stalingrad—the site of massive urban casualties in World War II.[45] The plan was much improved, yet on May 23 the president stated publicly that there were "no war plans on my desk."[46] What he did have in mind was a new strategic concept for the United States.

A New Strategy of Preemptive Attack

> The war on terror will not be won on the defensive. We must take the battle to the enemy, disrupt his plans, and confront the worst threats before they emerge . . . be ready for preemptive action when necessary to defend our liberty and to defend our lives.[47]

In the late spring of 2002, President Bush revealed a new strategy, quite appropriately in a speech given during the graduation ceremony at the U.S. Military Academy at West Point.[48] This "Preemptive Attack" strategy, later labeled the "Bush Doctrine," radically changed the strategic approach of the United States toward global threats.[49] The basic tenets of this new strategy, shaped by the cataclysmic events of 9/11, were that the United States could no longer sit back and wait for an attack to unfold from across the sea, but must proactively analyze and act to prevent attacks from reaching its shores. In part this was the simple realization that globalization and advances in communications and the international transportation system had so changed the global environment that the United States was no longer protected by the vastness of the Atlantic and Pacific Oceans. More importantly, however, it also reflected the change in attitudes of U.S. policymakers that the nation would no longer be naively idealistic in its approach to security. For Iraq, and the unrelentingly bombastic words and actions of Saddam Hussein, this change had very real consequences.

Had the Bush administration continued the philosophical approaches of previous governments confronted by military threats, it would have been constrained by reacting to the military attacks, or at least the observed military preparations for war, of its likely enemies. Given the recent actions of non-state actors such as Al Qaeda, such a change seemed necessary, if not prudent, for the capabilities of non-state actors had significantly increased at the same time that their ability to reach the United States in real time (less thatnt-wenty-four hours) had also increased. Unfortunately, though the strategy of preemptive attack made imminent good sense to many, when faced by the threats posed by non-state actors, the extension of this strategy to include state actors such as Saddam Hussein took the world largely unaware.

This is not to say that the hoped-for byproduct of the strategy, when combined with the serving of notice to states identified in the "axis of evil," did not prove productive; Libya, under Muammar Kaddafi, clearly did see itself under the threat of preemptive attack as a member of the axis and did eventually reach out to the United States and Great Britain to renounce and dismantle its WMD stockpiles. Unfortunately, though Kaddafi seemed to understand the intentions of the U.S. government, Saddam Hussein never did see that President Bush really meant what he said and that both Congress and the American people were so affected by 9/11 that they would give their president the full support needed for preemptive military action against another sovereign state that had not directly attacked the United States (though many in the policymaking sphere in Washington could accurately point to attacks against American aircraft involved in the no-fly zone operations as attacks on the United States itself.

Military Preparations for War: The Hybrid Start

Through the summer of 2002, General Franks and the CENTCOM staff rarely stopped working to improve the 1003V plan for war in Iraq. By August the pressure was so great that he told his commanders that they needed to be ready to attack on a moment's notice. The plan had evolved again by that time, so that it had taken the name "Hybrid Start" to demonstrate the compromise the current version had achieved in time and forces over the more risky "Running Start" version.[50] Still, there remained a host of concerns that continued to drive the CENTCOM leadership to find answers to complex problems.

This mindset extended more or less automatically to many other senior members of the U.S. armed forces. "Major General Henry 'Hank' Stratman, the deputy commanding general for support of Third Army and the CFLCC [Combined Forces Land Component Command] observed that from 9/11 on, the assumption in Third Army concerning war with Iraq was not whether, but when."[51] The Third Army staff even began building staging bases in Kuwait, named for the states where the 9/11 attacks had occurred (Virginia, Pennsylvania, and New York) before President Bush made the decision to go to war.

Prudent military preparations often must include developing plans for a wide range of possible conflicts, but rarely does the Department of Defense actually spend money to prepare unless operations are considered highly likely. By spring of 2002, $550 million had been allocated to support the military force buildup necessary to prosecute the war out of Kuwait.[52] By August 2002, the Army was already deploying crucial, limited supply transportation assets to the Gulf—the clearest indication that war was likely—months before the Bush administration delivered its ultimatum to the government of Saddam Hussein.[53]

Soon after Lieutenant General David McKiernan assumed command of Third Army in September 2002, he had a number of hand-picked Army officers assigned to his staff, augmented it with seventy Marines (including Major General Rusty Blackman to serve as chief of staff) and replaced most of his key colonel staff chiefs with general officers (including Major General James "Spider" Marks as C2, and Major General James "J. D." Thurman as C3), to ensure that it was the best-manned headquarters in the Army. Quickly thereafter, Air Force Major General Dan Leaf joined the staff to direct the air coordination element, as did British Major General Albert Whitley, to act as the senior advisor for British forces.[54] As Army Chief of Staff General Eric Shinseki noted in October 2002, "from today forward the main effort of the U.S. Army must be to prepare for war with Iraq"[55]—and so it was.

The Power of Poor Assumptions—The Bane of Military Planners

All of this massive planning effort had to be based upon a certain number of assumptions: key unknown facts that required answers in advance of execution. It was typical for military staffs to base their efforts on assumptions because war was a complex and nearly unknowable phenomenon—some things simply had to be assumed for even the simplest of plans to be completed. Unfortunately, the significant lack of understanding in the United States about Iraq and the Iraqi military led to a number of false and dangerous assumptions, many of which would not be revealed until after the combat forces had begun their drive toward Baghdad.

Some of the assumptions proved valuable. The strategic timing of the attack in late winter, assembling the force without sparking combat through the use of spikes in air activity, and changing the order of the air and ground campaign starts proved accurate. On the other hand the assumption that the Turkish government would support U.S. requests for overflight and transit through its territory proved to be a severely limiting inaccuracy. General Franks and Air Force General Joe Ralston, his counterpart at the United States European Command (in whose area of responsibility Turkey lay), had visited the chief of the Turkish armed forces in November 2002 to gain his support for the use of Turkish territory for the northern pincer of the attack plan.[56] They thought that the Turkish government as a NATO ally would support their requests to move forces through its territory, but in the end a newly elected government in Ankara refused to allow the transit and the entire northern flank of the attack had to be reset in the last weeks.

Most critically, the strategic assumption that the Iraqi people would quickly welcome the coalition forces and turn to their aid proved dangerously inaccurate. So too was the assumption that Iraqi expatriates would return to their homeland to rapidly establish a functioning government supportive of the coalition efforts in Iraq.

The Diplomatic Process and Secretary Powell

By the fall of 2002, the major contributions of the State Department under retired General Colin Powell were several. First, Powell had worked to moderate the movement toward war, and had specifically discussed the ugliness of "owning Iraq" with President Bush during a summer meeting in 2002. But he did not argue against going back to war.[57] He also oversaw the development of the international coalition against Iraq, which was a much more difficult task than forming the coalition against Afghanistan. Under his direction, the United States proposed a new Security Council resolution against Iraq. That resolution, UNSCR 1441, passed on November 8, 2002, by a unanimous 15–0 vote, with Russia, China, France, and even some Arab countries voting in favor—which gave UNSCR 1441 wider support than even the 1990 resolution against Iraq.

Finally, and perhaps of most influence on the decision for war, Powell made the Bush administration's strongest case for an enforceable UNSCR against Iraq by making the case for war before the United Nations on February 5, 2003. In his speech Powell argued convincingly in favor of military action. Citing numerous anonymous Iraqi defectors, Powell asserted that "there can be no doubt that Saddam Hussein has biological weapons and the capability to rapidly produce more, many more."[58] Powell also stated that Saddam Hussein was working to obtain key components to produce nuclear weapons. After the completion of his speech in New York, the Security Council still failed to pass any further resolution, but the Bush administration and other UN members remained convinced that Iraq was in material breach of UN Security Council Resolution 1441.

Post-Conflict Planning—National to Operational

The U.S. military was not the only institution in Washington planning for a continuation of the conflict with Iraq. Less than one month after the September 11 attacks, the State Department began a detailed study of Iraq, the "Future of Iraq Project," to support planning for a possible conflict there:

> Under the direction of former State official Thomas S. Warrick, the Department organized over 200 Iraqi engineers, lawyers, business-people, doctors and other experts into 17 working groups to strategize on topics including the following: public health and humanitarian needs, transparency and anti-corruption, oil and energy, defense policy and institutions, transitional justice, democratic principles and procedures, local government, civil society capacity building, education, free media, water, agriculture and environment and economy and infrastructure. Thirty-three total meetings were held primarily in Washington from July 2002 through early April 2003.[59]

One of the State Department officials who participated in the study project was Ryan Crocker, who would become the U.S. ambassador in Baghdad in 2007.

The State Department's Iraq study was fairly comprehensive, and even though it did not treat all aspects of Iraqi society equally, it did develop several key findings and recommendations for re-establishing governance in a post-Saddam Iraq that would have been extremely important to commanders in the wake of the Iraqi leader's fall. Among the findings were the high likelihood of looting and criminal behavior, the negative impact of the sanctions regime on critical infrastructure in Iraq, the need to reform the police to reduce corruption, and perhaps most importantly the need to retain but retrain the Iraqi military as a pillar of society.[60] Still, even though one government agency was studying the Iraqi transition that did not mean that the rest of the government benefited from the study. In fact, the Future of Iraq Project was largely ignored by members of the Defense Department who would play the key roles in post-Saddam planning.

Although post-conflict concerns had been discussed from the very first briefings involving CENTCOM and the president, the question of which government agency would direct American activities after the fall of Saddam was not formally determined until January 24, 2003, only weeks before combat operations began. During a National Security Council meeting on that date the president determined that the Defense Department would direct activities in the immediate aftermath of Saddam's removal. Soon thereafter, President Bush signed National Security Presidential Directive 24.[61]

Very quickly after that determination of post-conflict responsibility, Secretary Rumsfeld's staff developed the concept for the Office of Reconstruction and Humanitarian Assistance (ORHA), which was to manage those activities in Iraq. The National Security Council (NSC) did assign a senior director and an executive group to oversee Iraq policy implementation, but that organization left the planning and implementation tasks to the Department of Defense (DoD).

As the official U.S. Army history of the war stated,

> Despite the misgivings about nation-building, the DoD did commit resources to the planning of post invasion operations. In retrospect, however, the overall effort appears to have been disjointed and, at times, poorly coordinated, perhaps reflecting the department's ambivalence toward nation-building. Within the department, most of the responsibility for the planning would fall on the shoulders of CENTCOM. . . . And Franks' planners did prepare for operations after the fall of the regime. Still, given the short time it had to prepare CONPLAN 1003V—and the fact that the command was simultaneously prosecuting the war in Afghanistan—the CENTCOM staff dedicated most of its planning effort to the invasion itself. Also, despite guidance about CENTCOM's role in Phase IV of the campaign, Franks did not see postwar Iraq as his long-term responsibility. He later wrote that he expected a huge infusion of civilian experts and other resources to come from the US Government after CENTCOM completed the mission of removing the Saddam regime. Franks' message to the DOD and the Joint Chiefs was, "You pay attention to the day after, and I'll pay attention to the day of combat."[62]

In the Pentagon, the Joint Chiefs of Staff did try to assist in the planning for post-hostilities operations in Iraq by creating an organization called Combined Joint Task Force-IV (CJTF-4), which was to plan for post-Saddam activities, and possibly to be deployed to manage them. CJTF-4 was created by U.S. Joint Forces Command and commanded by Army Brigadier General

Steve Hawkins. The relationship between CJTF-4 and CENTCOM and its CFLCC was unclear. "Though Hawkins' organization completed some initial planning before the war, its work did not influence CFLCC planning and by early April 2003 it slowly disbanded as its personnel drifted off to join other commands in and out of the theater of operations."[63] So, while General Garner and ORHA were officially the lead organization for planning within the Defense Department, "staff officers in CJTF-IV, CFLCC, and CENTCOM continued to develop their own Phase IV plans."[64] None of these plans were very well integrated with the others.

General McKiernan's CFLCC staff developed the most comprehensive of these plans. His chief planner, Colonel Kevin Benson, was perhaps the most experienced planner in the army at the time and he directed the largest and most comprehensive effort in preparation for the post-hostilities phase.

> Once Benson and his planners received the mission and intent statements, they began to develop a list of problems and issues that CFLCC would face once PH IV operations began. The list grew and included major challenges, such as general lawlessness, humanitarian assistance, and assessment of the oil infrastructure. After careful analysis to include war games that tested U.S. actions in the most likely scenarios of PH IV, Benson concluded that this phase was growing so complex it required its own separate plan. On 20 March 2003, the day Coalition forces crossed into Iraq, Lieutenant General David D. McKiernan approved the creation of a new plan, and Benson's planners began work on what was called ECLIPSE II, after the original Operation ECLIPSE that served as the plan for the occupation of Germany after World War II. This new plan, really a sequel to COBRA II, would be published on 12 April 2003, almost a week after Coalition forces entered Baghdad.[65]

The Final "Five Attacks Plan" and Back to the Future: Cobra II

By December 2002, the plan was executable and CENTCOM was able to rehearse it during its annual exercise "Internal Look," which was conducted in Qatar with Rumsfeld in attendance. During that rehearsal General McKiernan presented a reinforced generated start modification for his CFLCC plan known as Cobra II, in reference to the VII Corps attack in Desert Storm, and at that point it was endorsed as the final land component concept of operations. Then, the following month, another exercise named "Victory Scrimmage" was conducted in Germany, wherein Lieutenant General William S. Wallace, the V Corps commander, was able to refine his tactical concept, including the coalition's transition to the role of occupying power after the fall of the Saddam regime.[66] With a final resourced plan ready for execution all that was required were the final unit deployments, positioning for the assault, and the execute order from the president of the United States. Very little could have stopped execution after January 2003.

Chapter 7

IRAQI FREEDOM:
EXECUTION OF THE INITIAL THRUST

> For the sake of peace in the world and security for our country and
> the rest of the free world . . . and for the freedom of the Iraqi people.
> —PRESIDENT GEORGE W. BUSH, MARCH 19, 2003[1]

The strategic environment for Operation Iraqi Freedom (OIF) was quite different from that of Operation Desert Storm. In 2003, the United States and its coalition partners had to execute combat operations against Iraq without widespread international support and without significant time to build up combat power in the theater of operations. The mix of strategic tools employed was also very different from the formula that had been used in 1991; in particular the lack of widespread support and the minimal time available to marshal forces drove the development of a very different scheme of maneuver, based predominately on speed.

General Franks and his staff knew from the beginning of their planning effort that the main objective of the operation was the toppling of Saddam Hussein and his Ba'ath Party. The scheme of maneuver was designed to achieve this quickly, and it was successful in this regard. But its formulation was based on what proved to be fallacious assumptions about the situation in Iraq. As a result, the forces employed were insufficient for the task of transitioning Iraq from authoritarian rule to some other more open form of governance.[2]

Setting the Stage for Conventional Combat

In late 2002, strategic timing issues drove much of the final preparations for the invasion of Iraq. The issue of weather was especially influential. Summers in Iraq are brutally hot, and thus likely to have a debilitating effect on the conduct of military operations—in particular, operations in which speed and agility were the main predicates of success. Given their concerns about the heat, and in expectation that forty-five days of high-intensity combat would be required to complete their mission, the CENTCOM planners determined that early spring of 2003 would be the optimal time for attacking Iraq. Also affecting the decision for a spring 2003 start date were issues pertaining to the training cycles of the Iraqi forces, the availability of strategic reconnaissance assets during the winter lull in Afghanistan, and the desire to keep international pressure (such as it was) on Saddam.

Assembling the force for the invasion of Iraq was made much more feasible because ongoing operations in the no-fly zones and the intensity of force movements directed at the ongoing fight in Afghanistan made deployments easier to camouflage. The first phase of the deployment was the reinforcement of logistics facilities and transportation infrastructure and the movement of Army transportation units to Kuwait which had started back in the spring of 2002.[3] This took place largely unseen by the Iraqis. As additional combat forces arrived, however, many U.S. officers were concerned that their movements would trigger a reaction by Saddam, so every effort had to be made to minimize the signature of unit deployments.

The "spike plan" conceived by Air Force Major General Gene Renuart, the CENTCOM J3 (director of operations), used an irregular series of dramatic increases in air activity in the skies over Iraq (spikes) to desensitize the Iraqis during the force buildup phase from the summer of 2002 to the beginning of combat operations in 2003. This seemed to work extremely well, but principally covered the movement of air assets. The naval forces also increased their presence through modifications of normal deployment schedules largely unnoticed by people in the region. The ground forces were much more difficult to hide. The Army had maintained a brigade in Kuwait since Desert Storm by keeping prepositioned equipment stocks in theater and rotating soldiers on six-month cycles through the area. In the summer of 2002, that rotating brigade was the 3rd Brigade of the 3rd Infantry Division. Then in September 2002, Third Army deployed the 2nd Brigade of the 3rd Infantry Division, commanded by Colonel Dave Perkins, from Fort Stewart in Georgia to Kuwait. That brigade would not rotate back at the end of its "normal tour" but would stay in theater for the duration of the invasion.

In October members of the forward headquarters of the corps/MEF and CFLCC staffs forward deployed to Kuwait to manage the expanding force arriving in Kuwait. Then on November 10, the British defense minister announced the deployment of the 7th Armored Brigade to Kuwait—a clear signal that Great Britain was deploying ground forces to the region. Later the same month, other American forces began to arrive in Kuwait to participate in CENTCOM's annual Internal Look exercise, that year rescheduled for December. The exercise was scheduled to help cover the influx of forces, but it was clear to most by the end of 2002 that the United States was increasing its troop levels in the region.

On January 6, 2003, the 3rd Brigade of the 3rd Infantry Division, commanded by Colonel Dan Allyn, began its deployment to theater barely preceding its sister 1st Brigade, commanded by Colonel Will Grimsley. By that date, a number of the main units of the MEF and V Corps were understood to be deploying to Kuwait as well. As in Desert Storm, the 7th Marine Regiment, commanded by Colonel Steve Hummer, was the lead Marine combat force into Kuwait; it was soon followed however by the 5th Marines, commanded by Colonel Joe Dunford, and then the 1st Marines, under the command of Colonel Joe Dowdy. The three units were part of the 1st Marine Division under the command of Major General Jim Mattis. Kuwait had two combat ready divisions in the sand by the end of February 2003. There was no doubt that America was preparing for possible combat.

Unknown to all but the most senior planners, one piece of the five attacks concept was not being prepared through troop deployments. The newly elected government in Turkey had resisted American pressure to permit the use of its territory as a transit location and staging base for an attack by the U.S. 4th Infantry Division on Iraq. Turkey's objection was the first significant shortfall in the planning, as it changed at least the means of insertion for any forces intended to operate in northern Iraq.[4] In response, planners identified the 173rd Airborne Brigade in Vicenza, Italy, as an available force that could be inserted by parachute in the north to replace the army's most technologically advanced division. The ideal force geometry was no longer possible, but by using the 173rd aggressively and magnifying its importance through the media, it was hoped that the Iraqi forces would remain fixed in place north of Baghdad for at least a few more weeks.

While the forces were assembling in the deserts of Kuwait there was a fear that the Ba'ath regime in Iraq could fold under pressure (no matter how unlikely) and General Franks had accordingly put Major General Dell Dailey's special operators in the Joint Special Operations Command at Ft. Bragg, North Carolina, on notice that they might have to respond on short notice and deploy to Baghdad in the event of the regime's sudden collapse.[5]

Preparing to Thrust North: Last-Minute Synchronization

President Bush gave an address from the Oval Office on Tuesday, March 18, offering Saddam Hussein one last chance to avert war—but only if the Iraqi leader and his sons left Iraq. No one expected Saddam to accept the offer, but it did demonstrate that President Bush was willing to take one last chance to overt war; some also saw the offer as an indication that the combat to come was aimed only at the Ba'ath regime and not the people of Iraq. Once all the details of the plan were synchronized, the initial attack into Iraq was scheduled to begin forty-eight hours after the ultimatum for Saddam and his sons to depart was issued by President Bush. That established D-day for Operation Iraqi Freedom as March 19, 2003. Unlike in 1991, the main attack was to be a near-simultaneous air and ground operation, with the air strikes beginning at 9 PM on the 21st and the ground assault starting just after dawn the following day. This main attack was to be preceded only by limited objective SOF insertions and simultaneous helicopter attacks designed to blind Iraqi observation posts in the south from observing the main coalition assault.[6] General Franks expected that the main attack on the 21st/22nd would generate considerable surprise because the Iraqis expected a long air campaign and would not react quickly to the ground activity. Although some believed that the Iraqi army would quickly capitulate, Saddam's forces were clearly preparing for combat in the days preceding the start of the conflict. Saddam supposedly met with his key staff and told them "to hold the coalition for eight days and leave the rest to him."[7]

As the evening of March 19 arrived, everything was set in the Kuwaiti desert south of Iraq. President Bush communicated with each of General Franks' component commanders[8] in a secure video teleconference to ensure each one had what they needed to begin the assault. After confirming that everything was in place, he told them that "for the sake of peace in the world and security for our country and the rest of the free world, and for the freedom of the Iraqi people, as of this moment I will give Secretary Rumsfeld the order necessary to execute Operation Iraqi Freedom."[9]

As often happens in combat, almost immediately things began to change. Intelligence reports revealed that fires were being set by the Iraqis around the oil fields in southern Iraq. Seizing and protecting the oil fields immediately across the border from Kuwait was one of the key objectives in the overall coalition effort, because Iraq was expected to compensate for the cost incurred during the operation by increased oil production after regime change—thus protection of Iraqi critical infrastructure was important from the outset. Saddam had set oil fires during Desert Storm, so it was natural that he would do so again. Because coalition planners knew that he expected that, the main attack would begin with air strikes. The hope was to occupy the Rumaylah oil fields before the Iraqis could react.

The oil fields in Rumaylah were important to the idea advanced by Deputy Secretary of Defense Wolfowitz and many others that the campaign would be self-financing, in other words, that Iraq could repay the investment of coalition through sale of its natural petroleum resources. The gas fires in Rumaylah were first noticed on the 19th, just as the coalition force was being set in its battle positions on the final timeline for execution.[10] When notified about the fires, General Franks quickly polled his commanders as to the feasibility of moving the entire attack schedule forward by forty-eight hours. This was extremely difficult for the master air attack planners, but the Army and Marine component commanders felt certain that they could execute early, so the ground attack was advanced to begin on March 20, thus actually starting the ground assault before the air campaign was begun as scheduled on March 21.[11]

Then, just as the entire force was adjusting to the new timing and sequencing, another opportunity injected stress into the already very complex military planning system. Saddam Hussein and his sons were reported by intelligence sources to be identified at a meeting place in the Dora Farms area near Baghdad. In a stellar, but risky example of emerging time sensitive, strategic targeting, Generals Meyers and Moseley managed to pull together an F-117 strike by two aircraft on the Dora Farms target site just as the invasion was to start. The information became available at 10 PM on the 19th, and a strike was planned for 4 AM on the following morning.[12] For its part the navy was able to scramble-program thirty-nine Tomahawk land-attack missiles to add to the firestorm envisioned against the Hussein clan at Dora.[13]

Forty-five minutes after the two Dora Farms attack aircraft executed their mission, President Bush addressed the nation to explain the unexpected start of the renewed offensive against Iraq. Later it was learned that the Dora raid was a bust—Saddam and his sons were not at the location—but the attack demonstrated the exceptional responsiveness of the coalition to emerging targets. That responsiveness would be used frequently over the following weeks of combat. The Iraqi armed forces did respond to the decapitation attempt, sending three short-range missiles from Basra aimed at Camp Commando (the Marine headquarters encampment of the MEF), Camp Doha (McKiernan's headquarters), and against the assembly area of the 101st Airborne Division. None of the Iraqi missiles did much damage, so the opening exchange of the conflict was a draw.[14]

By the time the announcement was made by the president special operations forces had already penetrated into Iraq to destroy observation posts and conduct their initial reconnaissance. About twelve hours later the air attack plan began with over five hundred strike sorties and other special operations forces attacking to seize Tallil airbase and significant river crossing points on the Euphrates. (See map, page 128.) As planned, at dawn the following morning, the MEF attacked into Iraq to secure the Rumaylah oil fields. The onus of command had shifted in less than twenty-four hours from President Bush to General Franks and on to his component commanders—most particularly the CFLCC, Lieutenant General Dave McKiernan.

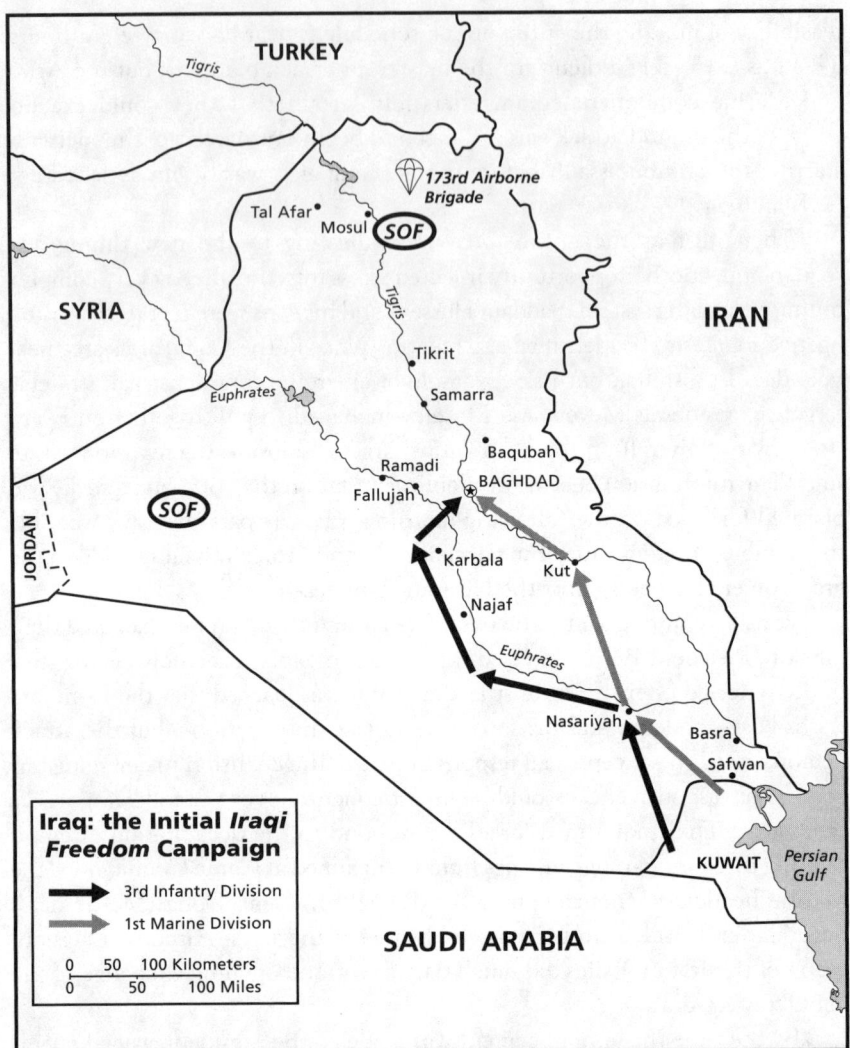

Iraq: the Initial *Iraqi Freedom* Campaign

→ 3rd Infantry Division

→ 1st Marine Division

0   50   100 Kilometers
0   50   100 Miles

Unexpected Encounters: The Problems of Combat on the Cheap

Although General Franks and his staff had spent over a year wrestling with Secretary Rumsfeld over the strategic parameters of the Iraq war plan, it was General McKiernan's Cobra II plan that was the real motive idea behind the impending ground assault. Within the ever shifting framework provided by CENTCOM, McKiernan's staff had coordinated in tremendous detail with the staffs of Generals Scott Wallace and Jim Conway to craft a penetration into Iraq that drew great power from its speed of advance and its design to avoid entanglements in urban areas. McKiernan wanted to maneuver around key infrastructure, not only to save it from destruction but also to minimize slow-downs and free his attacking forces from fighting in the cities on the way north to Baghdad.

Conceptually, the main effort for the assault was the Army's mailed fist (V Corps); the Marines of I MEF were to execute a supporting attack and protect the right flank of the army penetration while also driving north to keep the pressure on the Iraqi forces between Basra and Baghdad. V Corps would drive north along the Euphrates River until it passed through the escarpment northeast of Najaf and then through the Karbala gap to menace Baghdad directly from the west. The Marines would push north after passing through Nasariyah and eventually threaten Baghdad from the southeast after passing through the Iraqi town of Kut. It would be the longest ground attack, in terms of distance covered, in Marine history.[15] The British 1st Armored Division had been placed under MEF command, and it was responsible for taking the Rumaylah oil fields, after which it would turn toward Basra to liberate the citizens of that city. Along the way the Royal Marine Commando Brigade, with a U.S. Marine MEU attached, would seize and establish control over the port and waterways leading into Iraq.

The initial push to break through the Iraqi defenses went much better than expected, as did the movement to control the Rumaylah oil fields. As in Desert Storm twelve years before, the Iraqi military was largely caught off guard by the coalition axis of attack. Very quickly, however, it became obvious to the leaders on the ground that the real paucity of operational intelligence about Iraqi units and their leaders left coalition commanders uncertain about the locations and intentions of the Iraqi forces. As the penetration grew deeper it also became clear that the type of resistance expected was far from accurate.

At about 9 PM on March 20, with the news that the oil platforms were being torched, Marine Lieutenant Colonel Fred Padilla's battalion (1st Battalion, Fifth Marines) was the first conventional unit into Iraq, breaking through the Iraqi defenses as the lead element of its regiment, but followed closely by its sister battalion commanded by Lieutenant Colonel Sam Mundy. They were attempting to save the oil platforms, and even when confronted by Iraqi artillery, small-arms fire, and ignited oil in fire trenches, they managed to occupy all of their objectives during the night without any casualties.

The next day, the first American fatality of the campaign brought with it surprise and ominous implications. Early the following morning after securing his platform objective, Marine Lieutenant Shane Childers was struck by AK-47 fire from a tan Toyota pickup truck racing by the Marines carrying a number of Iraqis in civilian clothes. His men were uncertain what to do given their rules of engagement, since the Iraqis appeared to be civilians, but once the Iraqis began shooting the Marines returned fire and destroyed them and their truck. Childers was hit by a single round that passed completely through his body—there was nothing his medical corpsman could do to save him from massive blood loss. His death was not the result of Iraqi army action, but was instead due to an unconventional attack by Saddam's militia forces.[16]

With all of his battalions controlling their initial objectives inside Iraq, Colonel Dunford's Regimental Combat Team 5 (RCT-5) mission was complete only sixteen hours after the start of hostilities. To Dunford's right, Colonel Steve Hummer's RCT-7 Marines had similarly advanced into Iraq beginning at daylight and found nothing organized blocking their way north and east toward Basra and Zubayr. British Major General Robin Brims, with his 1st UK Division plus the Marine 15th MEU, moved up to take Basra and Umm Qasr, while the Royal Marine commandos attacked the Al Faw peninsula.[17] Along the way the coalition forces destroyed the Iraqi 51st Division and captured its commander.[18]

Unfortunately, though the coalition forces that penetrated early into Iraq met with great success—even greater than expected, in fact—when they were opposed, it was most frequently by Fedayeen Saddam militia forces, who mounted an irregular force battle of hit-and-run tactics, without wearing uniforms or employing the cohesive "conventional structure" that the coalition had anticipated. The use of hit-and-run tactics did not bode well for the coalition forces, which were pressing deeper into more inhabited areas of Iraq, particularly as the militia tended to use civilians as shields.

Within the first days of the attack in the Marine zone there were already some obvious incongruities that should have given planners pause and pushed operators to be more open-minded. First of all, the oil platforms were in serious disrepair (so much so that initially the coalition forces thought they had been destroyed by retreating Iraqi forces): as a result of the long sanctions regime and lack of funds, even the oil platforms—the most important infrastructure in the country—had fallen into a desperate state. Then there were several incidents that indicated how poor American strategic intelligence sources were in Iraq.[19] Finally, as the coalition continued the attack, it became increasingly clear that the restrictive rules of engagement (ROE) that were in effect (largely due to the "Iraqi welcome parades" assumption that caused commanders to expect Iraqi civilians to greet them warmly) did not match conditions on the ground; while it was true that most Iraqis were happy to see their "liberators," there were also significant numbers of militia that were fighting in the stead of the disintegrating Iraqi army.[20] These three factors were powerful signs that America's basic assumptions about the war needed to be reviewed.

The 3rd Infantry Division Drives North

The Marine thrust was intended only as the supporting attack for the main V Corps attack through southwestern Iraq along the Euphrates River toward Baghdad—that effort was spearheaded by the 3rd Infantry Division and its commander, Major General Buford "Buff" Blount. Blount had advised the Saudi Arabian National Guard in a previous assignment and he understood how to employ tanks in the desert.[21] His division was to advance as three heavy armored maneuver brigade combat teams (BCTs) and a cavalry advance guard. Initially it was to secure the corps' advance base at Tallil airbase, then press north toward Najaf and Karbala.

Blount attacked into Iraq at 2 AM, March 20, with two lead brigades (Colonel Will Grimsley's 1st BCT on the right, near the Marine zone, and Colonel Dan Allyn's 3rd BCT on the left.) Colonel Dave Perkins' 2nd BCT followed closely behind Grimsley's troopers; once the 1st BCT had punched a hole into Iraq it would then pass through and attack the initial morning objective at Tallil. As the plan had been written originally, the army maneuver brigades were to assault along the road networks moving north, but during the long period in the Kuwaiti desert since his soldiers had arrived in September 2002, Colonel Allyn had convinced the other commanders that the movement could be made faster and more effectively across the desert, so his brigade struck out "alone and unafraid" into the deserts of Iraq.[22]

Almost immediately, the soldiers of the 3rd Infantry Division began learning some of the same lessons as their Marine counterparts. Strategic intelligence was very poor,[23] and although the regular Iraqi forces of the 11th Division to their front did dissipate fairly easily, the irregular Fedayeen Saddam began to make a real difference in the conduct of the coalition attack as early as the morning of D+1. Blount's cavalry screen, the 3rd Battalion of the 7th Cavalry Regiment (3-7 Cav) under Lieutenant Colonel Terry Ferrell,[24] was supposed to secure two bridges over the Euphrates at the town of Samawah and then quickly continue the attack up the eastern side of the river toward Baghdad. This line of attack was crucial because it was part of a deception plan to make the Iraqis believe the main effort of the division's attack would come at Baghdad from the south—on the east side of the river. In reality, Blount had successfully argued for the V Corps plan to take his division around to the western side of the river, passing though Najaf to attack the Iraqi capital from the west.

Samawah and the Swarming of the Fedayeen Saddam

Unfortunately, what the troopers of the 3-7 Cav found at Samawah changed their plan. They took the bridges easily enough, but once they pushed into the town they were immediately counterattacked by the Fedayeen Saddam in significant numbers. Where they had expected flowers and a parade, they found a vicious fight.[25] One of the helicopter troop commanders in the fight reported that the Fedayeen were "using civilians to protect themselves. . . . [T]hey were dressed like civilians, and they intermingled with civilians, especially women and children."[26] The fighting at Samawah revealed fully that basic assumptions about the attack into Iraq were weak or false. Lieutenant Colonel Ferrell told General Blount over the radio, "This is nothing like we planned to fight."[27] The same sort of situation became evident in the small town of Kindr, another key choke point along the division's route.

Unhappy but decisive, General Blount called Colonel Allyn and made the decision to change the division plan, leaving Allyn's 3rd BCT to deal with the fighting in the division's rear areas and secure its long line of communications back to bases in Kuwait so that the remainder of his division could continue its attack with its rear secure. Allyn also convinced Brigadier General Lloyd Austin, the division's deputy commander for operations, to redirect 3-7 Cav to lead the assault up the west side of the Euphrates rather than slowing the advance by trying to push through Samawah.[28] By the morning of March 23, Allyn had redirected his battalions to begin security operations in the division's rear, but he did so in the most aggressive manner—not by digging-in in key areas and just responding to threats, but instead by conducting a series of punching attacks all along the zone, keeping the enemy off balance and always retaining the tactical initiative.

Although this reorientation of Allyn's brigade would normally have had only tactical significance, it in fact had a result that was symbolic of the significant gulf of misunderstanding between Saddam Hussein and his senior leadership on one side and the senior leadership of the coalition on the other. As Allyn's brigade began to punch against isolated strongpoints all along the western side of the Euphrates, Saddam Hussein came to believe that his forces were defending successfully in the southwest and staving off the coalition attack. In reality, Buff Blount's division was still racing north toward Saddam's capital nearly as fast as his huge diesel-inhaling tank engines could take it. Saddam was so convinced that he was holding his own against the coalition that he sent messages to the French and Russians asking them to stop efforts to gain a cease-fire; he may have even thought he was winning the war.[29]

At that point in the campaign, the effects of the big A-day air plan attacks were still to come, and although much of Iraq's infrastructure was off-limits to the coalition air planners (as a result of lessons during the previous campaign) the full weight of the coalition attack was far from obvious.[30] At that point too, the real motive force of the attack—speed—which would be the tool of choice to unhinge the Iraqi government, had yet to be fully employed.[31] The American public knew very little of the fighting at this early stage; General Franks was supremely confident; Saddam Hussein was confused, and his generals were far, far out of touch.

Special Operations Shaping and Reconnaissance

As the conventional military forces of the coalition drove north into Iraq they could anticipate at least some reconnaissance to be provided from the numerous special operations teams that were also inserted into Iraq. These teams (principally ODAs, or Operational Detachment Alpha) issued from the Special Forces (Green Beret) battalions of the U.S Army and the special operations units of the British and Australian armies, as well as American Civil Affairs and Psychological Operations units.[32] They had been assigned four principal missions by their commander, Brigadier General Gary Harrell: liaison with Kurdish Peshmerga forces in the north of Iraq; Scud basket reconnaissance in the western deserts of Iraq; key route reconnaissance along the designated routes of the conventional forces; and support to the conventional force attacks.

All four of these missions would turn out to be crucial over time. Even more importantly, these small SOF teams would become physical links that would literally bring together the very disparate parts of the coalition force as it moved north. And, they would oversee a very large part of Iraqi territory that the reduced number of conventional forces assigned in Iraq could in no other way control. The special operations activities during the conventional phase of the campaign played a far more important role than any SOF units had undertaken since the invasion of Panama in 1989.

It is also important to understand that behind these overt "white" special operators, who worked with and alongside the conventional forces, there were also a number of "black" covert special operations forces, under the command of Major General Dailey, who had much more specific, often covert national tasking and missions to perform.[33] Overall, the coordination of these activities, conventional operations and "white" SOF, "white" SOF and "black" SOF operations, and even "black" SOF and conventional force operations, was better than at any time before in American history. As the campaign continued, the coordination of these complex activities became so good that most would say that they were fully integrated with conventional operations. The SOF community had come a long way from Eagle Claw, and its role in Iraq was far more than a supporting effort; it was crucial to success and often became the supported mission as the campaign evolved.

Nasariyah and the Expansion of the Attack to the East

The next supremely important turning point in the war was planned to be the simple passage of lines at Nasariyah by Marine forces through the area controlled by Buff Blount's division. This passing of forces from one major command through an area controlled by another seems simple enough, but is actually a very complex undertaking—particularly in combat, when units can easily become intermingled and important momentum and control can be lost.

In order to keep General Mattis and his 1st Marine Division focused on continuing the attack north, General Conway had assigned the effort to conduct the passage of lines and take control of Nasariyah to Task Force Tarawa, a brigade-sized unit from the 2nd Marine Division commanded by Brigadier General Rich Natonski. Natonski had envisioned a fairly straightforward attack to seize the western bridges around the city once the handoff with 3rd Infantry Division had been accomplished and then as a follow-on mission he would task his regimental commander, Colonel Ron Bailey of 2nd Marine Regiment, with taking the eastern bridges over the Euphrates and then establishing control over the city.[34] March 23 was a day when little went according to plan, however.

The 3rd Infantry Division had attacked north and only bounded by, instead of moving inside, the Nasariyah city limits with a long tail of support units following it up the Euphrates valley. Many of these support units were not integral to the division, but were corps assets designed to play supporting roles for other units during future stages of the fight. Unfortunately, some of these varied organizations had never been trained to conduct road marches or movements to contact independently of their higher headquarters; in particular, one air defense support unit (the 507th Maintenance Company) became disoriented during the night movement of the 22nd and took a wrong turn into Nasariyah.[35] In the confusion, the soldiers of the 507th were attacked by Iraqis and eleven were killed; two other soldiers, including Private Jessica Lynch, were captured in the same action.[36]

The next morning, as Task Force Tarawa was moving toward Nasariyah, the lead Marine battalion, 1st Battalion, 2nd Marines (1/2), commanded by Lieutenant Colonel Ricky Grabowski, encountered soldiers from the 507th returning from the city. The company commander of the 507th, Colonel Grabowski, and Colonel Bailey were soon met on the ground by General Natonski, who pressed for the regiment to continue the attack into the city.[37]

Though they had little intelligence and no pre-planned fire support for an attack against an enemy who might have American prisoners and who was well aware of their impending action, Colonels Bailey and Grabowski pushed into the city.

Almost immediately the Marines of 1/2 were hit not only by small-arms fire, but by Iraqi tank fire. The defenders, a combined force of regular army troops and Fedayeen Saddam had been alerted and emboldened by the hapless 507th, and they reorganized to put up a decent defense against the attacking coalition forces. The Marines called in artillery and air support, but were mistakenly strafed by their own A-10 Air Force close air support aircraft as they were split across the bridges. RCT-1 under Colonel Joe Dowdy eventually was able to pass through Nasariyah in the afternoon of March 25, but the MEF advance north had been stalled for nearly an additional day by the fighting in Nasariyah. The fight to control the city would take Task Force Tarawa nearly a week. And once free of the entanglement crossing the Euphrates, the coalition forces were hit on the night of the 25th by "the mother of all sandstorms . . . with high winds stirring up massive clouds of sand and slowing operations to a crawl."

Meanwhile, General Mattis and his 1st Marine Division had passed through Nasariyah and were racing north along two axes: RCT-1 on Iraqi Route 7 toward Kut, and RCT-5 followed by RCT-7 on Route 1 up between the two rivers toward Diwaniyah and Hillah. The Marines of Dunford's RCT-5 attacked into Diwaniyah on the 26th while Dowdy and his Marines were fighting north through the cities and towns toward the junction of Routes 7 and 17.

The Escarpment and the Gap

General Wallace and his V Corps forces on the coalition left flank had not stopped attacking either. The lead brigades of the 3rd Infantry Division had continued north after leaving Allyn's brigade to deal with Samawah and by March 25, they were poised to take Najaf. Dealing with that city, however, presented some new challenges. First, intelligence sources indicated to General Blount that the Fedayeen Saddam militias were reinforcing in Najaf and, even more surprising, had indicated a willingness to attack out from the city against the American forces.[38] Second, Najaf was not only quite a large metropolitan area, it was one of the most holy cities in Islam; consequently, severe fires restrictions had been imposed on coalition forces in order to safeguard the religious sites in the city center. Finally, it was an old city with narrow streets, considered by the troopers of 3rd Infantry Division's armored units as a "deathtrap for tanks."[39]

General Blount decided to isolate Najaf rather than attack it, so he ordered Grimsley's 1st Brigade to seize the bridge and the town of Kifl to cut off Najaf in the north, and for Colonel Perkin's 2nd Brigade to isolate the city from the south and protect the corps' support base to its west (known as Objective Rams). The 3-7 Cav was given the mission to cross the river and close the hand-hold around Najaf from the south and east, eventually joining up with Grimsley's forces at Kifl.

Just as Lieutenant Colonel Pat Ferrell started his daring twenty-mile mile attack with 3-7 Cav around the east side of Najaf, his regiment was hit by the same blinding sandstorm that was thumping the Marines moving out of Nasariyah. In the midst of the sandstorm, Fedayeen Saddam swarmed around the lead element of the Cav regiment and destroyed two M1 Abrams tanks—an unprecedented event (previously no M1s had been lost in combat) that struck at the core of the cavalrymen of the force.[40] The 3-7 Cav continued the attack, calling in MLRS and B-1 bomber strikes on the opposing militia forces.[41] Apache Troop of the regiment conducted an all-night fight on March 25 at close range, expending some ten thousand rounds of ammunition and leaving thousands of Iraqi militiamen dead in a 360 degree arc around their position, with no loss of American life.[42]

The 3rd Infantry Division successfully isolated Najaf by the 27th, but the fighting around the city had taken many by surprise. In addition, the V Corps had been stunned by the damage suffered by the 11th Armored Helicopter Regiment, which had been rendered nearly combat ineffective during a regimental-sized attack from objective Rams on the night of 23–24 March against the Medina Division of the Republican Guard.[43]

The Operational Pause—The Last Days of March

Then on March 27, General McKiernan issued an order to both his subordinate commanders to halt their attacks. General Wallace and Blount's 3rd Infantry Division had encountered more opposition than expected on the left of the coalition attack and Conway and Mattis had encountered more of the same moving up in the center. Even more disconcerting to McKiernan and his staff was the fact that the enemy was fighting a different kind of war, something more akin to an irregular delaying action than a conventional fight. The CFLCC commander had to be concerned about his lines of communication as he drove his forces deeper into Iraq; he also understood that as he moved farther north, his forces (moving farther away from their bases of supply) would grow somewhat weaker, while the Iraqi defenders (recoiling together on Baghdad) would also grow comparatively more powerful as they massed onto fewer and fewer rear bases. Compounding this concern was the idea that he had very few forces available to ensure that his ever-expanding rear areas were safe in the face of the Fedayeen Saddam attacks. McKiernan decided he had to refine his approach, commit his reserve (the 82nd Airborne Division) to secure Samawah ,and direct a force-wide halt to secure his lines of communications across the zone of operations; meanwhile, he also wanted to confer with his subordinates.

After flying to Jalibah to meet face to face with Generals Wallace and Conway, the CFLCC commander became even more convinced that a halt was needed. Both subordinate commanders discussed the things they needed to do in order to prepare for the eventual attack on Baghdad, and McKiernan came away from the meeting with the clear impression that an operational pause, perhaps lasting a few days, was necessary.[44] McKiernan seemed to know that General Franks would not readily accept a significant operational pause, so he reformulated his plan into a briefing entitled, "The Way Ahead: The Destruction of the Republican Guard," though it was still formed upon the idea of a necessary operational pause.

Franks' perception of the fighting was quite different from that of his commanders on the ground, in part because during the sandstorm of March 25–26, he had shifted his focus to the employment of a massive air operation that struck the Iraqi forces all over central Iraq.[45] So Franks had continued the joint attack relentlessly from his perspective and, from his seat in Qatar, could discount the effects of the Fedayeen Saddam and the desperate nature of the fighting in Najaf and Nasariyah. Unfortunately, the decision to halt occurred at nearly the same time that the media was reporting negatively about the progress of the campaign, in particular quoting General Wallace saying, "The enemy we're fighting is different from the one we'd war-gamed against."[46] The article predicted a longer war than anticipated and the incident, coming as it did with the decision to pause, upset both General Franks and Secretary Rumsfeld. All of these things contributed to Saddam Hussein's belief that he could still win the war.[47]

Still, there can be no doubt that a halt of a few days was absolutely needed by the troops on the ground (many of whom had been fighting without sleep for four or five days); by the logisticians, who needed time to consolidate their supplies for the push on to Baghdad, and by commanders at all levels, who needed to reassess what was working and what was different. General Franks's inspirational phrase, "speed kills," still had value, but needed to be understood within a different context; the decision for an operational pause was both necessary and prudent.[48]

Driving Forward: The Escarpment and Kut

General McKiernan first put one brigade of the 101st Division into the fight on March 28 to conduct a deep attack, but then committed both the 82nd and the remainder of the 101st Division to secure the corps rear area and release the 3rd Infantry Division to attack north toward Karbala on the first of April.[49]

Karbala was a real concern, for although the entire 3rd Infantry Division was back together and on the move, it had to funnel all its forces through the very small gap of open terrain running between the western edges of the city and Lake Milh (Bahr al Milh). If there was a place where the Iraqi forces were most likely to defend against the attack route of the division it was at the Karbala gap—and that was also the place many feared Saddam might likely employ his chemical weapons.[50] General Blount tasked Dan Allyn's brigade with securing the gap, through which Blount would push Grimsley's and Perkins' brigades. Grimsley was to take a key bridge over the Euphrates (Objective Peach) and then Perkins would be free to punch his brigade north to a key intersection of Highways 1 and 8 just outside of Baghdad.

One of the key Iraqi problems in the campaign became obvious when the 3rd Infantry Division was able to pass through the Karbala gap easily. Although Allyn's 3rd Brigade did have to fight, it soon became obvious that no major forces were blocking the gap and the Fedayeen Saddam militia commander in Karbala had arrayed his forces to the south and southeast of the city, away from the route of march of the 3rd Infantry Division vehicles. Although Iraqi Lieutenant General Hamdani had positioned a brigade on the west side of the Euphrates and tasked it with moving toward the gap once the Americans appeared, it attacked too late to maximize the opportunity that the gap provided, and no Iraqi command mechanism existed outside Baghdad to permit Hamdani to coordinate his defense with the militia commander in Karbala. By the morning of April 1, Grimsley's first brigade was through the gap and attacking toward the al-Qa'id bridge on the Euphrates.

While Grimsley's forces were in the attack, General Hamdani had been called back to Baghdad to discuss strategy in one of the key meetings of the campaign. In that meeting he was informed that the attack he saw uncoiling from the south and west of Baghdad were simple diversions and that Saddam Hussein was convinced the main American attack would come from Jordan through the Iraqi city of Ramadi. Because of this insight Saddam had directed a reorganization of the defense of the Iraqi capital to shift to the northwest, taking units from Hamdani's corps.[51] Hamdani attempted to change the decision, but the minister of defense and Qusay Hussein were adamant. By the time the meeting was over the al-Qa'id bridge had fallen to the 3rd Infantry Division and Hamdani's corps was already under severe attack.

Southeast of the Iraqi capital the renewed attacks of the Marine regimental combat teams were also meeting with success. On April 2, Dunford's RCT-5 seized two keys bridges over the Tigris River near Kut, and then that regiment and Steve Hummer's RCT-7 destroyed the defending Baghdad Division of the Republican Guard on the following day. By April 3, the CFLCC forces were arrayed toward the Iraqi capital from both the south and the west. The battle for Baghdad was about to begin.

Iraqi Perspectives of the Fighting

It is likely that Saddam Hussein never believed that the Americans would attack Iraq with the goal of ending his regime. Based upon a belief that his French and Russian diplomatic partners could dissuade America from all-out war, and what he perceived to be an American tendency to give up before facing extreme casualties, Saddam assumed that President Bush would at most attempt to control the Shia-dominated areas of southern Iraq. "Through the distortions of his ideological perceptions Saddam simply could not take Americans seriously."[52] Plus, based upon his long experiences in the Iran-Iraq War, he believed his forces could hold off an attack on the central heartland of Iraq.

Saddam and his senior generals had been surprised when the coalition began operations without a preceding air campaign, but the initial feedback that he received from his commanders in the field observing the fighting in Samawah and Nasariyah reinforced the idea that he was succeeding in bloodying the coalition. But the most serious problem to plague the Iraqi regime was driven by Saddam's personality. His lack of trust and fearsome reprisals splintered his command structures, made coordination among groups nearly impossible, placed militarily ignorant people (including Saddam's son Qusay) in charge of operations, and tended to ensure that senior leaders never reported bad news about operations in the field or Iraq capabilities. In fact, once operations began, "Iraqi commanders at the rapidly moving front reported one success after another against the invading coalition forces."[53]

Coalition tactics added to the sense of confidence on the part of Ba'ath Party stalwarts. Avoiding combat in the cities made Americans look timid; the operational pause at the end of March reinforced that misperception, and when the American media claimed that the fighting was not going according to plan, Saddam probably felt supremely confident. He contributed to his own defeat in serious ways also. For example, his conviction that the feint from the north was the real attack caused his forces to be redirected at the best time for them to have blunted the coalition attack.

Ultimately the speed of the American forces sealed the fate of the Iraqi regime. Saddam and his generals had no idea that their opponents could move forces toward Baghdad at the speeds that were demonstrated over the last two weeks of March. Such movements were simply beyond their understanding of military operations and logistics capabilities.[54] The speed advantage that General Franks had pressed on his subordinates for tactical success had indeed been a major contributor to the strategic success of the campaign.

Penetrating the "Red Zone"

By April 3, three weeks into the invasion, coalition forces had crossed through the suspected "red zone," where they feared Iraqi counterattacks with chemical weapons, and had moved into the distant outskirts of Baghdad. Initially, V Corps had been assigned Baghdad as an objective, but that was when the 4th Infantry Division was planned to reinforce the 3rd Infantry Division. Once the coalition forces got close, it was clear that the MEF would have to share some responsibility for controlling the Iraqi capital, and General McKiernan made that official on April 3 when he issued an order assigning the Tigris River as a boundary and giving the Marines the eastern zone of Baghdad. At that point both V Corps and the MEF were to grip the city from the west and southeast and gradually move in, forcing the defending Iraqi forces into untenable positions in the city, and then attack them with precision air and artillery fires.

However, with most of the Republican Guard Forces Command units destroyed along the way, the major routes into the southern half of the city occupied, and the Iraqis convinced that the main attack would come from the north, the fighting in the city's environs seemed to come so quickly that there was no coherent command structure operating in Baghdad. The Marines suffered through heavy fighting in al Aziziyah, where a complex mix of regular and militia Iraqi forces and even some foreign fighters pushed back hard, but nothing could prevent the two strong penetrations. On the same day, with Baghdad close, General Blount called General Wallace and asked for permission to continue his division attack directly into Baghdad International Airport. Once given the green light, Will Grimsley's brigade launched at 3 PM; led by 3rd Battalion, 69th Armored Regiment, the brigade advanced without even a pause toward the coveted prize.

The division planners had studied the airport for some time but they were surprised to find it eerily quiet when the troopers of the 3-69 Armored Battalion bashed through the fence line and drove nearly on-line the length of the runway at 11 PM the same night.[55] There were no Iraqis in sight. For several hours nothing happened and then at 4:30 the next morning Iraqis seemed to pop up everywhere in the airport—they had simply been in their fighting positions asleep and had not even heard the armored attack against the sound of all the artillery shells falling around the area. The Iraqis fought hard, but they had never expected to encounter tanks and were soon defeated.[56]

Colonel Will Grimsley was able to announce the capture of Baghdad International the next day on international television news, but as his troopers coalesced around the airport they were almost immediately counterattacked by Iraqi forces from inside Baghdad. It was during one of these Iraqi attacks on the 2nd Battalion, 7th Infantry Regiment that Staff Sergeant Paul Smith won the first Medal of Honor of the war. Iraqis continued to attack fiercely from inside the city, but only on the tactical level. It seemed that 3rd Infantry Division's fight was soon to be over—the corps plan only included another single attack north around the city by Dan Allyn's brigade to seal off the city completely. None of these units wanted to give up the momentum of their attack, however.

Climax: The Thunder Runs and Firdos Square

General Blount had been convinced by his experiences fighting over the previous weeks that the Iraqi swere not up to urban warfare and he wanted to test his theory before the two sides settled into anything like a static defense. So he sold General Wallace on a limited advance to close up his lines of communications between his forward brigades. Once approved, the mission he gave Dan Perkins and his second brigade was to drive an armored force north into Baghdad and then turn it west through the best suburbs of the city and return to the airport and Will Grimsley's brigade. On April 5, a task force from Perkins' 1st Battalion, 64th Armored Regiment executed a trail balloon raid, later called a "thunder run,"[57] to test Blount's theory and rupture the remaining Iraqi defenses. It was an amazingly dangerous and risky operation; the troopers met heavy resistance, but were quite successful in reaching the airport. The next day, April 7, as directed by General Blount, Perkins' brigade conducted a similar armored raid but employed all three of his battalions,[58] attacked deeper into downtown Baghdad, and even occupied and held one of Saddam Hussein's palaces in fierce fighting. Perkins and his men did not exfiltrate; they stayed downtown, and the raid became a dagger thrust into the heart of the Ba'ath regime. The Americans were in Baghdad and Saddam was no longer in control.

The Marines also sought to maintain the momentum of their attacks into the city center from the other side of the coalition effort and though they had far less armor, they were still more than willing to conduct similar deep attacks. Even though General Mattis was increasingly concerned about the paucity of his logistics, all three Marine regiments had crossed the

Diyala River on April 5 and were pressing toward eastern Baghdad.[59] Three days later, with approval from CFLCC, they advanced with all three regiments into Baghdad itself. When his Marines seemed to encounter only limited opposition, General Conway authorized them to continue their advance deeper into the city.[60]

The RCT-7 sector included Baghdad's Firdos Square, with a huge statue of Saddam Hussein at its center. Late in the day on April 9, 3rd Battalion, 4th Marines rolled in, to finally be met in Iraq only by cheering crowds. The local Iraqis promptly decided to topple the statue (with the Marines' help). Within hours of the palace seizure by 3rd Infantry Division and with television coverage of the crowds in Firdos Square spreading throughout the globe, U.S. forces ordered Iraqi forces within Baghdad to surrender, or the city would face a full-scale assault. All the senior Iraqi government officials had disappeared, and although much of the Iraqi capital remained unsecured, with some fighting continuing within the city and on its outskirts, organized resistance was clearly ending. Colonel Dunford of RCT-5 thought April 10 was both the best and the worst day in Iraq; worst because he feared more intense fighting in the Iraqi capital and then best when his Marines found no more fighters but only cheering crowds; Baghdad had effectively fallen to the coalition.[61] Later, it became known that Saddam Hussein had left the city the day before.[62]

Lessons of the Conventional Campaign

The execution of the initial phase of Operation Iraqi Freedom demonstrated significant improvements over the conduct of Operation Desert Storm twelve years prior, but it also demonstrated that the United States and Iraq still did not understand each other and did not communicate well either. Although the Americans had clearly learned the lesson that the Iraqi army might fall apart upon being subjected to high-intensity combat, the number of prisoners of war anticipated in 2003 proved to be greatly excessive, and the effort required to control Iraqi towns and cities was also quite unexpected. The rules of engagement (ROE) initially authorized during the thrust north from Kuwait rapidly proved to be off the mark and adjustments were not immediately forthcoming.

Intelligence was poor for a variety of reasons, some of which may have been related to the poor assumptions that set the stage for so many misconceptions and misapplications of power during the operation. Because the coalition forces expected to be greeted with open arms by the people of southern Iraq, individual unit leaders at the tactical level were slow to understand the actions of the Fedayeen Saddam and other militias. This would have been more acceptable if strategic human intelligence failures had not also left commanders with little understanding of who was directing operations and who might have been available to help sort out friend from foe. Time and again, CIA coordination efforts and the quality of its information appeared faulty to unit commanders. These two facts were disconcerting and added to an overall feeling that the fight was wholly unexpected.

Overall, the level of conventional-SOF-agency coordination had improved a great deal over the previous decade (particularly between conventional forces and SOF); however, the level of coordination among U.S. government agencies involved in the support of combat operations must be judged as even less complete than had been demonstrated in 1991. In part this was due to the close-hold nature of the planning for Iraqi Freedom, and in part it was due to rivalries within the leadership of the various American executive branch government departments in Washington. Special operations forces played a very important role in Iraqi Freedom and accomplished their missions very well. The special operators began by effectively, if loosely, controlling the Scud basket zones in western Iraq and by conducting several important strategic reconnaissance efforts to give the conventional forces a bit wider window into what was actually happening in the towns and around the key bridges they were racing to control. Civil affairs and PSYOP forces were effective and well integrated.

Deception operations were both well planned and largely effective during the 2003 campaign. In particular PSYOPs helped pull the Iraqi forces apart, even without the extensive bombing effort that had been used in 1991. The significance and impact of the effort to keep a large portion of Saddam's best units focused on an attack from Turkey in the north has yet to be well recognized. Maneuver warfare as a sub-component of joint operational art reached a new height. The operational concept of Iraqi Freedom was superb and its execution was as flawless as can be imagined in modern Clausewitzian warfare, plagued as it will be by both fog and friction.

The combat decision-making of Generals Franks, McKiernan, Wallace, and Conway was certainly as good, if not better than that of Generals Schwarzkopf, Franks, and Boomer during Desert Storm. In particular, the rapid drive north was audacious and supremely effective; the much-debated operational pause in late March demonstrated both the accuracy of the "gut feeling" of these commanders that their subordinate forces needed to rest and rearm in order to confront the uncertain environment of an assault on the huge capital city of Baghdad; and the trust given Colonels Will Grimsley and Joe Dunford to conduct the thunder runs and Marine penetrations into the heart of Baghdad was exceptional and even more effective than dreamed. Tactically, commanders at several levels made good on the general assertion that American and British officers and NCOs are superbly professional, innovative, and adaptable.[63]

Catastrophic Success

As operationally successful as Iraqi Freedom was, important criticism remains. In particular, it became clear that efficiency in modern battle cannot mean doing only enough to defeat the enemy forces. The major shortfall in execution of the conventional phase of Operation Iraqi Freedom was the coalition's inability to properly assess the impact of its own highly successful synergistic attack on an opponent trained for a much more methodical battle. In fact, the efforts of V Corps and I MEF so far exceeded the expectations of most planners that the most senior commanders were unable to control the catastrophic results of their own impact on Iraq. They were unable to effectively transition their combat power after April 10 to develop some practical control over the wide array of activities in Iraq—particularly looting by the population—needed in order to manage events through some semblance of a transition to stability operations.

As strong as the coalition was in the period between March 20 and April 10, it quickly lost its momentum and lost control of events in Iraq by the last week of April. This was not primarily an operational failing, for Secretary Rumsfeld gave the clear sign that policing Iraq was not part of the coalition mission; but operational commanders certainly knew that the vacuum of power resulting from their decisions not to step in could be the midwife of other problems.

Dealing with uncertainty in combat—answering the question, "why things don't add up"—became even more important in Iraq than knowing what the enemy capability actually was at any given time. The coalition's inability to understanding the culture and society within the battlespace led to important errors. Unfortunately, these errors would not be corrected for over a year and their effects would slowly be magnified until they became significantly detrimental to the coalition effort in Iraq during 2004 and 2005.

Chapter 8

THE LOST YEAR OF THE COALITION PROVISIONAL AUTHORITY

O f the many useful lessons learned by the United States during its long conflict with Iraq, none remains more vital than the need to effectively manage the transition of national power from combat to post–hostilities-focused activities. The importance of that lesson was evident following Operation Desert Storm in 1991, but it became even more powerfully obvious during the summer months of 2003. The national cost resulting from the ineffective transition in those months was sufficiently severe as to warrant changes to the process and functioning of the executive branch of the U.S. government.

Although the immediate aftermath of the highly successful opening phase of Operation Iraqi Freedom called for the rapid turnover of responsibility in Iraq to retired Lieutenant General Jay Garner and his Office of Reconstruction and Humanitarian Assistance (ORHA) team, in practice the transition from primarily conventional combat operations to what was considered to be post-hostilities activities in Iraq was fraught with difficulty. This most complex of transitions, a seam in any operation, was tremendously complicated by three near-simultaneous actions taken by the U.S. government: first, ORHA was superseded by a new organization, the Coalition Provisional Authority, led by Ambassador Paul Bremer; second, the U.S military was given very clear guidance by the secretary of defense to begin a drawdown of forces as quickly as possible; and, finally, the Iraqi expatriates who had been identified to lead Iraq in the immediate post-Saddam era were woefully unorganized and inadequate to task. When combined with significantly greater destruction in Iraq and a general loss of civil order in the major Iraqi cities, these factors made April and May 2003 a critical turning point in the campaign.

Anti-Climax: The Loss of Leverage—April 2003

I would anticipate that the major combat engagements are over.
　　—Major General Stanley McChrystal, April 14, 2003[1]

With Saddam Hussein out of Baghdad and coalition forces still fighting isolated pockets of the enemy all around the city, Iraq was in a precarious situation for the first week after the fall of the statue in Firdos Square; no one was really in control. After decades of an iron grip around its neck, Iraq was largely unoccupied, ungoverned, and un-managed for the first time in most adult memories. The coalition had a minimal presence among the Peshmerga forces in the north and had cut three distinct but very thin swaths of control from south to central Iraq, through the largely Shia-dominated region of the country. There had at that point been almost no ground presence inside the major Sunni-dominated cities of central and western Iraq.

Also as each day passed, it became clear that there was an increasing loss of control in Baghdad itself as looters, long suppressed by the former regime, took out their frustrations on every symbol of the Ba'ath Party. Revenge was in many minds. The coalition had expected a different situation in Iraq—more order and more willingness among the Iraqis to step up and take care of everyday affairs. But that was nearly impossible in a place that had experienced no formal shift of political status, and where most officials in the former ruling party felt they could become targets at any time.[2]

The Drive to Tikrit

The situation in Baghdad was still uncertain, but General McKiernan had to turn his attention to the remainder of Iraq. The 3rd Infantry Division was so consumed with controlling Baghdad that the 101st Airborne, which had flown in to relieve that division in Najaf and Karbala, had been directed to send its last brigade into the Iraqi capital to assist. McKiernan also determined that he had to put some American forces in the oil-rich areas of northern Iraq, around Kirkuk and Mosul, and to control the Sunni heartland where the people were likely to be the most loyal to Saddam—his hometown of Tikrit.[3] After briefing General Franks, McKiernan tasked the MEF to drive north to extend the conventional force reach of the coalition.

Although the Marines of I MEF had far exceeded the normal limits of their lines of supply in the drive on Baghdad (as General Conway said, they were "far from salt water"), they quickly responded by creating an ad hoc task force consisting of three light armored reconnaissance battalions under the command of Brigadier General John Kelly to press north against Tikrit.[4] Although the short-notice mission had real risk and great uncertainty, the move into Tikrit went more smoothly than anyone believed possible. The area had already been visited extensively by special operations forces looking for WMD, capturing senior Iraqi officials,[5] and searching for prisoners of war.[6] On April 13, Kelly and his Task Force Tripoli bypassed Samarra and entered the city nearly without opposition. Local Iraqis from Samarra even helped the Marines find and recover two American prisoners of war held in that city during the move north.[7] Once Kelly and his Marines understood the situation in Tikrit, they did something rather remarkable: they immediately transitioned from combat operations to establishing stability in the town. Kelly established an ad hoc police force and disbanded militia checkpoints in order to start the transition to a post-Saddam government.[8] This shift was done effectively, all within a few days, in the hometown of the former dictator himself.

Unfortunately, this positive turn toward stability was not representative of the coalition's efforts throughout Iraq. In fact, when Kelly's Marines were relieved in Tikrit by the Army's 4th Infantry Division on April 21, all of their efforts to establish calm and order were overwhelmed by a much more aggressive, heavy-handed approach by the 4th Infantry Division, commanded by Major General Ray Odierno. There is some debate over the level of success on the part of the Marines and the degree of aggression by the soldiers who relieved them, but there is no doubt that the relative calm established in Tikrit was soon replaced by animosity if not opposition.[9] "The question of how best to deal with Iraq after the regime's fall remained a matter of dispute as resistance persisted and grew in coming months."[10]

Unfortunately, even as the coalition was consolidating its hold over Tikrit, the emphasis in Washington was already shifting away from the rigors of combat. "On April 15, President Bush convened a meeting of his top aides to consider the plan for withdrawing U.S. forces from Iraq."[11] The plan was less a concept for withdrawal of American forces than it was the recruitment of coalition forces to replace the American units, but the effect of the discussions was to further the idea that the U. S. military would not be conducting nation building operations in Iraq.

The following day, on April 16, after General Franks made his first trip into Baghdad, all of the CENTCOM component commanders met in the Al Faw Palace[12] in the western suburbs of Baghdad to hold a Secure Video Teleconference (SVTC) with President Bush. During that discussion they were surprised to receive guidance to pull their units out of Iraq within sixty days. They were informed by General Franks that the new units (namely, the 1st Armored and 1st Cavalry Divisions) scheduled to arrive in theater would stay no longer than 120 days after their arrival.[13] To even General Franks' dismay, even after his best attempts to stop it, one of those two reinforcing divisions (the 1st Cavalry) was later "off-ramped" from the deployment schedule by Secretary Rumsfeld on April 21.[14] Within two weeks of the fall of Baghdad the American military was mentally focused more on departing from Iraq than on establishing stability there.

Millions around the globe were astonished by the speed and relative ease with which the coalition had taken Baghdad and forced Saddam Hussein from power. But no one then realized that the very qualities that had shocked and toppled the Ba'athist regime had also carried the seeds of subsequent failure. Even under ideal conditions, such a rapid departure would have been challenging, but the extremely effective and relatively low-cost operation to decapitate the Iraqi regime had omitted one of the key characteristics required to set conditions for victory in war—it had failed to develop and maintain sufficient leverage over the enemy to control key activities after the most significant combat operations had been completed. Without such leverage, the military forces could do little to enable a transition to something more stable and enduring.

Large portions of Iraq had not yet been subject to the control of the coalition and did not yet feel that the yoke of Saddam had been loosened in any material way. Coalition forces had passed through the major cities of the south of Iraq but did not leave sizeable units behind to demonstrate control. Even in Baghdad, the coalition forces at hand were woefully insufficient to actually control activities in the city.[15] This was most evident in Al Anbar province, in western Iraq, where in the city of Fallujah on April 24 a shooting by soldiers from the 82nd Airborne Division, under Major General Charles Swannack, enraged the local population at a time when Saddam and his sons had most likely just visited the overwhelmingly Sunni and Ba'athist town.[16]

Something had to be done to reestablish the rule of law and civil order, but Secretary Rumsfeld was not supportive of the U.S. military assuming responsibility for that mission in Iraq—even if by normal international custom a military power has such responsibilities after defeating another country's national government. Rumsfeld famously said during a press conference on April 12: "Freedom's untidy, and free people are free to make mistakes and commit crimes and do bad things; they're also free to live their lives and do wonderful things. And that's what's going to happen here. Looting was not uncommon for countries that experience significant social upheaval. Stuff happens."[17] General Myers made a much more appropriate statement during the same press conference: "This is a transition period between war and what we hope will be a much more peaceful time."[18]

Despite the many tasks that obviously still needed to be completed in Iraq if the goals of Operation Iraqi Freedom were to be achieved in any permanent way, General Franks determined in late April that the transition for combat operations to post-hostilities needed to be clearly made by the United States. Franks asked Secretary Rumsfeld to make a public statement that major combat operations were completed so that the coalition troops that had served during the invasion would have their sacrifice applauded and also so that those nations that had indicated that they would provide forces for the post-hostilities phase in Iraq would get the clear message that they should proceed and deploy them.[19] Franks needed to make the public demarcation between his often cloudy hostilities and post-hostilities planning efforts for the benefit of many constituencies. Only later, after President Bush made a huge public display of flying onto the aircraft carrier USS *Abraham Lincoln* on May 2 and publicly praising the troops who had served did anyone realize that the words "major combat operations in Iraq are over" would be far from true in Iraq.

The ORHA Effort to Stabilize Iraq

Some Americans and Iraqis described the period between May and August as a window of opportunity that could have been exploited to produce the conditions for the quick creation of a new Iraq. Instead, several events and key decisions quickly shut that window. Perhaps the most important factor in that process was the escalation of looting, crime, and general disorder that began in late April.[20]

General Garner, the ORHA director, was not standing idly by in Kuwait. Originally scheduled to assume his duties in Iraq sixty days after the fall of Baghdad, he actively lobbied to arrive earlier.[21] He and his staff had developed a plan for the post-hostilities effort and although they were clearly a pickup team without much practice working together, they were all committed to the task of restoring Iraq's essential services. The expectation among Garner's team was that with Saddam out of the way, several Iraqi expatriates who had been advising the Pentagon over the preceding months (Ahmed Chalabi or Ayad Allawi, for example) would be welcomed by the Iraqi people as their new leaders; and, with that Iraqi leadership, Garner and his team would partner, ministry by ministry, to advise and assist the Iraqis to reform their government and quickly get their country back on its feet.[22] The problem was that by the time Garner and his advance team got to Baghdad, seventeen of the twenty-three Iraqi ministries were completely dysfunctional due to the chaos that followed the end of the Ba'ath regime.[23] And none of the Iraqi expatriates seemed to have any real influence over affairs in the Iraqi capital.

Upon their arrival on April 18, it was immediately obvious to the ORHA staff that conditions in Baghdad were much worse than they expected. The official U.S. army history of the war said it best, noting,

The institutions held together by Saddam's reign had collapsed along with his regime, furthering Iraq's descent into chaos. Long suppressed political, religious, and ethnic conflicts bubbled violently to the surface. The incredibly decrepit state of the Iraqi infrastructure became apparent once the veil of Saddam's tyrannical rule was lifted, and was made worse by unprecedented looting and destruction. Some Iraqis began to sense an absence of authority in their country, and, many, while happy to see Saddam Hussein removed from power, watched events unfold with increasing anxiety; other Iraqis saw an opportunity to pursue their violent goals. . . . At the same time, violent Islamist groups began targeting U.S. and coalition forces in Iraq as part of their larger terrorist campaign against Western interests.[24]

The first blunder of the post-conflict phase was the general failure to stop the looting throughout Iraq. The Bush administration had far underestimated the anger of the Iraqi people against the Ba'ath Party and the effects of the economic deprivation wrought by economic interwar sanctions regime. The Iraqis basically stole everything that was suddenly no longer under state management, from the copper wiring in state buildings, to storehouses of food and fuel, to the treasures of the national museums. Military commanders on scene in Iraq wrestled with the dilemma of trying to halt the looting, but General McKiernan never implemented martial law—basically, American forces were restricted from interceding to stop the looting.[25] McKiernan did not have sufficient troops to accomplish all of his critical, assigned tasks in Iraq and taking on suppression of criminal actions in Iraq would have also placed his forces in a very precarious legal position without any functioning rules of engagement to manage their actions against looters.

So, for a period of about two weeks after the fall of Saddam, the coalition forces largely ignored the growing chaos in Iraq, as the ORHA staff was becoming aware that their mission in Iraq was far larger than expected and their ability to influence activity in Iraq was nearly nil. Barbara Bodine, for example, who was to be the "mayor of Baghdad" under ORHA, found upon her arrival that she had no office spaces for the small staff, no way of identifying who had been managing the huge city in advance of her arrival, and no way of contacting key Iraqi city managers even if she could determine who they were (because she had no working telephones). As a result she was unable to exert any influence in the city for several days after her arrival.[26]

Garner did meet several times with key Iraqi leaders. On April 15 he met with representatives of various Iraqi tribes, ethnic groups, and religious sects at the ruins of the ancient city of Ur, a few miles from Nasariyah. Journeying north, on April 22 and 23 he met with Kurdish leaders Jalal Talabani and Massoud Barzani, with whom he had already established an excellent working relationship. Returning to Ur April 28 with U.S. special envoy Zalmay Khalilzad, he met with some 250 tribal chiefs, Shiite and Sunni clerics,

Kurdish leaders, and other invitees. Later that same day he attended meetings in Baghdad with the two Kurdish leaders, Ahmed Chalabi, Sunni leader Adnan Pachachi, Ayad Allawi, and Ayatollah Muhammad Bakr al-Hakim, leader of the Supreme Council for the Islamic Revolution in Iraq (SCIRI). Still, even at that late date in Baghdad, and while their leaders were meeting to form a new Iraq, sporadic fighting continued throughout the city and looters were still working to dismantle nearly every unoccupied government site in the capital.

> Garner also met with both Lieutenant General McKiernan and Lieutenant General Wallace in Baghdad, and the two military leaders agreed to provide ORHA with military escorts and security for its headquarters because of the continued fighting in Baghdad. V Corps focused on eliminating pockets of resistance in Baghdad, expanding its control out to the vast stretches of Iraq which it had not occupied, and moving its still arriving forces from Kuwait to Iraq. ORHA and CFLCC developed good initial working relationships, and both CFLCC and V Corps provided as much support as they could to ORHA.[27]

Still, the military in Iraq was depending upon Garner to accomplish the greatest part of the post-hostilities mission, and yet he was finding that his ability to influence the essential levers of governance in Iraq was grossly poor. Each time he had met with Iraqis, Garner promised a cooperative and relatively short effort to re-establish governance and prosperity in Iraq. He had no idea how short his experience in Iraq was to become.

The End of Both ORHA and American Strategic Assumptions

Without any prior notice given to Garner, former ambassador Paul Bremer was asked by President Bush to serve as the senior American official in Iraq.[28] In the Bush administration's eyes, Bremer would replace both Garner and Khalilzad and lead a new effort to help shape Iraq. President Bush publicly announced the decision on May 6, only seventeen days after Garner had arrived in Baghdad. The new organization was titled the CPA, or Coalition Provisional Authority, and its mission was to "restore conditions of safety and stability, to create conditions in which the Iraqi people can safely determine their own political future, and facilitate economic recovery, sustainable reconstruction and development."[29]

ORHA was never formally disbanded, and although some of its members joined the CPA, many—such as Garner and Bodine—were so shocked by the experience that they departed Iraq for good. ORHA was organized too late in the movement toward a second conventional conflict; it was significantly understaffed for the task it found itself facing in a very different Iraqi environment than it had anticipated and, perhaps most fatally, it did not get sufficient cooperation from the interagency system back in Washington to deliver the aid required. General Garner had a plan that might have worked in a more sedate and cooperative Iraq. He did his best under extremely trying circumstances to cope with the situation he found when he arrived, but he was under-resourced in almost every way. The CPA had many of the same weaknesses as ORHA, plus it had a leader that knew very little about Iraq or its people.

The Revolving Door of Generals

Change was taking place in the military sphere in Iraq as well. Just as obviously as they had made the CFLCC staff one of the best in the Army, the Pentagon leadership clearly indicated that the priority of effort in Iraq had shifted when they ordered General McKiernan and his CFLCC staff "dream team" to depart Iraq for Kuwait in June 2003.

> This transition began informally in late May when General Franks told both Lieutenant General Wallace, the outgoing V Corps commander, and the newly promoted Lieutenant General Ricardo Sanchez, the inbound commander of V Corps, that CFLCC was pulling out of Iraq to refocus on its theater-wide responsibilities. Franks ordered V Corps to become the nucleus of the senior military command in Iraq designated as CJTF-7 (Combined Joint Task Force 7). This move was sudden and caught most of the senior commanders in Iraq unaware. Sanchez and V Corps (an Army headquarters focused on ground operations at the tactical level) would now have to become a joint and combined headquarters, responsible for the theater-strategic, operational, *and* tactical levels of war.[30]

General Sanchez had only assumed command of the Army's V Corps on June 14, 2003, three days before he was to assume command of Coalition Task Force 7 (CJTF-7). As its commander, he became the leader of all ground forces in Iraq; he and his small staff would be tasked with more than any other corps had ever been required to do, with little augmentation. The operational staff created by the Army to conduct the invasion was "the dream team"[31]; the staff Sanchez retained was far less capable. The CFLCC staff that had run the ground assault was increased in size, augmented in grade (including the addition of at least six general officers), and reorganized functionally to be better postured to address functional warfighting concerns.[32] Garner had a very good viewpoint on the transition, and he noted, "You had Dave McKiernan as land component commander with the best staff I've ever seen in my 35 years of military [experience]. They're all general officers. They know what to do. They're can-do guys that have been working together for a year and a half. They know how each other thinks, and they make things happen. So overnight . . . Rick Sanchez and 5th Corps are put in. Rick Sanchez is the most junior three-star we now have in the Department of Defense. And this is no hit on Rick. . . . I know how small that staff is. You put them over [there] to do the hardest job the nation's faced thus far in this century? That doesn't make sense."[33]

As if it were not enough to have the dramatic shift in military staff quality in Iraq, when Sanchez and his staff assumed operational control in Baghdad they also had to create a completely new structure with which to command the many units from the coalition spread all over the country. CJTF-7 was a joint headquarters that should have included several hundred senior staff members from all four military services. Instead, Sanchez assumed responsibility for the entire military mission in Iraq with a staff less than half the size he needed.

General Sanchez was tasked with a mission that required him to continue offensive operations to eliminate any enemy forces remaining in country, provide direct support to the CPA, and provide aid for humanitarian assistance and the reconstruction of Iraq.[34] This was a huge mission, even for an army corps staff at full strength operating under a unified chain of command. With the CPA and Bremer as a partner in the effort and with his forces departing Iraq in significant numbers, it soon became an impossible tasking because other circumstances, some unforeseen, but some fully intentioned, intervened.

At the same time that the most crucial element of military command was changing in Iraq, its next higher headquarters, Central Command, was also undergoing a change of leadership. General John Abizaid was named as the new commander of U.S. Central Command on July 7, 2003, immediately following the retirement of General Franks.[35] General Abizaid was a natural choice to succeed Franks. He was an Arab-American who spoke the language and had extensive command experience, plus he had been Franks' deputy commander during the entire assault phase of the war and knew CENTCOM and the Iraq issues exceedingly well. Still, it was a very peculiar time for a commander to retire and be replaced by another leader, who if certainly as well qualified, had different approaches and a different philosophy of leadership.

The Two Great Blunders: De-Ba'athification and the Dissolution of the Iraqi Army and Police

Paul Bremer arrived in Iraq with all the authority of a conquering ruler.[36] He was appointed by the president of the United States to administer Iraq, and though he was paid by the Department of Defense and nominally worked through Secretary Rumsfeld (as the government's lead agent per NSPD 24), Bremer was clearly in charge in Iraq. He had met with both the president and Rumsfeld before his departure and had discussed at least a few key concepts with their staffs, but once he arrived in Iraq he directed affairs as he saw fit. He was aggressive, brilliant, and decisive; unfortunately, he was also unfamiliar with Iraq and a poor manager given the myriad of things that had to be accomplished in Iraq.[37] He also failed from the start to develop a good working relationship with his military commander, Lieutenant General Sanchez.

Ambassador Bremer's first official act upon arrival in Baghdad was to issue CPA Order Number 1, "De-Ba'athification of Iraqi Society," which ended all functioning of the Ba'ath Party in Iraq; his second major order, the "Dissolution of Entities" resulted in the formal dismissal of the Iraqi army and police. Both orders were discussed in Washington, and both in retrospect were mistakes.[38] They were not mistaken ideas, but were executed in a manner that made them counterproductive to the rapid development of a new Iraqi government and society.

CPA Order Number 1 was issued to ensure that no one in Saddam's regime had any claim to power in Iraq, and to ensure that the stranglehold of the Ba'ath Party over Iraqi society was broken forever. Like de-Nazification in post-war Germany, executing the order was fraught with problems as a result of the deep penetration of the Ba'ath Party in the everyday affairs of every service provided in Iraq. Many key officials noted that they expected the order would really only affect the senior levels of the party membership, but since Iraqi expatriates were charged with enforcing the order within Iraqi society—and they chose a very strict interpretation—it effectively cast out every official of any importance in the country, including teachers and the lowest-level ministry employees. The result was a widespread loss of bureaucratic expertise to the new nation of Iraq throughout 2003 and 2004.

Bremer's CPA and the Pentagon jointly coordinated the order to disband the Iraqi defense and security services. Bremer wanted to destroy the underpinnings of the Iraqi regime "to demonstrate to the Iraqi people that we have done so and that neither Saddam nor his gang is coming back," so he sent a proposal for the disbandment of the security forces to Secretary Rumsfeld on May 19, along with a recommendation that all former troops, save a few top intelligence, security, and Ba'ath Party leaders, be given severance payments.[39]

Under Secretary of Defense Doug Feith edited some of the draft text, and Bremer received permission from Secretary Rumsfeld to develop a policy for the new Iraqi military before briefing President Bush and subsequently signing the order on May 23.[40] The problem was that formally disbanding the army and the police put thousands of Iraqis out of work, and threw away the only effective means of controlling Iraqi society. Many of the newly unemployed soldiers and police were easily recruited for the insurgency. The disbanding of the security forces put effective control of Iraqi society by the coalition out of reach for months, if not years by sewing distrust of the coalition among all the former members of Saddam's security forces. Bremer strongly disagreed with criticism of his CPA orders; he felt those orders were a necessary means of preventing a return to power of the worst elements of Iraqi society.[41] That idea might have worked if post-Saddam Iraq had been a functioning state, as had been assumed before the invasion: unfortunately, Iraq was completely rudderless by June 2003, and the first two CPA orders only added to the challenge of rebuilding Iraq. They also very likely contributed to the development of the insurgency.

On July 22, 2003, Bremer and the CPA officially formed the Iraqi Governing Council and appointed its members. Bremer had started meeting with key potential leaders of Iraq in the first days after his arrival, but he found that gaining their active, productive involvement to be extremely taxing.[42] The men Bremer dealt with on a daily basis all held ancient agendas and had very little trust for one another—or anyone else, for that matter. In addition, they were largely expatriates with very uncertain support within Iraq. Only the major religious leaders who had remained in Iraq under Saddam held major influence over the Iraqi people; and they were increasing distrustful of the CPA.

The CPA–CJTF-7 Problem and Decentralized Execution

While Bremer and Sanchez were laboring hard inside the Al Faw Palace in Baghdad the rest of Iraq was almost completely ungoverned. With de-Ba'athification went all the provincial and town managers; and with dissolution of the army and police went every traffic cop and patrol officer in Iraq (with the exception of those in the Kurdish administered areas of the country in the north). Not only was the political structure of the country erased, the coalition was operating in a decentralized manner, where every regional approach was different. The British in the south were operating differently from the 101st Division in the north, which was even working quite differently than the 82nd Division in the west of the country. Baghdad had its own unique problems as well. This lack of centralized control made a very fertile field for any opponent of the new coalition structure to travel from place to place and find opportunities to wreck havoc with security and disrupt the efforts of the CPA. One learned critic of the period noted:

> Lieutenant General Ricardo Sanchez was the commander of military operations in Iraq. He never executed a campaign plan—as if, like Rumsfeld, he assumed that America was about to leave. As a result, there was no governing logic to the Army's myriad operations. T. X. Hammes, a retired Marine colonel who served in Baghdad in early 2004, said, "Each division was operating so differently, right next to the other—absolutely hard-ass here, and hearts-and-minds here." In Fallujah and Ramadi, Major General Charles Swannack, of the 82nd Airborne Division, emphasized killing and capturing the enemy, and the war grew worse in those places; in northern Iraq, Major General David Petraeus, of the 101st Airborne Division, focused on winning over the civilian population by encouraging economic reconstruction and local government, and had considerable success. "Why is the 82nd hard-ass and the 101st so different?" Hammes asked. "Because Swannack sees it differently than Petraeus. But that's Sanchez's job. That's why you have a corps commander."[43]

This approach was symptomatic of two interrelated problems. The first was that General Sanchez had been given no long-term mission in Iraq. He was essentially conducting operations while awaiting a political solution that would allow him and his forces to return home. Second, his force structure was diminishing every day, and he always had too few forces to develop any comprehensive security scheme nationwide. He was filling in where he could on a temporary basis. Bremer had begun to publicly state his concerns about the lack of forces in Iraq as early as July, but no one seemed to listen.[44] This was primarily because the Bush administration had promised a short campaign using only minimal forces, and it could not retreat from that idea—particularly after Saddam had been ousted so quickly.

August 2003—The Insurgency Begins in Earnest

The strategic problem that I had was I felt that, particularly again, in the period of September/October 2003, the military was not showing any high-operational tempo in the operations they were running against the insurgents. . . . I felt a lack of a real strategy to defeat this burgeoning insurgency, the Sunni insurgency that was coming up at

that point. That was [what] the strategic problem was: Did we have a
real strategy to defeat the insurgency?
—PAUL BREMER, JUNE 26, 2006[45]

A complex network of former regime intelligence (Mukhabarat) and military
leaders remained in existence even following the fall of Baghdad. This may
not have been by specific design (in other words it may not have been planned
as a follow-on operation by the Ba'ath Party officials), but the rapid dissolution
of the security forces in Iraq did nothing to lessen the effectiveness of an organization designed to observe every aspect of Iraqi society and to communicate
through a complex network of channels. Not only was this network in place
throughout Iraq, but it also had connections to Syria, which gave it access to
funding and other forms of external support in the immediate aftermath of the
fall of the Iraqi capital.

Even if Al Qaeda had no significant presence in Iraq in the summer of 2003,
the remnants of the regime and the decentralized organization of the Fedayeen
Saddam (which had never been completely destroyed in combat) could have
embarked upon a strong campaign to combat the efforts of the coalition in
Iraq. In addition to the network itself, and the obvious will of newly unemployed former party and security officials and their subordinates to carry on the
fight, there was the general understanding that the Americans were ill-suited
to prolonged irregular combat, as demonstrated by the experience of the U.S.
military in Somalia in 1993. (It has been said that "Blackhawk Down" was one
of Saddam's favorite movies and that he spoke often enough about this weakness for the close fight in conversations with his cronies.) There is also evidence to support an early reinforcement of the efforts of the dead-enders by
other Sunni Muslim supporters, to include members of Al Qaeda.

The Sunni areas of Iraq, primarily the Sunni Triangle (the area northwest
of Baghdad and northward to Tikrit encompassing Ramadi and Fallujah) had
yet to be subjugated by coalition forces. What forays had been made into these
larger cities were relatively limited in duration and were never comprehensive
enough to ensure that anti-coalition elements did not simply squirt out of the
hands of coalition units and into the countryside.

What is very clear is that by August 2003 there was a well-focused and
well-coordinated effort under way in Iraq to undermine the authority of the
coalition. Though the specifics of its leadership may remain unclear for some
time, this effort had a distinct goal—killing members of the coalition and making the environment unsafe for other key organizations that were important to
the legitimacy of the coalition effort, primarily the United Nations. Then the
insurgency struck in earnest. On August 19, the UN headquarters in Baghdad
was bombed and its special representative, Sergio Vieira de Mello, was killed.

Ten days later, on August 29, another bombing of a major mosque complex in Najaf killed the leader of the main Shiite faction in Iraq,[46] Muhammad Bakr al-Hakim.[47] Within a month, the insurgency had demonstrated it could kill some of the most influential people in the country in places where they should have been safe. That kind of insurgency was not haphazard and was not disorganized. From September onward, more and more key leaders in Iraq and the United States would realize that the coalition was not simply fighting dead-enders and criminals loosed by Saddam, but was instead fighting a much more organized and lethal network of enemies of the new Iraq.[48]

The Bremer Plan for Sovereignty

In early September Ambassador Bremer published an op-ed in the *Washington Post* that seemed to announce a new plan for the transition to Iraqi sovereignty.[49] That plan included seven detailed and even reasonable steps: the first was the creation of a twenty-five-member Governing Council; the second step had the Governing Council naming a committee to devise a way to write a constitution; the third and most important was putting day-to-day operation of Iraqi government in the hands of Iraqis; writing Iraq's constitution was the fourth step; which would be followed by popular ratification of the constitution, step five. The sixth step, election of a new government, followed a first open election. The seventh step was then the dissolution of the coalition authority and transfer of governance to a sovereign Iraqi government. It was a plan based very much on the model the British had used in the 1920s,[50] which would have been a phenomenally bad precedent to acknowledge with the Iraqis; as it turned out, the plan did not find favor in Washington, either. Policymakers in the United States were growing concerned that Bremer's plan would take too long.[51]

Bremer and his staff were working relentlessly to make such a transition happen, but it was difficult going. On September 1, 2003, the Interim Governing Council named its first cabinet of ministers to manage Iraq's essential services. Then, on November 15, the Governing Council and Bremer concluded an agreement on the timetable and agenda for the drafting of a new constitution and afterwards the holding of elections under that constitution. That agreement also included a target date for transition back to Iraqi control: June 30, 2004. The dominant question was whether a constitution could be drafted quickly enough to hold elections in Iraq before the end of the following June. That was doubtful in a peaceful Iraq, but the country was anything but calm by the winter of 2003.

Al Qaeda in Iraq

If the insurgency was a diverse conglomeration of groups, including former Ba'athists, as well as criminals and foreign fighters, the most ardent of the groups was clearly the faction initially known as al-Tawhid wal-Jihad, led by Jordanian Abu Musab al-Zarqawi. It was Zarqawi who had perpetrated the bombing attack of the UN headquarters in Baghdad in August.[52] Through the fall he made more contacts and recruited more members to his group, aided by the general lack of security and the unemployment of so many Iraqis—particularly Sunnis who felt completely disenfranchised.

Reputedly, "Usama Bin Laden's military chief, Muhammad Ibrahim Makawi asked Zarqawi to coordinate the entry of al Qaeda operatives into Iraq through Syria. Zarqawi readily agreed and by the fall of 2003 a steady flow of Arab Islamists were infiltrating Iraq via Syria. Although many of these foreign fighters were not members of Tawhid, they became more or less dependent on Zarqawi's local contacts once they entered the unfamiliar country. Moreover, given Tawhid's superior intelligence gathering capability, it made little sense for non-Tawhid operatives to plan and carry out attacks without coordinating with Zarqawi's lieutenants. Consequentially, Zarqawi came to be recognized as the regional 'emir' of Islamist terrorists in Iraq without having sworn fealty to bin Laden."[53] Regardless of the strength of his ties to bin Laden, in October Zarqawi had changed his group's name to Al Qaeda in Iraq, or AQ-I.[54] AQ-I would become over the following two and one half years the most significant threat to the Iraqi state.

The Bremer Plan Continues

Bremer unexpectedly returned to Washington for consultations on November 11, 2003.[55] Nine days before, insurgents had shot down a Chinook helicopter outside of the city of Fallujah, killing seventeen soldiers and wounding eighteen others—they had been on their way out of Iraq for some rest and relaxation. It was the deadliest day of the war since the Scud missile attack of February 1991.[56] Another helicopter was shot down near Tikrit on November 7, killing four more soldiers.[57] When Bremer arrived in Washington he voiced concerns privately with the president that the military leaders in Iraq did not seem to have a strategy to win; he noted that holding elections would be difficult in Iraq, but pressed for maintaining the June 2004 goal for sovereignty in the face of some who still lobbied for an immediate handover.[58] Bremer returned to Iraq to negotiate with the Governing Council the agreement that eventually set the June 2004 goal for the return of Iraqi sovereignty; it was signed on November 15. President Bush made a surprise visit to share

Thanksgiving dinner with the troops in Iraq, but the real concern was that November had witnessed 110 coalition deaths—approaching the same number that had been killed in action during Desert Storm.[59]

Finding Saddam

As Paul Bremer and the CPA staff were toiling away, attempting to develop the Iraqi Governing Council and reinstitute governance at the provincial level throughout the country, the coalition was still conducting security operations and searching relentlessly for Saddam Hussein. Based upon an unidentified tip, the Iraqi leader's sons, Uday and Qusay, had already been discovered by the soldiers of the 101st Division and special operations forces in a house in Mosul on July 22. The house was surrounded, and when the two men tried to defend themselves, everyone in the house was killed in the assault, including their nephew and a bodyguard. Immediately afterward, members of special operations Task Force 20, the CIA, and other U.S. personnel searched the complex for documents and any other information that could be used to locate Saddam.[60] It was later discovered that Saddam and his sons had fled Baghdad before it fell and traveled through Al Anbar province before splitting up to remain undiscovered. By the time the sons had settled in Mosul, all contact with the former Iraqi leader had been lost.

The coalition searched for Saddam for over four more months. On December 14, 2003, Paul Bremer announced that Saddam Hussein had been captured at a farmhouse near Tikrit by soldiers of the 1st Brigade Combat Team of the 4th Infantry Division, commanded by Colonel James Hickey, and members of the special operations task force. Saddam was hiding in a tiny hole in the ground, and armed with a pistol and a rifle, but he did not resist arrest. Images of the former leader, bearded and dirty from his period in hiding, thrilled people around the world. Saddam was given a physical examination, prisoner of war status, and incarcerated and interrogated for several months before being handed over to the Iraqi government for trial.

The capture of Saddam Hussein dramatically changed the context of the campaign in Iraq. With his incarceration there was little hope of any Ba'ath restoration among Iraqi Sunnis, and those who believed that the Iraqi leader had somehow organized the opposition to the coalition and the new Iraqi Governing Council had to look elsewhere for leadership of the insurgency.[61]

The Incident at Abu Ghraib Prison: October 2003–January 2004

From the beginning of the invasion, the coalition had taken Iraqis into custody during combat, and after June the continuing security operations only brought greater numbers of people into the few detainee camps used by the coalition forces. The most famous of these facilities was at Abu Ghraib on the western outskirts of Baghdad. It had been a notorious facility even under Saddam, where many Iraqis disappeared without a trace.

Most people detained in the coalition facilities passed through them within sixty days, after any useful information was obtained and their culpability was examined. But between October and December 2003, at the Abu Ghraib facility, numerous incidents of sadistic, blatant, and wanton criminal abuses were inflicted on several Iraqi detainees by members of the coalition. This abuse of detainees was perpetrated by several members of the military police guard force at the facility, which was composed of national guardsmen from the 372nd Military Police (MP) Company, 320th MP Battalion, assigned as part of the 800th MP Brigade, commanded by Brigadier General Janis Karpinski.

In 2004 information describing the abuse, including pictures showing military personnel abusing prisoners, became a media sensation when a CBS News 60 *Minutes II* television report shown on April 28, and an article by Seymour M. Hersh in *The New Yorker* magazine the following month, reported the story.[62] The U.S. military quickly conducted an investigation[63] which found a number of soldiers culpable; seven were charged with dereliction of duty, maltreatment, and other crimes; convicted in courts martial; dishonorably discharged from service; and sentenced to federal prison. Two soldiers, Specialist Charles Graner and Specialist Lynndie England, were sentenced to ten years and three years in prison, respectively. General Karpinski was demoted to colonel and retired.

Even with some justice done, however, the misconduct of members of the American military, and the apparent reluctance of senior military and civilian leaders to come forward with the details of the abuses even after they were informed of them, left a terrible stain on the entire U.S. involvement in the war. The Abu Ghraib incident colored international perceptions of America for years and added to the motivation of many insurgents to fight, when they interpreted the abuses there to indicate all U.S. soldiers would blatantly abuse innocent people and were free to insult and dishonor Muslims. Several media outlets called for Secretary Rumsfeld's resignation, including the *New York Times* on May 7, 2004. The incident also caused concern that the Bush administration might have authorized the torture of prisoners. As problems at the detainee facility in Guantanamo Bay, Cuba, appeared in the media over time, this concern became one of the most damaging and enduring allegations made against the policies of President Bush.

Phased Transitions

At the same time the Abu Ghraib abuses were taking place, the U.S. military was organizing for a longer campaign. Once the American military realized that its service in Iraq was not going to be completed by the fall of Saddam Hussein it had to consider how to maintain a force presence in the country over a longer period of time. Most of the forces that had been employed in the invasion the previous spring were quick reaction forces from the Army (part of its XVIII Airborne Corps) and expeditionary forces of the Marine Corps. They were not designed for sustained combat operations. The twelve-month replacement program of the Vietnam era was long discounted, so the Pentagon had to devise a way of deploying large units into Iraq on a rotational basis for a long-term commitment. The Army and Marine Corps took different approaches, based upon their success in deploying units at sea for six-seven month rotations, the Marines chose to maintain that deployment length for their units in Iraq; the Army settled initially on one-year deployments of individual units.

Once these concepts were determined, the forces that had arrived in the March timeframe in 2003 would be retained in country until they could be relieved in the same month of 2004. The Marines would assume responsibility for operations in the restive Al Anbar province—mostly because the Army considered that it did not have sufficient forces to maintain the entire American presence in Iraq alone. This established the first of what would become annual transitions of the major American commands in Iraq during the early spring timeframe: the changeover between the 82nd Airborne Division and the I MEF in the west; as well as the replacement of the 1st Armored Division under Major General Martin E. Dempsey in Baghdad to the 1st Cavalry Division (reinforced by a brigade from the Army National Guard in Arkansas) commanded by Major General Peter W. Chiarelli. Elsewhere in Iraq, General Odierno's 4th Infantry Division was to be replaced by the 1st Infantry Division plus the 30th Army National Guard Infantry Brigade from North Carolina under the command of Major General John R. S. Batiste. The 2nd Armored Cavalry Regiment was also being replaced by the 1st Brigade of the 1st Cavalry Division, and the 3rd Armored Cavalry Regiment was to be replaced by the Army's new Stryker brigade from Fort Lewis, Washington. These transitions facilitated the long-term presence in Iraq, but also created seams in the coalition's effectiveness as every sector in Iraq suffered under the control of less experienced units every year at the same time.

While Bremer and his staff were working to keep the Interim Governing Council (IGC) together, figuring out how to pay the new Iraqi police force and reintegrate Sunnis into the political process, drafting the Transitional Administrative Law (TAL) and developing priorities of work for the massive $18.6 billion appropriation for Iraqi reconstruction, the U.S. military was trying to adjust to a new ill-defined phase of the war.[64] American casualties were averaging forty deaths every month in early 2004, but the military expected the new phase of fighting to offer an improved chance for stability in the spring; they did not anticipate the growing anger and capability of the opposition in Iraq.

Major Combat Continued: The First Battle in Fallujah

Unfortunately, very soon after taking over responsibility from the 82nd Airborne in Al Anbar province, the newly returned I MEF and 1st Marine Division were directed to execute Operation Vigilant Resolve: the destruction of the insurgency in Fallujah.[65] This was in direct response to the killing of four Blackwater contract employees who ventured into Fallujah in a convoy during the morning of March 31; their bodies were burnt and later hung from the girders of the old bridge leading west out of the city. This incident horrified the world and directly affected the pace and conduct of counterinsurgency operations by the MNF in Iraq.

The irony was that the Marines had returned to Iraq with a very different and more integrated approach to their mission in mind. Unfortunately, the killings quickly drove them into a traditional assault on the city within a few weeks of their arrival. As with most combat operations in urban terrain, casualties to the civilian population were nearly unavoidable and when the casualties become front-page news these had a profoundly negative effect on world opinion, the CPA, and the ICG. By April 8, with bombs being dropped in the city, senior officials in Washington were questioning some of the tactics used in the fight. Iraqis in Baghdad very quickly urged restraint and began negotiations with the insurgents. Bremer soon directed a temporary halt in combat operations in order to reduce civilian casualties and damage to buildings and other infrastructure. By April 13, high-level negotiations had started and the operation to destroy the insurgents was effectively on hold. On April 16, negotiations at Camp Fallujah between the locals and the MEF developed the idea of a Fallujah Brigade to clean up the city, under the command of a local, retired Iraqi general.[66] By April 22 a cease-fire was in effect in the city.

By that time, a tactical post-combat concept had been developed to provide immediate humanitarian aid to the city using a Civil Military Operations Center (CMOC) to provide relief supplies to Fallujah. Over the course of the battle as many as 150,000 people were trapped in the city without regular supplies of food and fuel. The humanitarian plan was designed to be put into action preceding renewed combat operations in the city. It addressed aid, as well as work and cleanup projects for the residents of Fallujah and some road and building repair projects.

From late April the situation in Fallujah grew increasingly uncertain. The insurgents inside Fallujah were establishing defensive positions in mosques and hospitals; some analysts believed they would use the local residents as human shields when combat resumed. The insurgents clearly understood that civilian casualties and attacks on mosques and other normally restricted targets played in their favor in the international media. Great political pressure began to be applied to permanently halt combat operations and seek a negotiated settlement. The Fallujah Brigade, constructed from former Iraqi army soldiers, seemed a reasonable way to quickly restore order. It also appeared to be an ideal Iraqi solution to an Iraqi problem, but like most things in Iraq it turned out differently than expected.

The Fallujah Brigade was a unique and tenuous construct; its conceptual leader was a Major General Salah, but it was commanded in the field by another Iraqi, Brigadier General Latif. It was formed in the last week of April and began effective operations on the first day of May. Unfortunately, the brigade was infiltrated by insurgents and its leadership was in fact playing both sides of the confrontation. The real test of the Fallujah Brigade began on May 4, when General Latif agreed to reassert control over the city center. The coalition had already begun providing limited humanitarian assistance to the residents of Fallujah and had even developed a claims process for battle damage in the city. The cease-fire was holding and the coalition was planning to conduct a major convoy through the heart of the city on the May 10, but the city had yet to give up any crew-served weapons systems—one of the essential preconditions for a lasting cease-fire. Although the convoy went through on schedule, signs were already evident that the Fallujah Brigade was not going to make good on its agreement to gain control of the city.

The brigade quickly showed itself unable to oppose the Sunni insurgent forces in the town and soon thereafter dissolved as an effective military force. At the same time, the police in Fallujah, who were never very supportive of the coalition, began to side more and more with the insurgents. By June, it was clear that the city was no longer open to the coalition and its patrols. Insurgents increasingly gained control over the daily life of the residents of Fallujah and communications with the coalition leadership in the area soon became strained and then infrequent.

President George H. W. Bush *(DoD photo)*

President Saddam Hussein *(DoD photo)*

Generals Colin Powell and Norman Schwarzkopf (*DoD photo*)

President George W. Bush *(DoD photo)*

Secretary of Defense Donald Rumsfeld and General Tommy Franks *(DoD photo)*

Secretary of Defense Donald Rumsfeld and Lieutenant General Ricardo Sanchez
(*DoD photo*)

Ambassador Paul Bremer, General John Abizaid, and Secretary of Defense Donald Rumsfeld *(DoD photo)*

Generals George Casey and David Petraeus *(DoD photo)*

President Barack Obama and General Raymond Odierno in Baghdad, April 7, 2009
(*DoD photo*)

Problems in the South

About the same time that the coalition was shifting operations to the Fallujah Brigade in Al Anbar, fighting broke out in nearby Najaf at the instigation of the radical Shia leader Muqtada al-Sadr, the fourth son of the revered Shia cleric, Grand Ayatollah Mohammad Mohammad Sadeq al-Sadr and the son-in-law of Grand Ayatollah Mohammad Baqir As-Sadr—both of whom were very powerful Shia leaders in Iraq.[67] The elder al-Sadr's influence had always radiated from the city of Najaf, but Muqtada first came to prominence as the leader of the Shia Mahdi Militia, which he raised to oppose the coalition in the Sadr City area of Baghdad. Sadr City was an extremely poor Shia enclave in the capital city, where his words found fertile soil and his appeal grew to national significance.

By September 2003, after coalition forces moved into the area of Najaf, Sadr began calling for the overthrow of the Coalition Provisional Authority and had set up his own shadow Iraqi government in Sadr City.[68] Coalition forces had their hands full in the huge, densely populated city of Baghdad, and in Najaf a lack of reconstruction project funding and Mahdi Militia activities combined to discourage pilgrims from visiting the holy site of Imam Ali's tomb.[69] The resulting downturn in religious pilgrimages produced an economic slump and disappointment with the coalition.[70] Sadr took full advantage of these difficulties to press his agenda with the dissatisfied citizens of both cities. By the following spring, in March 2004, his rhetoric had become so extreme that the CPA shut down his newspaper—an action that only served to worsen the situation.

In early April, as a result of Muqtada al-Sadr's continuing opposition and the worsening economic conditions, open fighting broke out between elements of the Mahdi Militia elements and government forces in Najaf, Sadr City, and even in Basra. Ambassador Bremer declared Sadr an outlaw, based largely on his alleged participation in the murders of two prominent Najafis.[71] But the conflict in Najaf soon proved too great for the local Iraqi Security Forces to handle and Lieutenant General Thomas Metz assigned the 2nd Armored Cavalry Regiment (2nd ACR) to the region for over two months. Najaf province was too large for even an armored cavalry regiment to maintain order and the 2nd ACR concentrated its operations on the main supply routes running to the city and on countering the Mahdi Militia.

Luckily for the coalition, Grand Ayatollah Ali al-Sistani[72] stepped in to effectively mediate the violence, and a truce was implemented on June 4. The truce permitted the Mahdi Militia to remain in the city and called for restrictions on the employment of coalition forces in the area.[73] Similar to the truce that had ended Operation Vigilant Resolve, these conditions satisfied few and permitted anti-government forces to retain the initiative.

Hurried Transitions and the Development of the Interim Iraqi Government

These confrontations made life extremely difficult for Bremer and the CPA, but the political progress in Iraq continued through the spring, albeit at a decidedly irregular pace. The TAL had been approved after an all-night session with the IGC on March 1, and although the twin crises of Fallujah and Najaf nearly tore the IGC apart, particularly after the Abu Ghraib scandal broke in the press in late April, Bremer and his staff managed to keep the ICG together long enough to develop the plan for an Interim Iraqi Government (IIG) during May, with the help of Lakhdar Brahimi of the UN.[74] In the final hurried months of the CPA the one candidate among the Iraqi expatriates who seemed to be capable of directing a new Iraq and keeping the support of his fellow Iraqis among the great variety of sub-groups jockeying for power was Ayad Allawi.

Bremer diplomatically crafted a power-sharing structure for the IIG that would give each of the three major religious/ethnic groups in Iraq (Shia, Sunni, and Kurd) a seat at the leadership table in Baghdad. After negotiations with the leaders of the Iraqi Kurdish faction in mid-May, and considering a prominent Shia named Shahristani to assume the crucial post as prime minister in the new government, Bremer opted for another Shia member of the IGC, Ayad Allawi. Allawi was born into a Shia merchant family and studied to be a doctor. He had joined the Ba'ath Party in Baghdad before leaving his country to continue his studies in England. After graduation from medical school he reputedly conspired against Saddam and was attacked and severely wounded by Saddam's assassins. He later formed and led the Iraqi National Accord, which recruited Ba'athist defectors to oppose Saddam Hussein, and which was supported by U.S. funding. Allawi was well known to the coalition before the invasion of Iraq and was a clear choice to be appointed to the Iraqi Governing Council. On May 28, at Bremer's urging, he was unanimously selected by the IGC to become the interim prime minister of Iraq.

On June 28, the CPA turned over full sovereignty to the Interim Iraqi Government (IIG) in a surprise move two days prior to the announced date of the turnover. That same day Allawi assumed power as leader of the new Iraqi government—though not as president, a largely honorary office filled by Ghazi Mashal Ajil al-Yawer, a Sunni, with two vice presidents: Ibrahim Jaafari, a Shia, and Rowsch Shaways, a Kurd.

Allawi was a strong leader who was not reluctant to make difficult decisions; as such he was largely popular with the coalition leadership but grew increasingly unpopular with the Iraqi people as his decisions alienated many issue-focused constituencies. Though relative calm in July gave him a short period of weeks to develop a framework of government process (the new government operated under the TAL), August brought his administration a new, immediate, and serious set of crises.

Paul Bremer had accomplished a great deal in his fourteen months in Iraq, but there had never been sufficient time, troops, or the political will back in Washington to develop a real campaign plan to restore security in Iraq. That effort would have to be made by a new team from Washington. With Iraqi sovereignty, the United States appointed a new ambassador to Iraq as the senior U.S. official in the country, John D. Negroponte. Negroponte had previously served as the American ambassador in Honduras, deputy national security advisor in the Reagan administration, then as ambassador in Mexico and the Philippines before accepting a political appointment as the U.S. permanent representative to the United Nations from 2001 to 2004. At nearly the same time that Allawi was taking power with the exodus of the CPA, the military command structure in Iraq was also changing. General George Casey, the son of a general killed in combat in Vietnam, who had been serving as vice chief of staff of the Army, was selected to take the command in Iraq and bring the war to an end.

Chapter 9

THE CASEY STRATEGY, FROM FALLUJAH TO TAL AFAR: 2004–2006

We found that if we concentrated solely on establishing a large security force and targeted counterinsurgent combat operations—and only after that was accomplished, worked toward establishing a sustainable infrastructure supported by a strong government developing a free-market system—we would have waited too long. The outcome of a sequential plan allowed insurgent leaders to gain a competitive advantage through solidifying the psychological and structural support of the populace.

—Major General Peter W. Chiarelli, "Winning the Peace"[1]

After over a year of confused strategy and decentralized operations, on June 1, 2004, General George Casey assumed command in Iraq from Lieutenant General Sanchez and set up a new senior organization in Baghdad named the Multi-National Force-Iraq (MNF-I). Casey knew Washington's policies in Iraq well, and he arrived in Iraq to exert new command influence and to stimulate a more aggressive stance in order to finish the war. Casey's goal was to encourage the Iraqis to take ownership of their problems and accept responsibility for their own security. As the senior military commander in Iraq, he would focus on supporting the political development in the country, on training Iraqi forces, limiting the role of American forces, and transferring the burden for providing security to Iraqi forces. Meanwhile, the new U.S. ambassador in Iraq, John Negroponte, could focus on building and strengthening the Iraqi government led by Prime Minister Ayad Allawi and helping to motivate the Iraqis to hold elections. Allawi, Negroponte, and Casey formed a very effective team. Each knew well to stay in their own lane in order to fully empower the others, yet they worked well enough together to ensure that the three most critical elements of the counterinsurgency, the host nation government, international diplomacy, and military power were all synchronized. Such synchronization would prove critical as the ongoing turbulence in the cities of Iraq increased and economic and security problems continued to plague the new Iraqi government.

Within the military realm in Iraq, two other major headquarters were also created, under the overall strategic direction of MNF-I. Those two operational commands were named Multi-National Corps-Iraq (MNC-I) and Multi-National Security Transition Command-Iraq (MNSTC-I). MNC-I would run the day-to-day operational war in Iraq, focusing primarily on defeating terrorists and rooting out the insurgency, while MNSTC-I would focus on the training and development of the Iraqi security forces, police, army, navy, and air force. Initially, Lieutenant General Thomas Metz assumed command of MNC-I and Lieutenant General David Petraeus, who had commanded the 101st Airborne Division during the initial invasion phase of Iraqi Freedom, returned to Iraq to set up and command MNSTC-I.

This new command structure seemed to be focused appropriately on the key requirements of the war in Iraq. Casey could focus on the overall strategy and support the military functioning of the American pol-mil effort in the country, while Metz and Petraeus could specifically focus on fighting and training. Casey would not have long in command until his decision-making would be tested by a major battle.

The Battle of Najaf

Sunni opposition to the new government, and certainly to the MNF forces, was anticipated and well understood by most people working on the development of the new Iraq. What was potentially much more dangerous and what concerned them most, however, was the slow but clear growth in Shia opposition to the coalition and the Iraqi Interim Government (IIG). That opposition was made clear in Baghdad through the continuing strife in the slums of the largely Shia area known as Sadr City as the summer passed. It became even more dangerous with the growing demands of Muqtada al-Sadr and his demonstrations in the holy city of Najaf in late July and early August.

Najaf is one of the holiest and most important cities in Islam, and the spiritual center of Shiite Islam, because Imam Ali, who is buried there, was not just the son-in-law of the Prophet Mohammad, he is also seen as the first leader of the Shias. (See map.) The city holds such a revered place in Islam that even Iran's Grand Ayatollah Ruhollah Khomeini choose to live in exile there from 1964 to 1978. In 2004, it was a city of over 550,000 people and, because of its religious significance, it became a significant flashpoint for non-Sunni insurgent actions against the new Interim Iraqi Government and, even more unfortunately, the site of some of the most intense fighting of the summer. Under the guidance of the most respected of Shia leaders, and with certain rights provided by the truce agreement, al-Sadr had softened his opposition for nearly two months, only resurfacing in early August, after stating yet again his opposition

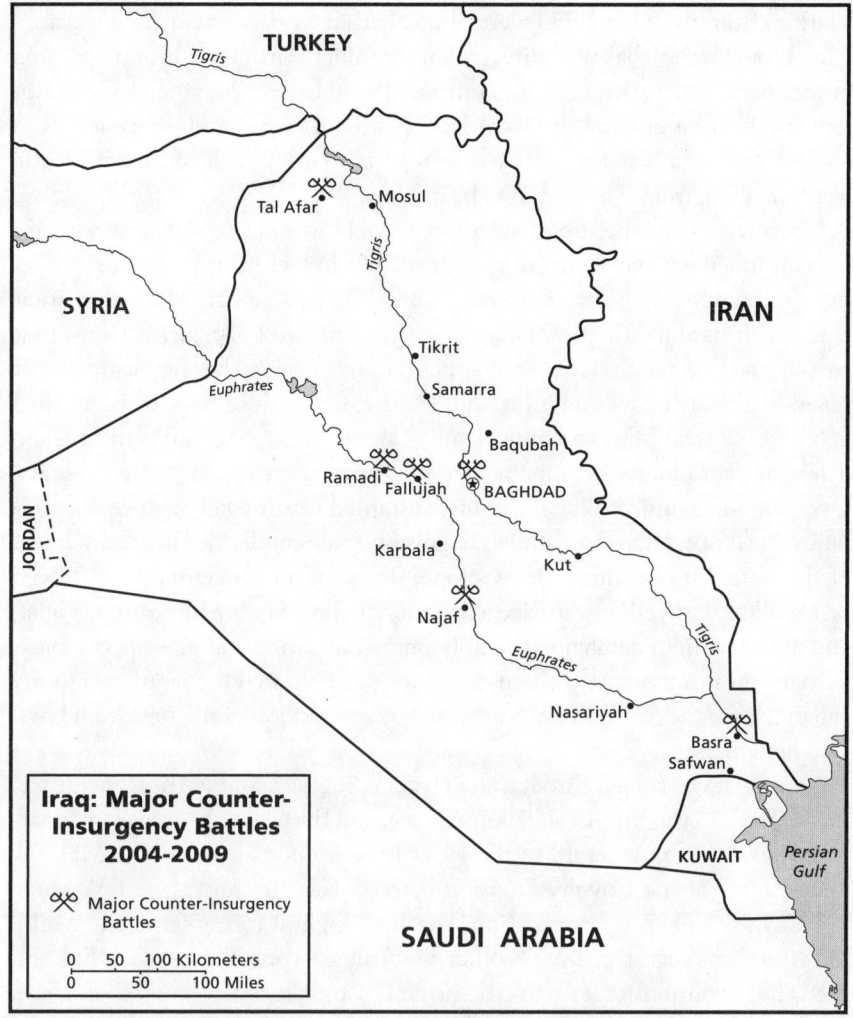

Iraq: Major Counter-Insurgency Battles 2004-2009

to the government. Sadr publicly boycotted an important Sunni conference, signaling his renewed effort to gain attention, and the Mahdi Militia stepped up their activities against local security forces around Iraq. Sadr's spokesman called for revolution and claimed his supporters controlled four provinces in the country.[2] They even attacked a newly arrived element of the 11th Marine Expeditionary Unit (11th MEU) on August 2.[3] The situation peaked again when Iraqi policemen and MNF forces were forced to surround al-Sadr's home and counterattack enemy forces on August 5 in response to a significant attack by the Mahdi Militia on the main Najaf police station the night before.[4]

When attacked by members of the Mahdi Militia, the Najaf police called for Iraqi army support, and by the early hours of Thursday morning, U.S.

Marines from the 11th MEU were also called in by the provincial governor.[5] This brought the coalition directly into conflict with al-Sadr and his Shia militiamen. When the fighting continued to escalate, provincial Governor Adnan al-Ziruffi ordered the local Iraqi National Guard and police forces to seal off Kufa and Najaf in response to reports that busloads of Mahdi Militia were traveling from Baghdad to fight in Najaf.

Some thought the use of such force would intimidate al-Sadr and deter his continued anti-governmental rhetoric, but in fact his followers grew ever more militant as additional force was applied. The MNF-I staff had not anticipated such hard fighting in Najaf province. Outside of al-Sadr's actions, that part of Iraq had been relatively quiet, but, in reaction to the significant threat posed by the anti-government Mahdi Militia, the 11th MEU was soon called upon by General Metz to conduct full-scale offensive operations in order to defeat al-Sadr's forces in Najaf and restore normal civil authority in the city. Over the following weeks, in the first sustained urban combat since the previous April operations in Fallujah, coalition forces under the tactical control of the 11th MEU commander, Colonel Tony Haslem, eventually destroyed or expelled the well-entrenched elements of the Mahdi Militia from Najaf, and did so without damaging the holy Imam Ali shrine and mosque complex. Perhaps most importantly, the fighting in Najaf showed a new Iraqi military capability for the first time, in the form of one battalion of the new Iraqi Civil Defense Corps.

Combat continued through the city on August 5 and 6; the difficult terrain of the city was intense and unforgiving, and the Mahdi Militia were fanatical defenders, so General Metz approved the reinforcement of the MEU by forces from the 1st Cavalry Division in Baghdad. On August 7, Task Force 1-5 Cavalry (TF 1-5) arrived from the Iraqi capital to reinforce the MEU. On Monday, August 9, I MEF officially assumed control of 11th MEU and the other coalition forces with the arrival of its forward command element, commanded by Brigadier General Dennis J. Hejlik. Upon his arrival, and for the duration of operations in and around Najaf, General Hejlik and Colonel Haslem conducted rounds of sustained peace negotiations with representatives of the IIG and Mahdi Militia officials, while still planning and supervising smaller-scale combat operations. The goal was to minimize the effects of the confrontation on the people of the region. An initial cessation of hostilities was planned for the following Wednesday, August 11.

As further reinforcement, TF 2-7 Cavalry arrived at Forward Operating Base Duke outside of Najaf on August 10. The following day, the MNF units were again engaged in the southwest, northwest, and northeast portions of the city. It was clear that the Mahdi Militia would not adhere to any peace agreement. General Hejlik put TF 2-7 into the fight, resulting in a three-battalion advance on the Imam Ali shrine complex at the heart of the holy city. On Thursday, August 12, after one full week of combat, coalition units and members of the 405th Iraqi National Guard Battalion conducted another raid near al-Sadr's house to destroy enemy forces in the area and gather intelligence. Later analysis of the information found in al-Sadr's house (numerous documents, computer hard drives, and other materials) produced much valuable intelligence implicating him and his key leaders in the worst acts of the militia. The same day, the Iraqi 36th Commando Battalion and the new Iraqi Counter-Terrorism Force (ICTF) conducted a direct action mission in the Sahlah Mosque in nearby Kufa. Coalition forces provided an exterior cordon around the site while members of the 36th Commando and ICTF established an inner cordon around the mosque and conducted the actual assault into the building.

A second cessation of hostilities was directed by General Metz on August 13 and, demonstrating the commitment of Prime Minister Allawi's IIG, the government ordered the reinforcement of the coalition in Najaf province with a battalion of the new Iraqi Intervention Force (IIF). The fighting nonetheless continued through the following week. Why the Mahdi Militia continued to fight in the face of continued coalition success is hard to determine. The militiamen may have been emboldened by the earlier success in Fallujah, or they may have benefited from a higher level of organizational cohesion inspired by their religious fervor. Slowly encircled and then cut off from outside support, al-Sadr's forces had no fighting chance against the combined efforts of the Marine and Army units and those of the Iraqi military and police. Even worse from the militiamen's standpoint, the local Najafis, who had never been very supportive of the militia's activities, grew increasingly opposed to their actions. Changing popular support is of course the key to success in any insurgency, and after the weekend of 21–22 August, al-Sadr's hopes in Najaf were pointless without popular support.

Sporadic fighting continued into the early afternoon of Thursday, August 26—three weeks into the fighting—until General Metz directed a halt to offensive operations in Najaf in order to give Iraqi political and religious officials the opportunity to peaceably resolve the removal of Mahdi Militia from the Imam Ali shrine and mosque complex in the city center. Finally, on August 27, the Grand Ayatollah Sistani received the keys to the shrine and mosque complex, finally signaling the end of hostilities in Najaf. The fighting in Najaf had demonstrated that the new Iraqi forces would fight, even if only in small numbers. It also demonstrated that Prime Minister Allawi and other Iraqi political leaders would support the ongoing military operations. Unfortunately, the signal of the Mahdi Militia resistance clearly indicated that Iraqi support was far from unanimous and that religious schisms posed serious threats to the development of the new Iraq.

Fallujah II—Operation Al Fajr

Unfortunately, after the failure of the Fallujah Brigade, insurgent and terrorist activity inside the city only grew more intense with each passing week. And by the time the fighting ended in Najaf, the MNF realized that the growing problem in Fallujah might not be solved by negotiations alone, and that plans for a second military assault needed to be developed. The second Fallujah operation would include an effort to split the enemy from its popular support base and a parallel reinforcing effort designed to draw the civilian population out of the city in advance of the fighting, thus reducing civilian casualties and better revealing enemy forces so that precision targeting could take a greater role in the operation. Shaping actions under the tactical control of I MEF would also deceive the enemy as to the actual point of the attack. The insurgent leadership could have no doubt that the attack would come, but the constant probing of the shaping phases helped convince them that the main attack would come again from the south and east, as had been the case in Vigilant Resolve.

Using the "Blackjack Brigade" from the 1st Cavalry Division, the MEF cut all the roads leading to Fallujah from the east, then moved a task force including the Iraqi 36th Commando Battalion up the peninsula west of the city to effectively seal it off. Once the city was surrounded the main combat forces of the 1st Marine Division moved into place on the northern edge of Fallujah. Beginning on November 8, the second fight for Fallujah employed overwhelming force by integrating Army, Marine, and Iraqi battalions, and attacking with two regiments side by side from north to south through the city. The assault was spearheaded by army mechanized and armored battalions followed up by infantry, which combined the shock effect of the armor with the large numbers of "boots on the ground" required for urban combat. The Iraqi soldiers facilitated clearing of sensitive sites, such as mosques. The MEF also fully integrated air power as well as numerous tactical sensors and SOF (whose snipers were particularly valued). The fighting in Fallujah was up-close, vicious, unpredictable, and very manpower intensive. Some buildings in the city were cleared multiple times. Tanks were used often and with telling effect. Indirect fires from 155mm artillery positioned less than five kilometers away in Camp Fallujah were used on a daily basis during the heaviest periods of fighting. Bulldozers were used on several occasions to push the walls of buildings in on stubborn defenders. Insurgents used armor-piercing bullets and even sewed grenades inside their clothing to kill and maim coalition troops at every opportunity.

Most of the fighters in the northern sections of the city were quickly overrun, but in the southern half of the city MNF forces found much more determined defenders, dug in with reinforcing positions. Operation Al Fajr employed traditional tactics as well as some very innovative procedures and command structures. Civil affairs teams and combat engineers followed the lead combat battalions to begin assessment of critical infrastructure and to facilitate population and resource control for any civilians left in the city. Because Vigilant Resolve had been halted due to widespread negative media attention, Al Fajr was designed to ensure that collateral damage was minimized and civilians could be cared for or evacuated as soon as possible. An aggressive public affairs (PA) stance was also critical to the maintenance of popular support. This in turn helped ensure the maintenance of Iraqi government resolve to conduct the fight. This was, after all, the first major *offensive* authorized and directed by Allawi's Interim Iraqi Government.

The initial objectives of the attack were secured early and the entire city was under MNF control after four days of very hard fighting. Although small pockets of determined, even suicidal insurgents would continue to fight for nearly a month, the MEF staff began to transition to local Iraqi control during the first week of combat. The city needed to be secure and made safe, essential services had to be restored to minimal levels, and the residents of the city had to have some semblance of normalcy in their lives before all the goals of Al Fajr would be met.

The basic concept of the operation depended upon a series of transitions, from combat, to restoration of security and essential services, to resettlement and return to local control by an Iraqi municipal government. The minimum requirements for conflict termination were identified prior to the assault. These included police forces for the city, a mayor to manage essential services, and reconstruction projects designed to rapidly restore the city's infrastructure to pre-conflict levels. The transition from combat operations to restoration of essential services and humanitarian assistance was envisioned to be spatial not time based; hence, while fighting continued in some areas of the city, MNF and Iraqi forces would be rebuilding pump houses and electrical substations and providing humanitarian relief supplies to the remaining Fallujah residents in other areas.

Though all the pre-requisites were never met, the IIG did appoint a military governor, Major General Abdul Qadir.[6] Unfortunately, the minister of the interior failed to provide police forces from outside the city and coalition soldiers, to include two battalions of newly formed public order battalions, were used instead to provide police in the city. Finally, both the MNF and the IIG did commit funds for the city's restoration, but at least initially there was no coordinating mechanism to determine who would accomplish which projects; and, not surprisingly, the MNF and Iraqi priorities for restoration were quite different.

The city of Fallujah was opened for resettlement on December 23, 2004, only six weeks after the initial assault. Many residents had been living for months in surrounding cities or in transient camps; the weather was turning cold with the onset of winter and their children were missing school, so they were anxious to return to their homes in the city. The IIG and the MNF were both very concerned about the re-infiltration of insurgents with residents, so the MEF decided to establish entry control points (ECPs) that restricted all access to Fallujah; the ECPs made for long lines on the roads leading back to Fallujah but also significantly reduced the number of insurgents who returned.

Prime Minister Allawi wanted to show the Sunnis that they would be cared for at least as well as the Shia populations in other areas of Iraq. Al Fajr required significant host nation leadership. The prime minister had to be personally involved on many occasions due to the sensitive nature of the fighting in the Sunni Triangle and the massive amount of funding required to rebuild and repair the city.[7] Fundamental questions of emergency law and re-establishment of police capability also required a high level of governmental involvement, particularly as several of the ministers were reluctant to cooperate with each other. Still, reconstruction of essential civic service sites, battle damage compensation, reimbursement for damaged homes, and funding for new economic development initiatives were already apparent in early 2005.[8]

The First Free Iraqi Elections: A Measure of Success and Missed Opportunity

On January 30, 2005, the Iraqi people went to the polls to chose representatives for the newly formed and transitional 275-member Iraqi National Assembly. The voting was the first general election in newly sovereign Iraq, and marked an important step in the transition from the interim structures established under the CPA to true Iraqi institutions. President Bush and other leaders around the globe hailed the event as a crucial step toward the future. The results showed an overwhelming victory by the Shia United Iraqi Alliance party, largely because Sunnis in Iraq felt alienated and threatened by insurgents and, as a result, most were too intimidated to vote. This gave the Shia parties a license to develop the new government in their own fashion and significantly restricted any Sunni input within the national government for years.

For the MNF, January 2005 had been important, as it witnessed the first free national election in recent Iraqi history, the insurgency in Fallujah had been destroyed, the Shia militias in Baghdad and the south of Iraq were rendered docile, and General Casey and his staff had been successfully managing security in Iraq under the authority of a sovereign Iraqi government. Casey and Ambassador Negroponte had formed an effective team and the MNC-I operational effort (soon to be commanded by Lieutenant General John Vines, one of the most proficient commanders in the Army) had demonstrated its value. Commanders at the tactical level in Iraq, such as Major General Pete Chiarelli in Baghdad, were already modifying their approaches to meet the new challenges of the evolving combat environment.

Meanwhile, at the national strategic level, President Bush had been elected to his final term of office with a significant 51 percent majority of the popular vote. It would have been an excellent opportunity for a thorough review of the progress of the war to date and potentially a very good time to alter the strategy if such a review indicated that sufficient progress was not being made.[9] In the aftermath of the elections, the new government coming to power in Baghdad certainly would have been open to a review of strategy. Unfortunately, no such review was undertaken and there was nothing other than head-down pushing toward the operational objectives that had been developed by Casey's staff the previous summer.

It is inordinately difficult for senior commanders to gain sufficient perspective to accomplish a thorough review of war progress while simultaneously engaging in combat operations. Still, such assessments must be accomplished if the ever-changing dynamics of a conflict are to be managed, and the coalition in Iraq had the tremendous advantage of having a strategic level staff (MNF-I) available to complete an assessment while the day-to-day battle was being managed by its subordinate operational headquarters, MNC-I. The January election had been supported by a fifteen-thousand-man troop plus-up (actually accomplished by holding forces in Iraq even after their replacements had already arrived), so that there were actually more forces in Iraq in February than were needed. The incidence of attacks that month, and for the months that followed, was half the number averaged during the previous three month period.

The Casey Strategy

The MNF-I strategy under General Casey can be summarized as "buildup and transition to Iraqi forces." It had been developed under the hand of Casey's predecessor, General Sanchez, and although Casey approved it and directed its execution in August 2004, it was not well adapted to the situation in which the coalition found itself. A well respected counterinsurgency analyst and later Pentagon official, Kalev Sepp, noted that the strategy "was a product that seemed to be toning itself down. It was written as if there were knowledge of this bad thing, an insurgency, that was coming up underfoot, and you had to deal with it, but you had to be careful about being too direct in calling it an insurgency and dealing with it that way, because then you would be admitting that it had always been there but you had ignored it up to that point. It did not talk about what you had to do to defeat an insurgency. It was not a counterinsurgency plan."[10]

In 2005 the strategy was being put into practice through the conduct of military operations designed to disrupt the flow of foreign fighters entering the country and the insurgent support lines that run into Iraq, while simultaneously training Iraqi troops to fill the security vacuum in the center and north of the country.[11] This was being accomplished using two primary levers: the MNC-I lever of tactical, kinetic operations (which was still decentralized into five sub-regional commands aligned with the Iraqi provinces and including one focused only on Baghdad)[12] and a Multi-National Security Transition Command-Iraq (MNSTC-I) lever focused completely on the development of the Iraqi security forces (military and police).[13]

MNSTC-I was commanded from June 2004 to September 2005 by Lieutenant General David H. Petraeus, who only six months prior had returned from Iraq to the U.S with his 101st Airborne Division.[14] While in Iraq with the division, Petraeus had been lauded as one of the most successful of the commanders in the initial invasion and pacification period, particularly as his sector in the north of Iraq had made better progress than many in the early months of the CPA.[15] MNSTC-I was responsible for developing, organizing, training, equipping, and sustaining the Iraqi security ministries (Ministry of Defense [MoD] and Ministry of Interior [MoI]) and their associated Iraqi Security Forces (ISF), which included not only traditional military and police units but also the border patrol and special site security units that were separate parts of the Iraqi security force system. It also had to develop Iraq's security institutions and build the associated infrastructure, such as training bases, police stations, and border forts required to provide security at the national level in Iraq.

MNSTC-I did this primarily by associating American military advisory teams within the individual Iraqi units that were being developed and by managing the equipment purchasing and training regime of the units themselves. Because Ambassador Bremer had disbanded the Iraqi security forces with his CPA Order Number 2, Petraeus and his subordinates had to create entire units instead of simply retraining the parts of the Iraqi security force structure that the coalition had called back into employment. As with everything the coalition found in Iraq in 2003, the Iraqi security forces were far less effective than had been assumed prior to the invasion; the job of MNSTC-I was technically very challenging and had the added complication that the units and their advisors were often put into combat situations well before their skill levels matched the requirements of modern warfare.

Therefore, it was the MNSTC-I mission that was truly the fundamental part of the U.S. strategy for victory in Iraq. It was only after MNSTC-I accomplished its mission to train the ISF that the Iraqis could become capable of defeating the insurgency and taking responsibility for maintaining security within the country. As the ISF became capable, the coalition could then reduce the number of its troops in Iraq and withdraw. The flaw in this concept lies in the core problem of developing security forces in a country plagued by open warfare (of a kind that had already manifested itself as an insurgency), rampant criminal activity, and increasingly frequent internecine fighting between the major factions of Iraqi society.

Later in 2005, Andrew Krepinevich would summarize the problem by saying, "After two years, Washington has made little progress in defeating the insurgency or providing security for Iraqis, even as it has overextended the U.S. Army and eroded support for the war among the American public. Although withdrawing now would be a mistake, simply 'staying the course,' by all current indications, will not improve matters either. Winning in Iraq will require a new approach. The basic problem is that the United States and its coalition partners have never settled on a strategy for defeating the insurgency and achieving their broader objectives. "[16]

Such comments were not limited to academic critiques; inside the U.S. military senior commanders were calling for change. General Chiarelli wrote at the time, "It is no longer sufficient to think in purely kinetic terms. Executing traditionally focused combat operations and concentrating on training local security forces works, but only for the short term. In the long term, doing so hinders true progress and, in reality, promotes the growth of insurgent forces working against campaign objectives. It is a lopsided approach."[17] Retired General Jack Keane made his assessment even more obvious by saying:

> In the summer of '04, after he [Casey] arrived, he put together a campaign plan to get everybody on the same page. The centerpiece to that was that we were going to transition to the Iraqi security forces. ... The political strategy was to stand up a representative democracy, a representative government, as quickly as possible. When you look back on that and analyze it, it's a short-war strategy. It's designed to get to a political objective, representative government, as quickly as possible, and secondly, transition to the Iraqi security forces so that

they can cope with the insurgency. Nowhere in there is a plan to defeat the insurgency, so we had no military strategy to defeat the insurgency. We were resting on a political strategy that would hopefully stem the violence because the Sunnis would come into the political process and therefore seek a political solution to the confrontation, no longer an armed solution. We over-relied on that. And then there was no forcing function, because we were not defeating the insurgents.[18]

Other analysts agreed that the "strategy" then in effect was not a feasible or acceptable method of winning the war. Krepinevich noted that "without a clear strategy in Iraq, moreover, there is no good way to gauge progress," meaning principally that the Casey approach relied more on abstract assessments of the state of readiness of the Iraqi security forces, rather than real measurable accomplishments of effects on the enemy.[19] It would have been possible to stand up a huge Iraqi security force structure, yet the forces contained therein could have been so riddled with problems (including counterproductive loyalties to tribes and religious sects) that even in large numbers, the force would remain ineffective against the insurgent threat.[20]

Lack of an effective strategy was not the only issue plaguing the American effort in Iraq at the time. Political progress was just as important to the future of Iraq as was controlling the insurgency, and in the spring of 2005 America's ambassador in Iraq, John Negroponte, was appointed director of national intelligence by President Bush. Negroponte returned to the United States, leaving Iraq without a U.S. ambassador until Zalmay Khalilzad's return to Baghdad four months later. During the summer of 2005 the newly elected Iraqi government would be working on the draft of the national constitution and preparations for the first elections of a national assembly in the winter—this was a crucial period requiring a great deal of mentorship in the difficult pathways of democracy. Although Khalilzad had worked wonders in Afghanistan and knew the National Security Council staff well, the improvement of governance in Iraq suffered a serious loss of momentum in the critical summer months of 2005.

Meanwhile, in the aftermath of the serious defeats suffered in the preceding months, the insurgency as a whole adapted and began shifting its strategy away from actions designed to damage coalition military forces and bases and toward assaults on the population of Iraq. This shift was certainly in part a reaction to the powerful blows it had suffered at the hands of Casey's forces, but it was just as much a purposeful shift away from attacks on the strengths of the coalition toward actions which would sow fear and discontent among the Iraqi people—who had already suffered far too long under conditions of Ba'athist oppression, twenty years of intermittent warfare, and the economic sanctions.

The Case of Tal Afar

A tactical illustration from one major battle of this period is instructive, particularly insofar as it shows the need for adaptation and the misalignment of the MNF-I strategy with conditions on the ground.[21] A city of nearly three hundred thousand people lying along the ancient smuggling route from Syria in the northwestern desert of Iraq, Tal Afar had been relatively peaceful in the months following the national elections in January 2005, but had experienced very uneven security since the fall of Saddam Hussein, largely due to the insufficient number of coalition forces. "In early 2004, the division that had occupied northwestern Iraq was replaced by a brigade, with one-third the strength. A single company—about a hundred and fifty soldiers—became responsible for protecting Tal Afar. Insurgents soon seized the city and turned it into a strategic stronghold."[22]

Then, in the spring of 2005, as a part of the normal rotation of units through Iraq, Colonel H. R. McMaster arrived in Tal Afar with his 3rd Armored Cavalry Regiment (3rd ACR). McMaster was both a combat veteran (having been awarded the Silver Star during Desert Storm) and a military intellectual (author of the prize-winning book *Dereliction of Duty*),[23] but neither skill served him very well in the early days of his unit deployment. The 3rd ACR was not new to combat either; the regiment had served in Iraq during the immediate aftermath of the fall of Baghdad, but it was shifted from site to site during its first tour in Iraq, so that its officers were never able to develop an understanding of the local people. Eventually, the regiment was assigned to Al Anbar province, where with far too few men to secure any area, it contributed to the problems in and around Fallujah prior to departing Iraq and being replaced by the 82nd Airborne Division.

The 3rd ACR and its commander initially approached their second Iraq tour of duty in Tal Afar with a typical, mostly kinetic mindset—focused on killing insurgents. This was understandable, for "when they arrived . . . the city was largely in the hands of hard-core Iraqi and foreign jihadis, who, together with members of the local Sunni population, had destabilized the city with a campaign of intimidation, including beheadings aimed largely at Tal Afar's Shiite minority."[24] McMaster admitted, "When we first got here, we made a lot of mistakes. We were like a blind man, trying to do the right thing but breaking a lot of things."[25]

The difference in Tal Afar was that, under McMaster, the 3rd ACR listened, learned, and adapted their approaches to the situation in the city, always keeping in mind the idea that they needed to develop security in Tal Afar for the longer term, regardless of the details of the MNF-I mission. Even though Tal Afar was largely controlled by Sunni extremists who were aiding Zarqawi and his Al Qaeda in Iraq followers, the officers of the 3rd ACR realized that their heavy-handed approaches were not helping this situation. Eventually they began to talk with the local leaders, spending "forty or fifty hours a week with sheikhs from Tal Afar's dozens of tribes: first the Shiite sheikhs, to convince them that the Americans could be counted on to secure their neighborhoods; and then the Sunni sheikhs, many of whom were passive or active supporters of the insurgency."[26]

This effort was not new in Iraq—members of the coalition had worked with the Iraqi population in the late spring and summer of 2003 (particularly in the north) and sporadically thereafter, but because they shifted around the country the American units rarely developed the affinity needed to make real inroads and develop trust. The Marines had recently developed good working relationships with the local leaders in Al Anbar province, but overall the civil affairs–oriented approach was not common, largely because it was difficult, slow, and decidedly "unmilitary." In Tal Afar, one of the American commanders, Lieutenant Colonel Chris Hickey, committed himself to a different approach with McMaster's support. "In painstakingly slow and inconclusive encounters, each one centering on the same sectarian grievances and fears, Hickey tried to establish common interests between the Sunnis and the Shiites. He also attempted to drive a wedge between nationalist-minded Sunnis and extremists, a distinction that, in the war's first year or two, American soldiers were rarely able to make; they were simply fighting 'bad guys.'"[27] George Packer noted, "At the highest levels of the Administration, the notion of acknowledging the enemy's grievances was dismissed as defeatist. But in Tal Afar I heard expressions of soldierly respect for what some Americans called the Iraqi resistance."[28]

Even with progress beginning to be felt in the civil relations approach, the problem in Tal Afar worsened to the point that it required the application of combat power. In September, the 3rd ACR executed Operation Restoring Rights, attacking with nearly equal numbers of Iraqi troops (approximately five thousand soldiers from the 3rd Division of the Iraqi Security Forces) "into the oldest, most dense part of the city, which had become the base of insurgent operations; there were days of heavy fighting, with support from Apache helicopters shooting Hellfire missiles.[29] Most of the civilians in the area, who had been warned of the coming attack, fled ahead of the action (unknown numbers of insurgents escaped with them)."[30] The destruction was significant, but not nearly as bad as Fallujah had experienced the previous November.

Because the ACR had managed to establish useful working relationships before the assault, McMaster was able to fully integrate his forces inside the city to hold his combat gains. "After McMaster's offensive, Hickey and a squadron of a thousand men set up living quarters next to Iraqi Army soldiers, in primitive patrol bases without hot water, reliable heat, or regular cooked meals."[31] Both American and Iraqi units helped with the restoration of security in Tal Afar. Packer noted, "The American patrol bases around the city stand next to Iraqi Army battalion headquarters; this allows for daily conversations among counterparts in the two armies and frequent sharing of information. The Americans are not just training an Iraqi Army; they are trying to build an institution of national unity before there is a nation."[32]

The results of Operation Restoring Rights were far-reaching; not only did conditions improve in Tal Afar, but other American officials took note of the tactics used to develop the rapport in the city. While on an inspection tour of Iraq for the secretary of state, Philip Zellikow happened to visit McMaster and the ACR in Tal Afar.[33] When asked about the concept for the obviously successful approach in the city, McMaster informed Zellikow that his approach was to clear out the insurgents, hold the terrain, and then begin to build up the city. Zellicow had been searching for a way of explaining the unclear strategy in Iraq and was sufficiently impressed to pass on the vision to Secretary Rice, who used the analogy in her next testimony before Congress on October 19, 2005.[34] "And that's the origin of 'clear, hold and build'—developing that as a catchphrase would just help people internalize that there's a strategy, and here's what it means."[35]

General Casey was taken aback by the secretary of state's testimony; he didn't think it was a reflection of his strategy in Iraq.[36] Donald Rumsfeld also disagreed. In his eyes, the coalition forces were not in Iraq to build a nation, but only to provide security for the developing Iraqi government and its forces.[37] Still, despite arguments at the top over whether Operation Restoring Rights was a true reflection of the U.S. strategy in Iraq, there was no doubt that "the Americans' achievement in Tal Afar showed that, in the war's third year, individuals and units within the Army could learn and adapt on their own. On his last night in the city, Colonel McMaster sat in his makeshift office and said, "It is so damn complex. If you ever think you have the solution to this, you're wrong, and you're dangerous. You have to keep listening and thinking and being critical and self-critical."[38]

The kind of approach used by Colonel McMaster was also popular with his troops, largely because they, nearly alone among the thousands of coalition men and women in Iraq, could see improvements resulting from their efforts. "During the 3rd Armored Cavalry Regiment's final weeks in Iraq, morale was remarkably high. Some soldiers expressed, almost under their breath, a reluctance to leave. Many of them had established strong bonds with Iraqis and didn't want to abandon the work they had done together. They brought gifts for the Iraqis' children when they returned from leave. The Iraqi Army units in Tal Afar had been watching McMaster's men carefully, and were showing signs of competence, taking the lead in small operations, learning to win the trust of local civilians, and often proving more adept than the Americans at securing good intelligence. They still faced enormous logistical problems—they lacked armored vehicles and a reliable system of paying salaries, and their ministry of defense was so weak and corrupt that Iraqi soldiers still depended on the American military's supply system to eat and to stay warm. As for the Iraqi police, they resembled less a neutral security force than a faction in the city's conflicts. Nonetheless, the American soldiers in Tal Afar felt that they had achieved something."[39]

Problems and Progress with the Iraqi Security Forces

In September 2005, General Petraeus departed MNSTC-I for another command at the U.S. Army's Combined Arms Center at Fort Leavenworth, Kansas.[40] By the end of his command, some one hundred thousand Iraqi Security Forces had been trained; Iraqi army and police were being employed in combat; countless reconstruction projects had been executed; and hundreds of thousands of weapons, body armor, and other equipment had been distributed in what was described as the "largest military procurement and distribution effort since World War II," at a cost of over $11 billion.[41]

One year before, Petraeus had written an article for the *Washington Post* outlining the progress being made by MNSTC-I in building Iraq's security forces; he also made very clear the many challenges associated with the training and equipping effort, saying "Although there have been reverses—not to mention horrific terrorist attacks—there has been progress in the effort to enable Iraqis to shoulder more of the load for their own security, something they are keen to do."[42] Some of the challenges involved in building security forces had to do with accomplishing this task in the midst of a tough insurgency. The command was also plagued by allegations of corruption. Two years later, the *Washington Post* would state that, according to a government report, MNSTC-I "lost track of about 190,000 AK-47 assault rifles and pistols given to Iraqi security forces in 2004 and 2005 . . . raising fears that some of those weapons have fallen into the hands of insurgents fighting U.S. forces in Iraq." The same article quoted an official in the General Accounting Office who said that the weapons distribution was "haphazard and rushed and failed to follow established procedures."[43]

As the key element of the effort in Iraq, the performance of the MNF in building the Iraqi security forces and the efforts of MNSTC-I in particular should be assessed. Performing such an assessment was difficult. One author noted in the spring of 2006:

> No one knows how many Iraqi security personnel there are today. The Pentagon can tell us that as of March 21, 2007, 329,800 Iraqi security personnel had been "trained and equipped," however, this number counts only how many Ministry of Defense (MoD) and Ministry of Interior (MoI) personnel have completed Coalition training programs. While it can tell us whether or not the Coalition is meeting its training targets, it doesn't tell us how many Iraqis are in uniform. It does not take into account deaths, desertions, or Iraqi police who are on the job but have not received Coalition-sponsored training. It fails to convey the fact that some quarter of military personnel and unknown number of police aren't at their jobs at any given time (they're on leave, taking their paychecks home, or just not there). Nor does it include thousands of other agents of the government in uniform and with guns. Iraqi officials are also not sure how many security personnel there are today. They may be able to calculate whom they are paying, but the fact is that they're still paying some unknown number of people who aren't actually working.[44]

The ISF included some one hundred thousand members in October 2004; that number increased to 130,000 in January 2005, and stood at 160,000 in June of the same year. By the time general Petraeus departed the number was over 200,000. However, building an army requires more than assembling units and equipment. The real proof in the effectiveness of MNSCT-I was not the simple number of units under arms, but the effectiveness of the Iraqi forces across the span of all their missions: military, police, and security. Assessments of Iraqi efficiency vary, but overall there was a clear and increasing growth in the ability of the Iraqi units to shoulder the real burdens of the war after December 2005.

The New Iraqi Constitution—October 2005

The new Iraqi constitution was drafted in 2005 by members of a constitutional drafting committee. It was needed to replace the Law of Administration for the State of Iraq for the Transitional Period (TAL). The TAL had been developed between December 2003 and March 2004 by the Iraqi Governing

Council and the CPA; but the TAL was not an Iraqi constitution, and the newly sovereign state needed one in order to frame its government.

Still, the obvious problem was that due to the Sunni boycott of the January 2005 elections, there would be very little Sunni input into the drafting of a constitution that could well determine the future of all Iraqis. The drafting and adoption of the new constitution was not easy, because sectarian tensions heavily affected the process. Some officials, particularly those of the Supreme Islamic Council of Iraq (SCIRI) made statements interpreted to mean that there would be little or no compromise on desired Sunni inputs. The deadline for the conclusion of drafting was extended four times because of a lack of consensus on key religious language in the document. In the end, Sunni leaders were split as to whether to support the constitution. Fortunately, the biggest Sunni block, the Iraqi Accord Front, did finally support the document after receiving promises that it would be reviewed and amended to take into account their views. Under this key compromise brokered before the referendum by Zalmay Khalilzad, it was agreed that the first parliament elected under the new constitution should sponsor a constitutional review to determine whether any portion of the constitution should be amended. Any amendments agreed would have to be ratified by a similar referendum to the one that originally approved it. After this agreement was entered into, the Sunni-majority Iraqi Islamic Party agreed to support the referendum on October 15, 2005.[45]

Electoral Commission officials stipulated that 78 percent of voters backed the charter and only 21 percent opposed it. Of the eighteen Iraqi provinces, two recorded no votes, which was only one province short of a veto. Two-thirds rejection votes in three of Iraq's provinces (Mosul, Al Anbar, and Salahaddin, those with Sunni majorities) would have required the dissolution of the Assembly, fresh elections, and the recommencement of the entire drafting process. Still, even with controversy, the development of a new constitution for all Iraq was a fundamental step forward in governance of the new nation.

The Incident at Haditha Dam—November 2005

On November 19, 2005, a small Marine unit on a resupply convoy from 3rd Battalion, 1st Marines (3/1) arrived in Haditha and was struck by an improvised explosive device (IED). Lance Corporal Miguel Terrazas was killed, and two other Marines, Lance Corporal James Crossan and Private First Class Salvador Guzman, were evacuated by helicopter with severe wounds. In response to the IED attack, the Marines, led by Staff Sergeant Frank Wuterich, ordered five Iraqi men out of their car, The Iraqis were then shot dead in the.

street. Very soon after their deaths, Lieutenant William Kallop arrived at the site and the Marines began reporting receiving small-arms fire, which they thought was coming from a nearby house. Kallop ordered the Marines to "take the house." In the resulting firefight, twenty-four Iraqis, including women and children as young as two years old, were killed in three adjacent houses that the Marines assaulted with grenades and automatic rifle fire.

After video evidence that conflicted with the initial Marine report was released, General Chiarelli, the MNC-I commander, ordered an investigation on February 14, 2006. In mid-March, U.S. officials confirmed that the Marines, not insurgents, killed the majority of the Iraqi civilians. Army Major General Eldon Bargewell looked into how the incident was reported through the chain of command. The Naval Criminal Investigative Service looked into the criminal aspects of the incident and a third investigation was launched by the Iraqi government. As a result of the investigations the commanding officer, Lieutenant Colonel Jeffrey Chessani, and two company commanders were removed from their duties. General Bargewell's investigation found that "statements made by the chain of command during interviews for this investigation, taken as a whole, suggest that Iraqi civilian lives are not as important as U.S. lives, their deaths are just the cost of doing business, and that the Marines need to get 'the job done' no matter what it takes. These comments had the potential to desensitize the Marines to concern for the Iraqi populace and portray them all as the enemy even if they are noncombatants."[46]

On December 21, 2006, the U.S. military charged eight Marines in connection with the Haditha incident, including Staff Sergeant Wuterich, who was charged with twelve counts of unpremeditated murder against individuals and one count of the murder of six people. Lieutenant Colonel Chessani was recommended to face a court-martial, but all charges against him were later dropped by a military judge. Staff Sergeant Wuterich was never convicted on any of the charges placed against him.

The incident shocked people around the world and played into the hands of those who decried the United States, providing them with evidence that violations of the law of armed conflict were being committed by members of the coalition in Iraq. That remains a serious charge; however, and just a importantly, the attitudes displayed by the Marines at Haditha demonstrated that the coalition forces in Iraq had strayed a great distance from the ideals that brought them to Iraq initially and that they were in fact acting in ways that were directly counter to the real objectives of their operations: the development of a new democratic Iraq.

Maturation of the New Iraqi Government—December 2005

Following the success of the first post-Saddam national elections in Iraq in January 2005, and the ratification of the Constitution of Iraq on October 15, 2005, a general election was held on December 15 to select a permanent 275-member Iraqi Council of Representatives. Because of the huge number of political entities in Iraq, the legislative elections took place under a list system, with voters choosing from among a list of parties. The 230 seats were apportioned among Iraq's eighteen governorates. Then an additional forty-five seats were allocated under a complex system designed to compensate those parties whose percentages of the national vote exceeded the percentage of the total seats that had already been allocated, bringing the total seats to 275. Women were required to occupy 25 percent of those 275 seats.

Voter turnout was high and the level of violence during polling was relatively low. The results of the election produced a government headed by Nouri al-Maliki, the secretary general of the Islamic Dawa Party. Maliki was a Shiite who had opposed Saddam before escaping into exile in 1979; afterwards he lived in Jordan, Syria, and Iran before returning to Iraq, where he worked on the de-Ba'athification committee before being elected to the transitional national assembly in 2005 and then helping to write the new constitution. The new government was not fully representative of the Iraqi people, but the election did demonstrate further progress toward a functioning Iraqi state.

The Bombing of the Golden Mosque in Samarra

Thus, 2006 began as a year with much promise; every indication of modern warfare would have shown that the coalition was winning the war in Iraq. "In January 2006, the mission is to continue to hand over more and more territory and more and more responsibility to Iraqi forces," President Bush said; "that's progress."[47] Unfortunately, the year was only to bring frustration and an ever-increasing death toll to the Iraqi people. The Golden or (al-Askari) Mosque is one of the most holy sites in Shia Islam, but on February 22, 2006, insurgents dressed as Iraqi police officers entered the shrine and detonated two bombs inside it, collapsing most of the dome.[48] It was a tremendously important attack that could only have been designed to insult and anger the Shia majority population of Iraq.

Although Al Qaeda in Iraq denied any involvement in the attack, Iraqi National Security Advisor Mouwafak al-Rubaie later revealed that a captured Tunisian named Abu Qudama had confessed to taking part in the attack and had given a detailed account of how the attack took place. Rubaie said that the mastermind of the mosque attack, Haitham al-Badri, was the Iraqi leader of an Al Qaeda in Iraq cell.[49] In an August 2006 press conference President Bush indicated he agreed with that assessment,[50] and later, before his death, Zarqawi listed among his goals the incitement of a civil war between Iraq's Shiites and Sunnis.[51] Haitham al-Badri was killed in August 2007.[52]

As expected by the leadership of Al Qaeda in Iraq, the bombing of the Golden Mosque led almost immediately to tremendous outbreaks of sectarian violence in Iraq. Members of the Sunni minority were victimized by Shia militia in retaliation for the years of suppression as well as for the bombing of the mosque. In response, armed Sunni militia attacked Shiite pilgrims and assaulted predominately Shia neighborhoods. The coalition forces could do little to stop the sectarian combat, which largely took place in the cities and towns, at night and out of coalition observation.

Staying the Course . . .

In the first months of 2006, General Petraeus had written an article wherein he summarized his observations on the war in Iraq. His fourteen lessons learned included the admonishment that "*success in a counterinsurgency requires more than just military operations.* Counterinsurgency strategies must also include, above all, efforts to establish a political environment that helps reduce support for the insurgents and undermines the attraction of whatever ideology they may espouse."[55] He also noted that "it goes without saying that success in Iraq—which clearly is important not just for Iraq, but for the entire Middle East region and for our own country—will require continued military operations and support for the ongoing development of Iraqi Security Forces. Success will also require continued assistance and resources for the development of the emerging political, economic, and social institutions in Iraq— efforts in which Ambassador Zalmay Khalilzad and General George Casey and their teams have been engaged with their Iraqi counterparts and have been working very hard." All of this sounded very positive, and it was basically true from the standpoint of the U.S. military, but unfortunately it was the Iraqi people who were to decide the outcome of the insurgency confronting their government and the coalition, and their lives and outlooks would dramatically worsen in the months to come.

Chapter 10

2006:
DESCENT INTO CHAOS

The first, the supreme, the most far-reaching act of judgment that the statesman and commander have to make is to establish…the kind of war on which they are embarking; neither mistaking it for, nor trying to turn it into, something that is alien to its nature. This is the first of all strategic questions and the most comprehensive.

—CARL VON CLAUSEWITZ, ON WAR

Iraq came pretty close, I think, to just unraveling in the course of that year.

—AMBASSADOR RYAN CROCKER, SEPTEMBER 11, 2007[1]

The success of the December 2005 provincial elections in Iraq had generated a great deal of optimism among American officials as 2006 began. The accomplishments of the coalition seemed to be making a difference in restoring security in Iraq, and particularly in several of the key towns and cities (such as Fallujah, Basra, Tal Afar, and Mosul) daily life was returning to a more normal state of activity. Many expected that the new members of the Iraqi provincial governments would contribute still more to the stability in Iraq and that the coming year might actually show cause for a reduction in U.S. forces, as the Iraqi Security Forces grew in number and capability.[2] Tragically, the events of 2006 would incinerate all these rosy expectations in a series of horrific sectarian clashes and car-bomb explosions.

The Samarra Shock

Several suicide bombings were conducted in Iraq in 2005 in the midst of Shiite religious celebrations, causing numerous casualties, but none of those attacks was as significant as the February 22, 2006, bombing of the Shiite Golden Mosque in Sunni-inhabited Samarra, in Salahaddin province. That attack largely destroyed the golden dome of the mosque and touched off widespread Shiite reprisals against Sunnis nationwide. For most, it is considered to have sparked the Iraqi-on-Iraqi violence that approached a civil war from the time of the bombing until late in 2007. The climate of chaos that resulted from these multiple, retribution attacks seemed to indicate that Iraq was on a downward spiral with little hope for recovery.

Most analysts attribute the Samarra bombing to AQ-I; the bombing certainly seemed to support the goals of Zarqawi and his organization. On several occasions, even President Bush seemed to imply that with the bombing of the Golden Mosque, Zarqawi had succeeded in his goal of destabilizing Iraq and discrediting the new Iraqi government in the eyes of its people. Indeed, by early 2007, most U.S. officials saw AQ-I as the driving force behind the insurgency, even though AQ-I had very different strategic goals than its minority partners in the contest against the coalition and the Iraqi government.[3] Although major bombings inspired by AQ-I constituted only a small percentage of overall attacks in Iraq (which in early 2007 numbered about 175 per day), they garnered a huge part of the international media coverage and were most influential in dampening the expectations of the American people concerning victory in Iraq; most of the U.S. combat deaths resulted from roadside bombs and direct or indirect munitions most likely employed by local Sunni insurgents.[4]

At the time of the Samarra attack the MNC-I was changing leadership; Lieutenant General John Vines and his XVIII Corps staff were handing over operational control of the coalition forces in Iraq to Lieutenant General Peter Chiarelli and the staff of V Corps from Germany.[5] General Vines had conducted Operation Hunter in the border region between Iraq and Syria, Operation Restoring Rights in Tal Afar, Operation National Unity in Baghdad, and Operation Carentan in Diyala and Salahaddin provinces. Chiarelli had previously commanded the 1st Cavalry Division in Baghdad in 2005, so he not only was very familiar with the situation in Iraq but had also tried a number of innovative techniques in Baghdad to win over the residents of the city using tools other than conventional military force.[6] Under General Chiarelli, MNC-I would attempt a number of creative operations designed to produce an end to the insurgency, all of which would be severely hampered by lack of support in the very areas he most valued (economics and rule of law) as well as ineffectiveness within the government of Iraq.

The Growth of Sectarianism in Iraq

By October 2006, the Office of the United Nations High Commissioner for Refugees (UNHCR) and the Iraqi government estimated that more than 365,000 Iraqis had been displaced since the bombing of the Golden Mosque; no one had any accurate idea of how many Iraqis had been killed by their neighbors over the same period.[7] Department of Defense estimates of sectarian violence and deaths by execution in Iraq between February and July alone numbered some 4,800 lives lost.[8] It was a period of horrible violence and almost daily press coverage of explosions and killings all around the country. At the same time, when the Iraqi Security Forces were supposed to be taking primacy in Iraq, they were rent by sectarian divisions.

Also during this period the Iraqi government was expected to make great steps forward to resolve many of he key domestic political issues in the country, yet in the spring of 2006 there was no prime minister in Baghdad to oversee this effort. A new Iraqi government had been selected in the general election held on December 15, 2005, but the new 275-member Iraqi Council of Representatives was slow to form and develop procedures. Most importantly, it took six months of negotiations to form a "government of national unity" between the parties receiving the majority of votes: the United Iraqi Alliance, the Iraqi Accord Front, the Kurdistani Alliance, and the Iraqi National List. It was only in May 2006 that a functioning government was formed under the leadership of the new prime minister, Nouri al-Maliki.

The Revolt of the Generals Begins

Many of the veteran commanders of the 2003 Iraq campaign had returned to the United States to prepare for future deployments back to Iraq or Afghanistan and to think about the changes that had taken place in warfighting since the start of the most recent combat operations in Iraq. By April 2006, support for the war back in the United States was waning significantly; everyday American citizens had opposed the war in small numbers in 2003, and those who voiced opposition had grown increasingly over time. But what changed significantly in the spring of 2006 was that for the first time senior military officers started to speak out (in retirement), and not just about the philosophical justice of the war but also about mismanagement of the war by the leadership in the Pentagon.[9] Retired generals such as Charles H. Swannack Jr., who commanded the Army's 82nd Airborne Division in Iraq; John Batiste, who commanded the 1st Infantry Division; Anthony C. Zinni, who commanded Central Command; Gregory Newbold, who served as the director of operations on the Joint Staff in the Pentagon; and Paul D. Eaton, who commanded the Coalition Military Assistance Training Teams in Iraq from 2003 to 2004, all publicly broke ranks with Rumsfeld over his conduct of the war.[10] General Swannack said in an interview, "I do not believe Secretary Rumsfeld is the right person to fight that war based on his absolute failures in managing the war against Saddam in Iraq."[11]

The opposition voiced by these generals was neither new, nor more vehement than the criticism of some other analysts; however their comments seemed to pose questions not only about the hallowed tradition of civilian control of the military in America, but also about the creeping suspicion in some minds that the American citizens had been misled by the Bush administration about the war. Had these negative comments been short lived, or had they run counter to a narrative of success in the field, they would have been insignificant. Since they did endure and did reflect the growing disappointment with the progress of the war, they would over time undermine public support for the war, and in doing so promote an anti-war sensibility that was at times reminiscent of the Vietnam War era.

Although the so-called revolt of some military leaders was gaining the attention of the press, another much more influential current of review was ongoing elsewhere within the American military establishment. Deeply concerned by the seemingly ineffective nature of the ongoing combat operations in Iraq, many leaders throughout the Pentagon were analyzing ways inside the system to reform and adapt procedures for fighting an insurgency. Chief among these efforts was the work of two of the most experienced commanders of the war, Lieutenant General David Petraeus and Lieutenant General James Mattis. These two men were co-leading groups from the Army and Marine Corps, respectively, that were working together on the development of a new field manual that would refine and explain how the U.S. military should fight in a counterinsurgency effort. That manual, which would be known as Field Manual 3-24, *Counterinsurgency*, would not only contain the combined wisdom of military and academic counterinsurgency experts from across the globe, but would also reshape the approach of all American forces in the years to come in the war.[12]

SOF and the Death of Zarqawi

Since 2003 the role of special operations forces (SOF) had grown in Iraq. Initially the special forces had served as adjuncts to the conventional assault on Saddam's military, but as the campaign shifted into a counterinsurgency mission, the unique capabilities of special forces units became increasingly important, and their numbers in Iraq grew accordingly.[13] By 2006, most of the American special mission units that performed direct action, strategic reconnaissance, and counterterrorist operations were either already in Iraq, had just returned from combat in that country, or were preparing to fight under MNF-I control in the future.

Lieutenant General Stanley McChrystal masterminded the hunt for terrorists and commanded the Joint Special Operations Command in Iraq under

General Casey. General McChrystal worked creatively to improve the integration of SOF into conventional operations, to maximize conventional force support for his own counter-terrorist and intelligence gathering operations and developed innovative ways of improving the fusion of intelligence and shortening the sensor-to-shooter linkage to make special operations missions more effective and more successful in the hunt for terrorists.

The most significant achievement of the special operators in Iraq was the successful identification and killing of the head of AQ-I, Abu Musab Zarqawi outside Baquba in June 2006.[14] "Before his death, Zarqawi had largely set AQ-I's strategy as an effort to provoke all-out civil war between the newly dominant Shiite Arabs and the formerly pre-eminent Sunni Arabs. Zarqawi apparently calculated that provoking civil war could, at the very least, undermine Shiite efforts to consolidate their political control of post-Saddam Iraq."[15] Had Zarqawi been successful, his strategy could have pushed the United States to leave Iraq by significantly undermining public support for the war effort, and leaving the Maliki government in Iraq vulnerable to continued AQ-I and Sunni insurgent attacks. Although Zarqawi had come to symbolize the link between the core of the Al Qaeda movement under Osama bin Laden and the ongoing anti-government insurgency in Iraq, his death did not cause the demise of AQ-I (which simply took a new leader) or an end the fighting, which had largely shifted to sectarian violence and Iranian-supported attacks on the MNF by the time he was killed. Still, the death of Zarqawi was a significant proof of special operations forces capability and the improvement of intelligence fusion in the campaign. In the wake of his death a number of other insurgent leaders were located and captured, striking a severe yet non-mortal blow to AQ-I.[16]

Just as Zarqawi was dying in the bombed rubble of a simple Iraqi house, President Bush was at Camp David listening to criticisms of the Iraq strategy; and in response he decided to make an unannounced visit to Baghdad to meet with Maliki and get a sense how the war progressing and how the new Iraqi government was functioning. Bush seemed to be pleased with what he saw and heard in Baghdad. He made a public statement saying, "I assured them [the Iraqi leaders] that we'll keep our commitment; I also made it clear to them that in order for us to keep our commitment and be successful, they themselves have to do some hard things. They themselves have to set an agenda. They themselves have to get some things accomplished."[17] Bush returned from Baghdad with renewed faith in the war effort, but also seemed to sense that the Iraqi government was in trouble.

Together Forward

Once in command, General Chiarelli had not been slow to begin opera-tions in Iraq designed to increase security as the new Iraqi government was being formed in the face of growing sectarian violence. In March he started Operation Scales of Justice in Baghdad. This operation significantly increased the number of forces in the Iraqi capital and netted some eight hundred sus-pected insurgents in its first two months, but didn't seem to make a dent in the overall violence in Iraq. Then in the summer of 2006, MNF-I launched a new major operation that was designed to fully integrate Iraqi Security Forces into a more broadly representative coalition with Iraqi forces taking a more promi-nent role; it was known as Together Forward.

Operation Together Forward was directed by Prime Minister Maliki and planned as an operation to be led primarily by Iraqis with coalition support. Beginning on July 9, Multi-National Division-Baghdad (MND-B) soldiers supported by Iraqi Security Forces (ISF) killed or captured over four hundred suspected insurgents, conducted some thirty-two thousand combat patrols, and seized numerous weapons and ammunition caches. On August 7, MND-B soldiers and the ISF began Phase II of Operation Together Forward designed to further increase security and reduce violence in and around the Iraqi capital. The goal of Phase II was to capitalize on the progress made during Phase I and give Iraqi forces the chance to operate with more autonomy than previously. In support of Phase II, six thousand additional Iraqi forces were to be sent to Baghdad as well as about thirty-five hundred soldiers of the 172nd Stryker Brigade Combat Team. But only two of the planned six Iraqi battalions were committed to the operation and that insufficiency in Iraqi forces was seen as a reason for the operation's lack of overall success. The coalition was able to clear certain areas of insurgents, but the combined MND-B and ISF force was unable to keep the insurgents and militia members from funneling back into the cleared areas of Baghdad.

A second major operation, Together Forward II, was executed in August 2006. Like in its predecessor operation, the coalition forces were to move into neighborhoods, clear the area of extremists, and hold those areas while building up essential services and infrastructure to better support the needs of the local population. Unfortunately, Together Forward II placed a far greater emphasis on the pace of clearing operations than on holding and rebuilding the neighborhoods that had been cleared.

The Iraq Study Group Report, directed by James A. Baker III and Lee H. Hamilton and published in December 2006, determined that recent opera-tions in Iraq had been failures. The authors noted that

The results of Operation *Together Forward II* are disheartening. Violence in Baghdad—already at high levels—jumped more than 43 percent between the summer and October 2006. U.S. forces continue to suffer high casualties. Perpetrators of violence leave neighborhoods in advance of security sweeps, only to filter back later. Iraqi police have been unable or unwilling to stop such infiltration and continuing violence. The Iraqi Army has provided only two out of the six battalions that it promised in August would join American forces in Baghdad. The Iraqi government has rejected sustained security operations in Sadr City. Security efforts will fail unless the Iraqis have both the capability to hold areas that have been cleared and the will to clear neighborhoods that are home to Shiite militias.

Among the several recommendations of the report was the clear indication that "changes in course must be made both outside and inside Iraq."[18] It also noted that "the United States should significantly increase the number of U.S. military personnel, including combat troops, imbedded in and supporting Iraqi Army units. As these actions proceed, we could begin to move combat forces out of Iraq."[19]

Changing Strategy during Combat

The challenges in Iraq are complex. Violence is increasing in scope and lethality. It is fed by a Sunni Arab insurgency, Shiite militias and death squads, al Qaeda, and widespread criminality. Sectarian conflict is the principal challenge to stability. The Iraqi people have a democratically elected government, yet it is not adequately advancing national reconciliation, providing basic security, or delivering essential services. Pessimism is pervasive.

—THE IRAQ STUDY GROUP REPORT[20]

When it was conceived in the summer of 2004, the "Casey Strategy" of building Iraqi Security Forces had one extremely weak assumption: that the host nation security forces could be developed and trained for combat in a relatively short time, based upon the existence of an old Ba'athist army and security force structure. This assumption was not just weak, it was in fact fundamentally flawed because of two linked and critically important misconceptions about security in Iraq. The first misconception was that the Iraqi police were relatively professional and semi-independent of the army, so that they could be rapidly rebuilt after de-Ba'athification was completed. In fact, the

Iraqi police under Saddam Hussein were rarely well trained and commonly held in low regard by the population.

The second misconception was that the Iraqi army was demobilized but available for recall, and that once recalled it would consist of cohesive units independent of government influence. A professional army in the American sense was a very different thing than the force that had previously existed in Iraq. If only these two factors had been at work the Casey Strategy may have begun to bear fruit by late 2006. General Casey in fact was correct, from his frame of reference, to argue against more forces and for the continuation of his strategy to allow it the time to mature. Unfortunately, once the Samarra bombing unleashed the powerful elements of sectarian division that had been dormant in Iraq for years, the minimal conditions required for the near-term success of the Casey Strategy were no longer attainable.

Magnifying the depth of the shortfall in capacity was the unforeseen eventuality that the Iraqi government (at least the government of Prime Minister Maliki) would not be a willing or able to partner in the conduct of counter-terrorism and counterinsurgency operations during 2006. The failure of Operations Together Forward and Together Forward II demonstrated convincingly that the Iraqis were unwilling and unable to work in the development of their own national security.

Another Strong Current: Change in Ramadi

The two battles for Fallujah in 2004 had driven Al Qaeda in Iraq from that city. But even though certain sheikhs and imams within the Iraqi resistance begin backing the political process after the re-opening of Fallujah, AQ-I simply shifted its emphasis to the neighboring provincial capital of Ramadi, which it came to call "The Capital of the Islamic State of Iraq."[21] AQ-I could offer money and jobs, social mobility, and an ideological appeal—jihad against the infidel to potential supporters—whereas the national government in Baghdad was offering nothing to Al Anbar province. Plus, sectarianism allowed AQ-I a role as the protector of the Sunnis in a new Iraq that seemed dominated by Shiites.

Continued violence in Ramadi, a city whose mostly Sunni citizens had always been hostile to the coalition and had refused to vote in the January 2005 national elections, pushed Al Anbar province nearly into the category of "the impossible win." Marine intelligence analysis repeatedly said that the coalition effort was untenable in Al Anbar—yet, in 2006 even that extreme prognosis began to be reversed, unexpectedly and from a surprising direction.

In a classic example for any future insurgency effort, the horrific acts of AQ-I in Ramadi and other areas inside Iraq began to exceed even the extremely high tolerance of Iraqis who had become nearly immune to pain by years of repression. There had been an attempt at reconciliation in late 2005; in November a conference with the resistance was held that offered government support for tribes that worked with the new government, and elements of the Al Anbar resistance did work to secure the December 2005 elections. In retaliation AQ-I killed many of the key leaders of the tribes that had attended the conference over the following three months and punished anyone found to be cooperating with the government or the coalition. By the early spring tolerance for AQ-I in Ramadi had lessened significantly.

"It is true that al-Qaeda has become unwelcome in the city," a leading Ramadi sheikh said in February 2006.[22] "Al-Qaeda still insists that it is justifiable to kill any Iraqi linked to the Government, including local Sunni policemen, an ideology increasingly rejected by local residents who want a stronger Sunni representation in the security forces." The previous month, an AQ-I suicide bomber stepped into the line during a recruiting drive for Iraqi police at the only industrial site in the city, a glass factory, killing more than fifty people and wounding at least sixty more. Al Qaeda was immediately condemned by Sheikh al-Miklif, whose tribe comprises 40 percent of the provincial population around Ramadi and which stood to gain the most from the jobs that had been made available. Abu Musab al-Zarqawi was still the leader of AQ-I, but he was losing popularity in the only area of Iraq he seemed to rule. "There is a hatred for Zarqawi in Ramadi now," a resident said. "People are exhausted by what he has done. Six months ago he was still accepted, though not 100 percent. Now we see him continue to target locals and their sons and kill our leaders, and we reject him totally."

Kenneth Katzman of the Congressional Research Service wrote of this period:

> Other Iraqi Sunnis resented AQ-I practices in the regions where AQ-I fighters congregated, including reported enforcement of strict Islamic law, segregation by sex, forcing males to wear beards, and banning all alcohol sales and consumption. In some cases, according to a variety of press reports, AQ-I fighters killed Iraqi Sunnis found violating these strictures. Some interpret the resentment among Iraqi Sunnis as economic—that the constant fighting in the Sunni areas had shut down almost all commerce and deprived Iraqi Sunnis of their livelihoods. Others believe that the strains between AQ-I and Iraqi Sunni insurgent fighters were a competition for power and control over the insurgency. According to this view, Iraqi Sunni leaders no more wanted to be dominated by foreign Sunnis than they did by Iraqi Shiites or U.S. soldiers. During 2003–2006 these strains

were mostly muted as Iraqi Sunnis cooperated with AQ-I toward the broader goal of overturning the Shiite-dominated, U.S.-backed power structure in Iraq. The first evidence of strains between AQ-I and Iraqi Sunni insurgents emerged in May 2005 in the form of a reported battle between AQ-I fighters and Iraqi Sunni tribal militiamen in the western town of Husaybah. Still, U.S. commanders had not, at this point, articulated or developed a successful strategy to exploit this rift, and Zarqawi was temporarily successful in countering the strains developing between AQ-I and the Iraqi Sunni political and insurgent structures. In January 2006, AQ-I announced formation of the "Mujahidin Shura Council"—an umbrella organization of six groups including AQ-I and five Iraqi Sunni insurgent groups, mostly those with an Islamist ideology. Forming the Shura Council appeared to many to be an attempt by AQ-I to demonstrate that it was working cooperatively with its Iraqi Sunni hosts and not seeking their subordination. To further this impression, in April 2006, the Council announced that an Iraqi, Abdullah Rashid (aka Abu Umar) al-Baghdadi, had been appointed its leader, although there were doubts as to Baghdadi's true identity. Iraqi Sunni insurgent groups dominated by ex-Baath Party and ex-Saddam era military members apparently did not join the Mujahidin Shura. AQ-I continued to operate under the Mujahidin Shura umbrella at least until Zarqawi's death.[23]

I MEF and its commander, Major General Richard Zilmer, developed a plan for another major operation during April and May, and the American brigade in Ramadi surrounded the city with checkpoints, but the main part of the operation was delayed until the new Maliki government was formed in late May. Progress in security was still tied to political progress. Throughout the spring, the new commander in the Ramadi area, Army Colonel Sean MacFarland of the 1st Brigade, 1st Armored Division, conducted increasingly aggressive operations in the city, aided by growing support from locals. In June his brigade conducted operations to clear neighborhoods in the city and then to establish outposts in order to hold the ground taken from AQ-I. His operations were so successful that the insurgents temporarily halted their attacks, but they soon resumed them again. MacFarland continued his efforts, working methodically through the city, neighborhood by neighborhood, but even by August he seemed to have made little tangible progress.

A Local Reassessment

The bombing of the Golden Mosque in Samarra the previous February and the severe sectarian fighting that followed that attack caused many Iraqis living in Al Anbar province to consider civil war in their country likely for the first time.[24] As 2006 progressed, Sunnis all over central Iraq suffered under more and more attacks, until they began to realize that they could not defeat both their own Shia countrymen (nor deny them the support they were receiving from Iran) as well as the coalition, even if they remained aligned with Al Qaeda.

With the U.S. public seemingly demanding an American withdrawal of forces, they were soon confronted with an even more stark reality—they would be decisively defeated in any future civil war without the moderating presence of the coalition forces. So, over the summer three rural tribes outside Ramadi started to back the fledgling Iraqi police. And eventually, Sheikh Abdul Sittar Eftikhan al-Rishawi ad-Dulaimi of the influential Abu Risha tribe publicly switched sides and began to work with the new Iraqi government forces and the coalition. While it is true that he was likely profiting from the black market, and that some of his tribesmen had certainly been active insurgents, Sheikh Sittar had grown so angry at AQ-I that he began to pressure other tribal leaders to change sides as well.

Then in August another local sheikh named Khalid Illiyawi was killed by AQ-I, which refused to return his body in time for a proper Muslim burial—an unforgivable insult. That act seemed to tip the balance, pushing even more local tribal leaders off the fence and against AQ-I. The following month, twenty-three Sunni tribal leaders in Al Anbar, led by Sheikh Sittar, formed an Anbar Salvation Council.

> As al-Qaeda's fighters tightened their grip on Ramadi, they became increasingly repressive and challenged the tribal leaders' power. Soon they were kidnapping and beheading innocent people as part of a campaign of extortion and intimidation. Some sheikhs fled to Jordan and Syria. Sheikh Sittar's father and three brothers were killed, his father during the holy month of Ramadan, and he says he has himself survived several kidnap attempts. This summer a fellow sheikh was ambushed and beheaded by al-Qaeda supporters, who piled insult on injury by keeping his body so it could not be buried immediately, as demanded by custom. "We began to see what they were actually doing in Anbar province. They were not respecting us or honouring us in any way," said Sheikh Sittar, speaking through an interpreter. "Their tactics were not acceptable." During the late

summer he began enlisting his fellow sheikhs in a movement called the Sahawat or Awakening, whose goal is to drive al-Qaeda from Anbar province.[25]

The Salvation Council recruited some thirteen thousand young Sunnis from around Al Anbar province to help provide security in Ramadi, Fallujah, and other provincial cities. Sittar told an American reporter, "They brought us nothing but destruction and we finally said, enough is enough."[26] The coalition leaders in Al Anbar understood the potential of the Salvation Council and they committed to additional work projects that gave tribal leaders the ability to offer patronage and salaries to fence-sitters that could offset financial offers from AQ-I. Over the fall and winter months the Awakening movement gained even more adherents and started to give AQ-I real competition for dominance in several locales.

Some twenty insurgent leaders were killed by tribesmen through the fall months; AQ-I was struggling to maintain dominance against the growing tribal security movement as 2006 drew to a close. Then, on November 25, some three dozen members of AQ-I attacked the small Albu Soda tribe living on the outskirts of Ramadi in an area known as Sufia, on the road between Ramadi and Fallujah. The tribe had not joined the Awakening, preferring instead to maintain neutral; but even neutrality angered AQ-I and it attacked the tribe fiercely in retaliation. Members of the tribe notified a local Iraqi army unit of the attack, the Iraqi unit notified Colonel MacFarland, and he changed the orders of one of his battalions directing it to immediately join in the defense of the Albu Soda tribe.[27] Once the American forces helped repulse the attack the Albu Soda tribe flipped completely to support the coalition. "It was like liberated France," said MacFarland, and tips began to flow in and the streets of Ramadi opened up for the MNF-I forces.[28]

By the end of the year, the security situation in Al Anbar province had shifted in obvious ways toward the coalition. The Iraqi government demonstrated it was willing to give tribes greater power and allow maintain tribal access to the black market; Baghdad even permitted the Al Anbar tribal leaders to control the local police, and the emergency response unit created in Ramadi. With the arrival of a new Fallujah police chief, Colonel Faysal, AQ-I intimidation within that city diminished significantly. Finally, late in the year the Albu Issa tribe began to actively fight AQ-I. "Sheikh Sittar and U.S. commanders believe that the tide is turning in their favour. 'Most of the people are now convinced that coalition forces are friends, and that the enemy is al-Qaeda,' the 35-year-old Sheikh claimed in his first face-to-face interview with a Western newspaper. . . . 'Al-Qaeda is now on the run,' said the local coalition commander, Colonel Sean MacFarland."[29] The tribes had rejected their former alliance with AQ-I and had switched sides to become the "counterinsurgency overseers" in Al Anbar province.

Insufficient Progress

Even with the changes in the security situation in Al Anbar province in late 2006, the overall situation in Iraq was probably worse than it had been at the beginning of the year. The level of violence and the lack of neighborhood security in Baghdad were particularly significant. The benchmark of the Casey Strategy—the development of the Iraqi army—was also doubtful at best. *The Iraq Study Report* noted,

> By the end of 2006, the Iraqi Army is expected to comprise 118 battalions formed into 36 brigades under the command of 10 divisions. Although the Army is one of the more professional Iraqi institutions, its performance has been uneven. The training numbers are impressive, but they represent only part of the story. Significant questions remain about the ethnic composition and loyalties of some Iraqi units—specifically, whether they will carry out missions on behalf of national goals instead of a sectarian agenda. Of Iraq's 10 planned divisions, those that are even-numbered are made up of Iraqis who signed up to serve in a specific area, and they have been reluctant to redeploy to other areas of the country. As a result, elements of the Army have refused to carry out missions.[30]

The report went on to list a number of other important shortfalls, including lack of leadership, equipment, personnel, and logistics support.

Perhaps even more significantly, the Iraqi government was still driven by sectarian agendas, characterized by inefficiency and dominated by Shia officials whose loyalties to the new Iraq seemed to be less strong than their devotion to other, often tribal interests. As a result the Iraqi government was "not effectively providing its people with basic services: electricity, drinking water, sewage, health care, and education."[31] In many sectors of the Iraqi economy, production in late 2006 was below prewar levels, and in Baghdad the situation was even worse. It was an untenable situation during a still-active insurgency.

Forcing Change

In late 2006, General Casey was doing his level best to execute his 2004 military strategy in Iraq, which was based upon recoiling coalition force units into ever fewer U.S.-run bases while building capacity within the Iraqi Security

Forces. At the time, however, popular opinion in the United States about the conduct of the was changing in a way that had a profound effect on oper-ations in Iraq. In part this change was due to the casualty rate among U.S. forces in Iraq, which was rising steadily in the fall of 2006. October of that year was in fact the sixth deadliest month of the war, with 106 American lives lost in combat. "Total attacks in October 2006 averaged 180 per day, up from 70 per day in January 2006. Daily attacks against Iraqi security forces in October were more than double the level in January. Attacks against civil-ians in October were four times higher than in January. Some 3,000 Iraqi civilians were killed every month."[32] To most Americans the cost of the war—especially the human cost—was exceeding the gains being made. It seemed that even after the death of terrorist leader Zarqawi in June 2006, the sectarian violence he had stoked with the bombing of the Golden Mosque in Samarra the previous February was steadily escalating, to the point that the government in Baghdad could do little to stop it. Calls for the ouster of Secretary of Defense Rumsfeld had begun to be voiced around Washington as early as the previous April.[33]

The U.S. military was not unaware of these anxieties. As a proactive organization, the Joint Chiefs of Staff in the Pentagon under the hand of its chairman, Marine General Pete Pace, began to study alternate strategies for the Iraq campaign in the summer of 2006. That effort gained new immedi-acy when General Casey came to realize that he could not reduce the force in Iraq down to twelve brigade equivalents given the widespread civil unrest evident in Iraq.

The Chairman of the Joint Chiefs of Staff, Marine General Pete Pace directed a strategy review inside the Pentagon in order to ensure that he could provide the president with the best possible military advice for dealing with the situation in Iraq. Pace was a full participant in the executive office's deliberations on Iraq and was well trusted by the president—Pace felt that he could effectively bridge the gap between the military, with its concerns about the conduct and course of the war, and the White House, which had to address other issues in addition to or in conjunction with those of the military. Pace noted that:

> We started out . . . wanting to have three separate groups working on the problem: General Petraeus and his team in Baghdad, whose focus and view, properly so, was on what was best for the way forward in Iraq; Admiral Fallon and his team in both Tampa and Qatar, whose focus and attention are properly focused on his region, to include Afghanistan and Djibouti and other places; and the six joint chiefs here in D.C., who were helped by a bevy of really smart colonels and

captains, whose responsibility is not only to ensure that the resources for the Central Command region were provided, but also to ensure that we were properly positioned should something else happen in the world that military force would be needed for. And we did that for several months, knowing that each was working on the problem, but not sharing our ideas so we would not get into some kind of a group-think as we were going through the options. We went through at the joint staff level about nine different options, to include everything from plusing-up, to maintaining the current status through as long as we could see into the future, to things like going out to the borders and letting the Iraqis take care of the center. . . . And then around the middle of August, General Petraeus briefed the Joint Chiefs and Admiral Fallon, Admiral Fallon briefed General Petraeus and the Joint Chiefs, and the Joint Chiefs briefed Admiral Fallon and General Petraeus, so we could all understand from each other how we saw the current situation and the way forward. Not surprisingly, we all saw the situation very much the same. So what the secretary said about unanimity amongst the eight four-star officers—General Petraeus, Admiral Fallon and the six Joint Chiefs of Staff—is absolutely accurate.[34]

As the active-duty military was conducting its multi-prong review of strategy, retired army General Jack Keane, a confidant and mentor of General Petraeus, was also staying involved. Keane had been the Army vice chief of staff and the acting service chief in the first year of the war. Since his retirement in 2003, he had remained a strong behind-the-scenes supporter of the officers (including Petraeus) he had developed in his career. Because he had been the army's number two officer when General Pace had served as the vice chairman, the two men knew and trusted each other well. In August 2006, General Keane decided that the path that the United States was taking in Iraq was not going to be successful.[35] Instead of going fishing, or writing editorials, he decided to act.

As the interim congressional elections neared in November, President Bush was hard pressed to show progress or to bolster the free-fall of public opinion toward his administration. Many were speaking out for a change— prominent among them was Republican Senator John McCain, who along with Democratic Senator Joe Lieberman visited Iraq over the Thanksgiving holiday period in November 2006.

The November congressional elections in 2006 were a disaster for the Bush administration, bringing in a new Democratic majority in both houses of Congress and serving as a referendum on the war. Unbeknownst to the

American people, Secretary Rumsfeld had submitted his resignation the day prior to the elections, with the congressional defeat obvious, and the president formally and publicly accepted Rumsfeld's resignation the day after the results of the election were announced, naming former deputy director of the CIA Robert Gates as the new defense secretary. Not only had Gates been deputy national security advisor for Bush's father during the Gulf War, he had more recently served as a member of the Iraq Study Group,[36] which had sought new ways of enhancing security in Iraq—he was well informed on matters of strategy and was a skilled decision maker.

With a new defense secretary at the helm in the Pentagon,[37] and Democrats in the House of Representatives clamoring for an end to funding for the war, in late November the president began a fairly open-minded search for new options in Iraq. He met with key members of the diplomatic corps at the State Department, as well as with a group of "Iraq experts" that included generals and historians on December 11; two days later he met with the members of the Joint Chiefs of Staff in the Pentagon. This Pentagon meeting "in the tank" with the Joint Chiefs of Staff revealed a decidedly negative mood among the military senior leadership of the United States.[38]

In his book *The War Within*, Bob Woodward later described how the meeting with the Joint Chiefs revealed that a rift had grown between the White House and the Pentagon over the war's strategy.[39] Essentially, the chiefs of the four military armed services had balked at the idea of increasing force levels in Iraq. They were paid to maintain their forces; therefore their counsel to the president had more to do with organizational health than it did with winning the war in Iraq. The chiefs felt that those proposals should come from the combatant commander and General Casey, so they felt fully justified in arguing against a "surge."[40]

The following day, December 12, yet another report on Iraq, by the American Enterprise Institute (AEI), was released by its authors, Frederick Kagan, Kenneth Pollack, and General Keane. Noteworthy among the many more pessimistic reports on the conflict, the AEI report called for a change in military strategy in Iraq, observing that "the basis of the Abizaid-Casey strategy is twofold: American forces in Iraq are an irritant and generate insurgents who want to drive us out of their country, and the Iraqis must be able to create and maintain their own stability lest they become permanently dependent on our military presence. Both of these arguments contain elements of truth, but realities in Iraq are much more complex." The AEI report specifically recommended a large and sustained surge of U.S. forces to secure and protect critical areas of Baghdad.[41]

The report and its recommendation were highly controversial. At a time when most Americans were looking for a way to end the conflict, and when the Congress appeared adamant that funding for the war was to be curtailed significantly, the AEI report described an increase in military forces in Iraq—seemingly running completely counter to the idea that America needed to shift the burden of combat onto the Iraqi forces. The report was lucid and persuasive, but if the president was to consider its adoption, he had not only to face the inevitable criticism of those who understood that increasing forces would increase casualties (at least in the short term), he also had to admit that the strategy he had so strongly advocated over the previous twenty-four months would not bring the desired result. It was a decision requiring significant moral fiber and risked a great deal of political capital.

Strategy Culmination: The Loss of Presidential Confidence

Although there were expectations that President Bush would announce a change in the Iraq strategy in December 2006, he did not make a formal announcement until January 10, 2007. In a speech to the nation from the White House, President Bush outlined the four key components of "The New Way Forward in Iraq."[42] Underlying these components was a continuation of the policy to "let the Iraqis lead," but also the decision that there would be a new effort to put down sectarian violence and bring security to the people of Baghdad. During his speech, the president announced the deployment of "more than twenty thousand additional American troops to Iraq." It was clear that President Bush had actually made the decision and had directed the Pentagon to execute the plan at an earlier date. The delay over the first days of the year had enabled the advanced deployment of troops of the 82nd Airborne Division, who were already arriving in Baghdad as the president spoke.

This decision to increase the troop level in Iraq was both historic and courageous. With his administration losing support and the ability to influence the public debate on the war, President Bush chose to commit more forces, and likely suffer more casualties, in order to achieve decisive victory in Iraq. Most Americans at the time expected the administration to back out of Iraq on a specific timeline, or to simply declare that its major objectives had been accomplished and depart without regard to the conditions on the ground. (All of the four key objectives announced for the war could have been justified at the time. Iraq had a weak but functioning democratic government, reasonably secure borders; and was a single, unitary state that could defend itself from external aggression.) But President Bush chose the more difficult route. Shortly thereafter he dispatched a new "command team" to Iraq, installing Ryan Crocker as ambassador and General David Petraeus as commander of MNF-I.

The Crucial Month: December 2006

The month of December brought more than just the president's decision to change the strategy in Iraq. It was perhaps the most momentous if least-heralded month of the long war. In Iraq, General Odierno concluded that General Casey's strategy would not produce victory, and he therefore decided, at the risk of his career, to engender support for the changed operational approach. On December 16, 2006, the counterinsurgency doctrine manual that Generals Petraeus and Mattis had labored so long and so well to produce, FM 3-34, was finally published, giving the entire U.S. military a new playbook for counterinsurgency operations and validating what many younger officers were discovering, mistake by mistake, at the tactical level in Iraq.

According to General Odierno, on December 19 "the coalition captured some mid-level al-Qaeda leaders just north of Baghdad. Upon them was a map that clearly depicted al-Qaeda's strategy for the total and unyielding dominance of Baghdad, betting that control of Iraq's capital and its millions of citizens would give them free rein to export their twisted ideology and terror. Indeed, al-Qaeda did operate with impunity in several areas surrounding the capital that we call the 'Baghdad Belts,' using these sanctuaries to introduce accelerants of violence. This strategy was similar to the way in which Saddam Hussein employed his elite Republican Guard forces to control the city. It was clear to us that Coalition forces would need to clear AQI from these belts and deny these enemies safe havens in order to control Baghdad."[43] The map and the importance of the "Baghdad Belts" became key to the new operational concept General Odierno was developing with his staff.

The new secretary of defense also took a much more aggressive stance than anyone expected in December 2006, and traveled to Iraq in the first days of his term in office. During a visit to Baghdad on December 20, Secretary Gates met with Iraqi Minister of Defense Abdul Qadir along with Generals Pace, Abizaid, and Casey to discuss the way ahead in Iraq. Then—finally—on the next to last day of the year, Saddam Hussein mounted the gallows where he had sent so many others to die and was hung. 2007 would be a very different year.

Chapter 11

THE PROTECTION STRATEGY AND THE 2007 BAGHDAD SURGE

No military operation by itself can resolve Iraq's problems. Success in Iraq can only emerge when political, economic, diplomatic, and reconciliation initiatives resolve underlying tensions and grievances and give the Iraqi people reason to accept the legitimacy of their government. The security situation in Iraq and particularly Baghdad is so grave, however, that political, economic, diplomatic, and reconciliation initiatives will fail unless a well-conceived and properly supported military operation secures the population first and quickly.

—Frederick W. Kagan, "Choosing Victory"[1]

One of the most noteworthy and far-reaching acts of the war was the 2007 decision by President Bush to change the national strategy in Iraq; a decision that came to be exemplified by the "surge," a reinforcement of the American forces in the country, when many thought the war all but lost. The decision was a difficult one to make, but once it was taken and implemented, the MNF-I forces in Iraq responded rapidly and decisively, with positive results. It is important to understand that the surge was in fact a complex process that integrated three distinct efforts into a single transformational undertaking.

First, the surge entailed change at the tactical level, on the part of coalition units engaged in combat all over Iraq: henceforth the emphasis was on protecting the Iraqi people, or "securing the population." This aspect of the surge had long been a feature of counterinsurgency theory, and had already been instituted as a common practice at the tactical level in a few places in Iraq as early as 2004; but it was not widely recognized as a primary objective of conventional operations until January 2007.[2] In order to achieve this objective, coalition forces were to move off bases and live among the Iraqi people, at least until the security force units in the local area could perform all essential security tasks by themselves. Additionally, in Baghdad barrier walls were erected to isolate and control individual neighborhoods until adjacent zones were secured, whereupon the walls would be removed. Overall, these efforts effectively reversed General Casey's approach, which kept U.S. forces on for-ward operating bases (FOBs), separate and isolated from the local populace.

Second, the surge entailed change at the operational level. Previously, priority had been given to merely training the Iraqi military; now the emphasis was on employing combined Iraqi and coalition forces in operations designed to clean out pockets of insurgent activity, establish enduring security for the local populace, protect key infrastructure, and build prosperity in Iraqi neigh-borhoods. The main effort would be directed at Baghdad and its surrounding "belts," where large-scale combat operations had not been conducted since 2003. The increase in forces was necessitated by the enormous size—and enor-mous population—of Baghdad and its environs.

Change at the strategic level was a third feature of the surge. This entailed the development of a new American national policy concerning Iraq from within the White House. The president of the United States took personal responsibility for altering the effort in Iraq by revealing in a speech to the nation on January 11, 2007, that: "The situation in Iraq is unacceptable to the American people—and it is unacceptable to me. Our troops in Iraq have fought bravely. They have done everything we have asked them to do. Where mistakes have been made, the responsibility rests with me. It is clear that we need to change our strategy in Iraq."[3] He explained how the new strategy would differ from those executed in the past, in particular noting the new emphasis on deploying forces among the Iraqi people. He further explained, "Many listening tonight will ask why this effort will succeed when previous operations to secure Baghdad did not. Well, here are the differences: In earlier operations, Iraqi and American forces cleared many neighborhoods of terror-ists and insurgents—but when our forces moved on to other targets, the kill-ers returned. This time, we will have the force levels we need to hold the areas that have been cleared."[4]

These three efforts together required personal courage and renewed com-mitment nearly five years into the Iraqi Freedom campaign. It is a clear testa-ment to the dedication of America's military personnel and no slight nod to the fortitude of President Bush that the United States was able to make such a significant change in the face of significant dismay about the situation in Iraq among the American people.

Petraeus and Crocker to Baghdad

The Friday prior to the president's announcement, Defense Secretary Robert Gates began to reveal some of the changes that would soon take place in the war by announcing that General Casey would leave his command in Iraq to be nominated to serve as the Chief of Staff of the Army. Lieutenant General

David Petraeus, former commander of the 101st Division and of the Multi-National Security Transition Command-Iraq would be named as Casey's successor in Baghdad.

General Casey had been in command in Iraq since July 2004—nearly thirty months service—when the president announced the change in strategy. Under any circumstances, Casey was due reassignment to the United States, and his performance in Iraq, though criticized by some, had more than justified his continued service on active duty as a general. Though it was time for General Casey to be reassigned, changing command in Iraq became imperative once the president decided on a new strategy that reversed much of what Casey had been saying would work during the previous months. As the Chief of Staff of the Army, Casey would develop the force necessary to continue the work he had been doing in Iraq. Casey's successor in Iraq was well known as both a respected combat leader and a keen intellect who had directed the development of the new counterinsurgency doctrine of the Army and Marine Corps. General Petraeus was also a keen student of General Westmoreland's mistakes in Vietnam, and he would bring amazing new energy and new focus to the operations in Iraq. But he was not the first to start changing approaches in Iraq.

Protection of the Population—The Conversion of Odierno

Even with the increase in the number of brigades serving in Iraq, a significant change in the situation might not have occurred if the attitudes of the senior commanders in Iraq hadn't changed to reflect new priorities and greater effort. General Petraeus brought new focus at the strategic level, and although his influence was clearly felt all the way down to the battalion level, the corps commander in Iraq was actually the coordinator and orchestrator of the operational and tactical actions in the country, and he had to be fully committed to any new strategy for it to succeed. The new multinational corps commander who had just taken charge of operations in Iraq in December 2006 was Lieutenant General Ray Odierno, who had formerly been the commander of the 4th Infantry Division in the Sunni Triangle in 2003.

At the start of Operation Iraqi Freedom in 2003, Odierno's division was to have entered Iraq through Turkey, but after the Turkish Parliament denied the United States the use of its national territory, the division joined the other CFLCC units as a follow-on force in April 2003, moving from Kuwait to attack into the area around Tikrit and Mosul south of the 101st Airborne's area of responsibility. The 4th Infantry Division remained in the Sunni Triangle north of Baghdad for several months, and it was Odierno's troops who captured Saddam Hussein in December 2003.

Even though his division had accomplished a great deal in Iraq, General Odierno had received some important negative comments resulting from the heavy-handed approaches that he had fostered while in command in Iraq.[5] He had followed his first combat tour in Iraq with assignments as the special assistant to vice chief of staff of the Army, and then as assistant to the Chairman of the Joint Chiefs of Staff, where he principally served as the military advisor to Secretary of State Rice. These duties gave him a new perspective on the war. When he took command of III Corps and Fort Hood, Texas, in May 2006, he knew he would assume the responsibilities as the MNC-I commander in Iraq later the same year, so he resolved to study the situation in Iraq and develop a new baseline with his staff for understanding the conflict. After studying the problem, he determined that he would take a very different tack in Iraq, one that he knew would bring him into a bit of conflict with his boss in Iraq, General Casey.

Planning for the Surge

The impact of Odierno's arrival in Baghdad in December 2006 was much more important than anyone believed at the time; after all, several other highly capable corps commanders had preceded him in Iraq and none of them had managed to make a significant difference in the actual prosecution of the war. The difference was that Odierno (who had a reputation for being tactically aggressive) had taken that time to study the actual situation in Iraq for the first forty-five days after his arrival. Many thoughtful strategists subscribe to Clausewitz's dictum that understanding the war one is fighting is a first, fundamental requirement for successful execution, yet few actually study the nature of the conflict that they are dealing with in its early stages, before they become completely absorbed by the chaos of war.[6]

General Casey had tasked Odierno with conducting operations in such a way as to break the cycle of violence then tearing Iraq apart and bring sufficient stability to the country so that the Iraqi government could begin to develop enough political progress to solve Iraq's long-term problems. So, the mission given Odierno and his staff was not new, but it was combined with the idea that he would also have to cut the number of forces in Iraq by as much as one-third.[7] It would have been a challenge for any commander to accomplish Odierno's assigned mission; many had already tried, but to do so with fewer troops than his predecessors would be even more difficult.

Thankfully, in carefully studying conditions in Iraq, Odierno and his staff found a new way of looking at the problem. For Odierno, reducing the violence required more than kinetic attacks on insurgents; he saw that he had to secure the population at the same time if he had any hope of stopping the horrific cycle of attacks and reprisals that were tearing the country apart. His team recognized that although previous efforts to clear Baghdad of insurgents had met with some success, these gains were temporary because the coalition forces were not committed to holding the areas they had cleansed of insurgents; once they departed, the enemy moved right back in to punish the people who had befriended the coalition soldiers.

Unfortunately, holding the key areas in Iraq (including many sectors of Baghdad) would require not only a change in the FOB-based approach then in execution, but would also require many more troops than the number he would inherit when he assumed command, even though everyone in Iraq and even most in the White House had been talking only about troop reductions over the past two years.[8] The Casey troop reduction strategy assigned to Odierno was called the "Bridging Strategy"; some might have called Odierno's new idea a bridge too far, but December 4, 2006, when he was formally briefed on the Casey plan, Odierno was not afraid to do something almost completely different, even if his approach was bound to rankle his boss George Casey.

Odierno still had strong ties back to Washington, including a strong working relationship with retired General Jack Keene, one of his mentors, who had also been working to change the strategy in Iraq, and the two men promoted the then very controversial idea of a force increase in Iraq to a network of people in the U.S. government. When Secretary Gates visited Iraq in December, very soon after taking office, Odierno lobbied him for a troop increase. Gates, who had been a member of the Iraq Study Group commission, also recommended to President Bush that he order a temporary troop increase to help stem the violence. President Bush announced what came to be known as the surge in January 2007 and ordered five additional combat brigades to Iraq.

With tactical commanders already improving their working relationships in Iraq due to their past combat experiences and in accord with the ideas codified in the new FM 3-24; with General Odierno already planning to use more forces; and with General Petraeus on the way to take over the strategic leadership of the war, the conflict turned slowly but decisively in a new direction in the early months of 2007.

2007—Implementing a New Strategy in Iraq

The surge did more than turn around the situation in Iraq—it made possible a major strategic victory in the broader war on terror. For the terrorists, Iraq was supposed to be the place where al Qaeda rallied Iraqis to drive America out. Instead, Iraq became the place where the Iraqis joined forces with America to drive al Qaeda out. As a result, al Qaeda suffered more than a military defeat in Iraq—it suffered an ideological defeat as well. Across the region, people saw that al Qaeda in Iraq could be vanquished, and that a future of terror was not foreordained.

—MARC A. THIESSEN, *A CHARGE KEPT*[9]

On February 10, 2007, General David Petraeus took command of MNF-I from General Casey in the Al Faw Palace in Baghdad. The change of command marked a clear change in both the leadership of the Iraq war and the strategy that would be the driving force behind the coalition effort in Iraq, but change at that level would take time, and had to be based upon Iraqi political improvements in governance as well as tactical efforts to end the insurgency.

General Odierno and his team had already decided that creating stability in Iraq required more than just greater resources; it required a change in mindset. They determined that the coalition forces had to make the protection of the population, creating safe neighborhoods and markets, and allowing Iraqis to go about their daily lives a first priority. They also decided that the coalition needed a more balanced approach in its targeting of extremists, and they were convinced the Iraqi government could no longer give Shiite militia groups the freedom to commit extra-judicial killings.[10] As the additional brigades began to arrive in the first months of 2007, the coalition forces also began moving off large bases and into small outposts in population centers all across Iraq, but especially in and around Baghdad.

During a series of early offensives commanded by Odierno, MNC-I forces also renewed the emphasis on providing essential services, encouraging local governance, and separating the "irreconcilables" from those willing to make peace with the legitimate government of Iraq. While conducting these initial operations, General Odierno also worked to deepen the growing alliances with groups of "concerned local citizens" that had agreed to work with his forces to bring security to their neighborhoods. The "Awakening" started in Al Anbar province in 2007 and began to spread across much of the country. Many of who took part in the Awakening were former insurgents who had rejected the program of violence and chaos wrought by AQ-I and decided instead to support the new Iraqi government. Later they came to be known as "Sons of Iraq."

February—Operation Fardh al-Qanoon

Operation Fardh al-Qanoon, or Enforcing the Law, began on February 13, 2007. Fardh al-Qanoon was significantly different in concept than either Together Forward I or Together Forward II of the previous year insofar as it reflected the new emphasis on security for the people identified by General Odierno's study the preceding winter. It also took advantage of the Major General Joseph Fil's 1st Cavalry Division being on its second tour in Iraq, this time as the head-quarters for MND-B, where almost all of the commanders were veterans of previous combat in Iraq. Fardh al-Qanoon featured troops living in the neighborhoods, interacting with residents, and gaining real human intelligence about the insurgent threat. MNC-I forces moved out of their forward operating bases (FOBs) in and around Baghdad, into smaller joint security stations (JSSs) and combat outposts (COPs) located in every neighborhood covered by the operation. In the combat outposts, coalition forces, Iraqi police, and units of the Iraqi army shared the same living conditions and worked together to execute better coordinated security operations.

During Fardh al-Qanoon, the "clear, hold, and build" strategy of 2005 and 2006 was replaced with a new "clear, control, and retain" strategy. This new strategy focused on controlling and retaining neighborhoods to provide real, lasting security for the population and also to prevent enemy re-infiltration into the neighborhoods cleared. Once safe, those neighborhoods were turned over to Iraqi forces, which were augmented by embedded American advisory teams, and the American combat units were shifted to overwatch positions. The new Fardh al-Qanoon approach also placed greater emphasis on rebuilding essential services and on long-term investment in neighborhoods and their supporting political and economic institution, than had been done in the past. Perhaps most significantly, since Prime Minister Maliki had been converted to the idea that the militias were a major threat, during Fardh al-Qanoon coalition forces conducted operations against extremist elements inside the Shia-dominated Sadr City area of Baghdad, which had previously been forbidden territory—a status that had contributed to the failure of the 2006 operations in Baghdad.

The first of the surge brigades arrived in Baghdad in February 2007 at the start of Operation Fardh al-Qanoon. That same month, additional U.S. and Iraqi forces were shifted into Baghdad from other towns in Iraq. Eventually, seven U.S. combat brigades conducted operations as part of the Multi-National Division-Baghdad (MND-B) during Fardh al-Qanoon. Once deployed into the city, individual U.S. battalions were paired with Iraqi brigades and assigned to work together within a structure of ten districts spanning Baghdad. The deployment of all these forces in the core of Iraq caused new command structures to be developed. Prime Minister Maliki had previously designated Iraqi Lieutenant General Abboud Qanbar to coordinate all Iraqi army activity in the capital. Assigned two him were to major generals who commanded Iraqi forces in the eastern and western sides of the Tigris River, which divided the city. The Karkh Area Command controlled the western half of the city and the Rusafa Area Command controlled the eastern half. General Odierno also created an additional division headquarters for command and control purposes: Multi-National Division-Center (MND-C) under the command of Major General Rick Lynch of the 3rd Infantry Division. These changes established a new, more complex, but better-integrated command structure for military operations in and around Baghdad.

Strategic Design

General Petraeus knew well that General Creighton Abrams had orchestrated a far-reaching survey of operations in Vietnam before taking command in Saigon from General Westmoreland on June 10, 1968, and he elected to do the same thing by creating the Joint Strategic Assessment Team (JSAT) in Iraq under the direction of Colonel H. R. McMaster, the former commander in Tal Afar, and including many of the same experts that had worked together to write FM 3-24 the previous year.[11] McMaster and the JSAT studied the Iraq problem for three months, delivering a full recommendation to the MNF-I commander in April 2007; that recommendation would be the primary guide for the development of a new joint campaign plan which would be drafted and approved by both General Petraeus and Ambassador Crocker in late July.

Meanwhile, Petraeus had to make some initial prioritization decisions so that General Odierno at MNC-I could maintain momentum against the insurgency and employ the arriving additional brigades to best effect. Essentially, he had to determine how much of his available military power he should devote to killing insurgents and how much to protecting the population; those two things did not always coincide. Specifically, General Petraeus had to determine how to weight the military effort in Iraq against three geographically divergent objectives: the special operation– dominated counterterrorism effort against AQ-I (which had shifted its activities to Baqubah after being run out of Ramadi), the conventional force effort to control Baghdad, and the conventional force effort to control the borders of Iraq against insurgent support from Syria and Iran.[12] Adding to the complexity of the problem was General Odierno's discovery that controlling the belts around Baghdad was also crucial to the success of any effort to control the city; that added geography would require additional units in order to develop better security in the huge central region around the city of six million inhabitants.[13]

The MNF-I commander eventually supported a main effort against Baghdad and the belts around the city that would become the central offensive of the new campaign. It would eventually take some twenty-eight battalions to secure the population of the city itself, and another twenty-six battalions to conduct clearing operations through the surrounding belts.[14]

Meanwhile, an assessment of the new, ever-expanding Iraqi army made it clear that mentoring the mid- and higher-level Iraqi unit commanders would be an important prerequisite for conducting the kinds of operations required under the new FM 3-24 approach. All armies can benefit from command mentoring, but in particular the Iraqi army was creating so many new units and new headquarters to manage them, that Iraqi military leaders were being promoted faster than their experience was preparing them to lead. Operation Fardh al-Qanoon, already under way, demonstrated the shortfalls in senior Iraqi command and control and military leadership, but new embedded U.S. military advisory teams that worked alongside Iraqi commanders and helped tie together the Iraqi and U.S. portions of any operation were a key improvement for future operations.

The New Command Team in Iraq

The arrival of General Petraeus reset the strategic military approach of the coalition in Iraq, but it was less than half of the change needed at the national level if the new strategy was to have longstanding results. General Petraeus knew well that his relationship with the new ambassador in Iraq and their collective relationship with Prime Minister Maliki would be crucial to sealing the success of any operational leverage that General Odierno might be able to develop in the aftermath of Fardh al-Qanoon. Luckily, the new ambassador, Ryan Crocker, was an old Middle East hand and probably the finest choice for the position. Crocker had served in four other Middle Eastern posts as ambassador (Lebanon, Kuwait, Syria, and, most recently, Pakistan); he had worked as a member of the Future of Iraq Project back in 2002, and had served as the deputy assistant secretary of state in the Near East Bureau before being assigned to Islamabad. Indicative of his energy, once named to the post in Baghdad, Crocker flew directly to Iraq, before even being ceremonially sworn in by Secretary Rice in Washington.[15]

Once Ambassador Crocker arrived on March 29, he and General Petraeus determined to act always as a team—particularly when meeting with Prime Minister Maliki.[16] The two American leaders were different temperamentally, but they shared many interests, most of all a fierce commitment to finding solutions for the problems in Iraq. The two worked out of offices located side-by-side in the Al Faw Palace and would redesign the new U.S. embassy facility to do so there as well. Crocker reached out to the best and brightest Middle East hands at the State Department to form his senior leadership team (including former Ambassadors Pat Butenis, Marcie Ries, and Charlie Ries);,and many of them attended the daily MNF-I update briefs to ensure that both the political and military sides of every problem were considered.[17]

General Petraeus understood full well that doing his job effectively required political improvement in Iraq; indeed many of the key benchmarks that would be used over the coming year to judge success in the war were strictly in the Iraqi domestic arena and almost completely out of his direct control.[18] Still, he was determined to work as seamlessly as possible with Crocker to inspire and push the Iraqi government for needed reforms and domestic quality-of-life improvements.

Unfortunately, Prime Minister Maliki was focused in the early months of 2007 on a very different agenda. His government was fraught with divisions and infiltrated with members who were far from cooperative; plus it faced a massive number of issues for which there was little consensus. As a former long-time Iraqi exile and manager of guerilla movements against Saddam, he was secretive and ever wary of threats—particularly from other groups inside Iraq. General Petraeus had cajoled him into visiting Ramadi for the first time ever in March to show him the progress Sunni Iraqis were making, but it took a significant effort by Petraeus and Crocker to show him that "interfering" in the military chain of command and turning a blind eye to efforts by Muqtada al-Sadr and even the Iranians in Iraq were extremely counterproductive to developing a unity government for all Iraqis. It was only after two highly successful special forces raids in Iraq in March revealed the depth of Iranian meddling in Iraq and the specific involvement of Hezbollah personnel and Iranian Revolutionary Guard al-Quds Force support in Iraq that Prime Minister Maliki saw the threat posed by some of his associates.[19]

June—Operation Phantom Thunder

A series of operations under the overarching title of Phantom Thunder was launched on June 16. Phantom Thunder demonstrated the first full employment of *all of* the surge forces newly arrived in Iraq and also marked the combat debut of the new MNF-I team of Petraeus and Crocker. The operation was designed to protect the Iraqi people, ease reconciliation among the religious sects, defeat AQ-I and other extremists, and continue to develop the Iraqi Security Forces.

South of Baghdad, Multi-National Division-Center, which had been created specifically for the operation, employed four brigade combat teams, including the 2nd Brigade of the 3rd Infantry Division, in clearing enemy safe havens along the Tigris River near Arab Jabour. This area was known for producing car and truck bombs, and had not seen coalition forces in nearly three years. On the east side of the Tigris River, the 3rd Infantry Division's 3rd Brigade simultaneously conducted clearing operations in the vicinity of Salman Pak while blocking enemy movement into Baghdad and Baquba.

At the same time that all five brigade combat teams from Multi-National Division-Baghdad were operating inside Baghdad a sixth brigade combat team was operating in Taji, north of the city to seal off a major insurgent exit route. The focus of all these operations was clearing the Baghdad districts of Adhamiya, Rashid, and Mansour, where sectarian fault lines existed and where most of the violence inside the city had taken place. The initial results of these linked operations inside Baghdad were mixed—some districts showed progress while others remained violence-prone—but progress was evident.

In Multi-National Division-North, three brigade combat teams conducted supporting operations in the north and east of Baghdad, and three more brigade combat teams operated in general support outside the city. The 3rd Brigade, 2nd Stryker Brigade Combat Team began Operation Arrowhead Ripper on June 18 in Baquba, the capital of Diyala province; it was designed to secure the population by conducting clearing operations in that city, known as a hotbed of AQ-I activity. The 4th Brigade, 2nd Stryker Brigade Combat Team fought in the zone between Baghdad and Baquba to destroy known AQ-I operatives and Shiite extremists. By the end of June, over 750 people had been detained, more than 150 insurgents had been killed, and some 125 caches were found; 300 IEDs and 7 VBIEDs (vehicle-borne improvised explosive devices) were neutralized.[20]

Each of the two initial offensives in 2007—collectively, the first major effort to secure both Baghdad and its belts—showed flaws in the coalition's approach, but also demonstrated that slow progress was being made. In the two follow-on operations conducted later the same year, the deficiencies were corrected and obvious momentum began to build. The third offensive was known as Operation Phantom Strike; it was conducted for several weeks starting in mid-August, with the goal of having coalition and Iraqi forces maintain pressure on AQ-I operatives and other insurgent groups as they were flushed from sanctuaries in the capital. General Odierno's fourth major offensive was labeled Operation Phantom Phoenix; it began just weeks before his departure in February 2008, and was designed to pursue the enemy into Diyala province, provide essential services, and jump-start provincial government improvements in less-contested areas.

"The key to the success of these operations was the combination of breadth and continuity. All of them struck multiple enemy safe havens and lines of communication at the same time—in contrast with previous U.S. military operations that had generally attacked enemy concentrations one at a time. Enemy groups could no longer move easily from one safe area to another and those that tried to move suffered serious losses as they dispersed. The rapid movement from one operation to the next denied the enemy time to regroup.

As scattered insurgent leaders and fighters attempted to reconsolidate in new areas, coalition forces hit them again and again."[21]

Keeping Up the Pressure

The surge also added some four thousand Marines to the fight in Al Anbar province. These additional forces demonstrated renewed commitment to the province and encouraged Sunni Salvation Council members to continue recruiting volunteers to help secure their towns. Added to the effect of new facilities projects and improvements in the local economy, these efforts convinced the residents to increase even further their cooperation with the coalition forces (primarily through revealing insurgents and their safe-houses) in order to help reduce violence. "U.S. commanders even offered a $300–$350 per month wage and additional training to the Sunni volunteers recruited by the Council for security duties. These volunteers came to be known as the 'Sons of Iraq.' By 2008 there are some 75,000 Sunni Sons of Iraq throughout the country."[22]

In June 2007, at the beginning of the surge, General Petraeus had called security improvements in Al Anbar "breathtaking." He and other commanders were able to walk freely in downtown Ramadi, which had been a major battleground only months before. General Petraeus later testified that that Al Anbar province could be turned over to Provincial Iraqi Control by July 2008.[23] The positive trends observed in Al Anbar encouraged other anti–Al Qaeda Sunnis to join the Awakening movement. In May 2007, a Salvation Council of tribal leaders was formed in Diyala province. Beginning in early 2007, the town of Amiriyah was slowly stabilized through the emergence of former Sunni insurgents cooperating with the coalition as a force called the "Amiriyah Freedom Fighters." These fighters claim to have expelled AQ-I from their neighborhoods.

Even neighborhoods in Baghdad began to undergo similar transformations. The employment of the combat outposts and joint security stations in partnership with the ISF, along with a population willing to come forward with information about AQ-I, brought the Iraqi capital to the point where 75 percent of its districts were considered secure in late 2007. Prime Minister Maliki said on February 16, 2008, that AQ-I had been largely driven out of Baghdad.[24]

Results of the Surge

Although the augmentation of the force in Iraq was the centerpiece of the new strategy, it was not the only significant factor in the decisive change in the situation that eventually brought success. The effort in Iraq was conducted both in depth and in breadth and fully engaged both conventional and special operations force activities to produce a synergistic effect on the enemy. As Fred Kagan later wrote,

> Odierno worked with the U.S. Special Operations Forces under the command of Lieutenant General Stan McChrystal to make sure they kept up the pressure on key leaders within the terrorist network. Their precise and skillful attacks not only took out insurgent leaders but also provided valuable additional intelligence that Odierno used to refine his plans. And Odierno's operations to clear and hold key terrain would greatly facilitate the Special Forces' efforts by flushing key enemy leaders out of their safe havens. Odierno's kinetic operations developed a positive synergy with the more traditional counterterrorism approach, making both much more effective than either could have been alone.[25]

This comprehensive approach to counterinsurgency—conducting simultaneous, large-scale operations to strike multiple enemy concentrations and bases of support while continually focusing on protecting the populace and reconciling with those willing to make peace with the government—led to dramatic decreases in attacks through Iraq. In December 2006, coalition forces were sustaining more than 1,200 attacks per week, and the civilian death toll for the month was over 3,000.[26]

By late September 2007, there had been a 50 percent decrease in the number of attacks in Baghdad. The decrease in car bombs, mortar, and rocket attacks was even greater than 50 percent.[27] When Odierno and his team finished their tour in February of 2008, civilian casualties were down 70 percent and attacks on coalition forces had dropped to their lowest levels since 2004. In the Baghdad security districts, specifically, ethno-sectarian attacks and deaths had decreased by 90 percent. The situation in Iraq had been "utterly transformed."[28]

General Petraeus appeared again before four committees of the U.S. Congress on April 8–9, 2008, to discuss progress in Iraq. He testified that the assistance from the Sons of Iraq, coupled with "relentless pursuit" of AQ-I by U.S. forces, had "reduced substantially" the threat posed by AQ-I.[29] Whereas in his testimony the previous September, General Petraeus could only be guardedly optimistic, in April 2008 his outlook was distinctly positive—reflective of the very real progress that had been made against AQ-I and with the Iraqi Security Forces for the Iraqi people.

Iraqi National Politics and the Influence of Iran

In July 2007, General Petraeus and Ambassador Crocker had jointly approved a new Joint Campaign Plan that outlined the fundamentals of cooperation previously demonstrated and designated even greater goals for the forthcoming year. The Joint Campaign Plan emphasized improving governance, spreading the rule of law, and bringing about reconciliation between the various Iraqi factions; it also focused on the longer term. Colonel Steve Boylan, General Petraeus' press advisor, noted, "The campaign is intended to maintain a sustainable security capability throughout Iraq, starting with local security. We are trying to set conditions for them to negotiate a power-sharing agreement where they decide to quit fighting." It also recognized that "with the Washington clock ticking faster than the Baghdad clock, accomplishments in the Iraqi political arena have become the paramount issue. Thus, the main emphasis of this new plan will be along the political line, with supporting efforts in the other three areas."[30]

By the fall of 2007, the military situation in Iraq was showing clear signs of improvement. In his testimony before the U.S. Congress in September, General Petraeus had been very guarded in his optimism,[31] but by November, after Phantom Strike had further improved the security situation, the downward spiral of the previous year had clearly been reversed.[32] Still, a majority of the benchmarks considered by Congress and by many citizens in the United States as the real indications of progress remained largely unfulfilled. In many cases these shortfalls were due to the Iraqi government's failure to act in areas of reconciliation and equity. This increasingly became the focus of effort by the American leadership.

To improve the situation, "Petraeus also challenged the relationship between U.S. leaders in Iraq and their Iraqi counterparts. His predecessors' emphasis on encouraging the Iraqis to do things for themselves had led them to defer to Prime Minister Nouri al-Maliki whenever possible and to try to avoid confrontations with the inexperienced Iraqi leadership. Petraeus took a more activist approach and relentlessly pressured Maliki and other Iraqi officials to make critical decisions and to abandon counterproductive behaviors. Crocker supported this approach and added to the pressure on the Iraqis to make the hard decisions and to take risks they would have preferred to avoid."[33]

Thus, the main focus of effort in 2008 in Iraq would be improving governance in the provinces, passing several critical national laws, developing a process for reconciliation, and beginning the task of identifying how the coalition would depart from Iraq—and doing all these things while maintaining upward trends in security across the country. The unique problem that menaced all of these goals was the growing influence—both political and military—of Iran in Iraqi affairs.

Since 2003, Iran had actively supported several Shia militias within Iraq, including both Muqtada al-Sadr's Mahdi Militia,[34] which may have numbered some sixty thousand members by 2006 and, even more importantly, the Badr Brigade units, led by Hadi Al-Amiri, that had previously been trained and equipped by the Iranian Revolutionary Guards during the Iran-Iraq War. Though both existed within the Shia faction of parties in Iraq, the Mahdi army opposed the Badr Brigade at nearly every turn, so there was no real unity even within the Shia militias. From 2006 on, the major security problems in Iraq were not posed by insurgent attacks on coalition military forces but were instead the result of nearly constant sectarian violence waged by militia groups, largely in the urban centers of Iraq. In mid-October 2006, militiamen of the Badr Brigade attacked members of the Mahdi army in the town of Amarah, Iraq; the fighting continued for four days. By October 20, the Mahdi army was in control of the city, and the local police were powerless. It took negotiations between local, tribal, and political leaders and representatives of Prime Minister Maliki to bring a resolution to the crisis.

Eventually a battalion from the Iraqi army took control of the city. This display of militia strength underscored the weaknesses of the Iraqi Security Forces and the potency of the militias, which were able to operate nearly at will throughout Iraq. Though Maliki had been key to the resolution of the crisis his involvement also demonstrated how close the country was to all-out civil war. During the following year, Prime Minister Maliki and the majority Shia government in Baghdad appeared to let the militias run rampant in Iraq. In 2007, it was estimated that some twenty-thousand Badr Brigade members resided in Iraq; many had infiltrated various Shia militia groups, but were still strongly influenced by Iran. Although the totals were very uncertain, "one press report said there are 150 Iranian Qods Forces and intelligence personnel in Iraq."[35]

It was clear that Iran was taking an ever larger role in actively supporting anti-coalition and anti-Iraqi attacks, and was nourishing the sectarian violence in Iraq. In February 2007, military briefers in Baghdad provided what they claimed was specific evidence that Iran had supplied armor-piercing explosively formed projectiles (EFPs) to Shiite militias. Then in July, the MNF-I staff indicated that the Qods Forces was using Lebanese Hezbollah personnel to train and channel weapons to Iraqi Shiite militia fighters, and that Iran was giving up to $3 million per month to its protégé forces in Iraq. Finally, in August, General Odierno said that EFPs had accounted for one-third of the seventy-nine U.S. troop deaths in July 2007, and that the Shiite militias accounted for 73 percent of the attacks that killed or wounded U.S. soldiers that month. He added that Iran had supplied the Shiite militias with the 122mm mortars that were then increasingly used to fire into the International Zone in Baghdad.[36]

As if this military interference by Iran was not sufficient cause for alarm, it was also becoming quite clear to most in Iraq that the Maliki government was being severely tested by this complex and threatening linkage between Iran, the Shia militias, and the political parties that represented and often encouraged their militia activities. Such influence not only threatened Iraqi sovereignty, but it also came to threaten in early 2008 the very viability of the coalition that brought Prime Minister Maliki to power.

Coalition Continuity

General Odierno relinquished command of MNC-I in Iraq in February 2008 and was replaced by Lieutenant General Lloyd Austin and his staff in the XVIII Airborne Corps.[37] Odierno had been nominated to become the vice chief of staff of the Army, but was soon chosen to become the successor to General Petraeus in Iraq instead. After a short return to Fort Hood, Texas, he assumed command of MNF-I in September 2008, just as General Petraeus moved to take command of the U.S. Central Command in Florida. Ambassador Crocker remained at his post in Baghdad, reteamed with Odierno. Thus, a couple of related decisions enabled Petraeus, Odierno, and Crocker to continue their strategic partnership and continue to shepherd Iraqi security into 2008.

Chapter 12

THE IRAQIS TAKE CONTROL

> Victory will not look like the ones our fathers and grandfathers
> achieved. There will be no surrender ceremony on the deck of a bat-
> tleship. But victory in Iraq will bring something new in the Arab
> world—a functioning democracy that polices its territory, upholds
> the rule of law, respects fundamental human liberties, and answers
> to its people.
>
> —PRESIDENT GEORGE W. BUSH, JANUARY 10, 2007

The protection strategy of 2007 provided a way for the United States
to develop a broad level of minimum security in Iraq. Such security
was necessary if the war was to be won (after the coalition had stayed
in Iraq to build a government in 2003), but it was not sufficient to defeat the
insurgency itself. In order to develop the conditions identified by President
Bush for victory in Iraq, the Iraqi government had to show itself capable of
defending its borders, policing its territory, and protecting the basic elements
assured the people in its constitution. That required the Iraqi government to
accept responsibility for the war, demonstrate its ability to lead, and provide
for its citizens.

In 2004, the Interim Iraqi Government under Ayad Allawi had tried to
accept responsibility, but it had none of the tools required to affect the conflict's outcome. The first Iraqi national government under Prime Minister
Ibrahim Jafari had been too weak in 2005 to make any attempt at controlling
events in Iraq.[1] Jafari lost power largely due to his inability to bring security to
the streets of Iraq and he was succeeded in office by Nouri al-Maliki, another
leader of the Dawa Party, principally through the efforts of the Ayatollah Ali
al-Sistani in May 2006 to create an effective coalition government. Initially,
that succeeding government of Prime Minister Maliki showed a similar lack of
fortitude, but in late November 2007, President Bush met with the Iraqi prime
minister in Amman, Jordan, and exacted a pledge for him to act more aggressively against the threats to Iraqi security—including threats posed by co-reli-
gionist militias in the south of the country.[2]

The Iraqi Government Steps Up: The Battle for Basra, 2008

Most of the well-known fighting in Iraq up to 2007 had taken place in central, north-central, and northwestern Iraq. However, the focus of the fight shifted suddenly when, in March 2008, Prime Minister Maliki decided to take Basra back from the town's Shia militias. The third largest city in Iraq, Basra formed a crucial part of the country's transportation infrastructure (being on the Shatt al-Arab waterway and at the junction of the Tigris and Euphrates rivers). And, because most of Iraq's oil—its most important natural resource—flowed through Basra, the city was also the nation's economic capital.

From late 2004 through 2005 the level of violence had increased in the city, even though it was nominally under British control. Basra was torn by battles among competing militia groups jockeying for control of its rich infrastructure and potential profits. In 2006, the Iranian influence grew much stronger within the city and the British forces became the victims of EFPs from Iran, which pushed them into bases, much as their American counterparts were doing at the same time. Then in mid-2007 the British contingent of the coalition, which had controlled the Basra province since the initial invasion in 2003, withdrew from the city center to their main base at the Basra airport on the outskirts of the city—a move that was viewed as a victory for the militias.[3] At about the same time, the Iraqi government created a Basra Operations Command, led by Lieutenant General Mohan al-Freiji, who managed both the Iraqi army forces and the police in Basra, along the lines of the command and control model then in use in Baghdad. Later that summer, the British officially handed over responsibility for their zone of action to General al-Freiji and the Iraqi government, and departed Iraq.

Basra had shown evidence of growing infiltration by Iranian influences for some time, but after the British departure violence flared up significantly and it became clear that the government would have to act or be proven powerless in the face of Shia instability. Still, competition between Shia political factions and their militias escalated unchecked. This presented a serious challenge to the Iraqi government of Prime Minister Maliki, which faced the prospect of looking weak immediately prior to the holding of provincial elections in late 2008.

In response to the growing problems in the city, Prime Minister Maliki fired the Basra provincial governor, Mohammed Waeli, on July 28, about the time the British were handing over control of the province. Waeli was a member of a competing Shia political party known as the Islamic Virtue, or Fadhila, Party. Fadhila was a rival to the Sadrists, gathering its support mostly from the Shia poor in the south of the country around Basra; in March 2007, the party had withdrawn from Maliki's ruling Shia coalition and vowed to continue as an independent bloc. In defiance of Maliki, Waeli refused to give up his position and nothing Maliki could do seemed to affect the situation in Basra.

Maliki's decision to act against the militias in Basra stemmed from economic, security, and political considerations. Widespread corruption, oil smuggling, and militia control of Iraq's shipping hub all posed a serious economic threat to a government beset by debt. And the security problems that resulted from escalating violence and militia control posed practical problems for the conduct of the provincial elections scheduled for October. If the Iraqi Security Forces were unable to secure the city, they surely would not be able to secure the polling stations and prevent voter intimidation. The Maliki government needed to combat the growing threat of malign Iranian influence in Basra. The precise nature and extent of that influence was well known to Maliki, thanks to information provided by the interrogation of three Iranian operatives (Qais Khazali and his brother Laith, both leaders of Iranian-backed Special Groups militia, and Ali Mussa Daqduq, a member of Lebanese Hezbollah) who were captured in Basra in March 2007. The prime minister also faced the political threat of a no-confidence vote and needed to bolster his appearance as a strong, effective leader.

General Petraeus had been in discussions with Iraqi National Security Advisor Mowaffak al-Rubaie and General al-Freiji on March 21, 2008, when he first learned of the prime minister's intent to act quickly against the Basra militias.[4] Petraeus and his staff were developing plans to address the problems in the city in the summer, after a planned coalition attack on Mosul that would finish the work that Phantom Thunder had started the previous fall, and at a date when Iraqi forces would be ready and available for such an operation. The next morning the Iraqi prime minister told the MNF-I commander that Iraq would attack in Basra in a matter of days, not months. General Petraeus was quite concerned, but he approached the problem diplomatically and agreed to support the Iraqi effort.

The battle of Basra began on March 25, 2008, when the Iraqi army launched Operation Saulat al-Fursan (Charge of the Knights) to drive the Mahdi army and other militias out of the city. The operation was the first major engagement planned and carried out primarily by the Iraqi army since the fall of Saddam. Unfortunately, because the Iraqis assumed the fight would be easy, their forces were thrown into combat in the city as soon as the first five battalions arrived only to face much heavier resistance than expected from the Mahdi army. The offensive stalled, and coalition air support and artillery fires were requested, and provided. By the first week of April the fighting had degenerated into a stand-off, and eventually a temporary cease-fire was brokered among the various Iraqi factions involved,[5] but some one thousand Iraqi soldiers had refused to fight and their parent formation, the 14th Division, had proven itself unsuited to independent operations (it had only been formed five weeks before the operation began).[6] The Iraq army had suffered one thousand casualties in six days of heavy fighting.[7]

To the coalition's credit, even after having been given little advance notice of the attack, General Petraeus had immediately sent senior officers and advisors to Basra to assist the Iraqi military leadership. Eventually, the deputy commander of MNC-I, Marine Major General George Flynn, and a team of planners joined the Basra Operations Command. On April 1, the best division in the Iraqi army, the 1st Iraqi Army Quick Reaction Force (QRF) Division, with embedded Marine Military Transition Teams (MiTTs), arrived from its base in Al Anbar province to reinforce the Iraqi division already in place.[8]

Once reinforced, the Iraqis planned and executed a more deliberate attack beginning on April 12, this time fully integrating the key lessons of the coalition operations in Baghdad, including the provision of humanitarian aid, a jobs program, and a significant national government investment in infrastructure improvements, announced by Prime Minister Nouri al-Maliki. The fighting continued with coalition support through the end of April and into the first weeks of May. Many of the Iraqi Security Forces members who had proven themselves incapable or unwilling to fight were dismissed and Major General Mohammed Jawad, who had commanded the 1st QRF Division, replaced General al-Freiji as the head of the Basra Operations Command. At the same time, Prime Minister Maliki opened discussions with the local tribes and also opened a highly successful recruiting campaign for residents of Basra to join the Iraqi army. The operation was completed with a robust reconstruction effort that did much to improve living conditions in the city.

Operation Charge of the Knights was a critically important demonstration that the national Iraqi government was willing to confront and could successfully defeat major Shia militia groups outside of Baghdad. Although it started badly, due to rushed execution, poor initial assumptions, and poor preparation of forces, once redesigned into a more deliberate operation it proved quite successful and showed how capable the Iraqi army could be in combat. The 1st QRF Division moved itself on short notice across Iraq, deployed into tactical formations, and integrated its scheme of maneuver with humanitarian and civil reconstruction projects while confronting a tough opponent. Even more importantly, Prime Minister Maliki lived up to his promises to take action against his fellow Shia militiamen and took a leading role in the political and military aspects of the operation. Operation Charge of the Knights also showed that the coalition could stand in support and allow the Iraqis full lead in a major fight. All of these developments were crucial to the next phase of the campaign: the transition to full Iraqi lead in the counterinsurgency effort.

The 2008 Election Season in the United States

By the time Operation Charge of the Knights was beginning in Iraq, the national election campaign in the United States had already been running for over a year. Many people believe that elections in democracies can have significant impact on the prosecution of ongoing military campaigns; however, even though the Iraq war was perhaps the major issue of the campaign, the election process itself did not affect operations, although it did reinforce the idea of eventual withdrawal from Iraq and regular announcements were made about the decreases in American force levels. The real impact of the campaign was to focus more clearly on how the force would be withdrawn—whether at a certain date or in a conditions-based manner. The major party nominees stood on opposite platforms on that issue, with Republican nominee Senator John McCain advocating a conditions-based scheme that would ensure victory for the troops, and Democratic Senator Barack Obama clearly expressing his opposition to the war and pressing continually for rapid withdrawal within sixteen months of the election.

When Senator Obama visited Iraq in July 2008, he met with Prime Minister Nouri al-Maliki, Vice President al-Hashimi (the senior Sunni in the government), and of course Ambassador Crocker and General Petraeus. Obama reiterated his view that Afghanistan should be the real focus of the global American military effort and reinforced the idea that the sovereign Iraqi government should be leading the entire effort in Iraq.[9] The real question threaded through the discussions was how quickly should the coalition forces withdraw given the clear need to let the Iraqis resolve the conflict while avoiding a power gap that might generate renewed violence. By July 2008 it was clear that America was no longer an opponent of Iraq, but was indeed moving to a position as a supporting partner in an Iraqi counterinsurgency campaign.

Summer Decisions in Iraq

Iraq's success in its counterinsurgency campaign was, however, still measured by a series of benchmarks, established in 2007, that required security capacity building, ethnic power-sharing, and improvements in reconciliation and justice.[10] Specifically, in the security realm, the Iraqis had already provided forces and supporting economic development schemes for the Baghdad Security Plan, and had adopted sufficient military command and control to lead operations. In the political realm, however, the Maliki government needed to show progress on constitutional review, ensuring that minority rights were protected, and developing a range of legislation concerning de-Ba'athification, distribution of hydrocarbon resources, provincial elections, amnesty, and militia disarmament. These were much more difficult issues to accomplish, particularly by a weak coalition government.

The government did develop but did not pass a hydrocarbon law in 2007; it passed a budget for 2008, and also passed, on January 12, the "Accountability and Justice Law," often also known as "de-Ba'athification reform" which opened the door for Sunni reconciliation. Maliki's leadership and willingness to tackle the militias in Basra did much to assist his government in accomplishing the benchmark tasks, and by July 2008 only three remained at unsatisfactory levels: militia disarmament, professionalization of the Iraqi police, and hydrocarbon resource distribution.[11] A "Provincial Powers Act" had been passed by the Iraqi parliament on February 13, but was not approved by the Presidency Council until October 2008; legislation concerning the status of Kirkuk and its oil resources would not be resolved before the provincial elections in January 2009. Still, conditions overall had greatly improved in Iraq and much progress had been made by its government as summer passed into fall in 2008.

The SOFA and Drawdown Options

In August 2007, President Bush and Iraqi Prime Minister Nouri al-Maliki had agreed in principle to the development of a Status of Forces Agreement (SOFA) between Iraq and the United States. The same month President Jalal Talabani, Vice Presidents Hashimi and Abd al-Mahdi, Kurdistan Regional Government President Massoud Barzani, and Prime Minister Maliki had called for an end to the Chapter VII status under which the UN Security Council had established and maintained the coalition relationship in Iraq. These agreements had led in November 2007 to a "Declaration of Principles for a Long-Term Relationship of Cooperation and Friendship between the Republic of Iraq and the United States of America." This document laid out a framework for the two countries to discuss the SOFA and related issues during negotiations. Those negotiations began in earnest in early 2008. The SOFA and an associated security agreement were eventually approved by the Iraqi Cabinet and the Iraqi Council of Representatives on November 27, 2008; on December 4, Iraq's Presidency Council endorsed that vote, approving the agreement on the Iraqi side.

Prime Minister Maliki needed to prove to the Iraqi public, before the next national election, that the withdrawal of the U.S. forces from Iraq would happen in an appropriate manner. He saw the approval of the SOFA before the U.S. national elections as an important political goal because he had no way of knowing what the approach of the new American administration might be following the departure of President Bush. Maliki also seemed to sense that President Bush's involvement would be key to any such agreement (the two men had for several months been conducting weekly video teleconferences), so Maliki pressed to ensure the agreement could be signed before the American president left the Oval Office in January 2009.

Maliki also saw the SOFA as another chance to present a strong image to the Iraqi people (and thus enhance his chances for re-election) as the official who had ended the "occupation" of Iraq. On December 14, 2008, President Bush and Prime Minister Maliki signed the Strategic Framework Agreement (SFA) and the SOFA. The SOFA gained most of the Iraqi and international media attention, while little attention was devoted to the SFA, even though it involved a broader range of more crucial issues.

More extreme Shia organizations in Iraq, such as Muqtada al-Sadr's Mahdi Militia, and some of the more conservative Sunni groups, like Harith al-Dari's Association of Muslim Scholars in Iraq, all looked to the SOFA as their opportunity to gain something from the United States, while simultaneously seeing the opportunity to oppose the agreement as a chance to de-legitimize the Maliki government prior to the upcoming elections. The Iraqi Kurds viewed the SOFA negotiations as a good way to delay any central government legislation concerning Kirkuk, hydrocarbon legislation, and greater federalism. With all of these diverging interests, the development of the SOFA became so complex that the Iraqi government did not open it to any public debate, and it was not subject to public referendum. Hence, when it was signed, it came largely as a surprise to the Iraqi people. (The Baghdad Pact had also been passed without any public discussion.)

A Department of Defense report later stated, "With the entry into force and implementation of the Strategic Framework Agreement (SFA) and Security Agreement, this period witnessed a historic transition in the nature of the relationship between the United States and Iraq. . . . [The] SFA begins to normalize U.S.-Iraq relations through economic, diplomatic, cultural, and security ties, and it will serve as a foundation for a long-term bilateral relationship based on common goals and interests."[12]

U.S. National Elections and Future Iraq Plans

Americans went to the polls in November 2008 in huge numbers to participate in one of the most long-argued and influential elections of their recent history. The election produced a number of firsts in U. S. presidential election history. It was the first election since 1952 in which neither the incumbent president nor the incumbent vice president was a candidate in the general election. Governor Sarah Palin was the first woman nominated for vice president by the Republican Party, and for the first time in history both major party nominees were sitting U. S. senators. When Senator Obama formally accepted his party's nomination, he became the first African American to be nominated for president by a major political party. Senator Obama won the election with 365 electoral votes to Senator McCain's 173; and Obama's share of the popular vote was 7 percent more than McCain's.[13] He became the first African American president of the United States on January 20, 2009.

President Obama's election determined several things concerning the ongoing war in Iraq. First, it seemed to indicate that the majority of the American people accepted an early withdrawal based upon a schedule of events, not a more nebulous conditions-based approach. Although that schedule had been determined by the SOFA negotiations developed and approved by President Bush, Obama's election ensured that the timetable would not be delayed. Second, the election of President Obama established a new relationship between the leaders of the two countries that was not based on previous agreements. Finally, the election would result in a shift of military priorities from Iraq to Afghanistan. That shift did not ignore the needs of Iraq, but it meant that commanders there would no longer have priority access to ever-diminishing resources. Indirectly, it meant as well that Iraq would nearly disappear from the major media coverage for the year to come, giving the Iraqi government more freedom of movement.

The outcome of the provincial elections in Iraq, also held in January 2009, showed several important improving trends. Although the voter turnout was down slightly, the process was largely peaceful and judged fair. In general the voting showed a trend away from sectarian movements and toward more secular parties.[14] The election was also a victory for Maliki's State of Law Party, which won the majority of votes in nine out of the fourteen provinces that held elections. It also promoted the consolidation of power within the Iraqi federal government. The results were also "a significant milestone in the progress of Sunni reintegration and reconciliation with the Shia population and the Government of Iraq. In the 2005 provincial elections, less than 2% of the Sunni population voted . . . in al Anbar, an overwhelmingly Sunni province, roughly 40% of the population voted in 2009 compared to the 2% turnout in 2005."[15] Not surprisingly, Prime Minister Maliki called the elections "a victory for all the Iraqis," an indicator of "the Iraqi people's trust in their government and in the elections," and "proof that the Iraqi people are now living in real security."[16] U.S. ambassador to Iraq, Ryan Crocker, hailed it as "the most important election to take place since the fall" of former Iraqi President Saddam Hussein.[17]

The Iraqis Assume Full Control

In a little-heralded event largely lost in the New Year's celebrations around the world, the new U. S. embassy was formally opened in Baghdad on January 1, 2009; more importantly, on that same date, the Iraqi government officially assumed control of the "Green Zone" in Baghdad and effectively accepted responsibility for the war effort over the entire country. Prime Minister Maliki declared, "This palace is the symbol of Iraqi sovereignty and its return is a message directed to the Iraqi people that Iraq's sovereignty has returned."[18] In another press report, Anthony Shadid of the *Washington Post* commented, "the war in Iraq is indeed over."[19]

The combat did not end on that first day of 2009, in fact a massive suicide attack on January 2 killed twenty-four prominent Sunnis and another the following day killed thirty-one. The attacks showed that the violence in Baghdad would not soon end; nonetheless, the role of the United States in the ongoing combat operations had shifted in a very important way. After the signing of the SOFA and the clear intentions of the incoming Obama administration made a long-term commitment in the lead untenable, the requirement for the Iraqi government to take full responsibility for operations within its own borders was undeniable.

The impact in Iraq was felt more clearly with every passing day. On January 3, the U.S. military took a first step toward pulling combat troops from Iraqi cities by moving out of a Baghdad military base and handing it over to Iraq. The base had been set up in March 2007 to repel Shia militias from the largely Sunni Adhamiya district as a part of the surge. Brigadier General Robin Swan, deputy commander of U.S. forces in Baghdad, said the transfer of Forward Operating Base Callahan was "tremendously significant."[20] The transfer of the base reflected both a narrowing of U.S. operations and improvements in security in Baghdad.

The End of the War: The Good Enough Solution[21]

The great tragedy of Iraq is that no one really credits our soldiers for doing the near impossible: they went into the heart of the ancient caliphate, took out a genocidal monster, stayed on to foster consensual government, endured often poisonous attacks from critics at home, and triumphed at a cost less than during a major campaign in World War II.

—Victor Davis Hanson, "The Good—Part III"[22]

President Barack H. Obama entered office on January 20, 2009, with a significant agenda of change, yet high on his list of new initiatives was the president's commitment to fulfilling his campaign promise to end the war in Iraq and shift national priorities back to the ongoing conflict in Afghanistan. He announced his resolve in his inaugural address and during his first day in office, in a face-to-face meeting with Secretary of Defense Robert Gates and General Petraeus.[23]

His predecessor in the Oval Office had said many times that the war on terrorism would not end with tumultuous parades and fancy ceremonies, but would most likely be resolved under quiet, conditions-based circumstances. His views on the end of the war in Iraq shifted over time but ultimately remained true to that staid vision.[24] Unlike the great ceremony held on the USS *Missouri* in Tokyo Bay in 1945 marking the end of the war with Japan, after the transition to Iraqi sovereignty in 2004, events marking the end of the Iraq war would resemble more the activities of the ratification of the U.S. Constitution—a long series of uncertain steps leading eventually to an uncertain agreement of principles and the enforcement of a new and tenuous social and political order. By January 2009, such a series of events (the Anbar Awakening, the strengthening of the Iraqi government, the signing of the SOFA and the hand-over of the Green Zone to Iraq, and the assumption of responsibility for the conduct of the war by the Iraqi government) had occurred, making the president's decision to withdraw military forces from Iraq a necessary but in no way completely determinant action. Symbolically, on the same day that the president was articulating a new mission in Iraq, the Iraqi government and its security forces were assuming full responsibility for the formerly restive city of Ramadi in Al Anbar province. Clearly, the situation on the ground in Iraq substantiated the reduction in troop levels and the effective termination of America's longest and most controversial struggle after twenty-nine years of conflict.

Less than two weeks later, the Iraqi people participated in a second national election process, and for the first time in its recent history the majority of Iraqi citizens voted. Sunni and Shiite, urban and rural, north and south, millions of Iraqis went to the polls in order to select from among some fourteen thousand candidates competing for 440 seats in fourteen of Iraq's eighteen provinces. Occurring without major incident and under the control of the Iraqi government (with the coalition in distant support), the election marked a significant step forward in Iraq's ability to demonstrate effective governance and security. One senior Marine officer said at the time, "One of the things I've always said was that we came here to 'give' them democracy. Even in the dark days my only consolation was that it was about freedom and democracy. After what I saw today, and having forgotten our own history and revolution, this was arrogance. People are not given freedom and democracy—they take it for themselves."[25]

In an address to service members at Camp Lejeune, North Carolina, on Friday, February 27, 2009, President Obama stated clearly his views on Iraq:

> Our review is complete . . . the United States will pursue a new strategy to end the war in Iraq through a transition to full Iraqi responsibility. This strategy is grounded in a clear and achievable goal shared by the Iraqi people and the American people: an Iraq that is sovereign, stable, and self-reliant. To achieve that goal, we will work to promote an Iraqi government that is just, representative, and accountable, and that provides neither support nor safe-haven to terrorists. We will help Iraq build new ties of trade and commerce with the world. And we will forge a partnership with the people and government of Iraq that contributes to the peace and security of the region.[26]

He further stated: "Let me say this as plainly as I can: by August 31, 2010, our combat mission in Iraq will end."[27]

The same day he nominated Christopher Hill, then the assistant secretary of state for East Asian and Pacific Affairs, to serve as Ryan Crocker's successor as the U.S. ambassador in Iraq. In January the fewest number of Iraqis had died than in any month since 2003; the next month the number of Iraqis killed soared back to 258, but the number of Americans killed in Iraq fell to nine— also the lowest to date since 2003. On April 7, the new American president flew to Iraq, where he visited with U.S. soldiers, but also discussed the political situation in Iraq with Prime Minister Nouri al-Maliki and President Jalal Talabani. Many suspected that he wanted to press them for continued progress. Obama noted while in Iraq, "We've made significant political progress in Iraq [but] there are a lot of unresolved issues that need to be dealt with."[28]

In May and June, the United Kingdom and Romania officially ended their military efforts in Iraq. The Estonian and Salvadoran contributions to the MNF had ended in January, so by the end of June the coalition included only the United States and Australia, which would end its military participation the following month. On June 30, 2009, the remaining American forces had been shifted out of the Iraqi cities and responsibility for security in the country was turned over to the Iraqi police and military; in Iraq they called it, "June 30: National Sovereignty Day." It was a day of great celebration, befitting the change in responsibility and also reflecting the lingering sense of occupation felt by many Iraqis.

If the key element of sovereignty is the ability to protect the nation's people, then Iraq's government had finally taken on the full measure of its responsibility. The United States was no longer at war with Iraq; it was no longer even the dominant partner in the effort to defeat the insurgency; Iraq was not fully at peace, but it was fully and democratically responsible for its own people and their security.

Beginning a Comprehensive Strategic Partnership

The months that followed the departure of American forces from Iraqi cities saw a great deal of progress in Iraq's development as a functioning nation, particularly in the form of improved governance and relations with its neighbors. Even so, there was no cessation to insurgency-sponsored violence and sectarian strife. In August an AQ-I suicide bomber killed ninety-five and wounded six hundred in central Baghdad near the Foreign and Finance Ministries. The attack demonstrated that AQ-I remained a threat to Iraqi society even as it seemed to show reluctance on the part of the Iraqi authorities to ask for American assistance in the immediate aftermath of the blasts.[29] In October simultaneously detonating bombs at the Justice Ministry and the provincial council buildings killed 150 and wounded at least three times that number. The bombers had evidently passed through several checkpoints before reaching their targets, leading some to believe that the security forces manning the checkpoints at least tacitly supported the attacks.[30]

The last major attack of the year, on December 8, was also blamed on security problems: divided by sectarian animosities, the Iraqi security apparatus lacked the cohesiveness, hence the capabilities, needed to gain control over the situation and prevent recurrent acts of violence. Public mistrust in the leadership of the police and security forces had grown accordingly, prompting Prime Minister Maliki to replace the head of security in the Iraqi capital.[31]

Notwithstanding the three bombings in Baghdad, the overall level of security across Iraq continued to improve as 2009 drew to a close. A new low for the number of Iraqi civilian deaths in November 2009 showed that the departure of the American forces had not resulted in a significant loss of control over the counterinsurgency effort. Despite problems in Baghdad, the ISF were conducting effective raids that resulted in the capture of a significant number of AQ-I members, including eighteen in Mosul on November 25.[32] General Odierno noted in December that "today, Iraq is a nascent democracy that is rebuilding its strategic depth as a regional power in the Middle East. . . . We are witnessing the principles of democracy taking hold in Iraq as Iraqis establish the foundations of their own representative government in accordance with their own constitution."[33]

Although the controversial hydrocarbon law (which was needed to better distribute oil profits across Iraq) had stalled in the Council of Ministers, the Iraqi parliament did finally pass a workable elections law in December, clearing the way for another national election which was set for the spring of 2010. Vice President Hashimi (a Sunni) had originally vetoed the election law on the grounds that minorities would be disadvantaged, but his veto was quickly overturned by the Iraqi courts. Although Hashimi's veto indicated that some still felt the system was biased in favor of the majority Shia population, the overturning of the veto showed that the Iraqi government had developed a functioning system of checks and balances that could ensure fairness. Unlike previous national votes where a numerous largely sectarian and relatively ineffective groups vied for power, six relatively mature and broadly representative, truly national parties were to face off for the first time in the 2010 election, demonstrating that democracy was finally well engrained within the Iraqi state. Even Muqtada al-Sadr and his followers were finally integrated into a party with a national base of support.

Iraq's relations with its neighbors also improved markedly after the American withdrawal from Iraqi cities showed the SFA's implementation to be progressing on schedule. The year 2009 witnessed a number of important visits by national leaders to and from Iraq. Turkey shifted from opposition to many Iraqi concerns to a more supportive stance and even began to work toward a new approach to the Iraqi Kurdish issue. Ankara planned to open a consulate in Irbil that allowed for better relations with the Kurds in Iraq.[34] Syria also made its support for the new Iraq clear, and even Iran changed its previous approach, indicating that it could accept a new type of state on its western border as long as it was not dominated by American concerns. Although Iraq named its first postwar ambassador to Saudi Arabia in 2009, relations between the two states remained cool because the Saudis found little to like in the Shia-dominated Maliki government.

Internally Iraq saw some of its displaced citizens return to their homes. It also developed a new national budget designed to improve its economy and the quality of life of its people. Oil exports did not reach anticipated levels due in large part to damage inflicted on the Iraqi pipelines, and although the production of electric power increased, it still fell short of the demand. Overall, despite strong Iraqi and significant international support, the Iraqi economy suffered under the global recession of 2009 and did not meet its goals. But this was true of nearly every economy in the world.

The Iraqi Security Forces still lacked important capabilities at the beginning of 2010. The Iraqi air force certainly lacked any credible ability to control or even accurately monitor its own airspace, and although the Iraqi army could respond quite effectively to localized threats, there remained some doubt whether it could respond simultaneously to both the ongoing internal threat and meet external threats while also protecting the full expanse of the nation's borders. By the spring of 2010 it was clear that a longer-term strategic security partnership with the United States was in Iraq's best interest, so that technology and specific capability shortfalls could continue to be remedied even after the full withdrawal of American forces in December 2010. It was likely even then that a new SFA would be valuable to Iraq in order to formally design an enduring American aid package for the coming decade.

For its part the American forces in Iraq led no combat operations after June 2009. The Multi-National Force-Iraq staff was not idle; it not only managed the drawdown of U.S. forces in Iraq but also participated in a wide variety of training and coordination functions all over the country. General Odierno said late in the year that it was "necessary and right that Iraqi Soldiers and Police assume security responsibilities for their people"[35]; and during a visit in December when he met with Iraqi Prime Minister Nouri al-Maliki, President Jalal Talabani, and the Presidency Council, Secretary of Defense Robert Gates condemned the continuing violence in Iraq and offered "whatever assistance was needed" to continue the recovery and prevent future attacks.[36] The United States had become a supportive strategic partner of Iraq.

Then a ceremony in Baghdad on the first day of 2010 marked another momentous evolution of U.S.-Iraq relations, as the coalition arrayed against Iraq officially ceased to exist and the five major international command groups in Iraq merged into a single command called U.S. Forces-Iraq. In the ceremony at the Al Faw Palace in Baghdad, General Odierno, the final Multi-National Force-Iraq commander, said good-bye to MNF-I, while all of his five subordinate commanders also rendered final honors and cased their military unit colors, signifying the coalition commands' official inactivations. General Petraeus, still commander of U.S. Central Command, traveled to Baghdad for the event and commented that the ceremony marked yet another significant transition in Iraq: the effective end of the international campaign against Iraq and the official start of a military effort designed only to assist the new, democratic Iraqi government. During the ceremony General Odierno noted, "Today, Iraq is uplifted by a real, though fragile, sense of hope for a bright and prosperous future. We remain committed to nurturing this hope."[37]

The war to remove Saddam Hussein ended when the Iraqi government that succeeded him in power was able to execute the obligations of a responsible nation-state. The termination of hostilities between Iraq and the United States after such a long conflict was not a glorious event, in fact it could not even be precisely identified in time, but it was extremely significant. American forces remained in Iraq to advise and assist their Iraqi counterparts for months to come, but the opposition between the two nations had clearly ended. The conflict between Iraq and the United States was a long war that spanned the gulf between the end of the Cold War era and the beginning of a new, more globalized and more networked century. In the same way that it had been conducted in a very different way than most Americans had envisioned, the war ended incrementally, through a process that few Americans fully understood. The end of the conflict was not marked by the huge parades that were held at the end of the World War II but it was also not met with the disappointment that followed the conflict in Vietnam. In fact, during the war the American people had gained a great new affection for their military. Perhaps most importantly, after so many years of strife, the conflict ended with the major objectives set for it largely achieved and with a very different, and much improved, future possible for the people of Iraq.

Chapter 13

A FINAL ASSESSMENT: THE IMPACT OF THE LONG WAR WITH IRAQ

The singular trait of the American way of war is the remarkable ability of our military to advance, absorb setbacks, adapt and ultimately triumph based upon the unique circumstances of a given campaign.
—Donald H. Rumsfeld, "One Surge Does Not Fit All"[1]

Although it is certainly premature to judge all of the key issues of the war with Iraq, there are nonetheless several clear lessons from the conflict that policymakers and future commanders should take into account whenever they consider the use of U.S. military power in the years ahead. Of all the potential benefits that may be accrued from the war (foremost among them being democracy in the Middle East, the end of an oppressive regime, and perhaps a more mature American approach to warmaking), none could be clearer or perhaps more beneficial over the long term than the need to better understand the culture and perceptions of other nations, particularly those in the Middle East. War is an irrational act, but the decision to make war should be the most rational of any made by a national leader. Making such a decision correctly requires both a full understanding of the geopolitical context and wisdom informed by an ability to see both sides of potentially fatal confrontations.

Much of the scrutiny leveled on the American government by critics of the war with Iraq focused on the rationale for continuing the war in 2003—the much-ballyhooed hunt for Iraqi weapons of mass destruction (WMD) which proved to be nonexistent.[2] This issue is exemplary for it addresses the most crucial larger element of the policy debate: under what conditions should the United States employ war as a means of policy? Prior to September 11, 2001, Americans believed that they would only engage in war if attacked, if it was deemed necessary by alliance relationships (if an ally were attacked), or by norms of the international community (after a United Nations Security Council resolution, for example). With the September 2002 advent of the Bush administration's National Security Strategy, those assumptions were changed, perhaps forever.[3]

Still, even when it became clear that Saddam Hussein's threats to use weapons he did not possess were idle, he still stood in violation of some sixteen United Nations Security Council resolutions.[4] This was sufficient grounds to renew the hostilities that had been appropriately authorized and near-universally accepted in 1991. Although sufficient, such grounds still may not have been appropriate as a rationale for war. For the United States to remain a respected global power, its leaders need to ensure that war as an instrument of national policy is only employed when it is both necessary, and in the long-term interests of the nation—a just cause.

In some ways, the U.S. conflict with Iraq displayed characteristics common to all wars— characteristics that should be held in mind whenever leaders are tempted to resort to combat, so they should always hesitate to take the decision which invariably causes the loss of human life. The war with Iraq was a horrible human tragedy that for all its benefits exacted a huge and painful toll on all the participant nations. Iraq was devastated and America and its allies suffered as well. Even though some portions of the war, most particularly the early weeks of Desert Storm and Iraqi Freedom, were accomplished in a way that made it seem that war can be conducted "according to plan," for the most part it required massive adaptation and extremely difficult decision-making, as unexpected and often unexplainable actions occurred nearly every year.

Tactical Implications

There were some important technical innovations and some tactical lessons learned from the fighting in Iraq that will influence warfare for decades. Most clearly, the later stages of the war demonstrated that technology is not an end but merely a means of war. The United States had vastly superior firepower and much more sophisticated weapons, but was most hurt in combat by the simplest of devices (the IED) often employed by largely untrained and ill-disciplined militia forces. The most deadly of the Iraqi weapons used in Desert Storm, the Scud, was no technological marvel at the time either, but it too added an unexpected dimension to the fighting that at least temporarily could have changed the outcome.

Overall, technology favored the United States and its industrial capacity delivered several very important technical advantages during the war. Among these were greatly increased tactical intelligence gained through the use of unmanned aerial vehicles (UAVs); the ability to track and quickly identify people using biometric measuring devices; enhanced position-locating tools based upon the global positioning system (GPS); and huge increases in life-saving resulting from numerous new tools of combat medicine. Finally, as in many past conflicts combat engineering was crucial to the construction of roads, bridges, and defensive works, but during the Iraqi Freedom campaign military engineers also worked wonders during local reconstruction efforts in towns throughout Iraq.

Operational Factors

With the exception of timing and tempo, the most significant lessons at the operational level of war had more to do with organization and coordination than with physical impact on the enemy. Command and control improved significantly over the duration of the war. Desert Storm was barely joint in execution, and it did not integrate special operations forces (SOF) very well into its overall scheme of maneuver. Iraqi Freedom, on the other hand, demonstrated significant improvement in the synchronization of conventional forces and SOF in combat. This was also true of the blending of civil affairs and PSYOPS capabilities with conventional forces; it was also evident in the coordination of conventional force operations and special ops counterterrorism missions in the later years of the war—primarily due to the innovative leadership of General Stanley McChrystal.

Coalition integration also improved after Desert Storm, although it was only very good among the nations that shared some of the same warfighting doctrine and training. Integration of Australian and British forces, particularly their SOF during Iraqi Freedom, was superb, but the tactical integration of many other coalition forces left much to be desired and opened seams in the coalition from which the insurgency often profited. The withdrawal of the Spanish contingent from Iraqi Freedom after the March 11, 2004, Madrid terrorist bombing by Al Qaeda opened a gap in terrain coverage in Iraq that the coalition had difficulty filling and sent a clear signal that disparate terrorist actions around the globe could weaken the resolve of governments and negatively affect coalition effectiveness.

One of the most noteworthy and undervalued aspects of Iraqi Freedom was the superb operational logistics functioning of the American military. The deployment of forces in Desert Shield and the massive swing west of the logistic support that preceded Desert Storm were crucial to success, but the enduring capacity in Iraqi Freedom to deploy and sustain over 130,000 troops for six years of combat operations was an amazing feat.

The fusion of intelligence from a variety of government sources improved during Desert Storm but reached new heights of effectiveness during Iraqi Freedom. The same should be said for cross-boundary coordination by conventional forces engaged against a very amorphous and mobile enemy.

A few small organizations adopted from elsewhere also made a significant operational impact during these campaigns. During Desert Storm the coalition liaison elements helped bring together an often very disparate group of national units so that they could work effectively in the same battlespace. During Iraqi Freedom military advisory teams (used previously in Vietnam to good effect) were essential for the rapid development and employment of the new Iraqi security forces. Provincial reconstruction teams (PRTs), pioneered in Afghanistan, also were crucial to the reconstruction efforts in many Iraqi provinces during the latter campaign.

Timing was critical for the conduct and success of both Desert Storm and Iraqi Freedom. Both campaigns used speed to create a devastating shock effect on the opposing Iraqi forces. They also were timed to ensure that major combat operations took place in the early spring, when the weather was optimal. General Schwarzkopf's decision to accelerate the attack of V Corps during the 1991 campaign was probably unnecessary given the "piston effect" of the Marine advance into Kuwait. Moreover, the focus of VII Corps' effort was directed too far south to have its intended effect on the Republican Guard to end the campaign, but Schwarzkopf probably could not have convinced President George H. W. Bush to allow the coalition into Iraq, given the trepidation of the coalition's Arab leaders—who were fearful that overthrowing Saddam Hussein (the inevitable outcome of a coalition invasion of Iraq) might inspire their own populations to press for regime change. Even more detrimental to the coalition victory effort was the poorly timed and poorly coordinated cease-fire meeting held before the Republican Guard formations could be engaged and defeated. The discussions at Safwan would have been much more productive had they been conducted after thorough analysis of what a cease-fire might accomplish with respect to finding long-term solutions to the threat that Saddam's regime posed to the Middle East.

Desert Storm showed masterful media management but a rather poor ability by American military leaders to assess possible outcomes of the offensive at the tactical level of war. Other problematic aspects of Desert Storm included the failure to formulate conflict termination criteria, poor operational assumptions, inaccurate assessments of the capabilities of the Iraqi forces, and poor planning for the treatment of beaten Iraqi units and prisoners of war. Iraqi Freedom was in some respects a repeat performance of Desert Storm, with the military exhibiting great expertise at dealing with the media while making the same or similar mistakes in the operational conduct of the campaign, especially during its early conventional phase. Moreover, both media management and the formulation of operational assumptions grew worse during the unconventional phases of combat that followed from 2004 to 2006.

Strategic National Issues

A significant achievement of the post–Vietnam era U.S. military was its ability to integrate National Guard and Reserve forces with regular units during combat. Reserve and National Guard participation in Desert Storm was useful, particularly in logistics and service support commands, but few of those units participated in combat directly alongside their active duty counterparts.[5] In fact, some National Guard units failed to achieve combat readiness in the time allotted. The situation had changed vastly by 2003, when Reserve and National Guard units were mobilized on very short notice, arrived in theater in a timely manner, and then fought alongside their active duty counterparts throughout the campaign. The integration of American National Guard and Reserve formations—up to division level—within active organizations became so effective during Iraqi Freedom as to become almost invisible. Although it is true that some of the tactical problems of the period were due to Reserve and National Guard units (the crimes committed by the 372nd Military Police Company at Abu Ghraib are a case in point), overall the performance of those units in Iraq was on a par with regular force commands. In truth, very little of the most important work of the post-invasion phase of the campaign could have been executed without Reserve and National Guard personnel. From the ministry advisors in Baghdad under the CPA, to civil affairs brigades and special forces teams spread across the country, and even to holding key terrain in combat, the Reserve and National Guard were crucial to success.

The strategic deployment of forces was also a great strength demonstrated by the United States during both campaigns. The admirable story of the Desert Shield deployment is well known, but the capacity for the United States to deploy large units over great distances in a very short amount of time, and to maintain high-deployment tempos for years during Iraqi Freedom, was remarkable. When combined with the willingness and the excess capacity to accommodate transporting multinational partners from as far away as Mongolia and South Korea to Iraq, the American strategic deployment system capability became truly phenomenal.

Both campaigns also amply demonstrated that the use of U.S. military power is most effective when it is employed in concert with allies. War no longer means the exclusion of the other diplomatic and economic elements of power—if it ever did. But gaining consensus across governments and synchronizing the use of these different elements of national power in the pursuit of a principal warfighting goal remains problematic. The post–Vietnam era doctrines of Caspar Weinberger and Colin Powell seemed well-crafted for the national requirements of the 1980s, but proved to be considerably less effective in the changed global context resulting from the fall of the Soviet

Union. In particular, although the Weinberger-Powell doctrines functioned quite well as a means of ensuring that the *decision* to use military force was made wisely, they provided no meaningful guidance for the *application* of such force on the operational and tactical levels—where serious flaws in the execution of combat operations could and did arise. The most significant and lasting contribution of the long war with Iraq on American national policy should be the absolute requirement for civilian and military leaders to focus national effort consistently, from the commencement of combat operations through conflict termination and beyond, until an effective, permanent resolution of the causus belli is attained.

Such an altered focus of effort cannot effectively be pursued by a single nation acting alone. As was discussed by nearly every team that assessed a way to resolve the conflict in Iraq in the period from 2005 to 2007, regional approaches always offer enviable advantages. Ensuring the effective, permanent resolution of most causes of war requires the active involvement of more than one nation, not always within the context of the UN or an alliance, but most effectively with the involvement of neighboring states that have a stake in the positive outcome.

The war between Iraq and the U.S. does pose a few interesting questions. Outside the specifics of execution, historians have already begun to debate the larger issue presented by the similarities between the Vietnam War and the Iraq War, namely: why doesn't the United States government learn from its mistakes and avoid making them in future conflicts? Are Americans blind to analogies? Do they fail to use intelligence products well enough to note similarities and differences? Are Americans so self-centered as to be blind to dominating regional and cultural factors? Finally, even when Americans learn about warfare, as did the army after 1968 in Vietnam, why does the military fail to institutionalize lessons so future generations of officers don't have to suffer through the same learning process?

The decision-making ability of the civilian Commander in Chief, particularly the U.S. president's role in making the decision to go to war, will certainly be one of the important concerns drawn from the entire period of the long war. Ultimately the main critique of the final phases of the war with Iraq will always center on the weak rationale that brought the United States back to conventional combat operations there. It appears certain, however, that although the influence of the "Neocons" was not in itself sufficient to drive the president to war, the momentum of events and his own preconceived notions of war after over a decade of engagement in Iraq seems to have heavily influenced the result.[6] Most Americans can accept the personal weaknesses of a flawed decision-maker, but few can accept a government that can allow war to occur without a well-deliberated and rational decision-making process, however flawed.

International Concerns

The waning influence of the United Nations was a key factor behind the scenes during the war between Iraq and the United States. In many ways the period of the long war between Iraq and the United States (1990 to 2010) spans the rise and the fall of the modern United Nations. Although the UN was a respected and powerful institution from 1950 to 1990, its global impact only grew after the success of the Desert Storm campaign. The level of involvement of the United Nations in the security affairs of its member states reached a new high during the 1990s. It was a period when many nations saw the UN as the arbiter of the globe, so the UN involvement in Iraq needs to be understood within the context of an international organization of much greater power and influence than ever before. The United Nations sponsored major military operations in four of its member nations during the 1990s, and minor efforts in many others. During each of these operations, the global influence and prestige of the UN grew, until in 1999 it actually served as the midwife for the birth of a new state: Timor Leste.

The United Nations Operation in Somalia (UNOSOM) was one of the first major interventions supported by the UN in the 1990s.[7] In April 1992, the Security Council established UNOSOM as a relief effort for famine-stricken Somalia. The Security Council authorized the deployment of some three thousand troops to provide security for the humanitarian aid effort. The situation continued to worsen, so in late 1992, the United States offered to organize and lead a major military operation to ensure the delivery of humanitarian assistance. The Security Council accepted the offer and authorized the use of "all necessary means" to establish a secure environment for the relief effort under Chapter VII of the UN Charter. In March 1992, the operations in Somalia transitioned to a new United Nations peacekeeping mission known as UNOSOM II. Although a great deal of aid was dispersed and some of the worst of the famine-induced suffering was relieved, the overall result of these intervention operations in Somalia was disappointing.

The United Nations Protection Force (UNPROFOR) in the former Yugoslavia was primarily an effort to stop ethnic cleansing within the framework of a multi-religious and multi-ethnic population.[8] UNPROFOR's mandate was enlarged to include the implementation of a cease-fire agreement and the monitoring of activities in Macedonia, then extended again geographically to include Bosnia and Herzegovina. In September 1992, UNPROFOR's mandate was further enlarged to deliver humanitarian relief, monitor a regional no-fly zone in Bosnia and Herzegovina (much like those then in force over Iraq), and establish safe areas around five Bosnian towns and the city of Sarajevo.

The most successful of the three UN interventions in the early 1990s was the United Nations Mission in Haiti (UNMIH).[9] In July 1994, the Security Council authorized supporting member states to form a Multi-National Force (MNF) and use "all necessary means" to return democracy to Haiti. UNMIH took over in early 1995 from the MNF to assist the Haitian government in maintaining a secure environment; UNMIH also helped to create, for the first time in the country's history, a national civil police. UNMIH was eventually replaced by three successive UN missions: the United Nations Support Mission in Haiti (UNSMIH) in 1996, the United Nations Transition Mission in Haiti (UNTMIH) in 1997, and the United Nations Civilian Police Mission in Haiti (MIPONUH), also in 1997, all of which were designed to improve security and, to a more limited degree, governance.

Most significantly, in June 1999 the United Nations sponsored a UN Mission in East Timor (UNAMET) to conduct a regional "popular consultation" wherein the people of East Timor were given a choice for full integration into Indonesia or independence. The Security Council then authorized a multinational force (International Force East Timor, or INTERFET), under a unified command structure headed by Australia, to restore peace and security in East Timor, to protect and support UNAMET in carrying out its tasks, and to facilitate humanitarian assistance operations. In October 1999, the Security Council established a United Nations Transitional Administration in East Timor (UNTAET) as an "integrated, multidimensional peacekeeping operation fully responsible for the administration of East Timor during its transition to independence."[10] The territory's constitution was approved in March 2002, and following presidential elections on April 14 of the same year, Xanana Gusmão, their former resistance leader, was appointed president-elect of East Timor. Under UN supervision the territory became a new nation, Timor Leste, in May 2002.[11]

Each of these United Nations efforts demonstrated the increasing power of the organization during the same period when it was growing ever less effective in the accomplishment of its own mandated mission in Iraq. In many ways, in fact, the Iraq experience belied the promise of the United Nations in the security sphere, and its failure in 2002 to prevent a resumption of hostilities would begin a serious descent in the global body's prestige and authority. Unfortunately, it immediately began to lose influence as it was manipulated and proved largely powerless in the face of renewed hostilities in Iraq only the next year.

Some have posited that the twenty-first century has ushered in the end of the Westphalian era.[12] They would view the increases in globalization, the spread of diasporas, the global economic challenges of 1997 and 2009, and the rise of global insurgent movements such as Al Qaeda as indications that the nation-state itself may be loosing preeminence on the world stage. The war certainly reinforced the lack of resilience in international borders and demonstrated the importance of international organizations of global reach. Still, much more will have to occur before the international legal framework moves past being nation-centric.

Philosophical Approaches

The uncontrollable nature of war was only reinforced by the conflict in Iraq. Along with just cause, war needs to be pursued with the firm conviction that flexibility and adaptability will be normal requirements; that the fog and friction inherent in combat will require leaders at all levels, and the diplomats, economists, and judges that support their efforts, to be supremely unaccustomed to routine and dogmatic approaches.

Thus, the first of the enduring lessons appropriate for national leaders remains that by its nature, war will always be horrific, chaotic, and unpredictable. Clausewitz is the most famous, but was far from the first practitioner of war who learned from painful experience that nothing could go as planned in combat. In his famous image of war as an ever-changing and constantly dynamic clash of forces, known as a trinity of passion, reason, and will, he adequately described even the non-conventional phases of warfare in Iraq in late 1991 and late 2003.

The long conflict between Iraq and the United States turned out very differently than was expected. The differences lay not only in the timeframe for the conflict, but also in the complexity of modern war. If war planners had been able to foresee more accurately the kind of war that they were considering, both in 1990 and in 2002, they certainly would have developed different concepts and differing resourcing for the combat to follow. Unfortunately, history shows that it is exceedingly rare for war planners to be able to forecast combat accurately—particularly in the strategic arena. That is the primary reason why Clausewitz and other past theorists of war have emphasized the uncertain nature of conflict. Preparation for war requires an understanding that significant aspects of combat cannot be controlled and that the enemy, not matter how feeble or incompetent, with still cause things to happen in unexpected ways. Because warfare is ultimately concerned with the loss of human life it is imperative that as people think about war in the future, they must realize that there are rarely any quick or low-cost solutions to international strife.

Nations must be prepared for the worst in war and must be open to adaptation and to changes in both ways of fighting and even the very objectives set for the conflict.

Saddam Hussein had a very healthy respect for the problems of insurgency, and much of the state organization he created was designed to deal with insurgencies. Americans seemed to forget their experiences fighting past insurgencies and had to ask over and again in 2006 whether victory was possible against such a threat. As 2007 unfolded, it again became clearer that winning such a conflict required not only commitment and willingness to sacrifice lives, but also the full integration of national power in a way that protected the population more than it emphasized hunting the insurgent in its midst. With that key lesson re-learned, the task now will be to keep it clearly in mind for any future like conflict.

Lessons of the Prolonged Theater Campaign

In many ways the most constructive assessment that can be derived from the conflict between Iraq and the United States should focus on the ability of nation-states, particularly wealthy industrial countries, to wage prolonged theater campaigns. In its most essential form, the conflict was a series of significant major combat operations conducted over an exceedingly long period of time, all focused toward a single overarching (but often forgotten) end—the reduction of the threat to the region posed by Saddam Hussein as the president of Iraq.

Desert Shield was a major military operation designed to protect Saudi Arabia from attack by Iraq and, if possible, to deter or coerce Saddam to free Kuwait through the threat of force combined with active diplomacy. It is now understood that Iraq had no intention of invading Saudi Arabia, but that was not clear at the time.[13] Unfortunately, Saddam was extremely difficult to coerce once his forces were deployed in Kuwait—a fact not well understood by Washington.

This lack of mutual understanding significantly constrained the effectiveness of the tools used during the subsequent period of negotiations and threats which continued for the remainder of the year. Once U.S. military forces were deployed in August 1990, they provided their own requirements: the need for force protection in the early days was paramount in the face of the size of the Iraqi force deployed in Kuwait. But by November, they represented a serious commitment of national will which would have been necessary to leaven the possibility of diplomatic success when dealing with Saddam.

Although it was conducted in a coalition environment, Desert Storm was a classic, conventional American military operation. It was designed to maximize shock and technology in the face of perceived overwhelming numbers of lesser skilled forces. It employed deception and indirect firepower approaches to maximum effort and was designed for a short conflict, and it minimized penetration and endurance for the advantage of speed and shock. As is well known, it succeeded much more rapidly that anyone of the post–Vietnam era military had envisioned and had to be terminated without a formal plan. For several reasons, its own kinetic success contributed to its ineffective termination and introduced yet another phase of conflict with Iraq: the sanctions regime.

During the sanctions regime period, the United States and a few of its original coalition partners maintained the northern and southern no-fly zones which provided the leverage needed to force Saddam to comply with the terms of the cease-fire agreement and the protections viewed as necessary to protect the Kurd and Shia minorities in Iraq that rose up in opposition to his rule in the immediate aftermath of Desert Storm. No one expected that these sanctions enforcement actions (known as Northern Watch and Southern Watch) would be required for a long period of time, and no one in the United States was prepared for the level of daily engagement by military (primarily air) forces that would be required to make their United Nations mandates effective. Eventually, as the focus of the world shifted to other more immediate issues, and as Saddam maneuvered to conceal and subvert the regime, time eroded the coalition's effectiveness and made the cost of enforcing sanctions nearly unbearable for the United States.

Without the paradigm shift resulting from the terrorist attacks of September 11, 2001, in the United States, the sanctions enforcement operations might have ended without result. The administration of George W. Bush took office in Washington in 2001 with the clear goal of reducing the American level of participation in long-term UN operations. However, with the threat to the U.S. homeland taking on a new priority the ongoing threats stupidly posed by Saddam Hussein became impossible to ignore, and ushered in a new period of coercive diplomacy, backed by the deployment of additional forces and the implied future use of significant military forces. Again the leaders of Iraq and the United States failed to understand each other and the two nations were driven back toward combat, unless concessions could be gained through some other means, which neither side thought likely.

Operation Iraqi Freedom was designed to topple Saddam Hussein from power and change the government in Iraq to one that would be less threatening to the region and inhospitable to terrorists. Like its predecessor, Desert Storm, it was designed to maximize advanced firepower and swift maneuver to defeat the Iraqi military, but failed through its own unexpectedly rapid success to develop conflict termination conditions conducive to the establishment of an effective replacement government in Iraq. It then led to a subsequent unnamed but very different type of operation, focused necessarily more on irregular warfare and counterinsurgency than on conventional maneuver and firepower actions.

Iraqi Freedom continued through three distinct phases, struggling to transform itself from a combat operation to a post-hostilities peace-enforcement operation, to a true counterinsurgency operation designed to protect the Iraqi population fromm internal threats. This transition process was traumatic for the United States and its extremely capable professional military. Clearly one of the most difficult challenges that any military must face in the service of its nation is the ability to continually assess progress and to adapt to changing circumstances, even with procurement and doctrine development processes that often lag far behind the realities of the frontline fighter.

One of the key challenges in the adaptation process is the periodic transition of forces that must take place in order to fight a long-term modern war. Gone are the days when armies went off to war and did not return until the fighting was done. Modern forces must be rotated over any conflict period that exceeds twenty-four months, and although nations always hope to resolve conflicts in periods of less duration than that, it is now logical to anticipate that modern war will require troop rotation policies to maintain capability in excess of that timeframe in normal course. In Iraq, forces settled into a deployment wave that witnessed major influxes of forces in the early spring and a lull in effective combat due to extreme weather conditions in the Middle East until the late summer. This made American forces predictable and provided an unnecessary advantage to the enemy.

On the other hand, the duration of the fighting gave some compensation to the United States. "The protracted nature of the conflict played to America's advantage, surprisingly, as new commanders were able to learn from previous examples and personal experiences even as they adapted to a changing situation and a fluid enemy."[14] Eventually, in 2007, Iraqi Freedom was employing new techniques, new doctrine, and new enabling technologies to protect the fledgling Iraqi government that had managed to take shallow root over the preceding three years.

Americans are almost genetically opposed to prolonged military operations. Although the United States conducted a series of operations against the native Indians in the late 1870s and 1880s, a similar campaign in the Philippines from 1899 to 1913, and another in Haiti from 1915 through 1934, these actions were never identified as campaigns and never well-enough publicized to attract popular scrutiny or understanding. Thus most Americans had come to believe that modern wars would be fought and won quickly. Iraqi Freedom disproved that misconception.

Iraq and the United States

Democracy in Iraq will never mirror democracy in the United States, but governance there has improved distinctly since the dark days of 2003. The war disrupted Iraqi society and killed untold thousands of Iraqis. The cost of the war to the United States has also been high in both financial and human terms, and America certainly lost significant prestige and respect around the world as a result of its missteps in the war. The long conflict between Iraq and the United States witnessed tremendous changes in the military capacity and doctrine of the American forces, and in the execution of its national security strategy. The war ushered in a new approach toward the Muslim world and opened the door for significant domestic changes within America as well. It was a watershed event in many ways.

Once the management of the insurgency in Iraq had been accepted successfully by the Iraqi government, the United States assumed a military support posture in the country. Very quickly thereafter, it also shifted its priorities back to the still ongoing conflict in Afghanistan, which became the main military effort under the Obama administration in 2009. During that shift, the administration also ended the use of the phrase "global war on terror"—effectively de-linking the conflict in Iraq with the larger effort against global extremism and terrorism.

The transformation of the Iraqi military was one of the best outcomes of the war. The Iraqi army was remade completely (albeit with coalition assistance in a Western mold), with proper tactical command and control, appropriate education and training for key commanders and staff, and newly empowered small-unit leaders. Additionally, at least at the higher levels, joint approaches were introduced and harmonized to improve the effectiveness of the entire defense organization. The Iraqi military has always been one of that nation's most important institutions and the reforms of the 2005–2010 period will be a significant hedge against future instability in Iraq.

The American defense establishment also made some significant changes as the war progressed. The Air-Land Battle doctrine that informed employment in the 1990s evolved to become more flexible and more comprehensive; joint approaches started after Goldwater-Nichols became truly commonplace, and synchronization improved across the four military services. Irregular warfare (defined as the struggle among state and non-state actors for legitimacy and influence over the relevant populations, to include counterinsurgency), also came to be viewed as equal in importance to conventional combat among military professionals.[15] Thus, counterinsurgency deserved the same level of training effort and resources as did conventional warfare. The traditional American way of war then evolved by the end of the conflict to include more than massed combat power and technological solutions; it had fully incorporated non-traditional actors, information operations, and the integration of other government agencies within its normal approaches. The American way of war was still unique, but had adapted to the norms of a new century.

The war between Iraq and the United States did witness striking successes and puzzling defeats. Both offensive operations (in 1991 and in 2003) were brilliantly executed; but both of them were followed by disappointingly ineffective transitions to vaguely defined "post-hostilities operations." Overall, the American strategies for conventional operations were superb, but those developed for stability operations were far less effective. The key presidential decisions to go to war appear to have been made in very different ways, with President George H. W. Bush using a more formal and coordinated approach, President Clinton using a less organized and less deliberate approach, and President George W. Bush employing a much more secretive and thus far less coordinated process. Operational decision-making improved significantly as the war progressed until by 2007 the MNC-I staff was employing very sophisticated operational integration that dominated the tempo of the fight and significantly reduced the opportunities for insurgents to act in a proactive manner. The critical political, strategic, and operational decisions that dramatically affected the outcome of the war will be instructive for years to come.

Although World War II still provided Americans with the dominant image of combat, by the end of the conflict with Iraq a new generation of Americans had been introduced to the painful nature of modern warfare. The incomprehensible war that was the American experience in Vietnam had been given new context, and replaced by a fresh appreciation for the complexities of combat. In some very important ways, the men and women of the Vietnam era were welcomed back into society in the United States with new-found respect as that younger generation of American families endured the hardships of a similar war for two decades. And, because the conflict with Iraq also ended without a distinct military victory ceremony, the "never-again" benchmark for American military doctrine and force employment established in the aftermath of the Vietnam experience was replaced by a new understanding of war in all its horrific dimensions. Imbued within that new generation of combat veterans was a fuller awareness of the need to understand other cultures, the desire to see common approaches to common threats, and the commitment to ensure that military capabilities are never again used without being well focused on the enduring national interests of the United States.

NOTES

Prelude: American Military Power in the Post–Vietnam Era, 1975–1989

1. Public Broadcasting Service (hereafter PBS), *Frontline: The Gulf War, Oral Histories of the Commanders*, found at http://www.pbs.org/wgbh/pages/frontline/gulf/oral/franks/5.html.

2. William Kristol, "The Defense Secretary We Have," *Washington Post*, December 15, 2004, A33.

3. During the final tactical actions of the fall of Baghdad in 2003, General Tommy Franks would make reference to his Vietnam experience when he christened the term "thunder run" to make the initial penetrations into the Iraqi capital. See Tommy Franks, *American Soldier* (New York: Regan Books, 2004), 517.

4. Dave R. Palmer, *Summons of the Trumpet: U.S.-Vietnam in Perspective* (Novato, CA: Presidio, 1978), xvii.

5. "Abrams, according to the doctrine, established this bond by creating a force structure that integrated Reserve and Active Components so closely as to make them inextricable, ensuring after Vietnam that presidents would never be able to again send the Army to war without the Reserves and the commitment of the American people." James Jay Carafano, "The Army Reserves and the Abrams Doctrine: Unfulfilled Promise, Uncertain Future," Heritage Foundation, April 18, 2005, http://www.heritage.org/Research/NationalSecurity/hl869.cfm.

6. General De puy commanded the 1st Infantry Division in Vietnam, where he won the Distinguished Service Cross for valor; General Starry commanded the 11th Armored Cavalry Regiment during the Vietnam War and won the Silver Star for valor.

7. A C-130 Hercules transport aircraft collided with a heavy lift RH-53 helicopter on a runway in the middle of the night and both aircraft were destroyed. A large black burn mark was clearly visible on the ground where the following eight Americans were killed: Air Force Major Richard L. Bakke, Marine Sergeant John D. Harvey, Marine Corporal George N. Holmes Jr., Marine Staff Sergeant Dewey L. Johnson, Air Force Major Harold L. Lewis, Air Force Technical Sergeant Joel C. Mayo, Air Force Major Lyn D. McIntosh, and Air Force Captain Charles T. McMillan II.

8. For the best treatment of the act, see James R. Locher, *Victory on the Potomac: The Goldwater-Nichols Act Unifies the Pentagon* (College Station: Texas A&M University Press,), 2004.

9. "Defense Organization: The Need for Change," Senate Armed Services Committee Staff Report, 99th Cong., 1st sess., Committee Print 99–86, 1985, 158.

10. United States Congress, Senate Committee on Armed Services, *Defense Organization: The Need for Change: Staff Report to the Committee on Armed Services, United States Senate* (Washington, DC: GPO, 1985 354) Known as "The Locher Report," See the "Historical Examples of DoD Organizational Problems," an appendix that presents six brief historical examples of organizational problems that have plagued U.S. military operations. The appendix includes two examples—the Spanish-American War and Pearl Harbor—from the period before the application of the concept of unified command. The other four examples are from the post-unified command period of U.S. military history: the Battle of Leyte Gulf, the capture of the USS *Pueblo*, the Iran hostage rescue mission, and the Grenada operation.

11. Jimmy Carter, "State of the Union Address, 1980," January 23, 1980, found at http://www.jimmycarterlibrary.org/documents/speeches/su80jec.phtml.

Chapter 1. The Decision to Go to War

1. These circumstances are best understood through a reading of Bob Woodward's fine book, *The Commanders* (Simon & Schuster: New York, 1991), 200–222. It should be noted, however, that planners in the U.S. Central Command and in the Defense Intelligence Agency had previously highlighted the possibility that Saddam Hussein might menace his neighbors with military force.

2. Source of U.S. Census figures is, "Crude Oil Imports into U.S., by Country of Origin," found at http://www.allcountries.org/uscensus/957_crude_oil_imports_into_u_s.html. In contrast, Iraq's exports to the United States represented 8 percent of the total; in 1990 Iraq's percentage would rise to 9 percent as then-occupied Kuwait's share fell by half.

3. Woodward, *The Commanders*, 223–225. The number of senior government officials who worked on the decision to commit military power against Iraq in both 1990 and 2002 is instructive. The list of important players making crucial decisions in both crises includes: Secretary of Defense (and later Vice President) Dick Cheney, Chairman of the Joint Chiefs of Staff (and later Secretary of State) Colin Powell, Under Secretary of Defense for Policy (and later Deputy Secretary of Defense) Paul Wolfowitz, and several others, including Robert M. Kimmitt and Andrew Card.

4. The Bush administration had already condemned the invasion at 11 PM on the day it started.

5. George H. W. Bush and Brent Scowcroft, *A World Transformed* (New York: Knopf, 1998), 317.

6. Woodward, *The Commanders*, 228.

7. H. Norman Schwarzkopf and Peter Petre, *It Doesn't Take a Hero: General H. Norman Schwarzkopf, the Autobiography* (New York: Bantam Books, 1992), 298.

8. Woodward, *The Commanders*, 231.

9. Bush and Scowcroft, *A World Transformed*, 316.

10. Margaret Thatcher, *The Downing Street Years* (New York: HarperCollins, 1993), 817.

11. Bush and Scowcroft, *A World Transformed*, 319.

12. Ibid., 321.

13. Ibid. Also found at http://www.margaretthatcher.org/archive/displaydocument .asp?docid=110709.

14. Minutes of NSC meeting, dated August 3, 1990, found at http://www.margaret thatcher.org/archive/displaydocument.asp?docid=110701.

15. Ibid., 2.

16. Bush and Scowcroft, *A World Transformed*, 323.

17. Minutes of NSC meeting, dated August 3, 1990, found at http://www.margaret thatcher.org/archive/displaydocument.asp?docid=110701, 9.

18. Ibid., 11.

19. Bush and Scowcroft, *A World Transformed*, 325.

20. Woodward, *The Commanders*, 241.

21. Ibid., 243.

22. This statement was negotiated by Secretary of State Baker and issued by Soviet Foreign Minister Edward Shevardnadze.—For the first time it showed the U.S. and the USSR aligned on the same side of an issue after the fall of the Berlin Wall. Bush and Scowcroft, *A World Transformed*, 326.

23. Woodward, *The Commanders*, 237.

24. Baker had just returned from his meeting with Edward Shevardnadze in Russia.

25. Woodward, *The Commanders*, 248–249.

26. General Chuck Horner, Schwarzkopf's air component commander, attended the meeting.

27. Woodward, *The Commanders*, 255.

28. Found at http://www.margaretthatcher.org/archive/displaydocument.asp?docid= 110704 and at: http://bushlibrary.tamu.edu/research/public_papers.php?id=2138&year =1990&month=8.

29. Bush and Scowcroft, *A World Transformed*, 333.

30. Meeting of the National Security Council, August 6, 1990, found at http:// www.margaretthatcher.org/archive/displaydocument.asp?docid=110716.

31. Bush and Scowcroft, *A World Transformed*, 353.

32. Found at the National Security Archive, http://www.gwu.edu/~nsarchiv/ NSAEBB/NSAEBB39/.

33. In the document, these goals are listed as "principles" that would guide U.S. policy. In some ways this terminology is more appropriate than the overly simple term goals, because "guiding principles" implies that as international perspectives shift in the natural course of interstate relations, principles can more flexibly

guide actions whereas goals could be interpreted as fixed, thus driving irrevocably to inflexible outcomes.

34. For details, see Dennis Ross, *Statecraft, and How to Restore America's Standing in the World* (New York: Farrar, Straus and Giroux, 2007), 82–84.

35. Bill Keller, "The Iraqi Invasion: Moscow Joins U.S. in Criticizing Iraq," *New York Times*, August 4, 1990, 1.

36. Ross, *Statecraft*, 87.

37. Ibid., 87–88.

38. James A. Baker III, *The Politics of Diplomacy: Revolution, War and Peace 1989–1992* (New York: G. O. Putnam's Sons, 1995), 305.

39. Ross, *Statecraft*, 89, quoting Michael Watkins and Susan Rosegrant, *Breakthrough International Negotiation: How Great Negotiators Transformed the World's Toughest Post–Cold War Conflicts* (San Francisco: Jossey-Bass, 2001), 194.

40. Terrence R. Fehner and Jack M. Hall, *The United States Department of Energy, A Summary History*, Office of Scientific and Technical Information, Oak Ridge Tennessee, 1994, 63–66.

Chapter 2. The Iraqi Context

1. Shivi Balaghi, *Saddam Hussein, A Biography,* (Greenwood Press Biographies (Westport, CT: Greenwood Press, 2006), 72. Phebe Marr, *The History of Modern Iraq* (Westview Press: Boulder Colorado, 2004), 22–23.

3. Found at http://wwi.lib.byu.edu/index.php/President_Wilson%27s_Fourteen_Points.

4. Marr, *History of Modern Iraq*, 23–24.

5. Ibid., 25.

6. Balaghi, *Saddam Hussein*, 12.

7. Marr, *History of Modern Iraq*, 28.

8. Nuri al-Said, a Sunni born in Baghdad, was a former Ottoman army officer and eventually deputy commander of the Iraqi army who had served with King Feisal during the war and remained his trusted confidant.

9. Marr, *History of Modern Iraq*, 37.

10. There is evidence that many members of the Iraqi leadership favored the Axis powers and were particularly supportive of German ideology during the early years of the war. The fact that a small contingent of the Luftwaffe flew in support of the Iraqi military against the British forces did nothing to reduce Allied anxiety about Axis influence in the region.

11. Rashid Ali, a Sunni born in Baghdad, had previously served as minister of justice and as prime minister in 1933.

12. The Anglo-Iraqi Treaty of 1930 gave the United Kingdom basing rights in Iraq. The British military principally used the Royal Air Force base at Habbaniyah.

13. Saddam made this incident famous throughout Iraq. It became the subject of two books and a movie—all of which were publicized in the period immediately after he took power in 1979.

14. The violence that followed the coup led to a prison sentence for Saddam and left him with a strong distaste for political infighting.
15. It is said that Saddam Hussein was one of two men standing behind al-Bakr when he appeared on television to announce the new Ba'ath government to the people of Iraq.
16. Balaghi, *Saddam Hussein*, 38.
17. Ibid., 47.
18. Ibid., 57.
19. Kevin M. Woods, *The Mother of All Battles: Saddam Hussein's Strategic Plan for the Gulf War* (Annapolis: Naval Institute Press, 2008), 31.
20. Other good treatments of Saddam Hussein include Efraim Karsh and Inari Rautsi, *Saddam Hussein: A Political Biography* (New York: Free Press, 1991), and Con Coughlin, *Saddam: His Rise and Fall* (New York: Harper Perennial, 2002).
21. Balaghi, *Saddam Hussein*, 72.
22. Some were said to have chanted the grand ayatollah's name as Saddam was hanged in 2006. The grand ayatollah was the father-in-law of Muqtada al-Sadr, the Iraqi theologian and political leader of the Mahdi Militia who would be very influential after the fall of Saddam.
23. For a succinct review of the war, see GlobalSecurity.org, at http://www.globalsecurity.org/military/world/war/iran-iraq.htm. Other useful studies include: Efraim Karsh, *The Iran-Iraq War, 1980–1988*, Essential Histories,(Oxford: Osprey, 2002) and Dilip Hiro, *The Longest War: The Iran-Iraq Military Conflict* (New York: Routledge, 1991).
24. This section is based largely upon the overview of the war outlined by the Iran Chamber Society, found at http://www.iranchamber.com/history/iran_iraq_war/iran_iraq_war1.php. For a much more detailed but largely similar description see Anthony H. Cordesman, *The Lessons of Modern War: The Iran-Iraq War 2* (Boulder, CO: Westview Press, 1990).
25. A report developed by the Stockholm International Peace Research Institute stipulated both Iran and Iraq used chemical weapons against each other in 1984. See the fact sheet found at http://books.sipri.org/product_info?c_product_id=363#.
26. Roger Hardy, "The Iran-Iraq War: 25 Years On," BBC News, found at http://news.bbc.co.uk/2/hi/middle_east/4260420.stm.
27. Iraq's main financial backers were the oil-rich Persian Gulf states, most notably Saudi Arabia ($30.9 billion), Kuwait ($8.2 billion), and the United Arab Emirates ($8 billion). From Global Security.org, found at http://www.globalsecurity.org/wmd/library/report/2004/isg-final-report/ch2_anxd_img06.jpg.
28. From the "Iraq Survey Group Final Report," of 30 September 2004, found at http://www.globalsecurity.org/wmd/library/report/2004/isg-final-report/isg-final-report_vol1_rfp-anx-d.htm.
29. Sarah Graham-Brown, *Sanctioning Saddam: The Politics of Intervention in Iraq* (New York: St. Martins, 1999), 2.
30. Ibid., 3.
31. Ibid., 4.

32. Woods, *Mother of All Battles*, 60.

33. Ibid., 64.

34. Ibid., 72.

35. The best brief summary of the attack can be found in Woods, *Mother of All Battles*, 81–88.

36. See, for example, Keith B. Payne, *The Great American Gamble: Deterrence Theory and Practice from the Cold War to the Twenty-First Century* (Fairfax, VA: National Institute Press, 2008), for a recent view on deterrence and its effectiveness.

Chapter 3. Desert Shield: The Line in the Sand

1. John S. Brown, "The Maturation of Operational Art, Operations DESERT SHIELD and DESERT STORM," in Michael D. Krause and R. Cody Phillips, eds., *Historical Perspectives of the Operational Art* (Washington, DC: U.S. Army Center of Military History, 2005), 452. Found at http://www.history.army.mil/books/OpArt/us5.htm.

2. United States Senate, "Statement of General H. Norman Schwarzkopf, Commander in Chief, United States Central Command, in Hearings Before the Committee on Armed Services, One Hundred First Congress, Second Session," 12 December 1989; 23, 24, 25, 26, 30 January; 2, 6, 7, 8, 21, 22 February; 7 March 1990 (S. Hrg. 101–70), 608, 626.

3. Headquarters, Army Forces Central Command, "COMUSARCENT OPLAN 1002-90 (Draft)," 16 July 1990, 4.

4. The best overview of the strategic deployment process and issues from the first Gulf War campaign can be found in James K. Mathews and Kora J. Holt, *So Many, So Much, So Far, So Fast: United States Transportation Command and Strategic Deployment in Operations Desert Shield and Desert Storm* (Joint History Office, May, 1996).

5. Frank N. Schubert and Theresa L. Kraus, eds., *The Whirlwind War: The United States Army in Operations Desert Shield and Desert Storm*, CMH Publication 70-30 (Washington, DC: U.S. Army Center of Military History, 1994), 53.

6. Even the secretary of defense knew that the initial forces were at risk. Colin Powell recounted a concerned phone call with Secretary Cheney on August 17, wherein Powell had to reassure an anxious Cheney that the risk was acceptable. See Colin L. Powell and Joseph E. Persico, *My American Journey* (New York: Random, 1987), 471.)

7. The 3rd MPS squadron was moving as well, with a similar equipment package from Guam.

8. The tremendous success of this initial deployment should rank as one of the most important and most challenging military actions of the entire long war with Iraq. The efforts of the newly established U.S. Transportation Command and the supporting staffs in CENTCOM, and particularly ARCENT (Third Army) and MARCENT (I MEF), deserve great praise.

9. Rick Atkinson, *Crusade: The Untold Story of the Persian Gulf War* (Boston: Houghton Mifflin, 1993), 108–114. The full Jedi team included Lieutenant Colonel Joseph

H. Purvis, Major Gregory M. Eckhart, Major William S. Pennypacker, and Major Daniel J. Roh.

10. As described by Collin A. Agee in his monograph, "Peeling the Onion: The Iraqi Center of Gravity in Desert Storm" (Fort Leavenworth, KS: School of Advanced Military Studies, U.S. Army Command and General Staff College ,1992), 26, the Jedi Knights under Purvis) had a tough task: "The mission they received on 18 September 1990 was straightforward: plan the ground offensive. They posted a list of 'Parameters' on the wall of their small cell; atop the list was: 'Outnumbered!'"

11. Thomas B. Allen, F. Clifton Berry Jr., and Norman Polmar, *War in the Gulf* (Atlanta, GA: Turner Publishing, 1991), 49.

12. The eight RGFC divisions included two armored, one mechanized, one special forces, and four infantry divisions organized into two corps of some 140,000 troops, supported by more than fifteen hundred tanks and infantry vehicles. The I Corps consisted of two armored units, the Hammurabi and Medina Divisions; one mechanized infantry unit, the Tawakalna Division; and a motorized infantry unit, the Al-Faw Division. The II Corps consisted of two motorized infantry units, the Nebuchadnezzar and the Adnan Divisions. The remaining, independent, mechanized infantry unit was the Baghdad Division, stationed in and around the Iraqi capital to serve as a deterrent to potential mutineers. The Republican Guard Forces Command also controlled several special forces (commando) brigades, and one naval infantry brigade.

13. Personal correspondence between Colonel Purvis and Collin Agee, quoted in "Peeling the Onion," 26–27.

14. Atkinson, *Crusade*, 110.

15. According to the U.S. Air Force, during the first Gulf campaign, the Checkmate organization expanded to nearly 150 people from throughout the air staff, intelligence community, and other armed services. They worked twenty-four hours a day supporting the "Black Hole" planners in Riyadh with strategic targeting information and analysis. The organization included Technical Plans and War and Mobilization Plans offices. The organization became a primary conduit of all-source intelligence and force-level planning assessments, and was considered to be a threat to the formal Joint Staff control of theater intelligence and planning. After the war, at the direction of the CJCS (General Powell) the Air Force disbanded the wartime Checkmate organization.

16. Atkinson, *Crusade*, 58.

17. Ibid., 59–60.

18. The Black Hole seemed to be named more for its secrecy than for its lack of technology and light.—It was in execution one of the most sophisticated and capable command and control facilities constructed up to that time.

19. Atkinson, *Crusade*, 110–111.

20. General Powell commented frequently thereafter that his approach was not based primarily on numbers, but was instead rooted in the idea that more forces also reduced the time of an operation and therefore the overall risk. As he

recounted in his memoir, Powell felt that it was necessary to "go in big and end it quickly. We could not put the United States through another Vietnam." See Powell and Persico, *My American Journey*, 487.

21. Atkinson, *Crusade*, 112–113.

22. Powell and Persico, *My American Journey*, 485–486.

23. Ibid., 447.

24. Woods, *Mother of All Battles*, 101.

25. Ibid., 97–98.

26. Ibid., 125.

27. The Popular Army was first used during the Iran-Iraq War, and was essentially composed of untrained militia; it was neither popular nor much of any army and was generally held in contempt by the regular Iraqi army. Woods, *Mother of All Battles*, 100.

28. Schubert and Kraus, *Whirlwind War*, 109.

29. U.S. Congress, Senate, *Crisis in the Persian Gulf Region: U.S. Policy Options and Implications, Hearings Before the Committee on Armed Services*, 101st Cong., 2d sess., 1990, 109.

30. Schubert and Kraus, *Whirlwind War*, 113–114.

31. The readiness ratings of the time designated C-1 as "combat ready," C-2 and C-3 ratings were designated for units whose personnel and equipment readiness for combat was substandard.

32. Schubert and Kraus, *Whirlwind War*, 123.

33. Marine Reserve units mobilized and deployed for combat included 14th Marines, 23rd Marines, 24th Marines, 25th Marines, 4th Reconnaissance Battalion, 4th Tank Battalion, 8th Tank Battalion, 4th Light Armored Vehicle Battalion, 4th Assault Amphibian Battalion, 3rd Civil Affairs Group, 4th Civil Affairs Group, 6th Engineer Support Battalion, 6th Motor Transport Battalion, 4th Landing Support Battalion, 4th Light Anti Air Defense Battalion, 4th Combat Engineer Battalion, 4th Maintenance Battalion, 4th Supply Battalion, 4th Medical Battalion, 6th Communication Battalion, 6th Engineer Support Battalion, 6th Motor Transport Battalion, Marine Aircraft Group-41, Marine Aircraft Group-42, Marine Aircraft Group-46, and Marine Aircraft Group-49.

34. John S. Brown, "The Maturation of Operational Art, Operations DESERT SHIELD and DESERT STORM," in Krause and Phillips, *Historical Perspectives of the Operational Art*, 452–453.

35. This was possible, perhaps for the first time, due to the maturation of the army corps into a semi-independent fighting force. "This trend had been recognized, and by the late 1980s had matured into the concept and then into the reality of the Capable Corps. Such a corps featured a sizable inventory of combat support and combat service support units that rendered it capable of sustaining combat operations for a prolonged period. Unlike the thinly manned command and control headquarters of World War II, the late twentieth-century corps had logistical attributes of the World War II army group. The net result was that DESERT STORM was fought on the ground with divisions as operational building

blocks and corps as practitioners of the operational art." Brown, "Maturation of Operational Art," in Krause and Phillips, *Historical Perspectives of the Operational Art*, 444.

36. Ibid., 452–453.

Chapter 4. Desert Storm: The 1991 Gulf War Campaign

1. H. Norman Schwarzkopf and Peter Petre, *It Doesn't Take a Hero: The Autobiography of General H. Norman Schwarzkopf* (New York: Bantam Books, 1992), 413.

2. General Schwarzkopf's career was indicative of many of his most senior peers in the American military—it was almost entirely based upon his service in Vietnam as a relatively junior officer and the quality of his senior staff service. In 1965, Schwarzkopf asked to serve in Vietnam and was assigned as a task force advisor to a South Vietnamese airborne division. On his second tour in Vietnam in March 1970, while serving as a battalion commander, Schwarzkopf received word that men under his command had encountered a minefield; he rushed to the scene and found several soldiers still trapped there. Schwarzkopf personally risked his life to extract his men from the field and was injured by one of the explosions, yet eventually led his men to safety. Schwarzkopf was awarded his third Silver Star for his actions. Later Schwarzkopf served as a brigade commander at Fort Lewis, Washington, and as assistant division commander (support) of the 8th Mechanized Division in West Germany. Then he was promoted to major general and given command of the 24th Mechanized Infantry Division at Fort Stewart, Georgia. During that posting he also served for a short period as deputy commander of the joint task force that invaded the tiny Caribbean island of Grenada. In 1986, Schwarzkopf was promoted to lieutenant general, and took command of I Corps at Fort Lewis, Washington. In 1988, he was promoted to general and appointed commander in chief of the U.S. Central Command, having not commanded in combat since he was a lieutenant colonel.

3. The airmen still did not fully trust either the Navy aircraft or the Tomahawk cruise missile. F-14 fighters were omitted from the early strikes because the Air Force planners considered them unsafe, and many TLAM targets were also covered by manned aircraft in case the missile failed. Even Colin Powell was said to doubt their reliability (see Atkinson, *Crusade*, 15.) In execution, the Tomahawk was startlingly accurate and reliable.

4. The Scud was a liquid-fueled ballistic missile originally developed by the Soviet Union during the Cold War and exported to many other countries. It had an operational range of approximately three hundred kilometers and could carry a warhead that weighed nearly a thousand pounds. Iraq first used the missiles during the Iran-Iraq War. Some eighty-five were fired during the 1991 campaign.

5. Promoted to general, Cody would later serve as the Army's vice chief of staff during *Iraqi Freedom*.

6. One of these bases, Al Taqaddum, would serve as a major coalition airbase during Iraqi Freedom.

7. Although coalition pilots had hoped otherwise, the first week of the air campaign saw very few Iraqi air force sorties. The Iraqi aircraft that did fly did little damage; only one coalition aircraft is known to have been shot down by the Iraqi air force, yet thirty-eight Iraqi MiGs were shot down by coalition aircraft. Soon after, the Iraqi air force began fleeing to Iran, with over one hundred aircraft flown to that country by their pilots.

8. In fact the Israelis did ready their ground forces in the Negev desert for a fight, but the Bush White House put as much reassurance and diplomatic pressure as they could muster on the government of Prime Minister Yitsak Shamir to prevent an Israeli response in order to preserve the largely Arab coalition that they had formed against Saddam over the preceding months.

9. Schwarzkopf and Petre, *It Doesn't Take a Hero*, 418.

10. See Robert A. Pape, *Bombing to Win: Air Power and Coercion in War* (Ithaca, NY: Cornell University Press, 1996), 215.

11. Iraq was eventually persuaded by the Soviet Union to propose a full and unconditional withdrawal from Kuwait without having won any concessions, but by that time the U.S. government insisted on a timeframe that did not allow Iraq to remove all its ordnance. As this would have seriously weakened it militarily, Iraq pressed for more time, but was finally rebuffed.

12. CENTCOM had only been created in 1983 and few thought war in its area of responsibility likely, so it suffered from a bit of strategic neglect. CENTCOM had not benefited significantly from the recent changes driven within the U.S. military by the Goldwater-Nichols DOD Reorganization act of 1986.

13. The air power argument was that by attacking the right strategic targets, Saddam's ability to orchestrate the combat phase would be so severely degraded as to cause him to lose control of his military and eventually be forced to end the conflict. The ground operational argument viewed the destruction of the RGFC as the key to destroying Saddam's military power-projection capability and thus ending his ability to threaten the use of force. The air power concept would emphasize striking targets in Baghdad; the ground effort would focus air power against the primary field forces of the RGFC in the south of Iraq. Because Horner had abundant weapons and a great deal of time, he was able to do a bit of both. The argument between the two philosophies continues.

14. Michael R. Gordon and Bernard E. Trainor, *The Generals' War: The Inside Story of the Conflict in the Gulf* (Boston: Little, Brown, 1994), 241–242.

15. Ibid., 244–245.

16. Marr, *Modern History of Iraq*, 236.

17. Woods, *Mother of All Battles*, 16.

18. Ibid., 18–23.

19. Schubert and Kraus, *Whirlwind War*, 162.

20. CNN correspondents John Holliman and Peter Arnett and CNN anchor Bernard Shaw relayed audio reports from the Al-Rashid Hotel as the air strikes began over Baghdad. CNN had previously convinced the Iraqi government to allow installation of a permanent audio circuit in their bureau. When the

telephones of all of the other Western TV correspondents went dead during the bombing, CNN was the only service able to provide live reporting. After the initial bombing, Arnett remained behind and was, for a time, the only American TV correspondent reporting from Iraq.

21. Schubert and Kraus, *Whirlwind War*, 164.

22. From the 1st Cavalry Division website, http://www.first-team.us/journals/1stndx08.html.

23. From the history of the 1st Battalion, 5th Cavalry Regiment, found at http://www.globalsecurity.org/military/agency/army/1-5cav-hist.htm.

24. This effort involved then Lieutenant Colonel Tommy Franks, the future CENTCOM commander during Operation Iraqi Freedom.

25. This exchange is covered in detail by the PBS *Frontline* investigative reporting program. The commentary of the main participants can be found at http://www.pbs.org/wgbh/pages/frontline/gulf/script_b.html.

26. Bahrain, Kuwait, Oman, the UAE, and Qatar.

27. *Report to Congress on the Conduct of the Persian Gulf War*, 258.

28. The coalition initially deployed a substantial amphibious force in the Persian Gulf which provided their only forced entry capability. By mid-January the amphibious force (2nd MEF) stood at some thirty-one amphibious ships carrying the assault echelons of both the 4th and 5th Marine Expeditionary Brigades and the 13th Marine Expeditionary Unit (Special Ops Capable). The force also had five Military Sealift Command (MSC) ships and two maritime prepositioning ships to carry the follow-on echelons. In total it had 17,095 personnel, 26 AV8B Harriers, 136 helicopters, 47 M60 main battle tanks, 112 amphibious assault vehicles (AAVs), 86 light armored vehicles (LAVs), 44 155mm howitzers, 8 105mm howitzers, 100 mobile TOW antitank systems, 80 Stinger air defense systems, and 2,271 wheeled vehicles. See P. Antill (26 February 2003), *Gulf War—Coalition Amphibious Operations*, http://www.historyofwar.org/articles/wars_gulf_amphibious.html.

29. Ibid.

30. Schwarzkopf and Petre, *It Doesn't Take a Hero*, 433.

31. Gordon and Trainor, *Generals' War*, 306–307.

32. Brown, "Maturation of Operational Art," in Krause and Phillips, *Historical Perspectives of the Operational Art*, 454.

33. General Powell said of this incident in his autobiography, "Whatever use the structure served, a large number of civilians died in the strike, which the whole world witnessed on television as victims were hauled from the smoking rubble. Schwarzkopf and I discussed this tragedy. Did we still need to pound downtown Baghdad over a month into the war? How many times could you bomb the Baath Party headquarters, and for what purpose? No one was sitting there waiting for the next Tomahawk to hit. Schwarzkopf and I started reviewing targets more closely before each day's missions. If nothing else, the Al Firdos bunker strike underscored the need to start the combined air/ground offensive and end the war." See Powell and Persico, *My American Journey*, 513.

34. Some of the fires burned out of control until November 1991, initially because the danger of combat operations prevented sending in firefighting crews, plus land mines had been placed in areas around the oil wells, and a general military clean-up of unexploded ordnance in the area was necessary before the fires could be effectively put out. Some seven hundred oil wells were set ablaze, and up to six million barrels of oil were lost each day that the fires burned. The cost to Kuwait of extinguishing the fires was estimated at nearly $1.5 billion. By the time they were extinguished the fires had burned for months and the byproducts of the petroleum burn had caused pollution in both the soil and air of Kuwait.

35. *Report to Congress on the Conduct of the Persian Gulf War*, 266.

36. Gordon and Trainor, *Generals' War*, 361–362.

37. General Franks had been planning to begin his corps assault at 5:30 the next morning, G+1.

38. *Report to Congress on the Conduct of the Persian Gulf War*, 270.

39. Brown, "Maturation of Operational Art," in Krause and Phillips, *Historical Perspectives of the Operational Art*, 461.

40. *Report to Congress on the Conduct of the Persian Gulf War*, 265–266.

41. Ibid., 277.

42. Brown, "Maturation of Operational Art," in Krause Phillips, *Historical Perspectives of the Operational Art*, 462.

43. Gordon and Trainor, *General's War*, 380–381.

44. Ibid., 383.

45. Brown, "Maturation of Operational Art," in Krause and Phillips, *Historical Perspectives of the Operational Art*, 465.

46. Robert H. Scales Jr. et al., *Certain Victory: The U.S. Army in the Gulf War* (Washington, DC: Office of the Chief of Staff, U.S. Army/GPO, 1993), 249.

47. Tom Clancy and Frederick M. Franks, *Into the Storm: A Study in Command* (New York: Putnam, 1997), 543.

48. Gordon and Trainor, *Generals' War*, 396.

49. Ibid., 418–419.

50. Woods, *Mother of All Battles*, 142.

51. Ibid., 14–17.

52. Ibid., 208.

53. Ibid., 189, 199, 207.

54. Ibid., 227.

55. Ibid., 228.

56. Ibid., 232.

57. Ibid., 241.

58. Brown, "Maturation of Operational Art," in Krause and Phillips, *Historical Perspectives of the Operational Art*, 464.

59. Scales et al., *Certain Victory*, 315.

60. From the history of the 1st Battalion, 5th Cavalry Regiment, found at http://www.globalsecurity.org/military/agency/army/1-5cav-hist.htm.

61. On the cease-fire, see, for example, Charles Duelfer, "How Baghdad Divided the Conquerors," *Los Angeles Times*, June 11, 2000, home edition, The World/ Iraq, 1, http://www.proquest.com/ (accessed July 3, 2008).

62. For an example of the immediate shift by the Iraqis to quell domestic revolt, see Nora Boustany, "A Trail of Death in Iraq; Shiite Refugees Tell of Atrocities by Republican Guard," *Washington Post* (pre-1997 Fulltext), March 26, 1991, final edition, http://www.proquest.com/ (accessed July 3, 2008).

Chapter 5. Interregnum: Iraq and the
UN Sanctions during the 1990s

1. Bill Clinton, "Iraq and the United States: Meeting the Threat of Predators," *Vital Speeches of the Day* 64, no. 10 (March 1, 1998): 290-293. Found at http://www.pro-quest.com/ (accessed July 3, 2008).

2. Marr, *Modern History of Iraq*, 241.

3. Global Policy Forum, "Iraq Sanctions: Humanitarian Implications and Options for the Future," August 6, 2002, 32.

4. Barton Gellman, "Allied Air War Struck Broadly in Iraq—Officials Acknowledge Strategy Went Beyond Purely Military Targets," *Washington Post*, June 23, 1991, A1.

5. United Nations, *The United Nations and the Iraq–Kuwait Conflict, 1990–1996* (New York, 1996), 186–188.

6. Maggie O'Kane, "The Wake of War," *The Guardian*, May 18, 1996, T034.

7. Patrick E. Tyler, "Excerpts from Two Statements by Bush on Iraq's Proposal for Ending Conflict," *New York Times*, February 16, 1991, 1.

8. Global Policy Forum, "Iraq Sanctions," 33.

9. "Reports complied by the World Food and the World Health Organization (WHO) compared the infant mortality rate (IMR) and the mortality rate for children under five for the years for the period 1989 to 1994. Over the period that the sanctions were in effect, the Iraqi IMR doubled and the mortality rates for children under the age of five had increased six fold." Ibid., 33.

10. Mark Tran, "Saddam Builds, Iraqis Suffer, Iraqi Leaders Spends Millions on Palaces," *Ottawa Citizen*, November 15, 1994, C1.

11. Madeleine Albright and Bill Woodward, *Madam Secretary: A Memoir* (New York: Macmillan, 2003, 275.

12. Global Policy Forum, "Iraq Sanctions," 10.

13. Ibid., 7.

14. Marr, *Modern History of Iraq*, 246.

15. Ibid., 248.

16. Ibid., 250.

17. Ibid., 251.

18. Again primarily by the United States, though thirteen nations participated in some way, with the processing of material contributions from thirty countries; forces from four other nations besides the U.S. participated in Operation Provide Comfort.

19. Provide Comfort was planned and executed by the U.S. European Command, and was commanded on the ground by Lieutenant General John Shalikashvili. Among those participating was Lieutenant Colonel John Abizaid.

20. For the official UN summary of UNSCOM, see http://www.un.org/Depts/unscom/index.html.

21. The best overall treatment of the UN effort is Charles Duelfer's *Hide and Seek: The Search for Truth in Iraq* (New York: Public Affairs, 2009).

22. See the UN official overview of UNSCOM at http://www.un.org/Depts/unscom/unscom.htm.

23. Ibid.

24. See the PBS *Frontline* interview with Robert Gates: http://www.pbs.org/wgbh/pages/frontline/gulf/oral/gates/2.html.

25. See the UNSCOM Chronology at: http://www.un.org/Depts/unscom/Chronology/chronologyframe.htm.

26. The text of UNSCR 715 is available at http://www.undemocracy.com/S-RES-715(1991).pdf.

27. See the Operation Southern Watch overview at GlobalSecurity.org http://www.globalsecurity.org/military/ops/southern_watch.htm.

28. See the operation overview at GlobalSecurity.org http://www.globalsecurity.org/military/ops/strike_930117.htm.

29. For additional background to include the fact that several of the plotters were found guilty by a Kuwaiti court, see http://www.fas.org/irp/agency/doj/oig/fbilab1/05bush2.htm.

30. See http://www.globalsecurity.org/military/ops/desert_strike.htm.

31. Cable News Network (hereafter CNN), "U.S. launches missile strikes against Iraq," September 3, 1996, found at http://edition.cnn.com/WORLD/9609/03/iraq.bombing/index.html.

32. Ibid.

33. Global Policy Forum, "Iraq Sanctions," 17.

34. Ibid., 18.

35. In 2006, one South Korean businessman named Tongsun Park was convicted in New York of conspiracy to launder money and acting as an unregistered agent of Saddam Hussein's Iraq. See Colum Lynch, "Park Sentenced to 5 Years in U.N. Oil-for-Food Bribery Scandal, South Korean Businessman Had Promised to Get Sanctions Eased for Hussein's Government," *Washington Post*, February 23, 2007, A11.

36. Ibid., A13. Three other UN officials were also charged with crimes related to the oil-for-food program.

37. Samuel Berger, "Saddam Is the Root of All Iraq's Problems," *Financial Times*, May, 4, 2000, found at http://www.fas.org/news/iraq/2000/05/000504-iraq-usia1.htm.

38. Global Policy Forum, "Iraq Sanctions," 13.

39. Ibid., 10.

40. See http://www.un.org/Depts/unscom/Chronology/chronologyframe.htm.

41. VX is an extremely toxic substance whose only use is as a chemical warfare agent. It was classified as a weapon of mass destruction by the United Nations in UNSCR 687. The production and stockpiling of VX was outlawed by the Chemical Weapons Convention of 1993. It is odorless and tasteless, and can be distributed as a liquid or as a vapor. VX blocks the action of acetylcholinesterase, thus resulting in sustained contractions of all the muscles in the body, which causes death by asphyxiation.

42. See CNN coverage at http://edition.cnn.com/WORLD/meast/9811/14/iraq.07/; see also GlobalSecurity.org, www.globalsecurity.org/military/ops/iraq_back.htm.

43. Linda D. Kozaryn, "Saddam Abused His Last Chance, Clinton Says," American Forces Press Service, found at http://www.defenselink.mil/news/newsarticle.aspx?id =41731.

44. See http://www.defenselink.mil/news/newsarticle.aspx?id=41727.

45. It was the first operation that used B-1B Lancer bomber aircraft in a combat role, and the first combat mission flown by female American pilots.

46. "Secretary of Defense and Chairman of the Joint Chiefs of Staff Briefing on Operation DESERT FOX," December 19, 1998, found at http://www.defenselink. mil/transcripts/transcript.aspx?transcriptid=1791.

47. Charles Duelfer admits that the U2 issue was perhaps an incorrect choice by UNSCOM. He does insist that the claims of Scott Ritter and others that UNSCOM did spy on the Iraqis were false. See Duelfer, *Hide and Seek*, 78, 182–183.

48. UNSCOM had previously written about its own accomplishments, noting in March 1996 that it had "uncovered significant undeclared proscribed weapons programmes, destroyed elements of these programmes so far identified, including equipment, facilities and materials, and has been attempting to map out and verify the full extent of these programmes in the face of Iraq's serious efforts to deceive and conceal. . . . UNSCOM has directed and supervised the destruction or rendering harmless of several identified facilities and large quantities of equipment for the production of chemical and biological weapons as well as proscribed long-range missiles." The report also listed examples of what it had uncovered since 1991: "the existence of Iraq's offensive biological warfare programme; the chemical nerve agent VX and other advanced chemical weapons capabilities; and Iraq's indigenous production of proscribed missiles engines. UNSCOM has supervised the destruction of the following proscribed items: 48 operational long-range missiles, 14 conventional missile warheads, 6 operational mobile launchers, 30 missile chemical warheads, 38,537 filled and empty chemical munitions, 690 tonnes of chemical weapons agent, more than 3,000 tonnes of precursors chemicals, 426 pieces of chemical weapons production equipment, the entire Al-Hakam, the main biological weapons production facility, and a variety of biological weapons production equipment and materials." See http://www.un.org/Depts/unscom/Achievements/achievements.html.

49. In addition to the Office of the Chairman with executive, legal, and liaison functions, UNMOVIC comprised four divisions (Planning and Operations,

Analysis and Assessment, Information, Technical Support and Training) as well as an administrative service. The commission maintained its headquarters at the United Nations in New York.

50. On June 29, 2007, the Security Council adopted resolution 1762 (2007) which terminated the mandate of UNMOVIC under the relevant resolutions. For the official UN summary of UNMOVIC, see http://www.unmovic.org/.

51. See UNMOVIC's "Compendium of Iraq's Proscribed Weapons Programmes in the Chemical, Biological and Missile Areas," http://www.un.org/Depts/unmovic/new/pages/compendium.asp.

52. Global Policy Forum, "Iraq Sanctions," 10.

53. Ibid., 15.

54. Ibid.

55. Many believed that Saddam was inciting aggression purposely. See, for example, Robin Wright, "Hussein Is Itching for a Fight, U.S. Officials Say; Persian Gulf: Members of the Clinton Administration See a Pattern of Iraqi Actions Aimed at Triggering a Military Response. U.N. Sanctions Might Be Casualties," *Los Angeles Times*, September 23, 2000, http://www.proquest.com/ (accessed July 3, 2008).

56. Rose Gottemoeller, "Evolution of Sanctions in Practice and Theory," *Survival* 49, no. 4 (December 2007): 101.

57. PBS interview with L. Paul Bremer.

58. L. Paul Bremer III, with Malcolm McConnell, *My Year in Iraq: The Struggle to Build a Future of Hope* (New York: Simon & Schuster, 2006), 18. See also Bruce R. Pirnie and Edward O'Connell, *Counterinsurgency in Iraq (2003–2006): RAND Counterinsurgency Study—Volume 2* (Santa Monica, CA: 2008), 9.

59. Michael Kelly "Properly Provoked," *Washington Post*, August 14, 2002, final edition, http://www.proquest.com/ (accessed July 3, 2008).

60. Kenneth Katzman, "Iraq and Al Qaeda," Congressional Research Service Report RL32217, April 28, 2008, CRS-2, found at http://fpc.state.gov/documents/organization/105195.pdf.

61. While most analysts reject the Saddam–Al Qaeda connection, the best counterarguments can be found in Stephen Hayes, *The Connection: How al Qaeda's Collaboration with Saddam Hussein Has Endangered America* (New York: HarperCollins, 2004).

62. CIA Director George Tenet in his memoir, *At the Center of the Storm*, confirms the activities of Zarqawi in Iraq and his relationship with Saddam's regime. See the extensive excerpts from the memoir in William Kristol, "Inadvertent Truths: George Tenet's Revealing Memoir," *Weekly Standard*, May 14, 2007, ahttp://www.weeklystandard.com/content/public/articles/000/000/013/615cglnt.asp (accessed August 20, 2007). On terrorist affiliations with Saddam, see also Lawrence Wright, *The Looming Tower: Al-Qaeda and the Road to 9/11* (New York: Alfred Knopf, 2006), 295–296.

63. An Arab expert's account of the inner workings of Zarqawi and Al Qaeda can be found in the work of the London-based journalist, Abdel Bari Atwan,

The Secret History of Al Qaeda (Berkeley: University of California Press, 2006), 179–206.

Chapter 6. Turning Back to War

1. Richard Perle, "Ambushed on the Potomac," *National Interest Online*, January 6, 2009, found at http://www.nationalinterest.org/Article.aspx?id=20486.

2. The pertinent paragraph in the Republican Party platform for 2000 reads: "A new Republican administration will patiently rebuild an international coalition opposed to Saddam Hussein and committed to joint action. We will insist that Iraq comply fully with its disarmament commitments. We will maintain the sanctions on the Iraqi regime while seeking to alleviate the suffering of innocent Iraqi people. We will react forcefully and unequivocally to any evidence of reconstituted Iraqi capabilities for producing weapons of mass destruction. In 1998, Congress passed and the president signed the Iraq Liberation Act, the clear purpose of which is to assist the opposition to Saddam Hussein. The administration has used an arsenal of dilatory tactics to block any serious support to the Iraqi National Congress, an umbrella organization reflecting a broad and representative group of Iraqis who wish to free their country from the scourge of Saddam Hussein's regime. We support the full implementation of the Iraq Liberation Act, which should be regarded as a starting point in a comprehensive plan for the removal of Saddam Hussein and the restoration of international inspections in collaboration with his successor. Republicans recognize that peace and stability in the Persian Gulf is impossible as long as Saddam Hussein rules Iraq."

3. Douglas J. Feith, *War and Decision: Inside the Pentagon at the Dawn of the War on Terrorism* (New York: Harper, 2008), 199.

4. Ibid., 200.

5. Significantly, Feith notes that Scooter Libby, chief of staff to Vice President Cheney, also advocated action against Saddam. See Feith, *War and Decision*, 203.

6. Ibid., 207.

7. Ibid., 210–211.

8. Ibid., 213.

9. During his 2002 State of the Union address, President Bush labeled those three countries as an "Axis of Evil." "States like these and their terrorist allies," he said, "constitute an axis of evil, arming to threaten the peace of the world. By seeking weapons of mass destruction, these regimes pose a grave and growing danger. They could provide these arms to terrorists, giving them the means to match their hatred. They could attack our allies or attempt to blackmail the United States. In any of these cases, the price of indifference would be catastrophic."

10. Douglas J. Feith, "Why We Went to War in Iraq," *The Wall Street Journal*, July 3, 2008, 11.

11. Traditionally, using the phrase "the decision to use force" implies an objective determination that extreme means are required in response to a threat. In the United States, only the president has the constitutional authority to make such a decision. However, the 2002 national security decision-making process that led to

renewed hostilities did not follow this model. Most significantly, unlike the case of his father in 1990, no specific decision by President Bush has been recorded. It is far more accurate to write that the process of defending the United States led the national command authority to employ military force against Iraq. The notion that the nation could initiate combat operations without a formal decision should be of concern.

12. George P. Shultz, "Act Now; The Danger Is Immediate. Saddam Hussein Must Be Removed," *Washington Post*, September 6, 2002, A25, found at http://www .proquest.com/ (accessed July 3, 2008).

13. Soon to be labeled terrorists once the real objective of the attacks became clear.

14. Most of this analysis is informed by the first person explanation of Defense Under Secretary for Policy Douglas Feith in his previously cited book about the war, *War and Decision*. For his recounting of the secure video teleconference conducted by President Bush on September 13, see *War and Decision*, 13–17.

15. Kelly, "Properly Provoked."

16. Many believe that the resolutionviolations alone were sufficient provocation for a return to hostilities with Iraq. Given a strict interpretation of the resolution that secured the cease-fire in 1991, they are correct.

17. Fantastically, Iraq fired on a reconnaissance drone within the no-fly zone on September 11 itself.

18. Feith, *War and Decision*, 15.

19. Doug Feith explains the president's logic: "When the president ultimately decided that the Iraqi regime must be ousted by force, he was influenced by five key factors: 1) *Saddam was a threat to U.S. interests before 9/11.* The Iraqi dictator had started wars against Iran and Kuwait, and had fired missiles at Saudi Arabia and Israel. Unrepentant about the rape of Kuwait, he remained intensely hostile to the U.S. He provided training, funds, safe haven and political support to various types of terrorists. He had developed WMD and used chemical weapons fatally against Iran and Iraqi Kurds. Iraq's official press issued statements praising the 9/11 attacks on the U.S. 2) *The threat of renewed aggression by Saddam was more troubling and urgent after 9/11.* Though Saddam's regime was not implicated in the 9/11 operation, it was an important state supporter of terrorism. And President Bush's strategy was not simply retaliation against the group responsible for 9/11. Rather it was to prevent the next major attack. This focused U.S. officials not just on al Qaeda, but on all the terrorist groups and state supporters of terrorism who might be inspired by 9/11—especially on those with the potential to use weapons of mass destruction. 3) *To contain the threat from Saddam, all reasonable means short of war had been tried unsuccessfully for a dozen years.* The U.S. did not rush to war. Working mainly through the U.N., we tried a series of measures to contain the Iraqi threat: formal diplomatic censure, weapons inspections, economic sanctions, no-fly zones, no-drive zones and limited military strikes. A defiant Saddam, however, dismantled the containment strategy and the U.N. Security Council had no stomach to sustain its own resolutions, let alone compel Saddam's compliance. 4) *While there were large risks involved in a war, the risks of leaving Saddam in power were*

even larger. The U.S. and British pilots patrolling the no-fly zones were routinely under enemy fire, and a larger confrontation—over Kuwait again or some other issue—appeared virtually certain to arise once Saddam succeeded in getting out from under the U.N.'s crumbling economic sanctions. Mr. Bush decided it was unacceptable to wait while Saddam advanced his biological weapons program or possibly developed a nuclear weapon. The CIA was mistaken, we all now know, in its assessment that we would find chemical and biological weapons stockpiles in Iraq. But after the fall of the regime, intelligence officials did find chemical and biological weapons programs structured so that Iraq could produce stockpiles in three to five weeks. They also found that Saddam was intent on having a nuclear weapon. The CIA was wrong in saying just before the war that his nuclear program was active; but Iraq appears to have been in a position to make a nuclear weapon in less than a year if it purchased fissile material from a supplier such as North Korea. 5) *America after 9/11 had a lower tolerance for such dangers*. It was reasonable—one might say obligatory—for the president to worry about a renewed confrontation with Saddam. Like many others, he feared Saddam might then use weapons of mass destruction again, perhaps deployed against us through a proxy such as one of the many terrorist groups Iraq supported." Douglas J. Feith, "Why We Went to War in Iraq," *Wall Street Journal*, July 3, 2008, 11.

20. Richard B. Myers and Malcolm McConnell, *Eyes on the Horizon: Serving on the Front Lines of National Security* (New York: Threshold Editions, 2009), 163.

21. The White House [National Security Council], "A National Security Strategy for A New Century" (Washington, DC: Government Printing Office, 1999), 19.

22. The Taliban is a Sunni Islamist, predominately Pashtun, movement originally headed by Mullah Mohammed Omar and characterized by an extremely strict and "anti-modern" ideology. Omar's supporters were a mix of former military, teachers, and Afghan refugees who had studied at Islamic religious schools; most members of the Taliban were from southern Afghanistan and western Pakistan. It is strongly suspected that the Taliban initially received training and supplies from the Pakistani government and its security services. The Taliban took control in Kabul in 1996 and instituted increasingly severe and restrictive laws; the following year the Taliban seemed to form an alliance with Al Qaeda and actively supported its training camps. The Taliban's destruction of the two Buddhas of Bamyan on March 21, 2001, received international condemnation.

23. Though there were a few analysts who envisioned a link between Al Qaeda and other national governments (Sudan, for example) none of those governments had the wherewithal to attack the United States conventionally.

24. The United Nations Security Council was never asked to authorize the campaign in Afghanistan. Although there little debate over whether UN authorization was required, the operation there was clearly viewed as an act of self-defense provided for under Article 51 of the UN Charter. The U.S. government did not officially declare war, but instead labeled the Taliban and its supporters terrorists no different than the individuals who made the attacks. Over time the Bush adminis-

tration determined that the fighters in Afghanistan could be labeled enemy non-combatants and thus denied the protections of the Geneva Convention.

25. See http://www.globalsecurity.org/military/ops/enduring-freedom-plan.htm.

26. Useful analysis of the Enduring Freedom campaign can be found in the following: Carl Conetta, *Strange Victory: A Critical Appraisal of Operation Enduring Freedom and the Afghanistan War—Project of Defense Alternatives Research Monograph 6* (Cambridge, MA: Project on Defense Alternatives, Commonwealth Institute, 2002); Norman Friedman, *Terrorism, Afghanistan, and America's New Way of War* (Annapolis: Naval Institute Press, 2003); Michael Radu, "This Afghan War is Different," *U.S. Naval Institute Proceedings* 127 (December 2001): 48–49; Daniel Bergner, "Where the Enemy Is Everywhere and Nowhere," *New York Times Magazine* 152 (July 20, 2003): 38–47; Gregory K. Herring, *The War in Afghanistan: A Strategic Analysis* (Carlisle Barracks, PA: Army War College, April 2003); Michael E. O'Hanlon, "A Flawed Masterpiece," *Foreign Affairs* 81, no. 3 (May/June 2002): 47–63; Milan N. Vego, "What Can We Learn from Enduring Freedom?" *U.S. Naval Institute Proceedings* 128, no. 7 (July 2002): 28–33.

27. Franks, *American Soldier*, 268.

28. Another example of a policy decision designed for Operation Enduring Freedom that eventually affected operations in Iraq was the establishment of the holding facility in Guantanamo Bay, Cuba. The detention camp at that facility, known commonly as Gitmo, was originally created in January 2002 to house captured members of the Taliban and Al Qaeda, mostly those captured in the field in Afghanistan. At that time, there were already some three hundred detainees in U.S. custody who were not recognized as having prisoner of war status (they were considered "illegal combatants") and the United States needed a location where they could be kept and where intelligence information could be gathered. Afghanistan was too hazardous and holding them on American soil would have entitled the detainees to rights under U.S. law—rights that some attorneys advising the Bush administration thought would inhibit intelligence-gathering efforts, which were the immediate priority. Marine Brigadier General Michael Lehnert, the facility commander, instituted procedures that would have treated the detainees as if they had authorized rights under the Geneva Conventions, but such humane treatment was later held in abeyance as the desire for intelligence pressed subsequent commanders to use much harsher methods of internment. By the summer of 2002, Gitmo held over five hundred detainees, and although some were released back to their home countries as early as October 2002, most of those in custody were held for years prior to release, most frequently either because they were considered a threat to the ongoing operations or because their native lands would not accept them back. As the detainments continued, the entire process at Guantanamo soon came under international scrutiny and was condemned by organizations such as Human Rights Watch. Member states of both the European Union and the Organization of American States, as well as Amnesty International, soon followed suit and Gitmo became a foreign policy nightmare for the United States government. Inasmuch as the United States had

always sought to represent the ideals of democracy and freedom for all peoples, employing a lesser standard for the treatment of its enemies after 2001 seemed hypocritical to many observers.

29. Rumsfeld served in the United States House of Representatives from 1963 to 1969, representing Illinois's 13th Congressional District; he then worked in the White House as director of the United States Office of Economic Opportunity. Subsequently he served as the U.S. ambassador to NATO.

30. Franks, *American Soldier*, 329.

31. Ibid., 337.

32. Ibid., 331.

33. Ibid., 329.

34. Ibid., 332.

35. The two men got along very well. Though born in Oklahoma, Franks considered himself a fellow Texan and actually attended the same high school as First Lady Laura Bush.

36. General Zinni was very aware of the problems identified in Desert Crossing and he became one of the early, vocal critics of the war with Iraq after his retirement in 2000. Zinni later stated: "It struck me then that we had a plan to defeat Saddam's army, but we didn't have a plan to rebuild Iraq. And so I asked the different agencies of government to come together to talk about reconstruction planning for Iraq. . . . I thought we ought to look at political reconstruction, economic reconstruction, security reconstruction, humanitarian need, services, and infrastructure development. We met in Washington, DC. We called the plan, and we gamed it out in the scenario, Desert Crossing. The first meeting surfaced all the problems that have exactly happened now. This was 1999. And when I took it back and looked at it, I said, we need a plan. Not all of this is a military responsibility. I went back to State Department, to the Office of Foreign Disaster Assistance, Department of Commerce and others and said, all right, how about you guys taking part of the plan. We need a plan in addition to the war plan for the reconstruction. Not interested. Would not look at it. So at Central Command before I left—I retired in 2000—I started a plan called Desert Crossing for the reconstruction of Iraq. Because I was convinced nobody in Washington was going to plan for it, and we, the military, would get stuck with it. So when I left in 2000 we were in the process of that planning. When it looked like we were going in, I called back down to Centcom and said, 'You need to dust off Desert Crossing. They said, What's that? Never heard of it.' So in a matter of just a few years it was gone. The corporate memory. And in addition I was told, 'We've been told not to do any of the planning. It would all be done in the Pentagon.'" See "Straight Talk from General Anthony Zinni," found at http://www.international.ucla.edu/burkle/article.asp?parentid=11162.

37. George W. Bush, "State of the Union Address," January 29, 2002.

38. Franks, *American Soldier*, 342.

39. Ibid., 349–351.

40. Ibid., 355–356.

41. Harlan K. Ullman and James P. Wade, *Shock and Awe: Achieving Rapid Dominance* (National Defense University Press, 1996). The approach was conceived by a team that included Admiral L. A. "Bud" Edney, General Fred M. Franks, General Chuck Horner, and Admiral Jonathan T. Howe.

42. Franks, *American Soldier*, 370.

43. Ibid., 366.

44. Michael R. Gordon and Bernard E. Trainor, *Cobra II: The Inside Story of the Invasion and Occupation of Iraq* (New York: Pantheon, 2006), 44.

45. Gordon and Trainor, *Cobra II*, 50–51.

46. Ibid.

47. Michael Barone, "The Road to Baghdad," *U.S. News & World Report*, June 17, 2002, as well as Gerry J. Gilmore, "Bush: West Point Grads Answer History's Call to Duty," American Forces Press Service, found at http://www.defenselink.mil/news/newsarticle.aspx?id=43798.

48. One wonders how many of the cadets listening in the audience could possibly imagine how different their lives were to be because of this new strategy.

49. Thomas E. Ricks and Vernon Loeb, "Bush Developing Military Policy of Striking First New Doctrine Addresses Terrorism," *Washington Post*, June 10, 2002, A01.

50. Gordon and Trainor, *Cobra II*, 67–68.

51. Gregory Fontenot, E. J. Degen, and David Tohn, *On Point: The United States Army in Operation Iraqi Freedom*, AUSA Institute of Land Warfare (Annapolis: Naval Institute Press, 2005), 31.

52. Ibid., 32.

53. Ibid., 36.

54. Ibid., 42–43.

55. Ibid., 29.

56. Franks, *American Soldier*, 407–408.

57. Feith, *War and Decision*, 246–248; Bob Woodward, *Plan of Attack: The Definitive Account of the Decision to Invade Iraq* (New York: Simon & Schuster, 2004), 150–152.

58. Colin L. Powell, "Remarks to the United Nations Security Council," New York City, February 5, 2003, found at http://www.globalsecurity.org/wmd/library/news/iraq/2003/iraq-030205-powell-un-17300pf.htm.

59. "New State Department Releases on the 'Future of Iraq' Project," found at http://www.gwu.edu/~nsarchiv/NSAEBB/NSAEBB198/index.htm.

60. Ibid.

61. NSPD 24 has yet to be made public.

62. Donald P. Wright and Timothy R. Reese, *On Point II: The United States Army in Operation Iraqi Freedom, May 2003–January 2005: Transition to the New Campaign* (Ft. Leavenworth, KS: Combat Studies Institute Press, 2008), 70.

63. Ibid., 71.

64. Ibid.

65. Ibid., 72–73.

66. Ibid., 78.

Chapter 7. Iraqi Freedom: Execution of the Initial Thrust

1. Franks, *American Soldier*, 431.

2. "In postwar situations, speed does not substitute for mass. It takes a lot of troops to control a nation of 24 million." Gordon and Trainor, *Cobra II*, 53.

3. As during Desert Storm and almost every U.S. operation since 1990, the heroic efforts of the Army 7th Transportation Group and its subunits made a huge contribution to the war effort; they never get the recognition they deserve. Fontenot et al., *On Point*, 35–39.

4. Saddam Hussein had a significant portion of his army garrisoned in northern Iraq as a guard against Kurdish activity, and the coalition wanted to keep those forces in the area long enough to prevent them from massing against the coalition assault from the south.

5. Gordon and Trainor, *Cobra II*, 171.

6. Ibid., 164.

7. Ibid., 166.

8. In addition to Lieutenant General McKiernan as the land component commander and Lieutenant General Buzz Moseley as the air component commander, Marine Lieutenant General Earl Hailston served as the Marine component commander, Vice Admiral Tom Keating served as the naval and maritime component commander, and Army Brigadier General Gary Harrell served as the joint special operations component commander.

9. Franks, *American Soldier*, xvi.

10. Gordon and Trainor, *Cobra II*, 166. This was the worst possible time to consider changing the execution timeline as many of the logistics support functions essential for success were extremely difficult to alter.

11. Ibid., 168.

12. Ibid., 169.

13. Ibid., 175.

14. Ibid., 180.

15. Ibid., 184. The Marine assault battalions were ordered by General Mattis to go "logistics lite" in order to cover the great distance while in combat. Extra fuel bladders were strapped to vehicles; Marines were told to eat all of their Meals Ready to Eat (MRE) because there would be nothing extra to spare; logistics units were trained to defend themselves; and the main source of resupply was planned to be by air, as were the main means of fire support in order to reduce artillery consumption. For the best coverage of the tactical fight from the Marine perspective, see Bing West, *The March Up: Taking Baghdad with the United States Marines* (Bantam, 2004).

16. Gordon and Trainor, *Cobra II*, 191–192.

17. Ibid., 196–197. This operation between two Marine organizations started out as a superb demonstration of allied interoperability, but after the nighttime crash of one of the American helicopters in very dim visibility the coordinated attack fell apart.

18. Ibid., 194.

19. Ibid., 202–203.

20. Ibid., 200, 208: "The Iraqis were using guerilla tactics: they were not marshaled in conventional formations. . . . And they were not surrendering, but fighting tenaciously."

21. For the best coverage of the tactical fight from the perspective of the Army forces in Iraqi Freedom, see Jim Lacey, *Takedown: The 3rd Infantry Division's Twenty-One Day Assault on Baghdad* (Annapolis: Naval Institute Press), 2007.

22. Ibid., 21.

23. Ibid., 25, 27, 46.

24. 3-7 Cav has a long history in American arms, including service at the Little Big Horn.

25. Lacey, *Takedown*, 45.

26. Ibid., 48.

27. Ibid., 49.

28. Ibid., 54.

29. Ibid., 58.

30. Gordon and Trainor, *Cobra II*, 209.

31. General Franks said several times, "The key is speed . . . speed kills, the enemy." Franks, *American Soldier*, 466.

32. The Special Forces battalions involved in the initial assault operations into Iraq included the 5th Special Forces Group, which had the "Scud-hunting" mission in the western deserts of Iraq to prevent the launch of Iraqi missiles against coalition forces and Israel. In northern Iraq, the 10th Special Forces Group plus one battalion from the 3rd Special Forces Group worked with the Kurdish militias to fix the Iraqi divisions stationed along the boundary known as the Green Line and prevent their reinforcing Saddam's army in Baghdad.

33. The division of SOF into "white" and "black" components is in many ways overly simplistic. Soldiers, and even Marines, sailors, and airmen, move between the two kinds of units regularly, the Ranger Regiment does a bit of both, and commanders can employ mixtures of all kinds of forces. But during Iraqi Freedom there was always one strategic SOF Joint Task Force in theater that performed "black" operations nearly exclusively. That unit handled some of the most sensitive missions in Iraq, including strategic attack, sensitive site exploitation, WMD recovery, strategic intelligence collection, and other specialized functions essential for success. That unit was initially commanded by Major General Dell Dailey and later by Lieutenant General Stanley McChrystal.

34. Nicholas Reynolds, *Basra, Baghdad and Beyond* (Annapolis: Naval Institute Press, 2005), 75.

35. The 507th, from Fort Bliss, Texas, was the last unit in a column of some six hundred vehicles. For a detailed discussion of this fight, see Fontenot et al., *On Point*, 154–160.

36. Those killed included Specialist Jamal R. Addison, Master Sergeant Robert J. Dowdy, Private Ruben Estrella-Soto, Private First Class Howard Johnson II, Specialist James M. Kiehl, Chief Warrant Officer Johnny Villareal Mata, Private

First Class Lori Piestewa, Private Brandon Sloan, Sergeant Donald Walters, Specialist Edward J. Anguiano, and Sergeant George Edward Buggs.

37. Reynolds, *Basra, Baghdad and Beyond*, 76.

38. Lacey, *Takedown*, 89. This was particularly serious because the major supply base for the continuing operations of the V Corps (Objective Rams) was just to the west of Najaf and within easy striking distance—it had to be protected if the advance was to continue successfully toward Baghdad.

39. Lacey, *Takedown*, 90.

40. Ibid., 92–93. It was later determined that the tanks had been hit during the sandstorm by friendly fire from a Bradley armored fighting vehicle to their rear.

41. Ibid., 94–95.

42. Ibid., 99.

43. For a detailed discussion of this fight, see Fontenot et al., *On Point*, 179–189.

44. See Reynolds, *Basra, Baghdad and Beyond*, 92; Gordon and Trainor, *Cobra II*, 304–305; and Lacey, *Takedown*, 119–121. General Franks had a very different perspective; see Franks, *American Soldier*, 508–509.

45. Franks, *American Soldier*, 502–504.

46. Rick Atkinson, "General: A Longer War Likely, Logistics, Enemy Force Reevaluation," *Washington Post*, March 28, 2003, A01. The author stated, "The Army's senior ground commander in Iraq, Lt. Gen. William S. Wallace, said today that overextended supply lines and a combative adversary using unconventional tactics have stalled the U.S. drive toward Baghdad and increased the likelihood of a longer war than many strategists had anticipated."

47. Kevin M. Woods and Michael R. Pease, *The Iraqi Perspectives Report: Saddam's Senior Leadership on Operation Iraqi Freedom from the Official U.S. Joint Forces Command Report* (Annapolis: Naval Institute Press, 2006), 32.

48. It is difficult to measure statistically, but there can be little doubt that the V Corps and I MEF forces would have been beyond their operational reach in days had they not paused; it is likely also that the fortitude and good judgment displayed during the fighting in Baghdad might not have been as evident without the halt. "Secure LOCs were a fundamental precondition for the corps to launch its attack on Baghdad." Fontenot et al., *On Point*, 209.

49. The entire corridor of the corps rear area was divided into two areas of operations, one for each division. Fontenot et al., *On Point*, 214.

50. The Iraqi commander of the Republican Guard II Corps, Lieutenant General Hamdani, had hoped to defend Karbala with a division, but he was directed to keep his forces on the eastern side of the Euphrates River to defend Baghdad. Lacey, *Takedown*, 134.

51. Ibid., 150–151.

52. For this perspective I am indebted to the analysis in Woods and Pease, *Iraqi Perspectives Report*, viii, 31.

53. Ibid., ix.

54. Ibid.

55. See Lacey, *Takedown*, 197–199.

56. Ibid., 199.

57. General Franks would later claim that the title "thunder run" as his own reference to a similar tactic used during the Vietnam War; see Franks, *American Soldier*, 517.

58. Lacey, *Takedown*, 218–219.

59. Reynolds, *Basra, Baghdad and Beyond*, 106.

60. While passing through the Saddam City sector of Baghdad the Marines began to observe Iraqis looting in large numbers, but could do little at the time to prevent it.

61. Reynolds, *Basra, Baghdad and Beyond*, 110.

62. Gordon and Trainor, *Cobra II*, 434.

63. To be most fair, American and British troops were key, but the Australians and the Poles (if only in very small numbers) were also present at the invasion and made important contributions to the takedown of the Saddam regime.

Chapter 8. The Lost Year of the Coalition Provisional Authority

1. Sean Loughlin, "Pentagon: 'Major combat' over, but smaller fights remain," CNN Washington Bureau, April 14, 2003, found at http://www.cnn.com/2003/US/04/14/sprj.irq.pentagon/index.html.

2. This problem was exacerbated by the fact that the Ba'ath Party included many of even the most low-level functionaries in Iraq (nearly everyone who had any power) and the fact that many party members were as fearful of retribution by their countrymen for abuses of power as they were concerned that the coalition forces would detain or target them.

3. The 173rd Airborne Brigade, commanded by Colonel Bill Mayville, was directed to Kirkuk, which was found to be relatively quiet, soon after the Peshmerga arrival.

4. Gordon and Trainor indicate that the mission was originally to be directed at Kirkuk, but the Kurdish Peshmerga forces had already raced there to establish their own control over the oil-rich area (*Cobra II*, 436.) According to Nick Reynolds, there had been some limited contingency planning by the MEF to move on Kirkuk if the army forces in the north were unable to control the all-important oil city. In time, as the situation in the north of Iraq stabilized, Kirkuk fell to the Kurdish forces and the furthest extent of the advance from the south was reduced to Tikrit. See Reynolds, *Basra, Baghdad and Beyond*, 114–116.

5. In a raid on a small town south of Tikrit, special operators captured five of Saddam's bodyguards, the chief of staff of the Iraqi air force, and several ministers just prior to the Marines' arrival in the area. Gordon and Trainor, *Cobra II*, 444. The important role of special operations in these early phases of the campaign has yet to be fully revealed.

6. Specifically Navy pilot Scott Speicher, who had been shot down during the opening days of Desert Storm; Captain Speicher was never found, even after years of intensive searching.

7. Warrant Officers Dave Williams and Ron Young had been shot down in their Apache helicopter during the 11 AHR raid on the Medina Division of the Republican Guard back on March 24.

8. Gordon and Trainor, *Cobra II*, 446.

9. One well respected author, Tom Ricks, said bluntly, "From its first days in Iraq in April 2003, the Army's 4th Infantry Division made an impression on soldiers from other units—the wrong one." Thomas E. Ricks, "It Looked Weird and Felt Wrong," *Washington Post*, July 24, 2006, A01.

10. Gordon and Trainor, *Cobra II*, 448.

11. Ibid., 457.

12. Later known as Camp Liberty and eventually Camp Victory, the complex initially known as the Abu Ghraib Palace in Baghdad served the home of the CFLCC staff and its commander, General McKiernan, and later served the same function for the headquarters of Coalition Joint Task Force-7 (CJTF-7), and eventually its successor Multi-National Corps Iraq. The CPA and later, the staff of the Multi-National Force Iraq and its commanders, Generals Casey, Petraeus, and Odierno were located in the Republican Palace in the center of Baghdad.

13. Gordon and Trainor, *Cobra II*, 459.

14. Ibid., 461.

15. This would be true through the spring of 2004. See Bremer *My Year in Iraq*, 356–357.

16. Gordon and Trainor, *Cobra II*, 462.

17. Sean Loughlin, "Rumsfeld on looting in Iraq: 'Stuff happens,' Administration Asking Countries for Help with Security," CNN, April 12, 2003, found at http://www.cnn.com/2003/US/04/11/sprj.irq.pentagon/.

18. Ibid.

19. Franks, *American Soldier*, 523–524.

20. Wright and Reese, *On Point II*, 25–26.

21. Gordon and Trainor, *Cobra II*, 463.

22. PBS interview with Lieutenant General Jay Garner on *Frontline: War, Truth and Consequences*, found at http://www.pbs.org/wgbh/pages/frontline/shows/truth/interviews/garner.html.

23. Ibid.

24. Wright and Reese, *On Point II*, 25–26.

25. Charles H. Ferguson, *No End in Sight: Iraq's Descent into Chaos* (New York: Public Affairs, 2008), 124–126.

26. Ibid., 88.

27. Wright and Reese, *On Point II*, 152.

28. Bremer, *My Year in Iraq*, 6–7.

29. Elaine Halchin, *The CPA: Origins, Characteristics and Institutional Authorities* (Washington, DC: Congressional Research Service, April 29, 2004), 4.

30. Wright and Reese, *On Point II*, 29.

31. Ricardo S. Sanchez and Don T. Phillips, *Wiser in Battle: A Soldier's Story* (New York: HarperCollins, 2008), 180.

32. Fontenot, et al., *On Point*, 43–44.

33. PBS interview with Lieutenant General Jay Garner on "Frontline: The Lost Year in Iraq," found at http://www.pbs.org/wgbh/pages/frontline/yeariniraq/interviews/garner.html.

34. Sanchez and Phillips, *Wiser in Battle*, 199.

35. Franks had been offered the job as Chief of Staff of the U.S. Army by Secretary Rumsfeld, but he declined and pressed for retirement instead. See Franks, *American Soldier*, 531–532.

36. Bremer even compared himself briefly to MacArthur. See Bremer, *My Year in Iraq*, 36.

37. Like ORHA, the CPA was an ad hoc organization that continually suffered from manpower shortages.

38. For the discussion in Washington, see Bremer, *My Year in Iraq*, 39, and Feith, *War and Decision*, 465.

39. Bremer, *My Year in Iraq*, 57.

40. Ibid.

41. Bremer later said, "I think the decision not to recall Saddam's army, from a political point of view, is the single most important, correct decision that we made in the 14 months we were there. The army was the central instrument of Saddam's repression of the Kurds and the Shi'a. The Kurdish leaders had made it very clear to me that if we recalled the army; they would secede from Iraq, which would have started an immediate regional war. Whatever calculations various colonels and majors made about how they could get these people to come back or not come back, the political argument against recalling the army was decisive." See the PBS interview with L. Paul Bremer.

42. Bremer, *My Year in Iraq*, 45, 87–103, 123–124, 167–168.

43. George Packer, "Letter from Iraq: The Lesson of Tal Afar, Is It Too Late for the Administration to Correct Its Course in Iraq?" *The New Yorker*, April 10, 2006, 51–52.

44. Bremer, *My Year in Iraq*, 107.

45. PBS interview with L. Paul Bremer.

46. Then called the Supreme Council of the Islamic Revolution in Iraq (SCIRI), renamed in June 2007 to become the Islamic Supreme Council of Iraq (ISCI).

47. Kenneth Katzman, "Iraq and Al Qaeda," Congressional Research Service Report RL32217, April 28, 2008, CRS-9, found at http://fpc.state.gov/documents/organization/105195.pdf.

48. Secretary Rumsfeld coined the term "dead-enders." See, for example, "Rumsfeld Blames Iraq Problems on 'Pockets of Dead-Enders,'" *USA Today*, June 18, 2003, found at http://www.usatoday.com/news/world/iraq/2003-06-18-rumsfeld_x.htm. Rumsfeld also refused to use the term "insurgency" or "guerilla war," even when commanders like General Abizaid felt the term correct. See "DOD News Briefing—Mr. Di Rita and Gen. Abizaid," *DefenseLink*, 16 July 2003, http://www.defenselink.mil/transcripts/2003/tr20030716-0401.html.

49. L. Paul Bremer III, "Iraq's Path to Sovereignty," *Washington Post*, September 8, 2003, A21.

50. Bremer, *My Year in Iraq*, 163.

51. Ibid., 167.

52. According to the U.S. State Department; see http://merln.ndu.edu/archive-pdf/terrorism/state/37130.pdf.

53. Gary Gambill, "Abu Musab Al-Zarqawi: A Biographical Sketch," *Terrorism Monitor* 2, no. 24, December 16, 2004, found at http://web.archive.org/web/20070930191559/http://www.jamestown.org/publications_details.php?volume_id=400&issue_id=3179&article_id=2369019.

54. Kenneth Katzman, "Iraq and Al Qaeda," Congressional Research Service Report RL32217, April 28, 2008, CRS-10, found at http://fpc.state.gov/documents/organization/105195.pdf.

55. Peter Slevin and Robin Wright, "Bremer Returns to Washington Amid Frustration in Iraq," *Washington Post*, November 11, 2003, 1.

56. Bremer, *My Year in Iraq*, 219.

57. Ibid., 222.

58. Ibid., 225–228.

59. Source is icasualties.org; 148 Americans died in battle during Desert Storm.

60. CNN, "Pentagon: Saddam's Sons Killed in Raid, U.S. Military Might Release Photographs of Bodies," July 22, 2003, found at http://www.cnn.com/2003/WORLD/meast/07/22/sprj.irq.sons/.

61. On June 30, 2004, Saddam Hussein was handed over to the interim Iraqi government to stand trial for crimes against humanity. On November 5, 2006, he was found guilty and sentenced to death by hanging. Saddam was hanged on December 30, 2006.

62. Seymour M. Hersh, "Torture at Abu Ghraib, American Soldiers Brutalized Iraqis. How Far Up Does the Responsibility Go?" *The New Yorker*, May 10, 2004, 42–43.

63. General Sanchez ordered the investigation as soon as he was informed about the incident; see Sanchez and Phillips, *Wiser in Battle*, 304. "The Taguba Report," submitted by Major General Anthony Taguba after his investigation was completed, can be found at http://www.dod.mil/pubs/foi/detainees/taguba/.

64. More properly known as the "Law of Administration for the State of Iraq for the Transitional Period," the TAL provided the only framework for law in Iraq until the new constitution could be written. It can be found at http://www.cpa-iraq.org/government/TAL.html.

65. Operation Vigilant Resolve was ordered on short notice, to be executed in less than Five days, with the goal of capturing or killing the insurgents responsible for the killing of the American contractors. It was also designed to re-establish law and order and prevent Fallujah from acting as a sanctuary for the anti-Iraqi forces. Vigilant Resolve was essentially a two-battalion attack, although four Iraqi battalions had been requested in support.

66. Camp Fallujah, not to be confused with the city itself, was a former Iraqi army training center designed for the use of an Iranian unit loyal to Saddam Hussein. It was a MNF military camp, located on the main highway less than five miles from the city.

67. Al-Sadr chose to fight in Najaf for a reason. His father had lived and taught there, becoming one of the most revered Shia leaders in Iraq before he was assassinated, along with two of his sons, by Saddam Hussein's henchmen.

68. The Najaf region was initially secured by American forces of the MEF, which departed Iraq in November 2003. The 1st Armored Division assumed control of the entire central south area of Iraq (Multi-National Division Central-South, MND-CS) following the departure of the MEF. Later, the Spanish contingent of the coalition was assigned to the area under the overall control of the Polish Division, which assumed the responsibility for MND-CS. An exclusion zone was set up comprised of the old city of Najaf, the cemetery, and the town of Kufa in order to minimize friction and the appearance of troops in the holy areas of the city.

69. Najaf is a major religious education center and pilgrimage destination because it is the site of the tomb of Ali ibn Abi Talib (Imam Ali), the cousin and son-in-law of the prophet Muhammad. The Shia faithful consider Ali to be the righteous caliph and first imam. It is estimated that only Mecca and Medina receive more Muslim pilgrims than does Najaf.

70. I MEF and 11th MEU staffs, "Battle for An Najaf, August 2004," *Marine Corps Gazette*, December 2004, 10.

71. Imam Abdul Majid al-Khoei and rival Shia leader Ayatollah Sayed Mohammed Baqir al-Hakim.

72. Grand Ayatollah Ali al-Sistani, who lives in Najaf, is the most respected of the Shiite imams in Iraq. His position was initially contested by other clerics, including Mohammad Sadeq al-Sadr, Muqtada al-Sadr's father, but his role as successor to his teacher Abdul-Qassem Khoei made Sistani the favorite of most Shia. The assassination of Sadr by Saddam Hussein made him the most influential Shia cleric in the country. In his role as ayatollah, Sistani oversees sums amounting to millions of dollars, which he distributes in various ways, including payment for the religious education of would-be scholars across the Muslim world. See http://www.sistani.org/html/eng/.

73. On June 17, a small battalion task force relieved the 2nd ACR after the truce. This second unit passed on very few of the pertinent factors of fighting in the area to the Marines who would follow them—another shortfall in transitioning critical information between units over the course of a relief in place.

74. Bremer, *My Year in Iraq*, 298–301.

Chapter 9. The Casey Strategy,
from Fallujah to Tal Afar: 2004–2006

1. Major General Peter W. Chiarelli and Major Patrick R. Michaelis, "Winning the Peace: The Requirement for Full-Spectrum Operations," *Military Review*, (July–August 2005): 4–17.

2. "This is a revolution against the occupation force until we get independence and democracy," al-Sadr's spokesman, Ahmed Shaybani, said in a telephone interview with Jackie Spinner of the *Washington Post*. See Spinner, "Cleric's Attack Tests Iraqi Leaders, Rebel Cleric Declares 'Revolution' against U.S. Forces in Iraq," *Washington Post*, August 6, 2004.

3. The 11th Marine Expeditionary Unit (11th MEU) had been assigned to the area on short notice, as the CENTCOM theater reserve, working directly for MNC-I (General Metz), after the Spanish contingent was withdrawn from the coalition. The Spanish government pulled its forces out following the intimidation of the Madrid bombings of March 11, 2004.

4. The local police were holding over one hundred Mahdi militiamen. I MEF and 11th MEU staffs, "Battle for An Najaf, August 2004," *Marine Corps Gazette*, December 2004, 12.

5. "A large number of aggressors, later confirmed to be members of the radical Shiite cleric Muqtada al-Sadr's Mahdi Militia, attacked the city of Najaf's main police station at 1 a.m. and were quickly repelled by the Iraqi police. Later, at 3 a.m., they attacked again, this time with heavy machine guns, rocket propelled grenades, mortars and small arms. Iraqi National Guardsmen from the 405th Battalion, 50th Iraqi Brigade, were notified and arrived on the scene and helped the IPs successfully defend the station from the Anti-Iraqi Forces." Chago Zapata, "11th MEU Battles Anti-Iraqi Forces in An Najaf," *Marine Corps News*, August 11, 2004. See also Spinner, "Cleric's Attack Tests Iraqi Leaders.

6. His full name was Abdul Qadir Mohammed Jassim Obeidi al-Mifarji'; he later became defense minister of Iraq under several governments and was a key Sunni member of the new Iraqi defense establishment through the negations for the end of hostilities in Iraq.

7. Sunni minority interests were always important and the prime minister understood well the fine line he needed to walk to gain inclusion, yet resist a negative reaction from other parties.

8. In the immediate aftermath of resettlement in Fallujah, Iraq held its first national elections in January 2005; this was in effect a semi-plebiscite for the Allawi government and a big indicator of popular sentiment. In Fallujah, where little or no significant reconstruction had begun at the time of the election, nearly one-third of the residents stood in long lines to vote. Elsewhere in Al Anbar province Sunnis were intimidated because every Iraqi who voted had his/her right index finger marked with blue dye, and insurgents had claimed all such fingers would be cut off; fewer than eighteen thousand people went to the polls. But in Fallujah a significant percentage felt safe enough to vote.

9. General Jack Keene has agreed, saying, "We had evidence to believe in the fall of '04 . . . that the Sunni insurgents believed that they were winning the war, and briefers thought that they were probably right because they were able to increase the level of violence rather considerably in '04 over '03. In my own mind, I believe when that violence in '05, in the spring, summer and fall, when I look back on it now, I can remember having anxiety because it increased over what it was in '04. That should have given us considerable pause right there. And I think what we should have done is let's go back and challenge our assumptions; let's go back and look at our basic premises for the development of the strategy, and are there some alternatives here that may be a lot more useful than what we're doing? That was probably the time to do it." PBS interview with General Jack Keene, found at:http://www.pbs.org/wgbh/pages/frontline/endgame/interviews/keane.html.

10. Packer, "Letter from Iraq," 52.

11. Dan Murphy, "US Strategy in Iraq: Is It Working? Major sweeps show results in western Iraq. But insurgents keep adapting and attacking," *Christian Science Monitor*, June 21, 2005, 1.

12. Linked to this kinetic lever but still conducting somewhat independent yet coordinated operations was a Special Operations Command whose mission was dominated by the fight against Al Qaeda in Iraq and other linked terrorist activities.

13. Coordination between the various commands in Iraq was not always optimum. Philip Zellicow noted: "And there are tensions. To outsiders, the military world looks very homogeneous. Within the military world, it's not homogeneous at all. So there's all kinds of tensions going on between Abizaid and Casey, and also even within Baghdad between the Multi-National Force command headed by Gen. Casey and the Corps command headed by Gen. Vines, then Gen. Chiarelli and now headed by Gen. Odierno. And actually the Multi-National Force headquarters and the Corps headquarters are in different locations. And a lot of what the Multi-National Force headquarters does is generate PowerPoint slides to use in briefing Washington, but the Corps is actually the people who have their fingers on what's going on in the field every day. " PBS interview with Philip Zellicow found, at http://www.pbs.org/wgbh/pages/frontline/endgame/interviews/zelikow.html.

14. General Petraeus was followed in command of MNSTC-I by Lieutenant General Martin E. Dempsey (September 2005–June 2007), Lieutenant General James M. Dubik (June 2007–July 2008), and by Lieutenant General Frank Helmick (July 2008–to date). It was headquartered in Baghdad.

15. The 101st had also been the unit that identified and eventually killed Saddam's sons Uday and Qusai in Mosul.

16. Andrew F. Krepinevich, "How to Win in Iraq," *Foreign Affairs* 84, no. 5 (September–October 2005): 87.

17. Chiarelli and Michaelis, "Winning the Peace," 15.

18. PBS interview with General Jack Keene, found at http://www.pbs.org/wgbh/pages/frontline/endgame/interviews/keane.html.

19. Krepinevich, "How to Win in Iraq," 87.
20. "In May of 2004, for example, following the insurgent takeover of Fallujah, General Richard Myers, chair of the Joint Chiefs of Staff, stated, 'I think we're on the brink of success here.' Six months later, before last November's offensive to recapture the city, General John Abizaid, the commander of U.S. forces in Iraq and Afghanistan, said, 'When we win this fight—and we will win—there will be nowhere left for the insurgents to hide.' Following the recapture, Lieutenant General John Sattler, the Marine commander in Iraq, declared that the coalition had 'broken the back of the insurgency.' Yet in the subsequent months, the violence continued unabated. Nevertheless, seven months later Vice President Dick Cheney claimed that the insurgency was in its 'last throes,' even as Lieutenant General John Vines, commander of the multinational corps in Iraq, was conceding, 'We don't see the insurgency expanding or contracting right now.' Most Americans agree with this less optimistic assessment: according to the most recent polls, nearly two-thirds think the coalition is 'bogged down.'" Krepinevich, "How to Win in Iraq," 87–88.
21. Packer, "Letter from Iraq," 48–65.
22. Ibid., 49.
23. H. R. McMaster, *Dereliction of Duty: Lyndon Johnson, Robert McNamara, the Joint Chiefs of Staff, and the Lies That Led to Vietnam* (New York: HarperCollins, 1997).
24. Packer, "Letter from Iraq," 50.
25. Ibid.
26. Ibid., 53.
27. Ibid., 54.
28. Ibid.
29. According to GlobalSecurity.org: "In this assault, the insurgents took heavy losses, 118 dead and 137 captured, before being driven out of the city. By September 13, the operation had been responsible for the deaths of numerous suspected terrorists and the detainment of 341 individuals. In addition, 22 weapons caches were uncovered, including mortar systems. Col. [McMaster] claimed that the operation also included the capture of many associates of Zarqawi. Examination of the western part of the city revealed that certain buildings had been rigged for destruction upon the entrance of coalition troops. One building contained barrels of chemicals that were intended to explode. After reconnaissance detected the threat, the area was cleared and the building was demolished. Operation Restoring Rights continued through October, with raids along the border between Iraq and Syria. During a 5-day-period in mid-October, more than 10,000 pounds of explosives were uncovered and destroyed." Found at http://www.globalsecurity.org/military/ops/oif-restoring-rights.htm.
30. Packer, "Letter from Iraq, 54.
31. Ibid.
32. Ibid., 56.

33. Condoleezza Rice had replaced Colin Powell as secretary of state in November 2004. She had of course been the administration's "point man" on Iraq from some time as the president's national security advisor, but in response to less than detailed responses to queries about the situation in Iraq from Rumsfeld's Defense Department, she began to gather her own information in order to make the international message concerning Iraq clearer.

34. Secretary of State Condoleezza Rice, "Iraq and U.S. Policy," testimony before the Senate Committee on Foreign Relations, found at http://foreign.senate.gov/testimony/2005/RiceTestimony051019.pdf.

35. PBS interview with Philip Zellicow, found at http://www.pbs.org/wgbh/pages/frontline/endgame/interviews/zelikow.html.

36. Bob Woodward, "Doubt, Distrust, Delay: The Inside Story of How Bush's Team Dealt with Its Failing Iraq Strategy," *Washington Post*, September 7, 2008, A1.

37. From Zellicow, Condoleezza Rice and the State Department immediately began to espouse a new approach toward winning the war based upon McMaster's "clear, hold, build" concept. It was not yet a national strategy—Secretary Rumsfeld flatly denied its use—and initially the White House did not fully understand the subtle differences in approach. Still, Zellicow's transporting of the concept back to the Washington bureaucracy would finally help the idea prosper, when via another route altogether the evolving approaches to wining in Iraq would reach up over the months to come from the ranks and to key members of the defense establishment in Washington through academia and the network of retired military officers.

38. Packer, "Letter from Iraq, 57.

39. Ibid.

40. General Petraeus was replaced in command by Lieutenant General Martin E. Dempsey (September 2005–June 2007), Lieutenant General James M. Dubik (June 2007–July 2008), and Lieutenant General Frank Helmick.

41. Fouad Ajami, *The Foreigner's Gift* (New York: Simon & Schuster, 2006), 295–298.

42. David H. Petraeus, "Battling for Iraq," *Washington Post*, September 26, 2004, B07.

43. Glenn Kessler, "Weapons Given to Iraq Are Missing, GAO Estimates 30% of Arms Are Unaccounted For," *Washington Post*, August 6, 2007, A01.

44. Olga Oliker, "Iraqi Security Forces: Defining Challenges and Assessing Progress," before the Committee on Armed Services Subcommittee on Oversight and Investigations, United States House of Representatives, March 28, 2007, found at:http://armedservices.house.gov/pdfs/OI032807/Oliker_Testimony032807.pdf.

45. The constitutional review committee was created by the Iraqi parliament on September 25, 2006, but it did not develop any changes to the document over the first three years of its existence.

46. Josh White, "Report on Haditha Condemns Marines, Signs of Misconduct Were Ignored, U.S. General Says," *Washington Post*, April 21, 2007, A01.

47. CNN, "Bush: Iraqi Forces Will Take More Control in 2006, President Predicts U.S. Force Levels Will Drop," January 4, 2006, found at http://www.cnn.com/2006/POLITICS/01/04/bush.iraq/index.html.

48. According to GlobalSecurity.org, the al-Askari Mosque, also known as the Golden Mosque, serves as a mausoleum to the tenth and eleventh imams, Imam Ali al-Naqi and Imam Hasan al-Askari. The golden dome on one shrine was presented by Nasr al-Din Shah and completed under Muzaffar al-Din Shah in the year AD 1905. Beneath the golden dome are four graves, those of Imam Ali al-Naqi (tenth imam) and his son, Imam Hasan al-Askari (eleventh imam). The other two are of Hakimah Khatoon, the sister of Imam Ali al-Naqi, who has related at length the circumstances of the birth of Imam al-Mahdi; and the fourth grave is of Nargis Khatoon, the mother of Imam al-Mahdi. See http://www.globalsecurity.org/military/world/iraq/samarra-mosque.htm.

49. Alex Rodriguez, "Suspect in Bombing of Shiite Shrine is Captured," *Chicago Tribune*, June 28, 2006, 13.

50. See CQ Transcripts Wire, "President Bush Holds a News Conference," August 21, 2006, found at http//www.washingtonpost.com/wp-dyn/content/article/2006/08/21/AR2006082100469.html.

51. Nelson Hernandez and Omar Fekeiki, "Insurgents Urge Sunni-Shiite War, Zarqawi Tape Threatens Goal of Iraq Unity," *Washington Post*, June 3, 2006, A1.

52. Reuters, "U.S. Forces Kill al Qaeda Mosque Bomber in Iraq," August 4, 2007, found at http://www.alertnet.org/thenews/newsdesk/L04311264.htm.

53. UN High Commissioner for Refugees, Division of Operational Services, "2006 Global Trends: Refugees, Asylum-seekers, Returnees, Internally Displaced and Stateless Persons," June 2007 (revised July 16, 2007), 13.

54. Department of Defense, "Measuring Stability and Security in Iraq," November 2006 Report to Congress, 24. The same report noted on page 17, "The most significant development in the Iraqi security environment was the growing role of Shi'a militants. It is likely that Shi'a militants were responsible for more civilian casualties than those associated with terrorist organizations. Shi'a militants were the most significant threat to the Coalition presence in Baghdad and southern Iraq."

55. Lieutenant General David H. Petraeus, "Learning Counterinsurgency: Observations from Soldiering in Iraq," *Military Review* (January–February 2006), 1–11.

Chapter 10. 2006: Descent into Chaos

1. Cited in Thomas E. Ricks, *The Gamble: General David Petraeus and the American Military Adventure in Iraq, 2006–2008* (New York: Penguin Press, 2009), 32. Carl von Clausewitz, *On War*. trans. and ed. by Michael Howard and Peter Paret (Princeton, NJ: Princeton University Press, 1976).

2. General Petraeus had even written in September 2005, "18 months after entering Iraq, I see tangible progress. Iraqi security elements are being rebuilt from the ground up. The institutions that oversee them are being reestablished from the top down. And Iraqi leaders are stepping forward, leading their country and their

security forces courageously in the face of an enemy that has shown a willingness to do anything to disrupt the establishment of the new Iraq." Petraeus, "Battling for Iraq," B07.

3. In his testimony before the Senate Armed Services Committee on February 27, 2007, the director of the Defense Intelligence Agency, General Michael Maples, called AQ-I "the largest and most active of the Iraq-based terrorist groups." See:http://www.investigativeproject.org/documents/testimony/268.pdf.

4. Kenneth Katzman, "Iraq and Al Qaeda," Congressional Research Service Report RL32217, April 28, 2008, CRS-11, found at http://fpc.state.gov/documents/organization/105195.pdf.

5. General Vines was Commander, Multi-National Corps Iraq in Baghdad, from January 2005 until January 2006.

6. He also wrote an excellent article in *Military Review* that outlined new approaches needed in Iraq. See Chiarelli and Michaelis, "Winning the Peace," 4–17. The article ended with the President Kennedy's insight that "few of the important problems of our time have, in the final analysis, been finally solved by military power alone."

7. UN High Commissioner for Refugees, Division of Operational Services, "2006 Global Trends: Refugees, Asylum-seekers, Returnees, Internally Displaced and Stateless Persons," June 2007 (revised July 16, 2007), 13.

8. Department of Defense, "Measuring Stability and Security in Iraq," November 2006 Report to Congress, 24. The same report noted on page 17, "The most significant development in the Iraqi security environment was the growing role of Shi'a militants. It is likely that Shi'a militants were responsible for more civilian casualties than those associated with terrorist organizations. Shi'a militants were the most significant threat to the Coalition presence in Baghdad and southern Iraq."

9. One of the early articles that may have spawned the name was Patrick J. Buchanan's "The Generals' Revolt" in *The American Cause*, April 15, 2006; see http://www.theamericancause.org/041506-print.htm. See also Katrina Vanden Heuvel, "The Generals Revolt: Opposition to Rumsfeld Far from Over," *The Nation*, April 17, 2006; "The Generals Revolt: There Are ManyRreasons for Donald Rumsfeld to Leave. Finger-pointing by Retired Officers Shouldn't Be One," *Washington Post*, April 18, 2006, A18; Perry Bacon Jr., "The Revolt of the Generals," *Time*, April 16, 2006; and Richard J. Whalen, "Revolt of the Generals," *The Nation*, October 16, 2006.

10. See David S. Cloud, Eric Schmitt, and Thom Shanker, "Rumsfeld Faces Growing Revolt by Retired Generals," *New York Times*, April 13, 2006, 1.

11. Ibid.

12. *The U.S. Army/Marine Corps Counterinsurgency Field Manual: U.S. Army Field Manual No. 3-24: Marine Corps Warfighting Publication No. 3-33.5* (Chicago: University of Chicago Press, 2007).

13. Normally considered part of the special operations community, Civil Affairs and Psychological Operations units continued to participate in all operations in

Iraq, normally in direct support of conventional force units. Their roles in Iraq were never fully recognized and their contribution to the overall success of the multinational force was greater than most understand.

14. Ellen Knickmeyer and Jonathan Finer, "Insurgent Leader Al-Zarqawi Killed in Iraq," *Washington Post*, June 8, 2006, A1, found at: http://www.washingtonpost .com/wp-dyn/content/article/2006/06/08/AR2006060800114.html.

15. Kenneth Katzman, "Iraq and Al Qaeda," Congressional Research Service Report RL32217, April 28, 2008, CRS-10, found at http://fpc.state.gov/documents/ organization/105195.pdf.

16. Knickmeyer and Finer, "Insurgent Leader Al-Zarqawi Killed," A1.

17. Jonathan Finer and Michael Abramowitz, "In Baghdad, Bush Pledges Support to Iraqi Leader, Visit Aimed at Buttressing Newly Formed Government," *Washington Post*, June 14, 2006, A01.

18. James A. Baker and Lee H. Hamilton, co-chairs; with Lawrence S. Eagleburger, Vernon E. Jordan, Jr., Edwin Meese III, Sandra Day O'Connor, Leon E. Panetta, William J. Perry, Charles S. Robb, and Alan K. Simpson, *The Iraq Study Group Report: The Way Forward—A New Approach* (New York: Vintage Books, 2006), 32.

19. Ibid., 48.

20. Ibid., 6.

21. See http://www.michaeltotten.com/archives/001514.html.

22. Anthony Loyd, "Murder of Sheikh Provokes Sunnis to Turn on al-Qaeda; Ramadi, Stronghold of the Insurgents, Has Turned against al-Zarqawi," *Times*, February 10, 2006, found at http://www.timesonline.co.uk/tol/news/world/iraq/ article729206.ece.

23. Kenneth Katzman, "Iraq and Al Qaeda," Congressional Research Service Report RL32217, April 28, 2008, CRS-12 and CRS-13, found at http://fpc.state .gov/documents/organization/105195.pdf.

24. In May 2006 some 80 percent in Al-Anbar saw civil war as likely, up from 50 percent in January. See http://www.ndu.edu/ctnsp/Stab_Ops/12Feb%20 Malkasian.pdf.

25. Ibid.

26. Todd Pitman, "Sunni Sheiks Join Fight vs. Insurgency," *Washington Post Online Edition*, March 25, 2007, http://www.washingtonpost.com/wp-dyn/content/ article/2007/03/25/AR2007032500600.html. (On September 13, 2007, Sheikh Sittar was killed by an AQ-I suicide bomber, but the council continued to function under his brother, Sheikh Ahmad al-Rishawi. The latter, along with Governor Mamoun Rashid al-Awani and other tribal figures, visited Washington, D.C., in November 2007 to discuss the progress of security in Al-Anbar province.)

27. Ricks, *The Gamble*, 69.

28. Ibid.

29. Martin Fletcher, "Fighting Back: The City Determined Not to Become al-Qaeda's Capital; A Power Struggle Is Taking Place in the Sunni Triangle, with Tribal Leaders and Coalition Forces Aligning against a Common eEnemy," *The Times*,

November 20, 2006, found at http://www.timesonline.co.uk/tol/news/world/iraq/article642374.ece?token=null&offset=0&page=1.

30. Baker et al., *Iraq Study Group Report*, 13.

31. Ibid., 20.

32. Ibid., 10.

33. For example, see David S. Cloud and Eric Schmitt, "More Retired Generals Call for Rumsfeld's Resignation," *New York Times*, April 14, 2006, found at http://www.nytimes.com/2006/04/14/washington/14military.html?_r=1&oref=slogin.

34. "DoD News Briefing with Secretary of Defense Robert M. Gates and Chairman, Joint Chiefs of Staff Gen. Peter Pace at the Pentagon Briefing Room, Arlington, Va.," September 14, 2007, found at http://www.defenselink.mil/transcripts/transcript.aspx?transcriptid=4037.

35. Ricks, *The Gamble*, 80–82.

36. As described in the U.S. Institute for Peace website, the Iraq Study Group, "was undertaken at the urging of several members of Congress with agreement of the White House. A final report was released to Congress, the White House, and the public on December 6, 2006. Leadership of the group was provided by two distinguished co-chairs: James A. Baker, III, former secretary of state and honorary chairman of the Baker Institute, and Lee H. Hamilton, former congressman and director of the Woodrow Wilson International Center for Scholars. The balance of the bipartisan group was comprised of Americans who have distinguished themselves in service to their nation: Robert M. Gates, Vernon E. Jordan, Jr., Edwin Meese III, Sandra Day O'Connor, Leon E. Panetta, William J. Perry, Charles S. Robb, and Alan K. Simpson."

37. Although only a few of the key decision-makers inside the Defense Department changed in the immediate aftermath of the resignation of Rumsfeld, the tone and activity of the Pentagon changed dramatically.

38. The meeting room inside the Pentagon where the chiefs of the military services often meet formally was known as "The Tank." Members of the Joint Chiefs of Staff at the time included Marine General Peter Pace as Chairman, Navy Admiral Ed Giambastiani as the Vice Chairman, Army General Pete Schoomaker as Chief of Staff of the Army, Marine General James Conway as Commandant of the Marine Corps, Admiral Mike Mullen, Chief of Naval Operations, and General Mike Moseley, Air Force Chief of Staff.

39. Bob Woodward, "Outmaneuvered and Outranked, Military Chiefs Became Outsiders," *Washington Post*, September 8, 2008, A1.

40. General Casey, however, was soon on his way to become the next Chief of Staff of the Army. Early the next month, it would be announced that Casey would leave Iraq and be replaced by Lieutenant General Petraeus—the principal force behind the new counterinsurgency doctrine.

41. Specifically, the report called for "a surge of seven Army brigades and Marine regiments to support clear-and-hold operations that begin in the spring of 2007 is necessary, possible, and will be sufficient to improve security and set conditions for economic development, political development, reconciliation, and the

development of Iraqi Security Forces (ISF) to provide permanent security." The formal title of the actual report was "Choosing Victory, A Plan for Success in Iraq, Phase I Report." It can be found at http://www.aei.org/docLib/20070105_ChoosingVictoryFINALcc.pdf.

42. The four "elements of the new approach" announced by the president were security, politics, economics ,and regional engagement.

43. Lieutenant General Raymond T. Odierno, "The Surge in Iraq: One Year Later," Heritage Lecture 1068, March 13, 2008, found at http://www.heritage.org/Research/NationalSecurity/hl1068.cfm.

Chapter 11. The Protection Strategy and the 2007 Baghdad Surge

1. Frederick W. Kagan, "Choosing Victory: A Plan for Success in Iraq, Phase One Report," American Enterprise Institute, December 2006. The publication lists the following members of the Iraq Planning Group at AEI: Frederick W. Kagan, General Jack Keane, U.S. Army (ret.), Lieutenant General David Barno, U.S. Army (ret.), Danielle Pletka, Rend al-Rahim, Colonel Joel Armstrong, U.S. Army (ret.), Major Daniel Dwyer, U.S. Army (ret.), Larry Crandall, Larry Sampler, Michael Eisenstadt, Kimberly Kagan, Michael Rubin, Reuel Marc Gerecht, Thomas Donnelly, Gary Schmitt, Mauro De Lorenzo, and Vance Serchuk.

2. For just one example of several well-known authors who developed studies of counterinsurgency that made the population a prized objective, see David Galula's *Counter-Insurgency Warfare: Theory and Practice* (London: Pall Mall Press, 1964), and his *Pacification in Algeria, 1956–1958* (Santa Monica, CA: RAND Corporation, 2006), originally published in 1963.

3. "President Bush Speaks to the Nation about Iraq, January 10, 2007, found at http://www.cnn.com/2007/POLITICS/01/10/bush.transcript/index.html.

4. Ibid.

5. See, for example, Thomas E. Ricks, *Fiasco: The American Military Adventure in Iraq* (New York: Penguin, 2006), 153.

6. One of the most frequently quoted phrases found in *On War* is Clausewitz's comment, "Now, the first, the grandest, and most decisive act of judgment which the statesman and general exercises is rightly to understand in this respect the war in which he engages, not to take it for something, or to wish to make of it something which, by the nature of its relations, it is impossible for it to be." Howard and Paret, *On War*, chapter 1, part 27.

7. Ricks, *The Gamble*, 111.

8. FOBs, or forward operating bases, were coalition military compounds, normally isolated from the rest of Iraq, where most soldiers and Marines lived when they were not conducting limited-duration forays into the rest of the country. They provided safe havens for the coalition, but also left the Iraqis to fend for themselves in the days and most nights when coalition forces were not present in the towns.

9. Marc A. Thiessen, ed., *A Charge Kept: The Record of the Bush Presidency, 2001–2009* (Washington, DC: Government Printing Office, 2009), 14.

10. Lieutenant General Raymond T. Odierno, "The Surge in Iraq: One Year Later," Heritage Lecture 1068, March 13, 2008, found at http://www.heritage.org/Research/NationalSecurity/hl1068.cfm.

11. Linda Robinson, *Tell Me How This Ends: General David Petraeus and the Search for a Way Out of Iraq* (New York: Public Affairs, 2008), 103.

12. Ibid., 104.

13. "Lieutenant General Peter Chiarelli, Odierno's immediate predecessor at MNC-I, had already recognized the need for a shift in approach and begun to reconnoiter the belts around Baghdad and areas within the city before he relinquished command in December 2006." Frederick W. Kagan and Kimberly Kagan, "The Patton of Counterinsurgency, With a Sequence of Brilliant Offensives, Raymond Odierno Adapted the Petraeus Doctrine into a Successful Operational Art," *Weekly Standard* 13, no. 25, March 10, 2008, found at http://www.weeklystandard.com/Content/Public/Articles/000/000/014/822vfpsz.asp.

14. Robinson, *Tell Me How This Ends*, 105.

15. Ibid., 148.

16. Ibid., 149.

17. Ibid., 171, 173.

18. Six of the eighteen key benchmarks were related in some way to reconciliation and governance reform in Iraq; see Robinson, *Tell Me How This Ends*, 170.

19. Ibid., 166–167.

20. See http://www.globalsecurity.org/military/ops/oif-phantom-thunder.htm.

21. Kagan and Kagan, "The Patton of Counterinsurgency."

22. Kenneth Katzman, "Iraq and Al Qaeda," Congressional Research Service Report RL32217, April 28, 2008, CRS-13, found at http://fpc.state.gov/documents/organization/105195.pdf.

23. Ibid.

24. Ibid.

25. Kagan and Kagan, "The Patton of Counterinsurgency."

26. See http://en.wikipedia.org/wiki/Raymond_T._Odierno.

27. See http://www.understandingwar.org/operation/operation-fardh-al-qanoon.

28. Kagan and Kagan, "The Patton of Counterinsurgency."

29. "Iraq and Al Qaeda, CRS-14."

30. Richard S. Lowry, "The Joint Campaign Plan: A Strategy for Stability in Iraq," *Weekly Standard*, August 2, 2007, found at http://www.weeklystandard.com/Content/Public/Articles/000/000/013/935tlkui.asp.

31. In September 2007, General Petraeus stated that "the military objectives of the surge are, in large measure, being met. In recent months, in the face of tough enemies and the brutal summer heat of Iraq, Coalition and Iraqi Security Forces have achieved progress in the security arena. Though the improvements have been uneven across Iraq, the overall number of security incidents in Iraq has declined in 8 of the past 12 weeks, with the numbers of incidents in the last two

weeks at the lowest levels seen since June 2006." See http://www.defenselink.mil/pubs/pdfs/Petraeus-Testimony20070910.pdf.

32. In April 2008, General Petraeus began by saying, "Since September, levels of violence and civilian deaths have been reduced substantially, Al Qaeda-Iraq and a number of other extremist elements have been dealt serious blows, the capabilities of Iraqi security force elements have grown, and there has been noteworthy involvement of local Iraqis in local security." See http://www.mnf-iraq.com/images/stories/Press_briefings/2008/april/080408_petraeus_testimony.pdf.

33. Kagan and Kagan, "The Patton of Counterinsurgency."

34. Also known as the Mahdi Militia or Jaish al Mahdi.

35. Kenneth Katzman, "Iran's Influence in Iraq," Congressional Research Service, Order Code RS22323, August 9, 2007, found at http://fpc.state.gov/documents/organization/91004.pdf, quoting, Dafna Linzer, "Troops Authorized to Kill Iranian Operatives in Iraq," *Washington Post*, January 26, 2007.

36. Katzman, "Iran's Influence in Iraq."

37. Odierno's III Corps staff was replaced in Iraq, by the staff of the XVIII Airborne Corps on February 15, 2008. General Austin turned over command of MNC-I to Lieutenant General Charles Jacoby in 2009.

Chapter 12. The Iraqis Take Control

1. Jafari and his Shia United Iraqi Alliance party led the Iraqi government from April 7, 2005, to May 20, 2006, by bringing together a political coalition based on the Jafari's own Islamic Dawa Party and the Supreme Council of the Islamic Revolution in Iraq (SCIRI) party.

2. Michael Abramowitz and Sudarsan Raghavan, "Bush Rejects Troop Reductions, Endorses Maliki, President Calls Prime Minister 'the Right Guy for Iraq' after Summit in Jordan," *Washington Post*, December 1, 2006, A24.

3. Marisa Cochrane, "The Battle for Basra, March 2003–May 31, 2008," *Weekly Standard*, Iraq Report #9, June 23, 2008, 4, found at http://www.understandingwar.org/report/battle-basra.

4. Ricks, *The Gamble*, 278–279.

5. Interestingly, the cease-fire was developed with Iranian support by the leader of the Iranian al-Quds force, Qassem Suleimani. Cochrane, "The Battle for Basra," 9.

6. Ibid.

7. Sudarsan Raghavan and Sholnn Freeman, "U.S. Appears to Take Lead in Fighting in Baghdad, U.S. Forces Battle Mahdi Army in Sadr City, Aircraft Target Basra," *Washington Post*, April 1, 2008, found at http://www.washingtonpost.com/wp-dyn/content/article/2008/04/01/AR2008040100833.html.

8. Cochrane, "Battle for Basra," 10.

9. Richard A. Oppel Jr. and Jeff Zeleny, "For Obama, a First Step Is Not a Misstep," *New York Times*, July 22, 2008, 1.

10. The eighteen benchmarks to gauge success in Iraq were drafted in coordination with Iraqi leaders and inserted into congressional bill H.R. 2206, "U.S. Troop Readiness, Veterans' Care, Katrina Recovery, and Iraq Accountability

Appropriations Act, 2007." H.R. 2206 was passed by Congress in mid-May 2007, and signed into law by President Bush on May 25, 2007.

11. Karen DeYoung, "U.S. Embassy Cites Progress in Iraq, Most Congressionally Set Benchmarks Met, Report Finds," *Washington Post*, July 2, 2008, A08.

12. Department of Defense, "Measuring Stability and Security in Iraq," March 2009 Report to Congress in accordance with the Department of Defense Supplemental Appropriations Act 2008 (Section 9204, Public Law 110-252), iii.

13. See the Federal Election Commission's official results tally at http://www.fec.gov/pubrec/fe2008/2008presgeresults.pdf.

14. Claire Russo, "Capitol Hill Briefing Notes: Provincial Elections in Iraq," February 19, 2009, found at http://www.understandingwar.org/print/525.

15. Ibid.

16. Hélène Frade and Lucas Menget, "Maliki Hails Iraqi Vote as 'a Victory,'" February 1, 2009, found at http://www.france24.com/en/20090201-maliki-hails-iraq-vote-victory-provincial-elections-polls-close.

17. See http://www.pbs.org/newshour/extra/features/world/jan-june09/iraq.html.

18. Amit R. Paley, "Green Zone Handed Off with Little Fanfare, Embassy Ceremony Hints at Uncertainty," *Washington Post*, January 2, 2009, 12.

19. Anthony Shadid, "In Iraq, the Day After, The War, in a Sense, Is Over. But a New Struggle Begins As Citizens Ask the Inevitable Question: What Next?," *Washington Post*, January 2, 2009, A01.

20. Tim Cocks, "U.S. Starts Pullout, Transfers Base to Iraq," *Boston Globe*, January 4, 2009.

21. For further explanation of this subtitle see the excellent book by Dominic J. Caraccilo and Andrea L. Thompson, *Achieving Victory in Iraq: Countering an Insurgency* (Mechanicsburg, PA: Stackpole Books, 2008).

22. Victor Davis Hanson, "The Good—Part III." found at: http://pajamasmedia.com/victordavishanson/784/.

23. General Odierno participated in the meeting via video-teleconference from Baghdad. See Peter Baker and Thom Shanker, "Obama Meets with Officials on Iraq, Signaling His Commitment to Ending War," *New York Times*, January 22, 2009.

24. Bush had identified the objectives of the war in several ways, but most consistently he described three determining factors. He said in 2005 that "victory will be achieved when the terrorists and Saddamists can no longer threaten Iraq's democracy, when the Iraqi security forces can provide for the safety of their own citizens, and when Iraq is not a safe haven for terrorists to plot new attacks against our nation." George W. Bush, "Remarks by President Bush on the War on Terror," at the Park Hyatt Philadelphia, Philadelphia, Pennsylvania, December 12, 2005.

25. Email from Major General John F. Kelly, USMC, February 1, 2009.

26. President Barack Obama, "Responsibly Ending the War in Iraq," speech given at Camp Lejeune, North Carolina, February 27, 2009, found at http://www.whitehouse.gov/the_press_office/Remarks-of-President-Barack-Obama-Responsibly-Ending-the-War-in-Iraq/.

27. Ibid.

28. CNN, "Obama Makes Surprise Visit to Iraq," April 7, 2009, found at http://cnnwire.blogs.cnn.com/2009/04/07/obama-makes-surprise-visit-to-iraq-2/.

29. Timothy Williams, "2 Blasts Expose Security Flaws in Heart of Iraq," *New York Times*, October 25, 2009, found at http://www.nytimes.com/2009/08/20/world/middleeast/20iraq.html.

30. Sam Dagher, "Bombings in Iraq, Deadliest Since 2007, Raise Security Issue," *New York Times*, August 19, 2009, found at http://www.nytimes.com/2009/10/26/world/middleeast/26iraq.html?_r=1.

31. Marc Santora and Riyadh Mohammed, "Iraq's Other Security Threat: Politics," *New York Times*, December 10, 2009, found at http://www.nytimes.com/2009/12/10/world/middleeast/10iraq.html?pagewanted=2.

32. U.S. Department of State, Bureau of Near Eastern Affairs, "Iraq Status Report, December 2, 2009," found at http://www.state.gov/p/nea/rls/rpt/c28011.htm.

33. Gerry J. Gilmore, "Odierno Cites Deliberate, Steady Progress," American Forces Press Service Wednesday, December 9, 2009, found at http://www.cjtf7.army.mil/index.php?option=com_content&task=view&id=28885&Itemid=128.

34. The Turkish foreign minister noted that "it was high time for the Arabs, Kurds and Turks to re-build the Middle East." See the "Turkey Opens Consulate in Northern Iraqi City of Arbil," *Turkish Weekly*, October 32, 2009, found at http://www.turkishweekly.net/news/92224/turkey-opens-consulate-in-northern-iraqi-city-of-arbil.html.

35. Gerry J. Gilmore, "Odierno: Time Right to Transfer Security," American Forces Press Service, December 10, 2009, found at: http://www.mnf-iraq.com/index.php?option=com_content&task=view&id=28895&Itemid=128.

36. See Donna Miles, "Gates Here to Talk Progress, Drawdown," American Forces Press Service, December 10, 2009, found at http://www.mnf-iraq.com/index.php?option=com_content&task=view&id=28893&Itemid=128.

37. Jim Garamone, "New Command Stands Up in Iraq, Marking Drawdown Milestone," American Forces Press Service, January 1, 2010.

Chapter 13. A Final Assessment:
The Impact of the Long War with Iraq

1. Donald H. Rumsfeld, "One Surge Does Not Fit All," *New York Times*, November 23, 2008, WK11.

2. See the key findings of the Iraq Survey Group Report, submitted by Charles Duelfer on September 30, 2004. See Charles Duelfer, "The Comprehensive Report of the Special Advisor to the DCI on Iraq WMD," 30 September 30, 2004, found at: https://www.cia.gov/library/reports/general-reports-1/iraq_wmd_2004/index.html.

3. That new strategy said in part, "We must be prepared to stop rogue states and their terrorist clients before they are able to threaten or use weapons of mass destruction against the United States and our allies and friends." "National Security Strategy of the United States of America," September 2002, 14.

4. The sixteen resolutions are: UNSCR 678 of November 29, 1990; UNSCR 686 of March 2, 1991; UNSCR 687 of April 3, 1991; UNSCR 688 of April 5, 1991; UNSCR 707 of August 15, 1991; UNSCR 715 of October 11, 1991; UNSCR 949 of October 15, 1994; UNSCR 1051 of March 27, 1996; UNSCR 1060 of June 12, 1996; UNSCR 1115 of June 21, 1997; UNSCR 1134 of October 23, 1997; UNSCR 1137 of November 12, 1997; UNSCR 1154 of March 2, 1998; UNSCR 1194 of September 9, 1998; UNSCR 1205 of November 5, 1998; UNSCR 1284 of December 17, 1999.

5. This was less true of the Marine Reserve and Air National Guard transport units.

6. See Irving Kristol, "The Neoconservative Persuasion: What It Was, and What It Is," *Weekly Standard* 8, no. 47, August 25, 2003.

7. Three significantly smaller UN missions had begun in 1991. The UN Angola Verification Mission II (UNAVEM II) helped Angolan Government and União Nacional para la Independencia Total de Angola (UNITA) carry out peace agreements, ending sixteen years of civil war. The UN Observer Mission in El Salvador (ONUSAL) began in July 1991. ONUSAL verified agreements between the government of El Salvador and the Frente Farabundo Marti para la Liberación Nacional to end a decade-long civil war. The United Nations Mission for the Referendum in Western Sahara (MINURSO) began in September 1991, following the agreement between the government of Morocco and the Frente Polisario. MINURSO was deployed to monitor the cease-fire and to organize and conduct a referendum that would allow the people of Western Sahara to decide the territory's future status. A fourth UN mission (ONUMOZ) began in Mozambique in 1992 and was tasked with monitoring the peace agreement and providing humanitarian assistance, including mine clearance, following the agreement between Mozambique's government and the Resistência Nacional Moçambicana in October 1992.

8. UNPROFOR was initially established in Croatia as an interim arrangement to create the conditions of peace and security required for the negotiation of an overall settlement of the Yugoslav crisis. For the official UN summary see http://www .un.org/Depts/dpko/dpko/co_mission/unprof_p.htm.

9. For the official UN summary, see http://www.un.org/Depts/dpko/dpko/co_mission/ unmihbackgr1.html. For additional perspective from the UN following the last of these interventions in Haiti, see http://www.un.org/Depts/dpko/missions/minustah/. See also John R. Ballard, *Upholding Democracy: The United States Military Campaign in Haiti 1994–1997* (Westport, CT:Praeger, 1998).

10. See the UN background note on the efforts in East Timor, found at: http:// www.un.org/Depts/dpko/dpko/co_mission/background.html.

11. See also John R. Ballard, *Triumph of Self-Determination: Operation Stabilise and United Nations Peacemaking in East Timor* (Westport, CT: Praeger Security International, 2006).

12. The Peace of Westphalia denotes the peace treaties of Osnabrück (May 15, 1648) and Münster (October 24, 1648) that effectively ended the Thirty Years'

War (1618–48) between the Holy Roman Empire and Spain, France, Sweden, and the Dutch Republic. The peace ushered in a new European political order wherein the nation-state was supreme.

13. Saddam Hussein probably did see his attack on Kuwait as a threat to the Saudis, nor to the other GCC states, serving his desire to demonstrate his enduring military capability as a lever in future economic and diplomatic efforts.

14. Kagan and Kagan, "The Patton of Counterinsurgercy."

15. See Department of Defense Joint Operating Concept, found at http://www.dtic.mil/futurejointwarfare/concepts/iw_jocl_O.pdf.

SELECTED BIBLIOGRAPHY

Books

Aburish, Said K. *Saddam Hussein: The Politics of Revenge*. New York: Bloomsbury, 2000.

Alfonsi, Christian. *Circle in the Sand: Why We Went Back to Iraq*. New York: Doubleday, 2006.

Allen, Thomas B. F., Clifton Berry Jr., and Norman Polmar. *War in the Gulf*. Atlanta, GA: Turner Publishing, 1991.

Andrews, William F. *Airpower Against an Army: Challenge and Response in CENTAF's Duel with the Republican Guard*. CADRE paper. Maxwell Air Force Base, AL: Air University Press, 1998.

Atkinson, Rick. *Crusade: The Untold Story of the Persian Gulf War*. Boston: Houghton Mifflin, 1993.

Balaghi, Shiva. *Saddam Hussein: A Biography*. Westport, CT: Greenwood Press, 2006.

Ballard, John R. *Triumph of Self-determination: Operation Stabilise and United Nations Peacemaking in East Timor*. Westport, CT: Praeger Security International, 1998.

_____. *Fighting for Fallujah: A New Dawn for Iraq*. Westport, CT: Praeger Security International, 2006.

Baroody, Judith Raine. *Media Access and the Military: The Case of the Gulf War*. Lanham, MD: University Press of America, 1998.

Bennett, W. Lance, and David L. Paletz. *Taken by Storm: The Media, Public Opinion, and U.S. Foreign Policy in the Gulf War*. Chicago: University of Chicago Press, 1994.

Billière, General Sir Peter de la. *Storm Command: A Personal Account of the Gulf War*. London: HarperCollins, 1992.

bin Sultan, Khaled, with Patrick Seale. *Desert Warrior: A Personal View of the Gulf War by the Joint Forces Commander*. New York: HarperCollins, 1995.

Bremer, L. Paul III, with Malcolm McConnell. *My Year in Iraq: The Struggle to Build a Future of Hope*. New York: Simon & Schuster, 2006.

Briscoe, Charles H. *All Roads Lead to Baghdad: Army Special Operation Forces in Iraq*. Fort Bragg, NC: USASOC History Office, 2006.

Bush, George, and Brent Scowcroft. *A World Transformed*. New York: Knopf, 1998.

Caraccilo, Dominic J., and Andrea L. Thompson. *Achieving Victory in Iraq: Countering an Insurgency*. Mechanicsburg, PA: Stackpole Books, 2008.

Chandrasekaran, Rajiv. *Imperial Life in the Emerald City: Inside Iraq's Green Zone*. New York: Alfred A. Knopf, 2006.

Clancy, Tom, with Fred Franks Jr. *Into the Storm*. New York: Putnam, 1997.

Clancy, Tom, and Chuck Horner. *Every Man a Tiger*. New York: Putnam, 1999.

Cohen, Eliot A., et al. *Gulf War Air Power Survey*. Washington, DC: Government Printing Office, 1993.

Cordesman, Anthony H. *Iraq and the War of Sanctions: Conventional Threats and Weapons of Mass Destruction*. Westport, CT: Praeger, 1999.

————. *The Iraq War: Strategy, Tactics, and Military Lessons*. Westport, CT: Praeger, 2003.

————. *The War After the War: Strategic Lessons of Iraq and Afghanistan*. Washington, DC: CSIS Press, Center for Strategic and International Studies, 2004.

Cordesman, Anthony H., with Patrick Baetjer. *Iraqi Security Forces: A Strategy for Success*. Westport, CT: Praeger, 2006.

Cordesman, Anthony H., and Ahmed Hashim. *Iraq Sanctions and Beyond*. CSIS Middle East Dynamic Net Assessment. Boulder, CO: Westview Press, 1997.

Darby, Phillip. *British Defence Policy East of Suez, 1947–68*. Oxford: Oxford University Press, 1973.

Dockrill, Saki. *Britain's Retreat from East of Suez: The Choice between Europe and the World, 1945–1968*. New York: Palgrave, 2002.

Etherington, Mark. *Revolt on the Tigris: The Al-Sadr Uprising and the Governing of Iraq*. Ithaca, NY: Cornell University Press, 2005.

Feith, Douglas J. *War and Decision: Inside the Pentagon at the Dawn of the War on Terrorism*. New York: Harper, 2008.

Ferguson, Charles H. *No End in Sight: Iraq's Descent into Chaos*. New York: Public Affairs, 2008.

Fick, Nathaniel. *One Bullet Away: The Making of a Marine Officer*. Boston: Houghton Mifflin, 2005.

Folsom, Seth W. B. *The Highway War: A Marine Company Commander in Iraq*. Washington, DC: Potomac Books, 2006.

Fontenot, Gregory, E. J. Degen, and David Tohn. *On Point: The United States Army in Operation Iraqi Freedom*. Annapolis: Naval Institute Press, 2005.

Franks, Tommy. *American Soldier*. New York: Regan Books, 2004.

Friedman, Norman. *Desert Victory: The War for Kuwait*. Annapolis: Naval Institute Press, 1991.

Galula, David. *Defeating Counterinsurgency Warfare: Theory and Practice*. New York: Praeger, 1964.

Gardner, Lloyd C. *The Long Road to Baghdad: A History of U.S. Foreign Policy from the 1970s to the Present*. New York: New Press, 2008.

Gardner, Lloyd C., and Marilyn Blatt Young. *Iraq and the Lessons of Vietnam: Or, How Not to Learn from the Past*. New York: New Press, 2007.

Gilbertson, Ashley. *Whiskey Tango Foxtrot: A Photographer's Chronicle of the Iraq War*. Chicago: University of Chicago Press, 2007.

Gordon, Michael R., and Bernard E. Trainor. *The Generals' War: The Inside Story of the Conflict in the Gulf*. Boston: Little, Brown, 1995.

_____. *Cobra II: The Inside Story of the Invasion and Occupation of Iraq*. New York: Pantheon, 2006.

Graham-Brown, Sarah. *Sanctioning Saddam: The Politics of Intervention in Iraq*. London: I. B. Tauris in association with MERIP, 1999.

Haass, Richard N. *War of Necessity, War of Choice: A Memoir of Two Iraq Wars*. New York: Simon & Schuster, 2009.

Hafez, Mohammed M. *Suicide Bombers in Iraq: The Strategy and Ideology of Martyrdom*. Washington, DC: United States Institute of Peace, 2007.

Hallion, Richard. *Storm over Iraq: Air Power and the Gulf War*. Smithsonian History of Aviation Series. Washington, DC: Smithsonian Institution Press, 1992.

Hashim, Ahmed S. *Insurgency and Counter-Insurgency in Iraq*. Ithaca, NY: Cornell University Press, 2006.

Herring, Eric, and Glen Rangwala. *Iraq in Fragments: The Occupation and Its Legacy*. Ithaca, NY: Cornell University Press, 2006.

Hersh, Seymour M. *Against All Enemies: Gulf War Syndrome: The War between America's Ailing Veterans and Their Government*. New York: Ballantine Publishing, 1998.

Hiro, Dilip. *The Longest War: The Iran-Iraq Military Conflict*. New York: Routledge, 1991.

Holmstedt, Kirsten A. *Band of Sisters: American Women at War in Iraq*. Mechanicsburg, PA: Stackpole Books, 2007.

Jadick, Richard, and Thomas Hayden. *On Call in Hell: A Doctor's Iraq War Story*. New York: NAL Caliber, 2007.

Johnson, Alison. *Gulf War Syndrome: Legacy of a Perfect War*. Brunswick, ME: MCS Information Exchange, 2001.

Kaplan, Lawrence, and William Kristol. *The War over Iraq: Saddam's Tyranny and America's Mission*. San Francisco: Encounter Books, 2003.

Karsh, Efraim. *The Iran-Iraq War: Impact and Implications*. New York: St. Martin's Press, 1989.

_____. *The Iran-Iraq War, 1980–1988*. Oxford: Osprey, 2002.

Karsh, Efraim, and Inari Rautsi. *Saddam Hussein: A Political Biography*. New York: Free Press, 1991.

Keegan, John. *The Iraq War*. New York: Knopf, 2004.

Kennedy, Greg. *British Maritime Strategy East of Suez, 1900–2000: Influence and Actions*. Routledge, 2003.

Koopman, John. *McCoy's Marines: Darkside to Baghdad*. St. Paul, MN: Zenith Press, 2004.

Lacey, Jim. *Takedown: The 3rd Infantry Division's Twenty-One Day Assault on Baghdad*. Annapolis: Naval Institute Press, 2007.

Levinson, Jeffrey L., and Randy L. Edwards. *Missile Inbound: The Attack on the Stark in the Persian Gulf*. Annapolis: Naval Institute Press, 1997.

Locher, James R., *Victory on The Potomac: The Goldwater-Nichols Act Unifies The Pentagon*. Texas A&M University Press, 2004.

Luizard, Pierre-Jean. *La formation de l'Irak contemporain. Le rôle politique des ulémas chiites en Irak à la fin de la domination ottomane et au moment de la construction de l'Etat irakien*. Paris: Éditions du CNRS, 1991.

Makiya, Kanan (original ed. under pseudonym Samir al-Khalil). *Republic of Fear*. Berkeley: University of California Press, 1998.

Marr, Phebe. *The Modern History of Iraq*, 2d ed. Boulder, CO: Westview Press, 2004.

Mathews, James K., and Kora J. Holt. *So Many, So Much, So Far, So Fast: United States Transportation Command and Strategic Deployment in Operations Desert Shield and Desert Storm*. Joint History Office, May, 1996.

Metz, Steven. *Iraq and the Evolution of American Strategy*. Washington, DC: Potomac Books, 2008.

Moore, Molly. *A Woman at War: Storming Kuwait with the U.S. Marines*. New York: Scribner's, 1993.

Murray, Williamson, and Robert H. Scales Jr. *The Iraq War: A Military History*. Cambridge, MA: Harvard University Press, 2003.

O'Donnell, Patrick K. *We Were One: Shoulder to Shoulder with the Marines Who Took Fallujah*. Cambridge, MA: Da Capo, 2006.

Packer, George. *The Assassins' Gate: America in Iraq*. New York: Farrar, Straus and Giroux, 2005.

Palmer, Michael A. *Guardians of the Gulf: A History of America's Expanding Role in the Persian Gulf, 1833–1992*. New York: Free Press, 1992.

Pauly, Robert J., and Tom Lansford. *Strategic Preemption: U.S. Foreign Policy and the Second Iraq War*. Burlington, VT: Ashgate Pub, 2004.

Pelletiere, Stephen C., and Douglas V. Johnson. *Lessons Learned: The Iran-Iraq War.* Carlisle Barracks, PA: Strategic Studies Institute, U.S. Army War College, 1991.

Raddatz, Martha. *The Long Road Home: A Story of War and Family.* New York: G. P. Putnam's Sons, 2007.

Record, Jeffrey. *Hollow Victory: A Contrary View of the Gulf War.* Washington, DC: Brassey's (US), 1993.

Reynolds, Nicholas E. *Basrah, Baghdad, and Beyond: The U.S. Marine Corps in the Second Iraq War.* Annapolis: Naval Institute Press, 2005.

Ricks, Thomas E. *Fiasco: The American Military Adventure in Iraq.* New York: Penguin, 2006.

———. *The Gamble: General David Petraeus and the American Military Adventure in Iraq, 2006–2008.* New York: Penguin Press, 2009.

Robinson, Linda. *Tell Me How This Ends: General David Petraeus and the Search for a Way Out of Iraq.* New York: Public Affairs, 2008.

Rosen, Nir. *In the Belly of the Green Bird: The Triumph of the Martyrs in Iraq.* New York: Free Press, 2006.

Roux, Georges. *Ancient Iraq.* London: Penguin Books, 1992.

Rudd, Gordon W. *Humanitarian Intervention: Assisting the Iraqi Kurds in Operation Provide Comfort, 1991.* Washington, DC: Center of Military History, 2004.

Sanchez, Ricardo S., and Don T. Phillips. *Wiser in Battle: A Soldier's Story.* New York: HarperCollins, 2008.

Scales, Robert H. Jr., et. al. *Certain Victory: The US Army in the Gulf War.* Washington, DC: Office of the Chief of Staff, United States Army/GPO, 1993.

Schubert, Frank N., and Theresa L. Kraus, eds. *The Whirlwind War: The United States Army in Operations Desert Shield and Desert Storm.* CMH Pub 70-30. Washington, DC: U.S. Army Center of Military History, 1995.

Schwarzkopf, H. Norman, with Peter Petre. *It Doesn't Take a Hero.* New York: Linda Grey/Bantam Books, 1992.

Simons, G. L. *The Scourging of Iraq: Sanctions, Law, and Natural Justice.* New York: St. Martin's Press, 1998.

———. *Targeting Iraq: Sanctions and Bombing in U.S. Policy.* London: Saqi Books, 2002.

Smith, Perry M. *How CNN Fought the War: A View from the Inside.* New York: Carol Publishing Group, 1991.

Spinner, Jackie, and Jenny Spinner. *Tell Them I Didn't Cry: A Young Journalist's Story of Joy, Loss, and Survival in Iraq.* New York: Scribner, 2006.

Summers, Harry G. *On Strategy II: A Critical Analysis of the Persian Gulf War.* New York: Dell, 1992.

Swain, Richard M. *"Lucky War": Third Army in Desert Storm*. Fort Leavenworth, KS: U.S. Army Command and General Staff College Press, 1991. Found at http://www-cgsc.army.mil/carl/resources/csi/Swain/swain.asp.

Swofford, Anthony. *Jarhead: A Marine's Chronicle of the Gulf War and Other Battles*. New York: Scribner, 2003.

Thompson, Robert. *Defeating Communist Insurgency: The Lessons of Malaya and Vietnam*. New York: F. A. Praeger, 1966.

Trinquier, Roger. *Modern Warfare: a French View of Counterinsurgency*. PSI Classics of the Counterinsurgency Era. Westport, CT: Praeger Security International, 2006.

Tripp, Charles. *A History of Iraq*. Cambridge: Cambridge University Press, 2007.

West, Francis J. *No True Glory: A Frontline Account of the Battle for Fallujah*. New York: Bantam Books, 2005.

West, Francis J. *The Strongest Tribe: War, Politics, and the Endgame in Iraq*. New York: Random House, 2008.

West, Francis J., and Ray L. Smith. *The March Up: Taking Baghdad with the 1st Marine Division*. New York: Bantam, 2003.

Winkler, David F. *Amirs, Admirals & Desert Sailors: Bahrain, the U.S. Navy, and the Arabian Gulf*. Annapolis: Naval Institute Press, 2007.

Wise, Harold Lee. *Inside the Danger Zone: The U.S. Military in the Persian Gulf, 1987–1988*. Annapolis: Naval Institute Press, 2007.

Wise, James E., and Scott Baron. *Women at War: Iraq, Afghanistan, and Other Conflicts*. Annapolis: Naval Institute Press, 2006.

Woods, Kevin M. *The Mother of All Battles: Saddam Hussein's Strategic Plan for the Persian Gulf War*. Annapolis: Naval Institute Press, 2008.

Woodward, Bob. *The Commanders*. New York: Simon & Schuster, 1991.

————. *Bush at War*. New York: Simon & Schuster, 2002.

————. *Plan of Attack*. New York: Simon & Schuster, 2004.

————. *State of Denial: Bush at War, Part III*. New York: Simon & Schuster, 2006.

————. *The War Within: A Secret White House History, 2006–2008*. New York: Simon & Schuster, 2008.

Zatarain, Lee Allen. *Tanker War: America's First Conflict with Iran, 1987–88*. Drexel Hill, PA: Casemate, 2008.

Articles and Papers

Agee, Collin A. "Peeling the Onion: The Iraqi Center of Gravity in Desert Storm." Unpublished paper, School of Advanced Military Studies, United

States Army Command and General Staff College, Fort Leavenworth, Kansas, 1992.

Boustany, Nora. "A Trail of Death in Iraq: Shiite Refugees Tell of Atrocities by Republican Guard." *Washington Post* (pre–1997 Fulltext), March 26, 1991, final edition, A1.

Carafano, James Jay. "The Army Reserves and the Abrams Doctrine: Unfulfilled Promise, Uncertain Future." Heritage Foundation, April 18, 2005, http://www.heritage.org/Research/NationalSecurity/hl869.cfm.

Chiarelli, Major General Peter W., and Major Patrick R. Michaelis. "Winning the Peace: The Requirement for Full-Spectrum Operations." *Military Review* (July–August 2005): 4–17.

Duelfer, Charles. "How Baghdad Divided the Conquerors." *Los Angeles Times*, June 11, 2000, home edition, The World/Iraq, 1.

Feith, Douglas J. "Why We Went to War in Iraq." *Wall Street Journal*, July 3, 2008, 11.

Kagan, Frederick W. "Choosing Victory, A Plan for Success in Iraq, Phase One Report." American Enterprise Institute, December 2006.

Keaney, Thomas A. "Surveying Gulf War Airpower." *Joint Force Quarterly* 2 (Autumn 1993): 25–36.

Keller, Bill. "The Iraqi Invasion: Moscow Joins U.S. in Criticizing Iraq." *New York Times*, August 4, 1990, 1.

Krepinevich, Andrew F. Jr. "How to Win in Iraq." *Foreign Affairs* (September–October 2005), 87–104.

Malkasian, Carter. "The First Battle for Fallujah." In *War in Iraq: Planning and Execution* by Thomas G. Mahnken and Thomas A. Keaney, 163–186. New York: Routledge, 2007.

Murphy, Dan. "U.S. Strategy in Iraq: Is It Working? Major Sweeps Show Results in Western Iraq. But Insurgents Keep Adapting and Attacking." *Christian Science Monitor*, June 21, 2005, 1.

Packer, George. "Letter from Iraq: The Lesson of Tal Afar, Is It Too Late for the Administration to Correct Its Course in Iraq?" *New Yorker*, April 10, 2006, 51–52.

Perle, Richard. "Ambushed on the Potomac." *National Interest Online*, January,6, 2009, http://www.nationalinterest.org/Article.aspx?id=20486.

Petraeus, David H. "Learning Counterinsurgency: Observations from Soldiering in Iraq." *Military Review* (January–February 2006): 1–11.

Ricks, Thomas E., and Vernon Loeb. "Bush Developing Military Policy of Striking First New Doctrine Addresses Terrorism." *Washington Post*, June 10, 2002, A01.

Rumsfeld, Donald H. "One Surge Does Not Fit All." *New York Times*, November 23, 2008, WK11.

Sattler, John F., and Daniel H. Wilson. "Operation Al Fajr: The Battle of Fallujah—Part II." *Marine Corps Gazette* (July 2005): 12–24.

Shultz, George P. "Act Now; The Danger Is Immediate. Saddam Hussein Must Be Removed." *Washington Post*, September 6, 2002, final edition, A25, http://www.proquest.com/ (accessed July 3, 2008).

Walker, George K. *The Tanker War, 1980–88: Law and Policy*. Unpublished paper. Newport, RI: Naval War College, 2000.

Woodward, Bob. "Doubt, Distrust, Delay: The Inside Story of How Bush's Team Dealt With Its Failing Iraq Strategy." *Washington Post*, September 7, 2008, A1.

Wright, Robin. "Hussein Is Itching for a Fight, U.S. Officials Say; Persian Gulf: Members of the Clinton Administration See a Pattern of Iraqi Actions Aimed at Triggering a Military Response. U.N. Sanctions Might Be Casualties." *Los Angeles Times*, September 23, 2000, home edition, 1, http://www.proquest.com (accessed July 3, 2008).

Government/Organizational Documents

Obama, President Barack. "Responsibly Ending the War in Iraq." Speech given at Camp Lejeune, North Carolina, Friday, February 27, 2009, found at http://www.whitehouse.gov/the_press_office/Remarks-of-President-Barack-Obama-Responsibly-Ending-the-War-in-Iraq.

Rice, Secretary of State Condoleezza. "Iraq and U.S. Policy," testimony before the Senate Committee on Foreign Relations, found at http://foreign.senate.gov/testimony/2005/RiceTestimony051019.pdf.

Taguba, Major General Antonio M. "Article 15-6 Investigation of the 800th Military Police Brigade," The "Taguba Report" on Treatment of Abu Ghraib Prisoners in Iraq, found at http://news.findlaw.com/hdocs/docs/iraq/tagubarpt.html#ThR1.9.

United States Congress. Senate Committee on Armed Services. *Defense Organization: The Need for Change: Staff Report to the Committee on Armed Services, United States Senate*. Washington, DC: GPO, 1985.

Internet Sources

The British Broadcasting Corporation (BBC): http://news.bbc.co.uk/hi/english/world/

Cable News Network: www.cnn.com/

The New York Times: www.nytimes.com/aponline/, and www.nytimes.com/library/world/asia/

The United Nations: www.un.org/News/ossg/hilites.htm

INDEX

ABOUT THE AUTHOR

John R. Ballard, PhD, is dean of Faculty and Academic Programs and professor of strategic studies at the Near East South Asia Center for Strategic Studies at the National Defense University in Washington D.C. He previously served as professor of strategic studies at the National War College, professor of Joint Military Operations at the Naval War College, and the Foundation Professor of Defence Studies at New Zealand's Massey University. A retired Marine veteran of the Iraq War, he commanded the 4th Civil Affairs Group in combat during Operation Iraqi Freedom.

The Naval Institute Press is the book-publishing arm of the U.S. Naval Institute, a private, nonprofit, membership society for sea service professionals and others who share an interest in naval and maritime affairs. Established in 1873 at the U.S. Naval Academy in Annapolis, Maryland, where its offices remain today, the Naval Institute has members worldwide.

Members of the Naval Institute support the education programs of the society and receive the influential monthly magazine *Proceedings* or the colorful bimonthly magazine *Naval History* and discounts on fine nautical prints and on ship and aircraft photos. They also have access to the transcripts of the Institute's Oral History Program and get discounted admission to any of the Institute-sponsored seminars offered around the country.

The Naval Institute's book-publishing program, begun in 1898 with basic guides to naval practices, has broadened its scope to include books of more general interest. Now the Naval Institute Press publishes about seventy titles each year, ranging from how-to books on boating and navigation to battle histories, biographies, ship and aircraft guides, and novels. Institute members receive significant discounts on the Press's more than eight hundred books in print.

Full-time students are eligible for special half-price membership rates. Life memberships are also available.

For a free catalog describing Naval Institute Press books currently available, and for further information about joining the U.S. Naval Institute, please write to:

Member Services
U.S. Naval Institute
291 Wood Road
Annapolis, MD 21402-5034
Telephone: (800) 233-8764
Fax: (410) 571-1703
Web address: www.usni.org